D1474211

The Roots of Educational Inequality

THE ROOTS OF EDUCATIONAL INEQUALITY

Philadelphia's Germantown High School, 1907–2014

Erika M. Kitzmiller

PENN

UNIVERSITY OF PENNSYLVANIA PRESS

PHILADELPHIA

Copyright © 2022 University of Pennsylvania Press

All rights reserved. Except for brief quotations used for
purposes of review or scholarly citation, none of this book
may be reproduced in any form by any means without
written permission from the publisher.

Published by
University of Pennsylvania Press
Philadelphia, Pennsylvania 19104-4112
www.upenn.edu/pennpress

Printed in the United States of America on acid-free paper
10 9 8 7 6 5 4 3 2 1

Library of Congress Cataloging-in-Publication Data
Names: Kitzmiller, Erika M., author.
Title: The roots of educational inequality : Philadelphia's
Germantown High School, 1907–2014 / Erika M. Kitzmiller.
Description: 1st edition. | Philadelphia : University of
Pennsylvania Press, [2021] | Includes bibliographical
references and index.
Identifiers: LCCN 2021014010 | ISBN 9780812253566
(hardcover)
Subjects: LCSH: Germantown High School (Philadelphia,
Pa.)—History. | Education, Urban—Economic aspects—
Pennsylvania—Philadelphia—History. | Education,
Secondary—Economic aspects—Pennsylvania—
Philadelphia—History. | Educational equalization—
Economic aspects—Pennsylvania—Philadelphia—History.
Classification: LCC LD7501.G475 K58 2021 | DDC
373.748/11—dc23
LC record available at https://lccn.loc.gov/2021014010

For my parents, Lisa and Richard

CONTENTS

PROLOGUE

On February 23, 2007, Frank Burd, a 30-year veteran teacher at Germantown High School, confiscated an iPod from one of his Algebra II students. School district policy stipulated that electronic devices were forbidden, but many teachers applied these rules inconsistently. While there were conflicting reports about what happened, video surveillance footage from the school's police station showed two students assaulting Burd in the hallway, cracking multiple bones in his neck and back. Philadelphia police arrested these students and charged them with aggravated assault and conspiracy. They pled guilty and were sentenced to prison. The incident launched the high school into the national spotlight and spurred a citywide debate about the escalation of violence inside Philadelphia's public schools as well as the intersection between public schools and the carceral state. Eventually, the furor subsided.[1]

When Burd's story circulated, I was volunteering at the Henry C. Lea Elementary School in West Philadelphia. One morning Lea's principal, Michael Silverman, told me that he had been hired as the next principal of Germantown High School and planned to leave Lea at the end of the year. I think he expected me to wish him well on this journey, but instead I asked him if I could follow him to Germantown to study his leadership. Silverman had a long track record of turning around challenging schools in the city, and I wanted to see how he did it at Germantown, to document his work and share it with others. Silverman agreed, and so I spent the year inside the high school watching him work.

When I spoke to teachers who had been in the school building the day of Burd's assault, many of them—both Black and white—told me that such incidents were commonplace in the school, that these reckless assaults were tied to the poverty and hopelessness that existed in the school community, and that I, as a white, upper-middle-class outsider, might not understand. During that year, many teachers warned me about getting close to students because they worried about the ongoing violence and unrest in the school. As they did this, they repeatedly assured me that the high school had once been a first-rate institution, an anchor in the community that drew middle-class families to Germantown for its public schools.

Their narrative of the school's decline and their warnings about my safety inside it troubled me. I grew up 180 miles west of Philadelphia, in a majority-white rural community, where I attended an under-resourced public school. My high school, like Germantown, was labeled a "failing public school," Corrective Action II, the lowest category, under the federal No Child Left Behind Act. As a high school student, I witnessed a significant number of altercations that would have been classified as "violent incidents" under the School District of Philadelphia's definition. In ninth grade, one of my peers hid his father's rifle in his duffle bag with the expressed intent of "shooting up a teacher." One of my peers alerted the principal about the situation. The student who brought the gun into the school was expelled and sent to a disciplinary school far from home. These incidents never made national headlines because they occurred in a majority-white public school in a rural community, not a majority-Black public school in the heart of Philadelphia. My experiences helped me recognize that Germantown was not unique and pushed me to question how race and racism shaped the narrative of public schools in the United States.

Moreover, from an early age, both of my parents helped me understand that class, gender, and race often shaped educational access and opportunities. My father shared his own schooling experiences with me and talked about the shortcomings of his under-resourced, racially integrated, postwar urban high school in Akron, Ohio. My mother, an Italian immigrant, shared her stories about how gender and race shaped her schooling experiences in suburban Cleveland. Their stories made me question the narrative about the once-glorious American high school that many Germantown teachers promoted.

Finally, as a first-generation college student, my undergraduate and graduate professors pushed me to recognize my own class and racial privileges and the ways that the schools I attended as a student and worked in as a teacher and administrator, both promoted mobility and replicated inequality.

My experiences and knowledge made me doubt the teachers' narrative about Germantown's storied past as well as their warnings about my safety in it. After talking with them, I knew I could not write the story that I had originally intended to tell.

Rather than focus on Germantown High School's 21st-century challenges and one principal's quest to address them, I decided to study the school's past to think about the alternative paths that the nation, city, and community might have taken to support this school, the ways that individuals resisted the inequities that existed in the community and its schools, and the long arc of American disinvestment in low-income communities, families, and youth, most notably in those places Black and Latinx families call home. Using the past to understand the present allowed me to combine two approaches: history and ethnography. This combination gave me a way to think deeply about the structural changes in one community and city and about youth experiences in one American high school.

I studied and worked in Germantown for seven years, first as a volunteer and then as a researcher, because the dedication and persistence of Germantown teachers, families, and youth, who fought for equity against great odds, inspired me. I met Germantown teachers outside in local restaurants and bars, families at citywide protests, and youth in clubs and activities. These teachers, families, and youth willingly shared their stories and assisted me in myriad aspects of this work—helping me find individuals to interview, typing names of graduates from school yearbooks, and suggesting questions for my interview protocols. These individuals routinely defied the stereotypes about "failing public schools"—disinvested families, unruly youth, and lazy teachers—that still shape our nation's policies and rhetoric. By telling their stories, and the stories of the generations that preceded them at Germantown, I hope to offer a new narrative about American high schools that counteracts these stereotypes and instead explains "failing" public schools as the product of more than a century of racial segregation, fiscal instability, and private funding.

I want my readers to listen to the stories and experiences of educators, families, and youth who have been fighting to be seen and heard for over a century. I have stayed connected to the school community for over a decade because I couldn't leave. And if I were still in Philadelphia, instead of 90 miles northeast in New York City, I'd probably still be in the Germantown community today, listening to the stories, testimonies, and experiences that made this book possible. I am so grateful to the individuals who opened their doors to let me listen and learn. Equipped with their stories, I finally felt empowered to tell my own.

This book is the story about one typical neighborhood high school in Philadelphia, but it is really the story of any high school that lacks the resources and supports for teachers, families, and children to thrive. There are thousands of these schools across our nation and our globe. I wrote this story to change the future. We are all responsible for past inequities and injustices, and as so many people in this story illustrate, we are also responsible for speaking up about these inequities and injustices in the hopes that our actions can alter what lies ahead.

INTRODUCTION

At the turn of the 20th century, Germantown, a community in Philadelphia's northwest corner, was home to a diverse group of individuals, but mainly to wealthy white residents who preferred the city's suburban periphery to its inner core. While Germantown's bourgeois residents beamed with pride about their isolated community, they were deeply concerned about their children, particularly their native-born white daughters, traveling to and from the city's limited set of high schools located in the bustling city center. Beginning in 1907, Germantown residents waged a successful seven-year campaign to build a majestic neighborhood high school tucked neatly away in their quaint secluded community.

When Germantown High School opened in 1915, the school offered a first-rate academic curriculum with coursework in Latin, Greek, Botany, and Rhetoric. Students were taught by teachers that were experts in their field, such as Dr. Anna Mullikin, the first woman to receive a doctorate in mathematics from the University of Pennsylvania.[1] After graduation, Germantown students enrolled in the nation's leading colleges and universities. Young men, like Forrest W. Brainerd, attended colleges such as Harvard, Princeton, and Haverford, while young women, such as Barbara Manley, went to schools such as Radcliffe, Wellesley, and Smith.[2] Eventually, many Germantown graduates assumed roles as leaders in Philadelphia's business and civic life. At the turn of the 20th century, Germantown High School was regarded as one of the leading secondary schools in the nation. Residents believed that it provided its graduates with a first-rate academic education and the necessary credentials to secure a prosperous future.[3]

Almost a century later, newspaper headlines featured Germantown High School. However, unlike earlier coverage that had celebrated the school's academic programs, this news signaled the school's demise. On December 13, 2012, William Hite, the superintendent of the School District of Philadelphia, announced that Germantown High School was one of 37 schools slated for

closure due to enrollment decreases, low achievement, and a district-wide
fiscal crisis. According to Hite's report, the school district's crisis stemmed
from decades of flight from the public school system, district mismanagement, and inadequate public aid.[4] In response, Philadelphians took to the
streets to denounce state officials who had slashed millions in educational
aid.[5] Principals begged their families to donate hundreds of dollars to make
up for these funding losses. And families did what they could—they opened
their checkbooks and wallets and donated their own money to guarantee
that their children's public schools had basic educational resources.[6] The reliance on private philanthropy bolstered budgets in the city's most affluent
public schools that served the city's most advantaged children; principals in
the city's poorest public schools had to find a way to cope with grossly inadequate public aid.[7] For months, Germantown High School administrators,
teachers, and alumni collaborated with elected officials and community
members to find a way to keep their nearly 100-year-old neighborhood high
school open. They hosted rallies, attended community-wide discussions,
and proposed alternatives. But school officials voted to close the school.[8] On
June 21, 2013, teachers packed their classrooms, moved their belongings, and
shut the doors to Germantown High School.[9]

   The Roots of Educational Inequality explores the political, economic, and
social factors that transformed American high schools and contributed to
the broader escalation of social inequality in America over the past 100 years.
This study deepens our understanding of urban school inequality by pushing the story further into the past to show how the interactions of class, race,
resources, and space help account for the ways that demographic change,
white flight, and white resistance transformed the American high school
and, in this case, ultimately led to closing of Germantown High. Despite the
wealth of scholarship on urban communities and schools, this is the first
book to trace the history of one high school in the context of its community
and city over the entire 20th century, deploying a longitudinal analysis that
investigates daily events rather than focusing solely on key turning points.[10]
While this approach required many hard choices about what to include, as a
teacher, researcher, and activist, I felt that telling this story in this manner
was the only way that I could do justice to the long arc of injustice, inequity,
and resistance in our nation's public schools and communities.

   The approach shows that Germantown High's 21st-century crisis stemmed
from choices that school leaders made over the course of the school's 100-year
history, beginning, of course, with the high school's founding. The challenges

of racial segregation, fiscal instability, and philanthropic subsidies are not the simple byproducts of postwar white flight, failed desegregation, and neoliberal reforms. These structural shortcomings have existed since American public high schools were founded at the turn of the 20th century. There were always alternatives, other paths that individuals might have taken, to create a more just and equitable system of schools. As this story shows, sometimes they took those paths; sometimes they did not.[11]

While *The Roots of Educational Inequality* acknowledges the role of postwar residential and economic flight, it insists that public schools never had sufficient public resources to operate effectively. Rather than raise taxes to the levels required to fund city schools, urban school districts instead relied on philanthropy to subsidize inadequate government aid. While this philanthropy provided essential support to urban public schools, the dependency on private funds generated spatial inequities based on race and class and often masked the inability of urban school districts to fund their schools with public revenues. This masking, of course, was more likely to occur in bourgeois white communities, such as Germantown, where upper- and middle-class residents could afford to supplement inadequate public school budgets with their own private funds. While many scholars have examined the connections between philanthropy and education, none of these works illustrates how local philanthropy historically created what I call *doubly advantaged schools*. Doubly advantaged schools served more white and affluent students and thus could leverage and rely on private philanthropy to subsidize inadequate public aid because the families that sent their children to these schools had more social and financial capital to give.[12] As this story shows, the location of these doubly advantaged schools changed as the city's spatial patterns of class and race changed over time. At the turn of the 20th century, Germantown High School was a doubly advantaged school, but by the turn of the 21st century, it was not.

While other cities, including Cleveland, Detroit, and St. Louis, relied on philanthropy to subsidize inadequate public school funding in the early 20th century, Philadelphia is an ideal place to study the ways in which class, race, resources, and space worked together to sustain and transform the public school landscape.[13] When Philadelphia expanded its system of public high schools in the early 20th century, critics argued that the city was poised to have one of the finest systems in the country. Only a year after Germantown High School opened, however, Philadelphia's school board argued that the city lacked the financial resources to fund its schools adequately and, instead, had to rely on philanthropy to make up the public budget short-falls.[14] Today, the Commonwealth of Pennsylvania has some of the nation's most inequitably funded public schools—high-poverty, majority-Black school districts, such as Philadelphia, often spend about 30% less per pupil than more affluent, majority-white school districts.[15] The School District of Phila-delphia, which serves the largest number of Black, Latinx, and poor youth in the state, spends approximately $13,000 per pupil each year. Lower Merion School District in the affluent, majority-white Philadelphia suburb that bor-ders the city's west side spends $23,000 per pupil each year.[16] In the 21st century, inadequate public school funding still disproportionately harms schools that serve the nation's most vulnerable youth.

When the School District of Philadelphia expanded its system of high schools at the turn of the 20th century, school officials allowed Black and white youth to enroll in Germantown High School. While the school was far from integrated, the fact that school officials never legally segregated Black and white youth into separate schools allows one to examine the ways that race and racism shaped student access to the high school from its founding. Furthermore, because Germantown is a comprehensive, neighborhood high school, it allows me to study an institution that, at least in theory, was open to everyone who lived in the neighborhood. The high school opened in the first wave of 20th-century high school expansion—a time when many indi-viduals hoped that American urban schools would serve as engines of de-mocracy. As my analysis shows, however, only a small percentage of urban youth attended high school, and the vast majority of those who attended were upper class and white. This finding challenges the very notion that ur-ban public schools served a democratizing function by offering opportuni-ties to all American youth. The expansion of high schools at the turn of the 20th century democratized attendance—many more American youth had the opportunity to attend school compared to the late 19th century—but the seeds of inequality, particularly with regard to class, race, and space, were sown into the foundation of high schools located in racially, ethnically, and economically diverse urban areas.[17]

Finally, Germantown is an ideal site to study this history because its residents have a deep appreciation and reverence for local history. German-town teachers, alumni, and activists have preserved many archival sources such as the high school yearbooks and student newspapers that were so critical to my work. As an ethnographer first and historian second, I devel-oped close relationships with these individuals. They willingly opened school storage areas, musty basements, and humid attics to share these sources with me. The oral histories that I did with Germantown youth, alumni/ae, and activists enhanced the archival sources tremendously. This diverse source base made it possible to tell the school's story from the inside—a point of view that is rarely documented in historical research on urban public schools.

Most scholarship links the demise of urban schools to postwar white racism and resistance to any policy that threatened to strip away the economic, educational, or social advantages of white middle-class families and their youth. Historians have documented the ways in which white middle-class families refused to integrate their neighborhoods, factories, and schools. They have also shown how, when white urban resistance proved useless, these families then purchased new homes and found new schools in the racially segregated suburbs.[18] But, this history often focuses on the postwar period, which downplays the importance of the early 20th century in setting the foundation for these practices in the postwar period and today.[19] In addition, it obscures the role that urban school finance has played in creating, maintaining, and promoting educational inequality.[20] In contrast, this book illustrates the ways that white residents blocked proposals to build affordable integrated housing units, to end discriminatory labor practices, and to integrate urban public schools beginning far earlier in the century. It also illustrates how the structures and spatial distribution of urban school finance have created significant resource disparities between white and Black schools since as early as the turn of the 20th century. This system has generated unequal access to educational resources along the lines of race and class and, since the 1920s, has proven to be impervious to educational reforms that would equalize opportunities for low-income youth of color mainly because none of these reforms addressed the inequitable structures of urban school finance.

This book focuses on three central themes: the social organization of education and the construction of urban and metropolitan space; the political economy of urban education; and the failures of educational policy. The first theme illustrates how the American metropolis shaped and was shaped by its system of public schools. Since the founding of Germantown High School in 1915, school officials have supported an unequal system of schools that has privileged white and middle-class communities and disadvantaged Black and low-income communities. The policies and decisions that officials made about school construction, catchment areas, and resource allocations have intensified racial segregation and educational inequality. Often, these policies corresponded neatly with existing patterns of class- and race-based segregation in the metropolis and its schools. School district policies and practices reinforced and intensified patterns of class- and race-based segregation. School officials caved to resident demands to build new, modern high schools, such as Germantown High School, on the city's periphery to retain and attract white middle-class families to the city's bourgeois enclaves. These policies privileged children of upper- and middle-class white families who moved from the city's center to its periphery and then out to its racially segregated suburbs.[21]

School officials played an active role in creating policies and practices that intensified inequality. Throughout its history, Philadelphia school officials have maintained and often promoted a separate and unequal system of public schools: one system that serves upper- and middle-class white youth and another that serves poor, Black, and Latinx youth. In the beginning of the 20th century, school officials preserved these two systems through gerrymandered school boundaries, racially biased hiring practices, and forced student transfers.[22] In the late 20th and early 21st centuries, school officials sustained this two-tiered system through market-based reforms aimed at expanding school choice and raising academic achievement. These reforms have forced the closure of public schools and left thousands of low-income youth of color in under-resourced schools struggling to survive. Meanwhile white families have used their social and financial resources to raise hundreds of thousands of dollars to support their children's public schools. Philadelphia's system of public schools has always been separate and unequal.[23]

The book's second theme centers on the political economy of urban education. In this book, political economy refers to the ways that public policy and government regulation shaped the economic, political, and social welfare of American youth. This happened in at least two ways. First, the policy decisions that government and school officials made about school construction, curricular programs, and resource allocations influenced the reputation of individual high schools. High schools with newer buildings, academic programs, and higher per pupil expenditures were perceived as better, more desirable institutions. As the racial demographics of Philadelphia's public schools shifted and white middle-class families moved first to the city's periphery and then its suburbs, the reputation of Philadelphia's high schools shifted. As schools became more bourgeois and white, the schools' reputations improved. As schools served more poor, Black, and Latinx students, their reputations declined. In other words, the reputation of the school often corresponded with the class and racial composition of the students inside the building. In the past and today, upper- and middle-class families, who had the financial and social capital to exercise choice on the educational marketplace, moved their families to the communities with the city's most reputable schools. These decisions ultimately affected the racial composition, and eventually the intensification of segregation, in Philadelphia's public schools. This chain reaction—district-level policies, demographic shifts, and individual choices—shaped the reputation of Philadelphia's public schools and the demographics of the students who enrolled in them.

Taken together, these factors also shaped the value of the high school credential. Even though every high school offered the same credential (a high school diploma), these educational credentials had vastly different values in the educational marketplace. The value corresponded to two things. First, it corresponded to the high school's reputation. Credentials from more reputable, academically oriented, and better resourced predominately white, middle-class schools had a higher value than those from less reputable, vocationally oriented, and poorly resourced Black and low-income schools. For example, a diploma from the elite Central High School or the bourgeois Germantown High School had a higher value in the labor market than a credential from a high school located in a Black community, such as Simon Gratz or Benjamin Franklin High School.[24] This was because school districts' officials implemented different curricular programs in each school. As the residential demographics of neighborhoods shifted, the curricular programs changed. Underfunded and ill-conceived vocational programs replaced prestigious and attractive academic programs as neighborhood schools moved from predominantly white and middle-class schools to predominantly Black and low-income schools beginning in the late 1930s and early 1940s. These curricular shifts and educational disinvestment, which were intimately tied to race and class, weakened the reputation, and in turn, the value of the credential from the high schools that served the majority of Philadelphia's poor youth of color.

Second, the credential's value often corresponded to a student's race once they graduated. This was due in part to the racial discrimination that students experienced in the high school and eventually in the labor market. Evidence demonstrates that Black youth, even those who graduated from

Germantown High School with an academic diploma, faced racial discrimination inside their schools and in the labor market that barred them from many of the economic opportunities that their white peers enjoyed. Germantown faculty routinely tried to dissuade Black youth from enrolling in the school's academic program and often encouraged them to select its commercial or vocational programs. Hundreds of Black youth defied this advice and earned an academic diploma, but then as this work shows, had to settle for unskilled and service jobs due to racial discrimination in the city's labor market. School-district policies, internal school practices, and labor-market discrimination created a stratified educational credentials market: a market that ascribed a higher value for a credential earned by Philadelphia's white and upper- and middle-class youth and a lesser value for a credential earned by the city's Black and working-class youth.[25]

In addition to the ways that the credentials both afforded and constrained opportunity and mobility, school funding policies and practices also influenced the political economy of urban education. Scholarship that attributes the demise of urban education to a decline in school funding argues that there was a golden age of education at the turn of the 20th century—when public officials and civic leaders used public dollars to fully fund urban public schools. According to these scholars, as white flight occurred, the tax revenues that once supported a robust system of urban public schools vanished.[26] This book directly challenges this view. It argues that state and city officials never funded urban schools adequately. Since the beginning of the 20th century, urban school districts have lacked the tax revenues needed to operate their schools. Rather than raising taxes, urban school districts such as Philadelphia, Detroit, and Cleveland instead relied on private philanthropy to subsidize insufficient government aid.[27] The dependence on philanthropy intensified educational inequality between and inside the city's schools. Upper- and middle-class white families, such as those in Germantown, supported their children's schools through private, philanthropic efforts. Schools in these communities were able to offer a first-rate education because upper- and middle-class white families supplemented grossly inadequate public budgets with their own funds. School administrators used these funds to purchase textbooks, modernize classrooms, and support extracurricular programs.

These philanthropic efforts extended beyond the schoolhouse. Bourgeois families also donated time and money to a dense network of recreational clubs, philanthropic organizations, and social agencies that provided an array of privately funded health and recreational activities outside of school in middle-class neighborhoods.[28] The spatial patterning of race and class (first by neighborhoods within the city and then between the city and its surrounding suburbs) benefited white upper- and middle-class youth by giving them access to educational and recreational resources that were largely unavailable to poor and Black youth because their families lived in different neighborhoods and lacked the private resources to compensate for shortfalls in urban school budgets.

This reliance on philanthropy generated significant funding differentials between schools in affluent white communities and schools in poor Black communities, which exacerbated racial and class-based educational inequality. These differentials created *doubly advantaged schools* like Germantown at the turn of the 20th century, and as we will see, like other schools in Philadelphia's Center City district at the turn of the 21st century. Doubly advantaged schools had more private funding because they served wealthier youth. Furthermore, the overreliance on philanthropy masked the school district's inability to fund its schools—a reality that became painfully clear to everyone at the end of the 20th century and into the 21st as the world weathered the 2008 recession and the COVID-19 pandemic.[29] This book demonstrates that money indeed matters.[30] Money has always provided upper-class, middle-class, and white youth with educational and social opportunities and advantages that poor, Black, and Latinx youth did not always have access to.[31]

This history also forces us to grapple with the fact that the boundary between the public and the private in education (and in other social welfare programs) has been much more porous than many scholars recognize. Private funding of public schools by families, foundations, and communities is not a 21st-century phenomenon.[32] Rather, the practice and dependency on philanthropy to fund American public schools has a long and storied history.[33] This book shows that better state funding for public schools has not and will not, alone, equalize resources among schools—not even among those within the same school district. That is because families in different neighborhoods do not have the same capacity to leverage private resources to benefit their children. Wealthy families have more social and financial capital, and thus, they can donate more money, resources, and time to their schools.

Finally, the book focuses on the failures of education policy to translate ideas and recommendations into school reforms that might create more just and equitable educational outcomes for all youth. For decades, educational reformers have tried to put policies in place to match high school curricula to labor market needs and students' vocational aims.[34] As this story illustrates, Germantown High School, at least initially, was immune from these reforms because it was a largely white upper- and middle-class institution with a mission to prepare its graduates for postsecondary schooling and futures as middle-class professionals and wives. Despite this mission, Germantown faculty routinely barred Black youth from the school's academic programs and instead encouraged them to enroll in the school's commercial program.

For decades, Black youth refused to comply with racist policies and practices in their schools. From 1920 to 1950, contrary to conventional wisdom, most Black graduates enrolled in Germantown's academic program. The Black youth who graduated from Germantown High School in the first half of the 20th century understood the racial discrimination that their families faced in the labor market. They knew that one avenue for social mobility was an academic diploma, and thus, if they attended high school, they fought to obtain an academic degree to avoid manual work and assume a professional position as a Black doctor, lawyer, or teacher.

Beginning in the Great Depression, the demographics of Germantown High School slowly began to change. First, the school enrolled more working-class white youth. Then, in the postwar period, it enrolled more working-class Black youth. As the demographics changed, school officials questioned the value of an academic degree for poor Black and white youth and expanded vocational programs that they believed matched the intellectual dispositions and future aims of youth, who in ordinary economic times, had never attended high school. The curricular reforms that school officials implemented, first in the poor Black schools such as Philadelphia's Simon Gratz High School and then later in Germantown High School, mapped neatly onto class and race.[35]

Through an analysis that weaves together the social organization of education and the construction of metropolitan urban space, the political economy of urban education, and the failures of educational policy, this book demonstrates how the convergence of class, race, and space generated a system of unequal access to educational resources and reinforced a system of racial and economic segregation. The story of Germantown High School forces us, as scholars, educators, and activists, to reckon with the fact that urban schools have remained largely impervious to education reforms, including those that focused on vocational education, school desegregation, and school choice.[36] None of these reforms addressed the structural and unequal distribution of race, space, and resources—both public and private—that have left low-income and youth of color in underfunded and under-resourced public schools since the turn of the 20th century.

This project leverages an interdisciplinary approach to scholarship that uses an array of quantitative and qualitative methodologies from education, history, and sociology and a diverse archival and contemporary source base. I examined graduate demographic data gathered from school yearbooks and the census to understand how the class, race, gender, and ethnicity of the Germantown student body changed over time.[37] Using quantitative methods and data for thousands of Philadelphia youth, I have analyzed these demographics to understand how class, ethnicity, gender, and race influenced students' educational opportunities and labor market outcomes. Using Geographic Information Systems (GIS) software, I mapped these quantitative data to show the spatial distribution of the community's youth by race and ethnicity. Qualitative methods—examining city and community newspapers, association meeting notes, political scrapbooks, and Philadelphia Board of Education annual reports—let me connect the political, economic, and social forces that shaped the history of the school and its community to larger historical changes (see appendix for statistical details). I also used school newspapers, yearbooks, and newsletters to document historical changes inside the school and to understand the perspectives that youth brought to these changes. I used ethnographic methods as well, filming oral history interviews with Germantown High School alums, teachers, and community activists and conducting participant observations at school events and rallies.[38] These interviews and observations allowed me to analyze how the district and school decisions affected the lives of adolescent youth and how the intersections of class, gender, and race shaped their experiences inside the school.

The Roots of Educational Inequality shows how class, race, and space have intersected with the political economy of urban education to create unequally resourced schools within one urban school district. It argues that our high schools are not actually broken, but that they are operating as they were designed to. These institutions were founded to provide different opportunities and resources to Black and white children. These differences can be traced to the fiscal policies that existed at the turn of the 20th century.[39] We can only see that by examining the history of one institution from its founding to its closure. This is the first book to do that. The story that follows—which focuses on one city, one school district, and one high school—sheds light on the broader transformation of urban communities and schools across America, on the ways that our nation has failed to provide Black schools with equal and adequate resources, and on the possible solutions to address their shortcomings in the hopes of creating more equitable and just outcomes for all youth.

CHAPTER 1

The Campaign for an Elite Public High School in Philadelphia's Suburban Sanctuary, 1907–1914

Shortly before the sun rose, Viola C. Fisher's mother knocked gently on her daughter's door to wake her for her first day of high school. Viola's mother had already pressed her finest clothes, a crisp, white blouse with a high collar bordered by a hint of lace and a long, black skirt that draped to the edge of her ankles. Viola looked at her new clothes with excitement. They epitomized refined femininity, marking her as a young woman with a bright future. Viola was one of a select group of girls privileged to attend one of the finest high schools in the city, the all-female Philadelphia High School for Girls. A diploma from Girls High virtually guaranteed white-collar employment and, for many, marriage to an appropriate suitor. Her mother beamed as she watched her daughter get ready for her first day of high school.

After Viola cinched her skirt and laced her black leather boots, she rushed down the oak staircase and gathered her belongings. She kissed her mother goodbye before leaving the safe confines of her family's Germantown home. Her father, Gilbert, a machinist, accompanied Viola on the half-mile walk from her home on Rex Avenue to Germantown Avenue, the main thoroughfare, with its historic cobblestone street and modern electric trolleys.[1] As they walked down their street, past Germantown's middle-class twin homes and upper-class stately mansions, Gilbert reminded Viola to keep to herself on the crowded electric trolleys that transported workers and students to and from the city's periphery to its bustling center. He wanted his young daughter to board the trolley, attend high school, and return home safely. However, as she left the protected confines of her quiet community and entered the chaotic city, he knew he could not protect her.[2]

Many of the upper- and middle-class white families who sent their children to high schools located in Philadelphia's city center shared Gilbert's fears. While they might have worried about their sons, they were particularly concerned about the perceived effects and risks of the commute on their daughters. As figure 1 shows, the Philadelphia High School for Girls was located far from Viola's home, but it was also located near the census tracts with the highest concentrations of Black and immigrant residents. Upper- and middle-class white families in Germantown, such as the Fishers, often imagined a city split into separate zones. The first zone included the city's secluded majority-white upper- and middle-class communities on the city's periphery where white bourgeois families felt that their daughters could travel freely; the second zone included the city's congested and majority-Black and immigrant working-class neighborhoods in the city's inner core where they, perhaps, could not. Viola and her peers who traveled to the city's inner core for high school challenged the gendered and racialized boundaries that had governed their young lives and raised newfound concerns about their moral and physical development.[3]

From 1907 to 1914, Germantown residents waged a citywide campaign to build a permanent high school in their community to protect women like Viola from the dangers of the urban core where Philadelphia's high schools were located.[4] The story of this campaign challenges the idea of the golden age of public education—an age, at the turn of the 20th century, when elected officials and the public willingly used tax dollars to fund a robust system of public schools.[5] In Philadelphia, the campaign illustrated the reluctance among many taxpayers and most elected officials to fund its public school system.[6]

Philadelphia's high school campaign moved across three distinct phases. In the first phase, Martin G. Brumbaugh, Philadelphia's school superintendent, asked taxpayers to approve a multimillion-dollar loan to improve the city's existing schools and build new schools to accommodate the city's ever-expanding school enrollment. Despite support from a Progressive coalition of civic groups and labor unions, Philadelphia voters blocked the loan. After this failure, Brumbaugh and his allies argued that Philadelphia needed more high schools to protect young, bourgeois, white women who lived in the city's periphery. This signaled the second phase of the campaign. Drawing on psychological theories of the day and referencing local stories about the dangerous commute, the leaders argued that by traveling to the

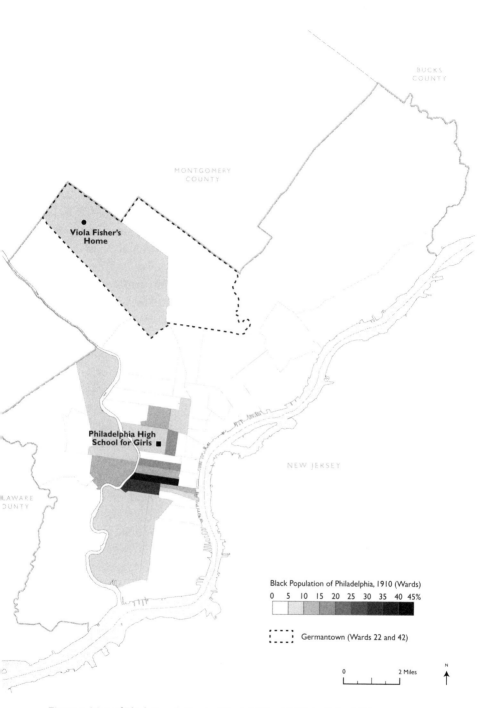

Figure 1. Map of Black Population by Ward, 1910, with Viola Fisher's Home and Philadelphia High School for Girls. Source: Ancestry.com; United States Census, 1900; *ARBPE-P*, 1907.

city center, these young white women risked their future lives as dutiful wives and loving mothers.[7] Philadelphia needed public high schools in the city's "suburban" communities to protect and preserve these women's morals and bodies.[8]

While there was widespread support for this argument in Germantown, Philadelphia's powerful Republican political machine refused to allocate funds to build high schools for the city's elite.[9] Even though this tactic failed, the decision to tie the high school campaign to the protection of female bodies revealed the class, gender, and racial hierarchies, the coded geographies, that defined urban space. Even at the turn of the 20th century, Germantown residents attached ideas and meaning to urban neighborhoods based on the class, ethnic, and racial composition of the residents who lived in them. These coded geographies, which were tied to anti-Black, anti-immigrant, and anti-working-class sentiments, generated anxieties and fears among elites in Philadelphia and other American cities. Germantown's majority-white residents worried about their daughters traveling to the city's inner core because many of them believed that the Black, foreign-born, and poor men who lived in the city's center posed a serious threat to their white native-born daughters. The decision to link the high school campaign to ideas about the fragility of women's bodies and morals revealed the beliefs that many early 20th-century educators and families held about the spatial distribution of race and class. Germantown residents wanted a new high school to protect their daughters and to segregate Germantown's bourgeois, white youth from poor, immigrant, and Black youth who lived in the city's center. In contrast to other scholarship that focuses on the expansion of high schools to relieve middle-class anxieties about their sons' economic futures, this chapter illustrates that school officials founded Germantown High School to address the middle-class anxieties about young women transgressing the racial and class codes that governed urban space.[10]

For almost five years, Philadelphia's Republican machine had refused to finance a public high school for Germantown's white elite. Elected officials argued that the board needed to reserve its funds to build elementary schools in the city's center. In 1911, the state passed a new school code. The passage of this code corresponded with the campaign's third, and final, phase. For the first time in the city's history, residents on the city's periphery paid the same tax rate as residents in the city's center. This new code gave Philadelphia's bourgeois elite leverage to procure the funds for their high school. In 1912, Brumbaugh allocated the funds to build Germantown's first-rate academic public high school. Germantown residents rejoiced that their children, particularly their daughters, could finally attend high school in their predominantly white secluded suburb in the city.

The New Superintendent Seeks to Modernize
Philadelphia's Outdated Public Schools

On July 1, 1906, Philadelphia's board of education appointed Martin G. Brumbaugh, Germantown resident and University of Pennsylvania professor, as its superintendent of schools.[11] When Brumbaugh assumed his role, thousands of children attended overcrowded and under-resourced schools on part-time schedules because the city did not have enough schools to accommodate Philadelphia's growing youth population. Educators complained that the temporary and antiquated school facilities, with their dark and dingy classrooms, impeded learning. Brumbaugh told residents that the dismal school conditions coupled with the insufficient number of high schools threatened Philadelphia's ability to compete economically with other cities.[12] In an effort to reform the system, Brumbaugh mobilized over 4,000 educators to protest the dire school conditions and fight for more school funds.[13] Philadelphia City Council, which controlled the purse strings, argued that the school district's problems stemmed from administrative mismanagement not insufficient funding.[14] Mayor John Reyburn toured several schools. Reyburn said that the superintendent had exaggerated the problems. Reyburn assured voters that Brumbaugh had enough funding.[15]

Frustrated with Philadelphia's political leaders, Brumbaugh appealed directly to Philadelphia voters for support. In a speech commemorating the opening of Philadelphia's Southern Manual Training High School for Boys, Brumbaugh pointed out that Philadelphia's high school population had nearly doubled over the past 10 years. Brumbaugh argued that "an army of girls and boys" from "honest and worthy families" had to forgo their high school education because the city's high schools did not have space to accommodate them. He asserted that the city lacked high schools because council had not provided the funds to build them. He told listeners that the city's current high schools were in the city's center, and the geographic location generated financial hardships for families who lived on the city's periphery in communities such as West Philadelphia and Germantown. Families who lived in the city's predominately white and bourgeois periphery had to

pay trolley and lunch fares for their children to attend high school. Brumbaugh argued that these expenses represented a "tax" on these residents. He
couched his argument in economic terms to persuade middle-class families
who lived on the periphery to approve his proposed loan.[16]

A few days later, Brumbaugh mobilized social clubs, labor unions, and
civic associations, including the Germantown and Chestnut Hill Improvement Association, to rally for the loan.[17] Brumbaugh told reporters that the
conditions in Philadelphia's public schools were much worse than any of the
schools he had visited "in the rural districts of Pennsylvania" or the "moun-
tains of Porto Rico [sic]."[18] The school board distributed a pamphlet that
outlined their plans for the loan, highlighted the unfair costs for families in
the outlying areas, and noted, "the reputation of Philadelphia is at stake."[19]
Brumbaugh hoped that this multipronged approach might convince voters
to approve his proposed loan.

Despite his hope, Philadelphia voters only approved a smaller loan, half
the amount that Brumbaugh had requested.[20] Brumbaugh pledged to use the
limited funds to build new elementary schools and vowed to fight for funds to
build new high schools in the future. Reiterating his earlier argument, Brumbaugh told his constituents that Philadelphia needed more high schools. He
said, "when a boy or girl must hang on a trolley strap to reach [high] school,
with carfares to be paid and a lunch to buy, that child's father is being taxed
too much."[21] Taxpayers could either support a school loan to build new high
schools or use their personal funds to pay this "tax." In the spring of 1908,
the board of education told taxpayers that Philadelphia ranked 23rd among
American cities in the percentage of its youth who enrolled in high school.
Brumbaugh blamed the low high school enrollment on the city council's
unwillingness to allocate funds to build new high schools.[22] After two years
of failed campaigns to convince taxpayers of the economic necessity of new
high schools, Brumbaugh and his supporters tried a different tactic: they
tied Philadelphia's high school campaign to national anxieties about coeducation, race suicide, and the fragile white female body.

American High Schools, Racial Suicide,
and the Fragile White Female Body

In the late 19th and early 20th centuries, high schools and colleges witnessed
a dramatic surge in the percentage of female graduates. This increase incited

an intense debate about the effects of academic study on white women's bodies. Beginning with Edward H. Clarke's *Sex in Education; or, A Fair Chance for Girls* (1875), scholars argued that the expansion of women's educational opportunities and increased academic study generated hysteria, anxiety, and infertility.[23] Feminist leaders denounced Clarke and his colleagues for publishing a book that lacked rigorous scientific evidence and slowed women's progress. Even with the vocal opposition to Clarke's work, college administrators implemented quotas to restrict female enrollment and provided routine medical examinations to monitor their health.[24] Statistical evidence from the 1900 US census bolstered Clarke's ideas. Data indicated that native-born white women had fewer children than either foreign-born white women or Black women.[25] Social scientists and political leaders blamed this trend on the growing numbers of high school and college-educated white women who had delayed or rejected marriage and childbirth. Worried about the effects of these trends, President Theodore Roosevelt said, "the man or woman who deliberately avoids marriage, and has a heart so cold as to know no passion and a brain so shallow and selfish to dislike having children, is in effect a criminal against the race." Roosevelt called the decline in the birthrate among native-born white Americans "race suicide."[26]

In 1904, G. Stanley Hall, a Harvard-trained psychologist, brought new evidence to these ideas with his highly acclaimed publication, *Adolescence*. Hall told readers that he had surveyed hundreds of the latest scientific studies conducted around the globe to verify the validity of sexual differences and the fragility of adolescent development. Hall characterized adolescence as a period of immense growth that contributed to male aggression and feminine maternity. He argued that this rapid development made adolescent youth susceptible to disease and infection.[27] These risks, he contended, were much greater for urban youth and young women. Cities with their dense populations and corrupt activities increased the chances that urban youth might contract a deadly disease or fall into despair. Hall worried that adolescence placed unique strains on the female body, making it vulnerable to illness and immorality. He wrote: "American girls come to this crisis [adolescence] without having much control or restraint, and with their habits and actions almost entirely unsystematized. They appear rosy and healthy because energies, which should go to perfecting other parts and functions, have been diverted to cerebration. Influences from those about her tend to make her give up free and girlish sports and romping, and to feel herself a woman too suddenly."[28] Hall asserted that adolescence presented grave dangers to young women because they were often unable to restrain their wild emotions and desires. He argued that academic study compounded these ailments and threatened to destroy a young woman's nerves, body, and morals and often provoked a deep aversion toward marriage and motherhood. Hall encouraged school officials to build high schools for girls situated "in the country in the midst of hills" to help them develop healthy breathing and strong bones.[29] Even though Hall's theories received considerable criticism, his work's positive reception influenced ideas about the risks of urban space and academic education for white upper- and middle-class girls.[30]

In the spring of 1908, the leaders of Philadelphia's high school campaign leveraged Hall's concerns about the effects of urban space and academic education on native-born white girls and urged the city council to allocate funds to build new high schools in the city's peripheral districts. On May 12, 1908, the Business Men's Association of Germantown and the Germantown and Chestnut Hill Improvement Association hosted a mass meeting to rally support for a new high school. Echoing Brumbaugh's earlier campaign, these men argued that Philadelphia's inadequate public school system threatened Philadelphia's economic standing. They also asserted that the trolley fares that families paid to send their children to high school placed a "serious drain upon the resources of parents" and forced most high school students to drop out of school before they graduated.[31] Then, they presented data that indicated that families that lived in Germantown were much more likely to send their children to high school compared to families from other communities in the city.[32]

Building on Hall's ideas and the coded geographies in the city that governed many of their bourgeois white daughters' lives, the members of these associations argued that "the remoteness of the existing high schools" made it difficult for Germantown youth to attend high school because the long commute to these schools presented a "grave risk to their [children's] physical health and moral well-being."[33] Once again, these men argued that the commute presented a grave risk for two reasons. First, it was long. Second, it forced Germantown's white elite female youth to cross geographies where the majority of Philadelphia's immigrant and Black residents lived. Germantown's business leaders asked the board of education to fund a high school annex for girls inside Germantown's YWCA. Even though the superintendent and several board members who lived in Germantown supported this proposal, the board of education refused it, arguing that it had to save its funds to build new elementary schools for immigrant and working-class youth in the city's center. Undeterred, Germantown elite mobilized to continue their fight for a neighborhood high school.[34]

Despite this setback, Brumbaugh, a member of Germantown's bourgeois elite, once again pushed the connections between the high school campaign and the preservation of native-born white female bodies and morals. In a citywide address at the opening of William Penn High School for Girls, Brumbaugh said that the city's existing system of high schools denied many Philadelphia youth the opportunity to earn a high school diploma. Repeating earlier statements, Brumbaugh argued that Philadelphia needed more high schools for female youth. Philadelphia had several high schools that admitted male students, but only two high schools that admitted female students. Moreover, the high schools that enrolled female students were in the center of the city far from outlying districts. Brumbaugh understood the coded geographies that shaped the lives of young women in Philadelphia and argued that the long commute to these high schools "endangered the physical strength, good manners, and sound morals" of women who attended high school located far from their homes in the city's center. Brumbaugh demanded that the city council allocate funds for new high schools in the city's periphery.[35]

Tensions Rise Between Bourgeois Elite Residents and Philadelphia's Elected Officials

The tensions between elites in the city's periphery concerned about their white bourgeois native-born daughters and Philadelphia's Republican machine, which depended on white working-class ethnic voters in the city's center, peaked in the winter of 1909.[36] On December 3, 1909, Brumbaugh and members of the Education Alliance, a citywide group focused on the campaign to build more high schools, testified before the city council. As Brumbaugh walked to the podium to speak, Councilman Joseph McAllister, the chairman of the school and finance committee, leapt out of his seat and chastised these men for pressuring the council to fund high schools in the city's wealthier outlying districts rather than elementary schools for the "poor boys and girls in [his] district."[37] McAllister reminded these men, there are "poor Jew and Italian [children] in the slums, where I come from, who have to either sit on soap boxes or stay away from the schools altogether" because the schools had no space for them.[38] The councilman argued that Brumbaugh and his allies were more interested in building high schools for wealthy residents than in providing additional schools in the center of the city for "poor children who now receive their education in the gutters and streets."[39] McAllister represented the city's center where most of the city's Black and immigrant residents lived; he did not want to fund more public schools for Philadelphia's bourgeois white native-born families on the city's periphery.

Brumbaugh challenged some of McAllister's claims. He reminded those present that the board had already used funds to build elementary schools in McAllister's district. Senator Ernest Tustin, who represented West Phila- delphia, told McAllister that his committee was not advocating on behalf of wealthy residents in the city's outlying areas who sent their children to pri- vate schools. Rather, Tustin wanted the council to pass the school loan to provide high schools for "the vast majority [of families] whose income [was] not sufficient to thoroughly educate their children [in private schools], and who must look to the State for assistance."[40] George Darrow, a Germantown resident and Education Alliance board member, used a slightly different tactic. Darrow said: "A practical high school education is not a luxury, but has become a necessity to meet the demands and competition of modern industrial and commercial life. Many a father and mother have told me that unless they are given the opportunity to continue the education of their children, they would have to move away, as that was the most important thing for them to consider. People, as a rule, are willing to pay for the things that they want."[41] Darrow reminded his listeners that if council did not give Germantown's bourgeois residents the public high school that they demanded, many of them would move across the city line to the nearby suburbs with modern high schools and lower tax rates. Germantown's elite had the finan- cial and social capital to move, taking their children and their city tax reve- nues with them.

Council refused to budge and once again only approved funds to build additional elementary schools in the city's center. In his 1910 annual report, Philadelphia's school board president, Henry Edmunds, reiterated the need for additional high schools in the city's outlying areas, which had the high- est rates of high school enrollment. To prove his point, he provided detailed statistics about the growth in high school enrollment and a map that indi- cated the mismatch between the location of Philadelphia's high schools and the places with the largest high school enrollment. Germantown had one of the highest concentrations and the highest number of high school students, but it lacked a neighborhood high school. Figure 2 illustrates these data and his point that the city's high schools were located in the center of the city, but the census wards with the highest percentage of youth in high schools were in the city's periphery.[42] In the superintendent's report, Brumbaugh once again argued that the long commute from Germantown to high schools in the center of the city threatened the well-being of adolescent girls who, he argued, were "at an age when they need and should receive the finest moral and physical protection." Brumbaugh once again used the coded geographies of the city to advance his claims. According to him, forcing young women to travel to and from the city's high schools endangered their moral and physical development and generated "a frightful loss to the future of womanhood and motherhood in the city."[43]

This phase of the campaign revealed the gendered geographies that divided the city into two distinct parts. Many individuals in Germantown and those that lived in the city's outer ring regarded the city's center, with its bustling commercial district and immigrant and Black enclaves, as a place for bourgeois white men to travel in the morning, spend the day at work, and leave in the evening. Germantown's white residents had little interest in having their children, particularly their daughters, leaving the boundaries of their secluded white bourgeois community to attend high school in the city's center. Even though Germantown's bourgeois were deeply concerned about the effects of their daughters traveling to and from the city center for high school, Councilman McAllister and the others who controlled council's purse strings had no interest in using public funds to build high schools for the city's elite in Germantown and other outlying districts. In 1910, the high school campaign leaders and the superintendent focused on convincing the state to pass a new school code.

The Board of Education Opens Separate and Unequal High School Annexes in Germantown

In the summer of 1910, overcrowded conditions in Philadelphia's high schools pushed the board of education to allocate $140,000 to open high school annexes in Germantown—one for girls and another for boys.[44] The skewed enrollment patterns once again illustrated the anxieties about sending girls to the city's center for high school. When the annexes officially

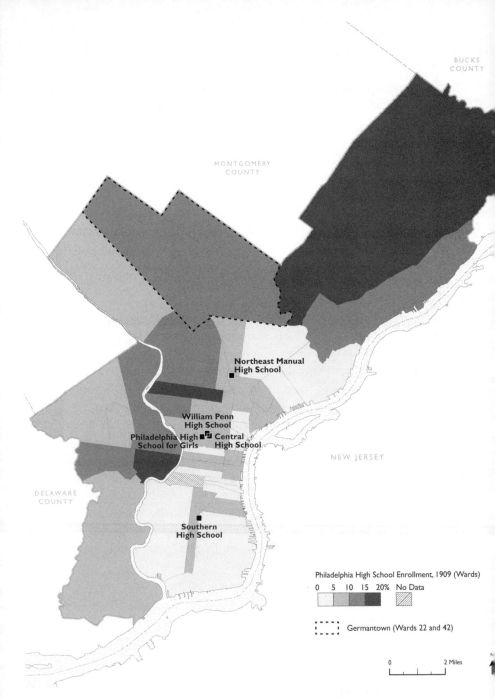

BUCKS
COUNTY

MONTGOMERY
COUNTY

Northeast Manual
High School

William Penn
High School

Philadelphia High
School for Girls

Central
High School

NEW JERSEY

DELAWARE
COUNTY

Southern
High School

Philadelphia High School Enrollment, 1909 (Wards)

0   5   10   15   20%   No Data

Germantown (Wards 22 and 42)

0   2 Miles

N

Figure 2. Percent of Philadelphia High School–Youth Enrolled in School by
Ward with Current High School Locations, 1909. Source: *ARBPE-P*, 1909.

opened, the boys' annex enrolled 35 students; the girls' annex had 175 students. Many residents worried that this imbalance might stall the community's ability to secure a permanent high school, and so, they encouraged Germantown families to send their boys to these local school annexes. Some families listened, but the enrollment remained skewed. In February 1911, 87 boys and 285 girls enrolled in Germantown's high school annexes.[45] Eventually, the annexes became overcrowded, forcing school officials to move 40 girls and 30 boys who had enrolled in the annexes to schools in the city's center. Frustrated with this outcome, Germantown residents organized a series of rallies and formed new committees to secure a permanent high school.[46] More than a year later, in the fall of 1912, the board passed a school loan with specific funds to build a high school in Germantown.[47]

The board's decision stemmed from several factors relating to changes in the 1911 school code. First, the 1911 school code finally gave the board the ability to pass a school loan without the city council's approval. Freed from council's fiscal control and oversight, school board president Henry Edmunds procured funds to expand Philadelphia's high schools so the city could "maintain a credible position among the cities of America in regard to its schools."[48] Second, as Edmunds explained in the 1913 annual report, before the 1911 school code, residents in the city's suburban or rural Philadelphia districts paid a lower municipal tax rate than residents in the city's urban districts. Because of these differential tax rates, residents in the city's outlying areas "received less in the way of school facilities than the sections paying the full tax rate." The city's skewed tax system generated inequities within the school district—the city's central areas had "fine [school] buildings, excellent equipment, and the best types of school organization" while the city's remote areas had "inferior buildings, meagre equipment, and very imperfect types of organization." The 1911 school code reformed this system and instituted a uniform tax rate across the city. Edmunds wrote: "In view of the fact that residents of suburban and rural portions of school districts are now contributing to the school funds on the same basis as those who reside in the built-up portions, they have a claim for improved school accommodations such as they have never had before. . . . Uniform tax rates have radically changed the situation. There is no longer any reason why the people living in the outlying portions of the city should be content and should be expected to be content with school facilities in any way inferior to those offered anywhere else in the school district."[49]

For nearly five years, the city council had refused to build a high school for Germantown's white elite, but the new school code made it impossible for council to block their demands. The board of education and the city's superintendent had ties to Germantown—Martin G. Brumbaugh and several of the board members lived in the community. For years, these men had promised their neighbors the high school that they demanded. The 1911 school code made that possible. For the first time in the city's history, residents on the city's periphery, including those in Germantown, paid the same tax rate as their city's inner-city residents. The board of education allocated the funds for a new high school in Germantown because the bourgeois elites had the social connections to convince them to do so and because they were finally paying the taxes to cover the nearly $4 million in capital costs to build it. Germantown's comprehensive high school gave these families a way to protect their daughters' bodies and morals from the city's corrupt inner core so that they might have secure economic futures as bourgeois wives and mothers.

A New High School Tucked Away in the Suburban Solitude

On September 14, 1914, thousands of residents gathered on Germantown Avenue, the community's main thoroughfare, for the high school's cornerstone ceremony. Local Civil War veterans dressed in their military regalia led a procession of hundreds of high school–aged youth down Germantown Avenue to the site of the new high school on Haines and High Street. Residents flanked both sides of the avenue waving small American flags.[50] The leaders of the high school campaign basked in what they had achieved: a public high school to serve Germantown's white middle-class families. In the first phase of the campaign, Philadelphia's new superintendent, Martin G. Brumbaugh, used an economic argument to convince conservative taxpayers and Philadelphia businesspeople to approve a school loan to modernize and expand Philadelphia's system of public schools. Even though this phase failed, it revealed the entrenched resistance to raise money to fund the city's public schools. Philadelphia's elected officials and conservative constituents refused to support Brumbaugh's call for more money. After this, Brumbaugh and his supporters connected the high school campaign to national anxieties about the effects of academic education on native-born women. Germantown's high school campaign exposed bourgeois ideas about the city's gendered geographies, which corresponded to the city's spatial distribution of race and class. It also revealed the residents' desire to build a new high school to segregate Germantown's upper- and middle-class white youth from the working-class immigrant and Black youth who lived in the city's center. In the end, the 1911 school code, which gave the board of education the right to raise funds and equalized the tax rate across the city, made it possible for Germantown residents to get what they had spent seven years campaigning for: a publicly funded institution for the city's bourgeois white elite that, when it opened, was regarded by many as one of the finest high schools in the nation.

CHAPTER 2

Philanthropy Sustains Philadelphia's Expanding Public School System, 1914–1920

On November 1, 1915, over 500 boys walked through Germantown High School's hand-carved wooden archway, up its pristine marble staircase, and into its magnificent assembly room. After the boys had settled, Dr. Harry Keller, the high school's first principal, eagerly welcomed them to their new school. When Dr. Keller finished his remarks, faculty escorted the boys to their classrooms tucked away on the east side of the school. As the boys filed out, approximately 800 girls found their seats in the assembly room where Miss Mary Holmes, the head of the girls' school, oriented them to their new school. When Holmes finished, the faculty walked the girls to their classrooms on the west side of the building. Even though Philadelphia school officials lauded their modern coeducational and racially integrated high school buildings, they still segregated boys and girls the moment they stepped into Germantown High School.[1]

The history of Germantown's early years sharpens our understanding of the factors that led to the 21st century challenges in urban schools by examining the ways that class, race, and space shaped educational resources and, in turn, educational inequality.[2] Although school officials in Philadelphia never officially segregated their students by race, they routinely implemented racist policies and practices that deprived Black youth of some of the city's most resourced schools. They did this in several ways. First, district officials built most of the city's new schools on its periphery, where the majority of white upper- and middle-class families lived. These decisions left working-class Black and immigrant youth in overcrowded and outdated schools in the city's center. Second, school administrators gerrymandered school boundaries and implemented discriminatory practices to maintain and create racially segregated schools. White youth routinely attended better re-sourced schools than did Black youth.[3]

In addition to these practices, the School District of Philadelphia never had the resources necessary to support its schools. Like other urban school districts across the nation, rather than raise taxes, school district officials in Philadelphia relied on philanthropy to subsidize inadequate public school budgets. When Germantown High School opened, upper- and middle-class families donated funds to supplement inadequate school budgets. The influx of private money provided Germantown youth with additional educa-tional resources and programs that would not have been available other-wise. However, the spatial patterning of class and race in Philadelphia's neighborhoods and schools, coupled with the overreliance on private fund-ing, intensified inequality. Upper- and upper-middle-class white families in Germantown had the social and financial capital to donate private funds and resources to their public schools; low-income Black and immigrant families in the city's inner core did not. As a result, the schools on the pe-riphery, such as Germantown, which served primarily upper- and upper-middle-class white youth, had more funding and resources than the schools in the city's inner core, which served primarily low-income Black and im-migrant youth. In other words, Germantown High School was a doubly ad-vantaged school.

Even though Germantown High School benefited immensely from the influx of private dollars and resources, when one looks inside the school, other inequities emerge. Germantown opened as a coeducational, racially integrated institution, but from its founding, Black and female youth did not have the same rights and privileges as their white male peers. School administrators and educators segregated male and female youth into sepa-rate spaces and routinely barred Black and female youth from extracurricu-lar programs. From the moment that the high school opened, Germantown youth and their families fought inequitable practices in the school and community.

The Promise of Opportunity Spurs Blacks to Migrate North

When Germantown High School opened, Black southerners were engaged in a mass exodus to northern cities such as Chicago, Detroit, and Philadel-phia in the hopes that they might secure the economic, political, and social rights that they had been denied for centuries in the South. Most migrants willingly went wherever they could find work. As one 30-year-old man living in Houston with a young family remarked, he wanted to move to Chicago or Philadelphia, but he did not care where he went "so long as I go where a man is a man."[4] As thousands of migrants settled in Philadelphia, the city's Black population rose from 5% in 1910 to just over 11% in 1930. In Germantown, on the other hand, the Black population decreased from 6.8% in 1910 to 4.3% in 1930 as white families moved from the city's center to its suburban and white periphery.[5] The great expectations about their new lives in the North shattered the moment Black migrants tried to find a job and a home.[6] Racial discrimination on Philadelphia's labor and housing markets made it difficult, if not impossible, for Black residents to secure decent housing and work. White managers routinely refused to hire Black workers; white landlords routinely refused to rent to Black residents. In the rare cases when white landlords allowed Black residents to live in their properties, white residents often retaliated by burning Black-occupied homes to the ground.[7]

Facing limited housing options and fearing the threat of Philadelphia's white mobs, Black residents remained concentrated in the city's historically Black communities in the center of the city and the small, but important, historically Black communities in West Philadelphia and Germantown. As Black families moved into these areas, white families began their slow but steady movement out of the city's center and into its periphery or nearby suburbs. As figure 3 illustrates, the in-migration of Black families and out-migration of white families intensified racial segregation between the city's core and its outer ring.[8] By 1930, Black residents made up more than 20% of the population in 15 of Philadelphia's 48 wards, up from 2 wards in 1910 and just 4 wards in 1920.[9] The patterns of Philadelphia's postwar racial segregation had already started to emerge.

Philadelphia School Leaders Implement Policies and Practices That Promote School Segregation

While no one could deny the fact that segregation in the city's neighborhoods affected racial segregation inside the city's schools, school officials implemented policies and practices that exacerbated race-based school

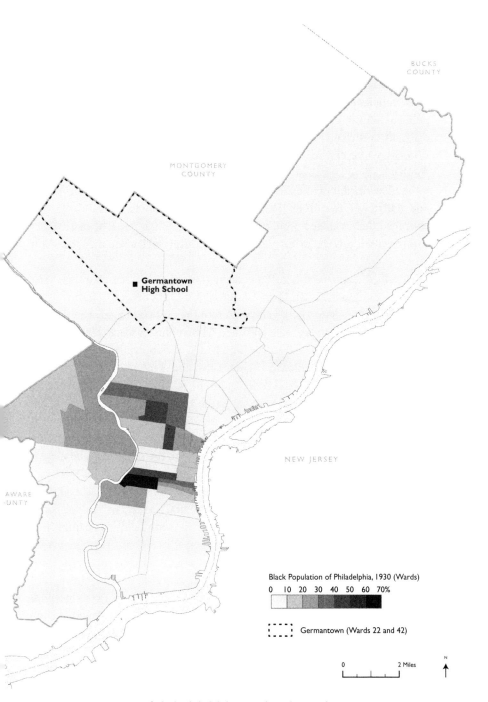

BUCKS
COUNTY

MONTGOMERY
COUNTY

■ Germantown
High School

NEW JERSEY

AWARE
UNTY

Black Population of Philadelphia, 1930 (Wards)

0   10   20   30   40   50   60   70%

┌╌╌╌┐
╎   ╎ Germantown (Wards 22 and 42)
└╌╌╌┘

0   2 Miles

N

Figure 3. Percentage of Black Philadelphia Residents by Ward, 1930.
Source: United States Census, 1930.

segregation.[10] Philadelphia school leaders and administrators gerrymandered school catchment boundaries and supported racially biased enrollment policies to create and sustain racial segregation among Philadelphia's
public schools.[11] From 1905 to 1920, school district officials built most of the
district's new elementary schools and all of its new high schools in or near
majority-white census tracts (see figure 4) and thus benefited the white
youth who lived in these areas. As the city built new schools in white communities, Black children attended schools that were much older, more crowded,
and had fewer resources than majority-white schools.[12] School officials
leveraged the racialized geography of the city to build new schools in white
communities, which, in turn, intensified educational inequality based on
race and space.[13]

Black educators and families actively resisted the school district's racist
practices and policies. Dr. Daniel A. Brooks, a Black educator, testified that
school officials had forced Black youth into the city's outdated schools with
facilities that did not promote learning. Classrooms in many Black schools
were "gas-lighted with coal stoves" and had "out-door water closets" for the
children to use. White children, in contrast, attended the city's newest schools,
which had electric lights and indoor plumbing.[14] Black families demanded
that their children have access to the same educational resources as white
children. Philadelphia school officials routinely blocked their requests. In
1926, Roscoe P. Douglas, a middle-class Black Germantown resident, tried
to register his son at the all-white Keyser School, the school located closest
to their home. The principal told Douglas that he could not enroll his Black son
at the school because the school only enrolled white children. He encouraged Douglas to register his son for the all-Black Meehan School located a
few blocks away. Refusing to relent, Douglas met with Louis Nusbaum, Germantown's regional school superintendent. Nusbaum confirmed the principal's remarks and told Douglas that he had to register his son at the Meehan
school because "there has never been a colored child" at the Keyser School.[15]
Douglas filed a legal complaint against the school district. In response, the
members of the board of education told the court that overcrowded conditions in the city's public schools made it impossible for them to guarantee
that students could enroll in the school closest to their homes. Even though
the all-white Keyser School was most likely less crowded than the all-Black
Meehan School, the court sided with the school board.[16] Black residents and
educators repeatedly pushed Philadelphia's white school leaders to end the

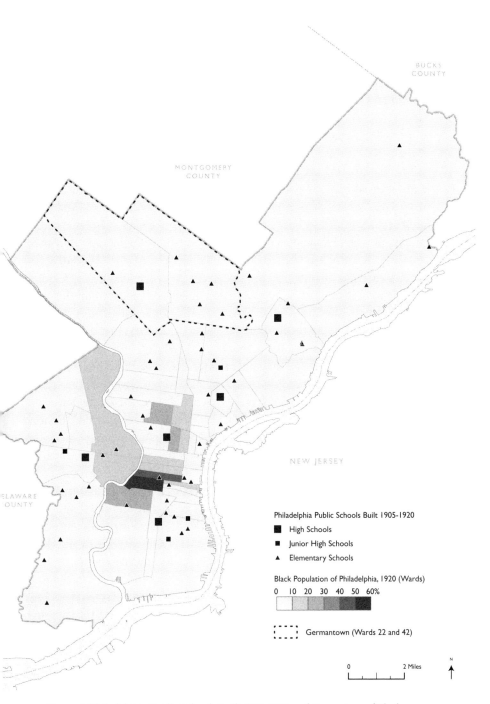

Philadelphia Public Schools Built 1905-1920

■ High Schools

■ Junior High Schools

▲ Elementary Schools

Black Population of Philadelphia, 1920 (Wards)

0 10 20 30 40 50 60%

┌ ─ ─ ┐
└ ─ ─ ┘ Germantown (Wards 22 and 42)

0   2 Miles

Figure 4. Philadelphia Public Schools Built 1905–1920 and Percentage of Black Residents by Ward, 1920. Source: United States Census, 1920; "Locations and Cost of Buildings and Sites Owned and Rented," in *ARBPE-P*, 1920.

racist policies and practices that forced Black children into separate and unequal schools.[17]

The Expansion of High Schools Generates a Fiscal Crisis

While Black residents challenged Philadelphia's gerrymandered boundaries
and racist admissions policies, high school enrollment across the nation
soared due to child labor legislation, compulsory attendance laws, and tech-
nological changes.[18] In 1890, 202,963 students in the United States enrolled
in high school; Philadelphia had 2,577 students in its high schools. In 1918,
the national figure had risen to 1,645,171; Philadelphia had 18,158 students in
high school.[19] As high school enrollment increased, school officials in Philadelphia and other communities worried about the costs of building and
operating these schools. High schools, with their ornate structures, modern
amenities, and credentialed faculty, were expensive to build and operate.
In 1916, Henry Edmunds, the school board president, announced that the
board of education lacked the funds to meet its operating expenses due, at
least in part, to the expansion of Philadelphia's high schools.[20] The school
board suspended public school construction and appealed to local and state
officials for more school aid.[21] City and state officials never provided the necessary funds.[22]

Rather than pressure the state for more aid, school officials relied on
the city's expansive network of wealthy donors, local philanthropies, and
cultural institutions to subsidize Philadelphia's inadequate public school
budget with private funding and resources. Elite residents raised millions
of dollars for the city's local Welfare Federation Drives to fund a variety of
school-based social centers and recreational sites for city youth and their
families.[23] They donated funds and resources to improve the nutritional
quality of public school lunches and to hire doctors and nurses to conduct
free medical, eye, and dental exams inside the city's public schools.[24] Philadelphia educators routinely engaged in what John P. Garber, the superintendent of the city's schools, called "practical and rational philanthropy,"
giving poor youth used clothing and money for school-lunch expenses and
trolley fares.[25] The Public Education and Child Labor Association used private funds to open several industrial and continuation schools to teach vocational skills to out-of-school youth.[26] The White Williams Foundation

donated money to cover school expenses for low-income youth to help them finish school.[27] Several local associations raised money to build public playgrounds and to sponsor free afterschool programs for city youth.[28] Local museums, such as the Philadelphia Museum of Art and the Commercial Museum, raised nearly a million dollars in private funds to support school-based programs.[29] School leaders praised these individuals, associations, and organizations for offsetting the school district's fiscal obligations with private money and other forms of "material assistance."[30]

Even though these private supports enhanced educational and extracurricular experiences, the reliance on philanthropy concealed the fiscal challenges inherent in the structure of urban school finance. Despite the influx of millions of dollars in private resources and supports, in 1920, school officials had to borrow money because the city did not have enough money to pay its teachers. Simon Gratz, Philadelphia's school board president, told his constituents that the board's reliance on loans for basic operating expenses, such as teacher salaries, seemed completely "indefensible from the standpoint of sound business principles."[31] In 1924, a national survey indicated that Philadelphia ranked 17th out of the nation's 19 largest cities in per pupil expenditures.[32] The school district's reliance on philanthropy often masked the fact that Philadelphia never had enough public dollars to operate and sustain a robust system of public schools.

Beyond the fiscal challenges that this approach created, Philadelphia's dependence on philanthropy to finance public goods, such as schools and playgrounds, generated educational and social inequities based on race and space.[33] For example, the Junior Employment Services (JES) Office, which opened in 1915 to support in- and out-school youth employment, benefited white youth more than Black youth. Between 1915 and 1922, white youth received over 98% of JES positions.[34] In Philadelphia, most educational and recreational facilities followed unwritten, but strictly enforced, racial codes. Facilities in white communities served only white youth; facilities in Black communities served only Black youth. Although residents pressured officials to build more social centers and recreational facilities for Black youth, most of the educational social centers and recreational facilities were built in white communities and thus were only accessible to white youth.[35] The city's racialized geographies influenced the allocation of private money and resources, which in turn, generated separate and unequal educational and recreational opportunities based on race and space.

Philadelphia's New High Schools Expand
the Educational Marketplace

The expansion of the city's high schools strained the school district's budget, but it also afforded families new and diverse secondary-school options. When Germantown High School opened in 1915, Philadelphia offered a variety of public, private, and parochial high schools, including two elite academic schools, the all-male Central High School and the all-female Philadelphia High School for Girls, as well as several comprehensive neighborhood high schools. The academic schools required an admissions exam; the comprehensive neighborhood high schools drew students primarily from their respective communities. Families who lived in Germantown's northwest region usually sent their children to one of three public schools: Central, Germantown, and the Philadelphia High School for Girls. Statistical analyses of data from high school yearbooks and the United States census help to explain the choices that Philadelphia families made about where to send their children to high school. First, demographic data indicate that upper-class youth made up the largest segment of the graduates in these three high schools. This pattern suggests that at the turn of the 20th century Philadelphia's public high schools, like those in other cities, educated the city's elite. Second, lower-middle-class youth made up a sizable portion of the graduates of these schools, as well, which reflects the growing anxieties among artisans and craftspeople about the economic changes that had left many of them under- or unemployed during this period. Lower-middle-class families were willing to send their children to high school to help them secure more prosperous futures as middle-income, white-collar professionals.[36]

However, differences between these three schools emerge when one compares the demographics of their respective graduating classes (see table 1 and appendix for statistical details). Regression analysis indicates that immigrant youth comprised a significantly greater proportion of the graduating classes at the city's two elite exam schools, Central High School and Philadelphia High School for Girls, compared to Germantown High School. Upper- and upper-middle-class male youth made up a significantly greater proportion of the graduating class at Germantown than from the all-male Central High School. Working-class female youth made up a significantly larger segment of the graduating class at Germantown than from Philadelphia High School for Girls. Finally, Black female youth made up a significantly larger proportion

Table 1. Graduate Demographics, Philadelphia, Citywide Exam and Northwest High Schools, 1920

	Central High School (n = 330)	Germantown High School[1] (n = 428)	Philadelphia High School for Girls (n = 148)
Race			
Black	2%	2%	9%
White	98%	98%	91%
Nativity			
Immigrant[2]	71%	18%	26%
Native Born	29%	82%	74%
Class			
Upper Class	47%	57%	48%
Upper Middle Class	12%	17%	18%
Lower Middle Class	35%	22%	27%
Working Class	6%	4%	6%

[1] These figures include female and male graduates.
[2] The immigrant category includes foreign-born youth and youth with foreign-born parents.
SOURCE: GHS, Central High School, and Philadelphia High School for Girls Yearbooks, 1919–1921; United States Census, Philadelphia County, 1920.

of the graduating class at Philadelphia High School for Girls than from Germantown High School.

The spatial distribution of race and ethnicity helps to explain why Black and immigrant girls were significantly more likely to attend Philadelphia High School for Girls and immigrant boys were significantly more likely to attend Central High School than Germantown. Figures 5 and 6 show the locations of the residences of Black and immigrant youth who graduated from Central, Germantown, and Philadelphia High School for Girls. These maps indicate that nearly all of the Black (100%, Central and Germantown; 85%, Girls) and most of the immigrant youth (65%, Central; 63%, Germantown; 54%, Girls) who graduated from these schools lived within two miles of the schools that they attended. Most graduates probably lived within walking distance of their high school to avoid the added costs and dangers associated with commuting to and from school in the city's center. In the early 20th century, class, ethnicity, race, and space shaped Philadelphia's high school demographics.

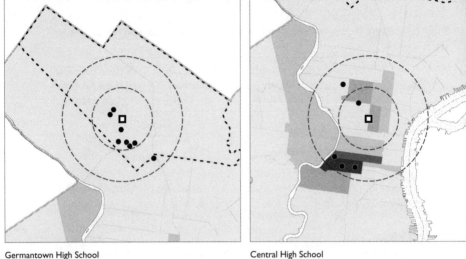

Germantown High School

Central High School

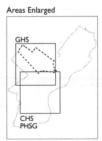

Areas Enlarged

Philadelphia High School for Girls

●   Residences of Black Students by High School
      (1920 Graduates)

□   High Schools

( )   1- and 2-Mile Distances from School

Black Population of Philadelphia, 1920 (Wards)

0   10   20   30   40   50   60%

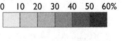

Germantown (Wards 22 and 42)

Figure 5. Residences of Black Graduates of Germantown, Central, and Girls High Schools and Percentage of Black Residents by Ward, 1920. Source: United States Census; *ARBPE-P*, 1920; Germantown High School Yearbook, 1919–1921; Central High School Yearbook, 1919–1921; Philadelphia High School for Girls Yearbook, 1919–1921.

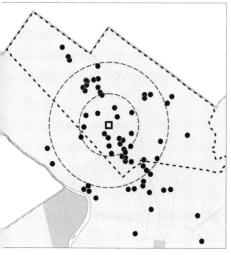

rmantown High School

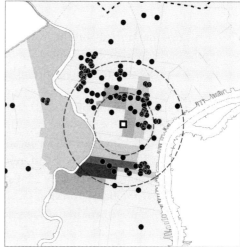

Central High School

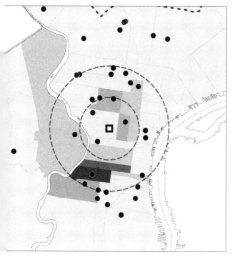

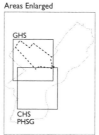

Areas Enlarged

GHS

CHS
PHSG

adelphia High School for Girls

Residences of Immigrant Students by High School
(1920 Graduates)

High Schools

1- and 2-Mile Distances from School

Foreign-Born Population of Philadelphia, 1920 (Wards)

10   20   30   40   50%

Germantown (Wards 22 and 42)

Figure 6. Residences of Immigrant Graduates of Germantown, Central, and
Girls High Schools and Percentage of Foreign-born Residents by Ward, 1920.
Source: United States Census; *ARBPE-P*, 1920; Germantown High School
Yearbook, 1919–1921; Central High School Yearbook, 1919–1921; Philadelphia
High School for Girls Yearbook, 1919–1921.

Economic need and the instability of the labor market also influenced the decisions that Philadelphia families made about their children's secondary schools. The credentials from the elite, exam high schools had a higher value on the labor market than a credential from Germantown's new high school. Male immigrant youth, particularly Jewish youth who made up a large proportion of immigrant youth at Central High School, enrolled in the city's all-male elite high school because their families hoped a diploma from that school would help their children move up the economic ladder.[37] At the beginning of the 20th century, Philadelphia High School for Girls had a special appeal for Black families. Graduating from this institution virtually guaranteed placement in the city's normal school and eventually a position as a teacher in the city's segregated schools. For example, Hattie Yarborough, the daughter of two southern Black migrants who held lower-middle-class positions as a chauffeur and housewife, most likely walked the short distance from her home to the school. She graduated in 1919 and secured a professional position as a public school teacher. This explains, at least in part, why Black females made up such a large percentage of its graduating class.[38]

Even though at the time less than 30% of American youth and only 3.2% of Philadelphia's Black youth attended high school, in 1920, these enrollment patterns illustrate the commitment to education as a means of advancement among Black and immigrant families.[39] Black and immigrant families were more likely to send their children to the city's elite exam schools because Black and immigrant families lived near these schools and because these schools provided their graduates with the city's most valuable high school credential, which in turn, increased the probability of social mobility for these youth.[40]

Racist educators also played a role in the fact that Black students made up such a small percentage of graduates (only 1.9%) at Germantown High School. Archibald Child, a Black man born in Germantown in 1912, recalled the first time he visited Germantown High School with his mother, Maude, a southern Black migrant who worked as a domestic in the community. Before leaving the South, Maude taught secondary school in a one-room segregated school, married Archibald's father, and had several children. When his mother visited Germantown High School, a teacher told Maude to enroll her son in the commercial program. His mother challenged the teacher and explained that she wanted Archibald to receive an academic education. Despite her pleas and Archibald's exemplary academic record, the teacher refused to admit

Archibald to the academic program. Rather than sacrifice her son's future in a school with racist educators, Maude sent Archibald to an all-Black segregated high school in Virginia where he earned the academic credentials to prepare him for college. After earning his college degree, Archibald secured employment as an educator with Germantown's all-Black Wissahickon Boys Club, a position that allowed him to contribute to racial uplift in his community and to have a more secure economic future.[41]

Despite the obvious inequities in the city's high school system, when Germantown High School officially opened in 1915, Henry R. Edmunds, the president of the board of education, argued that the city's expanded system of secondary schools marked "a new era in education for the city," remarking that "educational opportunity was at one time very far from being equally distributed to the young people of Philadelphia." According to Edmunds, building high schools "in all the sections of the city" provided new educational opportunities for youth in the city's outlying regions, who could not easily attend one of the centrally located high schools, and moved the school district even closer to its aim of having secondary schools "for all the children of all the people."[42] Edmunds believed that the early 20th century was the heyday of the American high school and that the expansion of these institutions provided access to schooling for working-class immigrant youth.[43] The expansion of Philadelphia's secondary-school system clearly provided new educational options, but as the 1920 graduation data indicate, the youth who enrolled in the institutions outside the city center did not represent "all the children of all the people." Germantown High School, which was part of Philadelphia's secondary-school expansion, had a majority-white, native-born, upper-class graduating class.

Germantown High School: A First-Rate Academic High School for the City's Elite

From its founding, faculty and residents of Germantown High School collaborated to create a doubly advantaged, academic high school that prepared its graduates for postsecondary education, professional careers, and bourgeois lifestyles. Germantown administrators replicated the academic curriculum at the city's elite all-male Central High School and hired teachers, such as Dr. Anna Mullikin, who had earned doctorates in their fields. The faculty established a college entrance committee to guarantee that students understood postsecondary admissions requirements and hosted events with local college alumni associations and foundations that provided hundreds of local and citywide scholarships to Germantown graduates. In 1920, students had the option of four curricular programs: academic, which prepared students for postsecondary education and professional careers; commercial, which enabled graduates to enter clerical and sales positions; domestic science, which educated young women on the scientific principles of homemaking; and mechanical arts, which prepared young men for college and managerial trade positions. The majority of Germantown graduates in the 1920 cohort selected the academic program (56%, see table 2).[44] Germantown's academic program and college-bound culture promoted the idea that this new high school was one of the finest in the nation. As that idea spread, hundreds of bourgeois, white families moved to the area to enroll their children in the community's new high school.[45] In 1920, white residents made up 92% of the population in the three neighborhoods located near the school—Germantown, Mt. Airy, and Chestnut Hill.[46]

Regression analysis of data on the demographics of Germantown's graduates indicate that upper- and upper-middle class graduates were significantly more likely to earn an academic diploma, which would help them prepare for college and preserve their class status, than a commercial diploma (see table 2 and appendix for statistical details).[47] Douglass Walter Eiseman, the white son of a manager and homemaker, earned an academic degree in 1921, attended Haverford College, and eventually became a banker.[48] Barbara Manley, the white daughter of a civil engineer and homemaker, earned an academic degree, enrolled in Swarthmore College, earned a chemistry degree, and married a college classmate who pursued a professional career while she stayed home to raise her children.[49] Upper- and upper-middle-class white graduates like Douglass and young women like Barbara used the academic program to help them maintain their class status as professional employees and bourgeois housewives.

Working-class families hoped that education might provide their children with a better future, and thus, they enrolled their children in high school. All of Germantown's 1920 working-class graduates earned either a commercial degree or an academic degree (see table 2) to help secure managerial and clerical positions after high school. Alice Craigmile, a white daughter of Irish working-class immigrants, graduated from the high school's commercial

Table 2. Course Enrollment by Gender, Race, Nativity, and Class, Germantown High School, 1920

	Academic	Commercial	Vocational
All Graduates ($n = 428$)	56%	30%	14%
Gender			
Female	59%	31%	10%
Male	48%	27%	25%
Race			
Black	88%	12%	0%
White	55%	30%	15%
Nativity[1]			
Immigrant	51%	35%	14%
Native Born	57%	29%	14%
Class			
Upper Class	63%	21%	16%
Upper Middle Class	55%	32%	13%
Lower Middle Class	42%	46%	12%
Working Class	44%	56%	0%

[1] The immigrant category includes foreign-born youth and youth with foreign-born parents.
SOURCE: GHS Yearbooks, 1919–1921; United States Census, Philadelphia County, 1920.

program in 1920. After high school, Alice lived with her family and later found a position as a secretary in a local private school.[50] Germantown's commercial program gave Alice the opportunity to develop the skills and earn the credentials to move into the middle class.

Black youth made up less than 2% of the graduates in the 1920 cohort. Even in 1920, most Black students lived in communities that were, or were nearly, majority Black (see figure 7). Most of the 1920 Black graduates were from lower-middle-class or working-class families. Many of their families migrated to Philadelphia from the South. Despite their class backgrounds, Germantown's 1920 Black graduates were significantly more likely to graduate with an academic degree than white youth (see table 2 and appendix for statistical details). Germantown High School's Black families had a deep belief in education and insisted on enrolling their children in the high school's academic program.[51] For example, John and Lilla Baugh, who had moved to Philadelphia from Virginia and settled in Germantown's Black neighborhood near the high school, enrolled their daughter, Florence E. Baugh, in

Figure 7. Residences of Black Germantown Graduates and Percentage of Black Residents by Enumeration District, Ward 22 and Adjacent Districts, 1920. Source: Germantown High School Yearbooks, 1919–1921; Ancestry.com; United States Census, 1920.

Germantown High School's academic program. John worked as a laborer while Lilla stayed at home and raised their family. After Florence graduated in 1920, she secured a position as a teacher in the city's segregated public schools, and in 1929 she married Orrin Evans, a reporter with the Black-owned *Philadelphia Tribune*.[52] The academic program at Germantown High School provided her with exactly what her parents had hoped for—access to a middle-class profession and a marriage that afforded their daughter the lifestyle they had never truly enjoyed. Despite myriad barriers that these young Black men and women faced, many of those who had the opportunity to attend and graduate from Germantown High School with an academic diploma were able to move up the social and economic ladder.

Germantown Residents Leverage their Social and Financial Capital to Support their New High School

Germantown's new high school represented an anchor, retaining the city's white elite who had threatened to move to the suburbs during the high school campaign, and a magnet, attracting more upper- and middle-class white residents to the community. Even before Germantown High School officially opened, Germantown residents willingly leveraged their own personal networks as well as their financial and social capital to ensure that their children not only had a majestic new building but that they also had additional resources, paid for through philanthropy, to subsidize the city's inadequate public school budgets. This influx of private funding, however, created inequality, based on class, race, and space, across and within Philadelphia's public schools. Upper- and upper-middle-class white residents, who made up the majority of Germantown residents and graduates, were much more likely to have money and resources to donate to their local public schools than low-income, Black, and immigrant residents whose children attended schools in the city's inner core. As a result, Germantown's young high school enjoyed an influx of private donations that few other schools had at their disposal. The private funding for a school that served a majority upper- and upper-middle-class and majority-white student body made Germantown a doubly advantaged school.

Current scholarship suggests that the availability of extracurricular resources is an essential, if overlooked, engine of social mobility.[53] Germantown residents recognized the value of extracurricular resources not only for their own children, but to attract new upper- and middle-class residents to the area and to care for low-income residents who did not have the resources to subsidize extracurricular opportunities for their own children. Inside the high school, Germantown administrators and families supported a diverse set of extracurricular activities, which included athletic teams, art programs, and other clubs, such as the engineering club, the debate club, and the HI-Y club. High school faculty volunteered their time, with no compensation, to operate these programs.[54] Germantown administrators ran a school senate, modeled after the United States Senate. The school senate included representatives from each advisory section and faculty from each department. The senate set the school governance procedures, including its disciplinary codes, and organized school-wide assemblies.[55] Germantown faculty and students organized a lavish annual overnight trip to Washington, DC, where soon-to-be graduates visited local museums, toured national monuments, and held an extravagant dance party at one of Washington's finest hotels.[56] Faculty and students expected their peers to participate in these programs to improve the reputation of the young high school. As one student told her peers, "Remember, it is the student body which makes a school successful and if you do not do your part you are detracting from the good reputation of our school. We expect everyone to help in bringing honor and glory to Germantown."[57]

The city's inadequate public school budgets could not fund all these programs, and so, residents raised funds and resources to support the high school's extracurricular programs. Families hosted tea parties and rummage sales to purchase athletic uniforms and classroom supplies.[58] Students sold athletic tickets and pennants to relieve the school "from a painful lack of funds."[59] The school senate collected class dues, held annual benefits, and charged poll taxes. Students who wanted to participate in school activities and elections had to pay their peers to do so. These funds subsidized school activities such as class trips and essential resources such as textbooks.[60] The school community also donated money to the Student Assistance Fund.[61] Germantown businesses and residents, including several university professors and Philadelphia orchestra musicians, donated their time and money to bolster the school's programs.[62] Although these supports might resemble present-day fundraisers, the school community raised millions in today's dollars to support the school and its programs. For example, the school community sold over $1 million in WWI Liberty Loan bonds and, beginning in 1928, sponsored a campaign to raise $400,000 to build a new athletic field.[63] Local associations and engaged residents raised thousands of dollars in scholarship and award funds to commemorate the accomplishments of Germantown High School youth.[64] The influx of private money made these public school programs possible. Germantown faculty, families, and students donated their time and money to support these extracurricular programs because they understood that they strengthened Germantown High School's budding reputation as one of the finest high schools in the nation.

Members of the school community leveraged their social networks and donated personal funds for a simple reason: they recognized Germantown High School's importance as a vital community asset that offered a first-rate educational experience to local youth and enhanced Germantown's standing as one of Philadelphia's premier communities for upper- and middle-class white families.[65] The influx of private funding purchased resources for Germantown High School that most schools in Philadelphia, particularly those that served the low-income immigrant and Black youth in the city's center, could not necessarily access. This differential in funding and resources generated inequities within the system—affluent, white communities like Germantown had more families with money and resources to give to their public schools and to local social service agencies that supported youth than did low-income Black and immigrant families. The fact that Germantown families could raise private funds for their public school created a doubly advantaged school—an institution that served primarily bourgeois, white youth and that relied on public and private funding to do so (figure 8).

Even though the influx of funding supported programs that increased the availability of educational and recreational activities, these extracurricular activities fractured Germantown youth along gender and racial lines. The school sponsored an all-male engineering club and an all-female hospital auxiliary club.[66] Despite the popularity of interscholastic sports teams, school officials barred female youth from competitive sports due to the perceived fragility of their bodies and reserved demeanors and instead sponsored less rigorous intramural sports for female youth.[67] Geneva E. Edney, a Black female who graduated from Germantown High School in 1925, also recalled the unwritten, but clear, racial lines that existed in the school. According to Geneva, Black youth rarely participated in extracurricular activities such as athletic programs because they were not permitted to swim in the all-white YMCA pool that the high school team used for its practices and competitions. They routinely opted out of school traditions such as an overnight

Figure 8. Germantown High School Library, circa 1920. Source: Germantown
High School Archives.

trip to Washington, DC, because racial codes barred them from the hotel. In
her interview, Geneva said, "I can't say for sure if we were barred [from
participating in the high school's clubs and activities], but we were never
permitted."[68]

Germantown residents also donated money to support recreational activities and programs outside the high school. During the Progressive Era,
Germantown residents sustained and expanded several social service facilities for local youth, such as the YMCA, YWCA, and Boys Clubs. These institutions provided tuition-free coursework for youth to develop vocational
skills and sponsored employment bureaus to help them find jobs.[69] The
organizations also hosted recreational activities, including sports teams,
citywide arts clubs, and tuition-free summer camps at the Jersey Shore and
in the Pennsylvania woods.[70]

From their founding, the local social services agencies also segregated youth by race and gender. Germantown had four Ys—the all-white Germantown YMCA, the all-Black Rittenhouse YMCA, and two YWCAs segregated by race—and several Boys Clubs, including the all-white Germantown club and the all-Black Wissahickon club. These institutions offered industrial and commercial courses to help boys find jobs and taught homemaking and cooking classes to help girls tend homes.[71] The all-Black Wissahickon was the only one of these organizations open on Sundays, which allowed its members to attend programs while some of their parents, many of whom worked as domestics, served Sunday dinner to Germantown's white elite. The Wissahickon Boys Club served a dual purpose: it provided Black youth with educational and recreational activities and it increased the availability of Black domestic labor.[72]

Although these institutional arrangements mirrored structural inequalities throughout the nation, the leaders of Germantown's social service agencies also used Germantown's segregated institutions to promote racial uplift and challenge social inequality. As the founder and superintendent, respectively, of the Wissahickon Boys Club, John T. Emlen and William T. Coleman Sr. worked together to address racial inequality.[73] In his 1911 annual report, Emlen urged the Wissahickon's board to recognize that its members faced "a double problem . . . the boy problem and the negro problem." He noted that local businesses and firms were often willing to hire white boys, but routinely refused to hire Black boys. Emlen drew on Du Bois's idea of the talented 10th and encouraged the organization to "guide our better and brighter boys into better paying work, so that they may have better homes and that the boys' wives in the homes may be able to give more time to the children."[74]

While Emlen tried to raise awareness about racism in the labor market, Coleman worked tirelessly to enhance the club's reputation and expand programs for Black youth. Coleman showcased the club's achievements in national publications, such as the *Boys Workers Round Table* and the *Southern Letter*. Coleman promoted the members' activities and achievements in local and national competitions. He also provided activities to shield his members from the racism in his community. Throughout his tenure, he screened movies at the club so that his members could be "spared the humiliation of sitting in the segregated section" of their local movie theatres. Coleman and other leaders counseled the boys about educational and employment opportunities and helped them secure scholarships and part-time work to defray the expenses of postsecondary education. He repeatedly reminded his members to reach for their goals and remain committed to their ideals despite the racism that they endured daily in their schools and community. Coleman also urged his staff to provide the supports and resources that the club members needed to realize their aims and hung a banner under the entrance to the club with the Wissahickon's motto: "A boy is a diamond in the rough; add character and you have a jewel."[75] He also worked closely with the Germantown police to curb juvenile delinquency. Coleman's oldest son recalled that his father asked the police to bring club members to his home rather than arrest them. In return, Coleman promised to speak to the offender and his family about the incident and discuss appropriate consequences for the member's actions.[76] Coleman's approach received national attention for being a more humane and effective way to reduce juvenile delinquency.[77]

Germantown residents supported these extracurricular programs and social service agencies because the availability of these resources promoted the idea that the community and its high school was a safe place to raise and educate upper- and middle-class children. The community could support these programs because many of the residents who lived in the area had the money and time to donate to the high school and these social service agencies. The extracurricular programs in the high school and these social service agencies provided essential support to upper-, middle-, and low-income Black and white youth who called Germantown home.

A First-Rate High School Built and Sustained with Public and Private Funds

When Germantown High School officially opened, Philadelphia was in the midst of dramatic demographic change. Thousands of Black migrants packed their bags and moved with their families hoping to find better economic and educational opportunities in the North. When they arrived, racism in the city's labor, housing, and educational markets barred them from Philadelphia's best jobs, neighborhoods, and schools. As these migrants settled in their new homes, the board of education struggled to fund its ever-expanding system of public schools. Rather than raise taxes to support its schools, Philadelphia relied on the influx of private funds from wealthy residents and local institutions to support programs and opportunities for its youth. While this philanthropy provided necessary funds to support the city's schools, it masked the district's fiscal insolvency and generated educational inequities based on the city's spatial distribution of race and class. This created a two-tiered system of schools. One tier consisted of under-resourced and over-crowded public schools in the city's center that served primarily poor Black and immigrant youth. These schools relied solely on public support. The other tier included the well-resourced, modern public schools in the city's periphery. These schools, the doubly advantaged schools, served wealthier white residents and relied on private and public aid. Germantown residents recognized the importance of a strong public school to its community, and thus, they donated hundreds of thousands of dollars to support and sustain the educational institutions and youth programs that supported their youth, including their young high school. The influx of private money provided Germantown High School and its community with resources and programs that could not be supported on tax revenues alone. But while the resources and supports that Germantown residents provided strengthened the high school's curricula, programs, and activities and helped to solidify its presti-gious reputation, as the Great Depression began, the economic challenges in the city and nation revealed the shortcomings of the community's reliance on philanthropy.

CHAPTER 3

Philadelphia's Reliance on Philanthropy Begins to Crack, 1929–1940

On a brisk autumn afternoon in 1929, 10-year-old Marion Garrison ended her school day as she always had. She walked out the school door and met the chauffeur who drove her each day in her family's magnificent nine-passenger limousine. During the school day, her father, C. Kenneth Garrison, a prominent Philadelphia stockbroker, watched the stock market plummet. Within a few weeks, Marion's father lost the lucrative career that had provided his family with a level of financial security enjoyed by only a small percentage of Americans. Faced with financial ruin, her family auctioned their exquisite limousine, liquidated their family jewels, sold their family mansion, and moved into a modest middle-class apartment in Germantown's commercial center. Marion's father sank into a deep depression. Eventually, he accepted a position at a small firm as a stockbroker, the only profession he had ever known. Marion's mother, who had never taken care of a house on her own, tried to accept her new status as a middle-class homemaker with no hired help. Marion's parents eventually transferred their children from their quaint private school to an all-white public school near their home because they could no longer afford to pay for private school. In 1936, Marion graduated from Germantown High School, a place she never truly enjoyed. Over 70 years later, Marion remembered, "when that crash came in October 1929, the bottom fell out of our world. You hear about people going from rags to riches. Well, we went from riches to rags."[1]

The 1929 market crash shattered the labor market, leaving thousands without work. By 1930, Philadelphia had the third highest unemployment rate in the nation, behind Detroit and Cleveland.[2] Young workers between the ages of 16 and 25 had the highest rates of unemployment.[3] The decimation of the youth labor market forced young workers out of the labor market and pushed them into their local schools. Over time, high school enrollment surged. To meet the new enrollment demands, school officials built new high schools, which cost the school district millions. As school enrollment increased, the city experienced a rise in delinquent real estate taxes—the school district's main revenue source—as homeowners struggled to survive. As school enrollment increased and public funding decreased, school officials had to find a way to educate more students with fewer public dollars. School officials, once again, relied on philanthropy to make up for the city's budget shortfalls. The school district's overreliance on private funding exacerbated inequality between the doubly advantaged schools—schools with majority-affluent, majority-white student bodies whose inadequate public budgets were subsidized with private funding—and the rest of the city's schools, which often relied solely on inadequate public funds.

Germantown High School reflected the city's challenges and changes. During the Great Depression, student enrollment increased, but the per-pupil expenditures that the school received from the city decreased. To offset these financial hardships, Germantown High School administrators urged families and students to donate what they could to sustain and promote the school's curricular and extracurricular programs. However, as unemployment and poverty increased, white, working-class students flooded the once elite high school. Frustrated with the pressures to donate to their academically oriented high school, many working-class youth challenged the legitimacy of Germantown High School's reliance on philanthropy, emphasis on academic learning, and focus on postsecondary placement. The Great Depression, which shattered the youth labor market, increased high school enrollment, and decimated public school budgets, ushered in the beginning of Germantown High School's transformation.

The Decimation of the Youth Labor Market Shapes the Educational Marketplace

When Franklin D. Roosevelt assumed the presidency, about half of Philadelphia's workers were unemployed. Black adult men and workers ages 16 to 25 had the highest rates of unemployment, at more than 50% in 1932.[4] The decimation of the nation's labor market forced thousands of youth, who in ordinary economic times had entered the labor force as soon as they could legally accept work, to reevaluate their futures. Some secured employment in federal youth employment programs, such as the Civilian Conservation Corps (CCC) and National Youth Administration (NYA), to gain practical skills, earn an income, or attend college.[5] However, the vast majority of American youth did something that they had no intention of doing before the stock market crashed—they stayed in high school.[6] During the Great Depression, high school enrollment in Philadelphia soared from 32,223 students in 1929 to 47,199 in 1939, which strained the already fiscally strapped school district.[7] Even though thousands more entered high school, only a small percentage of these youth actually earned a high school degree. In 1940, only about 14% of Philadelphia youth age 25 and over had a high school diploma. The rates were slightly higher for girls (16%) than for boys (12%) and much higher for native-born white youth (17%) than for foreign-born (6%) and Black youth (5%). Though high school enrollment increased, only a small percentage of Americans had a high school degree when the Great Depression ended.[8]

In the late 1920s, Germantown's attractive modern amenities, bustling commercial district, social service organizations, and reputable public schools attracted thousands of new residents to the Germantown area. Between 1920 and 1930, the community's population rose by 23%. Even though unemployment in Germantown was much lower than in the rest of the city, the economic downturn challenged the racial and class codes that governed where people lived and drew class- and race-based lines between the northern and southern parts of Germantown.[9] In 1930, Black residents made up 9% of the residents in Lower Germantown, near the high school, but less than 1% of the residents in Upper Germantown, which included Chestnut Hill and Mt. Airy.[10] For years, racial and ethnic covenants barred Black, Catholic, and Jewish families from owning homes in these two communities on Germantown's northern tip. However, after the market crashed, elite families in Chestnut Hill and Mt. Airy sold their single-family mansions to anyone who could afford them. A small number of affluent Black, Catholic, and Jewish families capitalized on this moment and purchased homes in these neighborhoods that had once only been available to the city's white, Protestant elite. The Great Depression catalyzed the slow, but steady movement of Black, Catholic, and Jewish families to the northern part of Germantown.[11]

The southern part of the community, which most locals simply called Germantown, remained a racially integrated and socioeconomically diverse community with small row homes for working- and lower-middle-class laborers, twin homes for middle-class workers, and single-family homes for upper-class professionals. Even though Black and white residents lived side by side, unwritten, but widely recognized, racial codes still dictated where and when Black and white residents could interact. Black residents recalled playing stickball and eating pasta with their white Italian neighbors as children, but they also remembered their mothers telling them to avoid the places where white residents "don't want you." Black children were not permitted to swim in white-only pools, to frequent white-only businesses, or to sit in white-only sections of the movie theatre. They were not allowed to visit all-white community-based organizations, such as the Germantown YMCA and YWCA.[12] While many families moved to the area during the Great Depression to take advantage of Germantown's reputable public schools, these unwritten racial codes influenced the decisions that these families and youth made about where to attend high school.

Between 1920 and 1930, school officials approved the construction of several new neighborhood high schools including two new schools in the city's northwest region to relieve the overcrowded conditions at Germantown High School: Simon Gratz High School (opened in 1925) and Olney High School (opened in 1932). Gratz was a few miles south of Germantown High School; Olney was a few miles east. Like Germantown, these schools served primarily youth who lived in their respective neighborhoods. Despite the geographic proximity of these three schools, they served distinct student bodies due to the differences in their neighborhood composition. In 1930, immigrant youth were significantly more often found among Gratz's graduating class compared to Germantown's (table 3; see appendix for statistical details). In 1940, immigrant, upper-middle-class, and lower-middle-class youth were significantly more likely to appear among the graduates at Gratz and Olney than Germantown (table 4; see appendix for statistical details). However, working-class youth were significantly more likely to appear in the graduating class of Germantown than from Gratz or Olney. Among these three schools, Gratz had the largest percentage of Black graduates (tables 3 and 4; see appendix for statistical details).

Spatial segregation in Philadelphia's neighborhoods based on class, ethnicity, and race shaped these findings. In 1930 and 1940 Philadelphia youth often attended and graduated from the high school closest to their home. The communities near Gratz and Olney High Schools had a higher concentration of ethnic white residents than did the neighborhoods around Germantown

Table 3. Graduate Demographics, Philadelphia, Citywide Exam and Northwest
High Schools, 1930

	Central High School (n = 302)	Germantown High School (n = 449)	Gratz High School (n = 356)	Philadelphia High School for Girls (n = 242)
Race				
Black	4%	4%	1%	12%
White	96%	96%	99%	88%
Nativity				
Immigrant[1]	79%	29%	58%	56%
Native Born	21%	71%	42%	44%
Class				
Upper Class	55%	45%	42%	48%
Upper Middle Class	10%	24%	24%	11%
Lower Middle Class	32%	25%	28%	29%
Working Class	4%	6%	6%	12%

[1] The immigrant category includes foreign-born youth and youth with foreign-born parents.
SOURCE: GHS Yearbooks, January and June 1930; Central High School Yearbooks, February
and June 1930; Philadelphia High School for Girls Yearbooks, February and June 1930; Simon
Gratz High School Yearbooks, June 1930; United States Census, Philadelphia County, 1930.

High School, and thus, immigrant youth were more often found in the graduating classes of Gratz and Olney than Germantown. The communities
near Gratz also had a higher concentration of Black residents.[13] Germantown, on the other hand, experienced a significant influx of working-class
white families. The spatial distribution of class and race, coupled with the
school district's decision to build these new high schools, generated new forms
of segregation and inequality based on class, race, and space (see figure 9).[14]

The citywide elite exam schools, which required an admission exam,
mirrored some of these trends. In 1930, Black and immigrant youth were
significantly more likely to be found among the graduates from the all-female
Philadelphia High School for Girls than from Germantown; immigrant youth
were significantly more likely to found among the graduates from the all-male
Central High School than from Germantown (see tables 3 and 4). Once again,
spatial demographics, which corresponded to race and nativity, shaped these
patterns. Black and immigrant families were more likely to live near these elite
schools than they were to live in Germantown, and thus, Black and immigrant youth were more likely to be found in the graduating classes from

Table 4. Graduate Demographics, Philadelphia, Citywide Exam and Northwest High Schools, 1940

	Central High School (n = 275)	Germantown High School (n = 638)	Gratz High School (n = 315)	Philadelphia High School for Girls (n = 325)	Olney High School (n = 608)
Race					
Black	11%	4%	6%	14%	0%
White	89%	96%	94%	86%	100%
Nativity					
Immigrant[1]	56%	12%	47%	41%	37%
Native Born	44%	88%	53%	59%	63%
Class					
Upper Class	53%	27%	29%	36%	36%
Upper Middle Class	9%	29%	13%	18%	15%
Lower Middle Class	28%	24%	49%	36%	39%
Working Class	6%	14%	9%	11%	10%

[1] The immigrant category includes foreign-born youth and youth with foreign-born parents.
SOURCE: GHS Yearbooks, January and June 1940; Central High School Yearbooks, January and June 1940; Philadelphia for Girls Yearbooks, January and June 1940; Simon Gratz High School Yearbook, June 1940; Olney High School Yearbooks, January and June 1940; United States Census, Philadelphia County, 1940.

Central and the Philadelphia High School for Girls. Even though these schools admitted students from all over the city, yearbook data indicate that 80% of Philadelphia High School for Girls's 1930 Black graduates and 54% of its immigrant graduates lived within a walkable one to two miles of the school. Similarly, 67% of Central's 1930 Black graduates and 65% of its immigrant graduates lived within that distance.[15]

For years, school officials had threatened to move Central High School out of the city's center. In 1939, they did. This move, coupled with the decimation of the youth labor market, attracted youth from the more middle-class Olney community surrounding the school's new location and shaped the school's class composition. In 1940, upper-class male youth were significantly more likely to be among Central High School's graduates than Germantown's. Between 1930 and 1940, the percentage of working-class youth in Germantown High School doubled as the poor youth labor market forced these youth into their local high schools. By 1940, working-class youth were

Germantown High School

Central High School

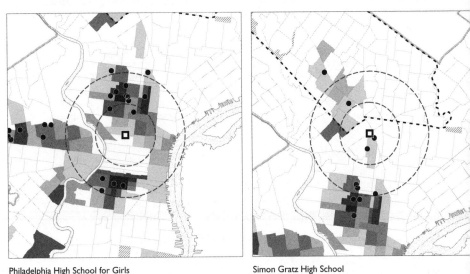

Philadelphia High School for Girls

Simon Gratz High School

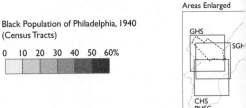

● Residences of Black Students by High School
(1940 Graduates)

□ High Schools

⌐⌐ 1- and 2-Mile Distances from School

┆┄┄┆ Germantown (Wards 22 and 42)

Black Population of Philadelphia, 1940
(Census Tracts)

0   10   20   30   40   50   60%

Areas Enlarged

GHS

SGH

CHS
PHSG

Figure 9. Residences of Black Graduates of Germantown, Central, Girls, and
Gratz High Schools and Percentage of Black Residents by Census Tract, 1940.
Source: United States Census, 1940; *ARBPE-P*, 1940; Germantown High
School Yearbook, January and June 1940; Central High School Yearbook,
January and June 1940; Philadelphia High School for Girls Yearbook, January
and June 1940; Simon Gratz High School, June Yearbook, 1940.

significantly more likely to be among the graduates of Germantown High School than from the two neighborhood high schools in the northwest region, Gratz and Olney, as well as from the city's two elite exam schools, Central High School and the Philadelphia High School for Girls (see tables 3 and 4).

In addition to the spatial distribution of class and race, the school district's open-enrollment policy also shaped these patterns. This policy gave families an opportunity to register their children at any neighborhood high school that had space for them. In theory, parents could use the open-enrollment policy and file a voluntary transfer to move their child out of their neighborhood school. In practice, race and racism affected who did and did not use this policy. White graduates were more likely to live more than two miles from their high schools than Black graduates. As figures 10 and 11 indicate, 92% of Germantown's Black 1940 graduates and 44% of Germantown's white 1940 graduates lived less than two miles from the school. This finding suggests that white families were more likely to use the school district's open-enrollment policy to enroll their children in Germantown High School. Moreover, these maps indicate that many of the white graduates who lived more than two miles from Germantown lived near Simon Gratz High School. These families most likely used the school district's open-enrollment policy to move their white children from a school with a higher concentration of Black graduates (Gratz) and into a school with a higher concentration of white graduates (Germantown). The availability of the open-enrollment policy and the choices that these white families made escalated the spatial segregation of race in the city's neighborhood public high schools.

Even though school district policies and practices clearly shaped the school's demographics, oral histories suggest that unwritten, but widely held racial codes, also influenced the decisions that families and youth made about where to attend high school. Born in 1916, Charles Cauthorn was raised in Philadelphia after his parents, Robert and Jennie, migrated to the city from the South. Robert owned his own landscaping business and tended Germantown's "classy neighborhoods." Jennie took care of her 10 children in their modern three-story home located in the heart of Germantown's historically Black community near Germantown High School.[16] Charles attended Germantown's all-Black Joseph E. Hill Elementary School and the racially mixed Roosevelt Junior High School. Even though Germantown High School was the high school closest to his home, Charles used the school district's open-enrollment policy to attend Simon Gratz High School. He recalled that his own educational experiences and the racial barriers on the

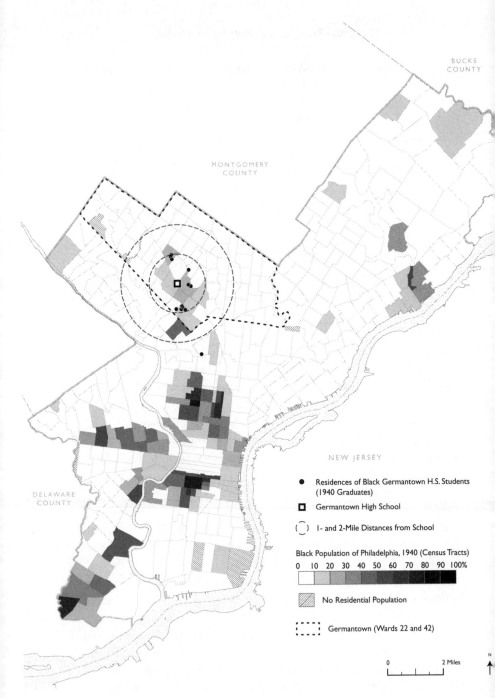

BUCKS
COUNTY

MONTGOMERY
COUNTY

NEW JERSEY

DELAWARE
COUNTY

● Residences of Black Germantown H.S. Students
  (1940 Graduates)

□ Germantown High School

(⁓) 1- and 2-Mile Distances from School

Black Population of Philadelphia, 1940 (Census Tracts)

0   10 20 30 40 50 60 70 80 90 100%

▨ No Residential Population

⌐⌐⌐ Germantown (Wards 22 and 42)

0   2 Miles

N

Figure 10. Residences of Black Germantown High School Graduates and
Percentage of Black Residents by Census Tract, 1940. Source: United States
Census, 1940; Germantown High School Yearbook, January and June, 1940.

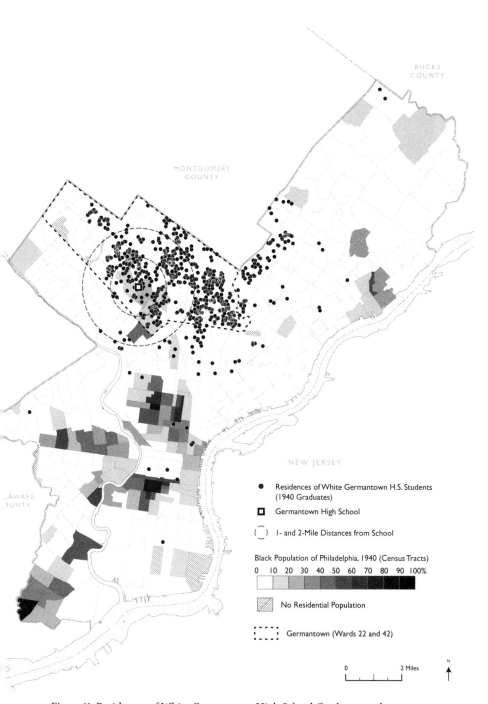

Figure 11. Residences of White Germantown High School Graduates and Percentage of Black Residents by Census Tract, 1940. Source: United States Census, 1940; Germantown High School Yearbook, January and June, 1940.

Legend:

● Residences of White Germantown H.S. Students (1940 Graduates)

□ Germantown High School

(⌐) 1- and 2-Mile Distances from School

Black Population of Philadelphia, 1940 (Census Tracts)
0 10 20 30 40 50 60 70 80 90 100%

▨ No Residential Population

⌐ ¦ Germantown (Wards 22 and 42)

0   2 Miles

N

city's labor market shaped this decision: "When I got to sixth grade, I guess I thought I knew everything and I stopped studying. . . . I had no incentive. There were minimum of jobs [sic] for people of my race. My parents and I did not realize that up the road there would be a better chance to get a better job if you had an education. We were looking for jobs as a street sweeper, chauffeur, take care of someone's lawn, work in some house, or things of that sort."[17] Like other working-class Black youth, Charles never thought he "could be a doctor or lawyer or something like that." In his words, "only the good students" went to Germantown. Charles enrolled at Gratz because he knew the Germantown faculty "would have made me study," and as a Black man with limited employment opportunities due to the racial discrimination on the labor market, he thought that Gratz's industrial courses, which Germantown did not offer at the time, more closely matched his career options. No one questioned his decision.[18]

Alyce Jackson Alexander, a Black girl who lived three blocks from Germantown High School, also used the school district's open-enrollment policy to attend Simon Gratz High School. Her father, Jesse, worked as a laborer, while her mother, Carinthia, a Southern migrant who graduated from Germantown High School, worked as a domestic for a local family and as a laundress for several local churches. Alyce's parents stressed the importance of education for their four daughters and insisted that they attend college. Despite the racism they experienced, Jesse and Carinthia believed that education might help their children "to get a step ahead." Like her mother, Alyce's oldest sister, Mildred, graduated from Germantown High School. However, Alyce decided to register at Simon Gratz High School, a school with more Black youth a few miles from her home. The racism that she and her family experienced in the community most likely shaped this decision.

Even in her mixed-race community, Alyce understood racial boundaries from an early age. Alyce's family lived in a modest home on East Haines Street, in a neighborhood a few blocks from Germantown High School. Although she described her block as "very friendly and very neighborly," she also noted the ways that racism and segregation shaped her childhood. For example, Alyce recalled that the Waterview Playground management, a city recreational center across the street from her home, segregated children based on race. The managers only allowed white children to use the facilities most days. They sponsored Black-only swimming days on occasion. Alyce's parents discussed racism with their children and urged them to ignore it. For example, rather than challenge the Waterview policies, her parents encouraged Alyce to swim at the all-Black Wissahickon Boys Club or the all-Black Rittenhouse YMCA.

Alyce attended the all-Black Hill Elementary School where her teachers provided a first-rate education even though the school lacked the resources that all-white public schools enjoyed. After Hill, Alyce attended Roosevelt Junior High School, Germantown's integrated junior high school. She recalled that her peers at Roosevelt were friendly, but that informal racial boundaries existed. Her parents often reminded her that she had to focus on her studies and prove her worth, as a Black girl, to others in the school. Alyce recalled that her parents always told their children: "You have to put your best foot forward at all times, because there is always somebody watching you. . . . A Black person can do things much better than, you know, the average white child in school. Because they [the white children] know they're going to get the job, but you're not going to get it unless you really work hard." When it was time for Alyce to register for high school, she refused to attend Germantown High School, a school for "rich, ritzy people," and instead enrolled at Simon Gratz High School. Alyce's older sister, who was one of six Black students at Germantown High School when she graduated, told her about the racist practices inside the high school. Alyce knew that Germantown faculty routinely barred Black students from the academic program and extracurricular activities and that faculty often graded Black students more harshly than their white peers. Alyce enrolled at Gratz because she wanted to attend a school "with my own people, with my own friends and stuff." Even though she experienced some racism at Gratz, she recalled that there were more Black youth at Gratz than at Germantown, which made the school seem more welcoming to her.[19] School district policies, individual-level choices, and widely understood racial codes intensified the differentiation of Philadelphia's high schools based on class, race, and space.

The School District of Philadelphia Faces a Fiscal Disaster

As Philadelphia's high school enrollment and unemployment levels soared, school officials searched for ways to educate more students with less funding. After the stock market crashed, thousands of Philadelphia homeowners defaulted on their mortgage payments and lost their homes. Thousands of others failed to pay their real estate taxes on time. The escalation of housing foreclosures and growing number of delinquent taxpayers had a dire impact on the school district's main revenue source: local real estate taxes.[20] In 1932, Philadelphia's school board announced that it lacked the revenues to operate its schools. To cut millions from its budget, the board reduced salaries, laid off teachers, instituted hiring freezes, and implemented program cuts.[21] The School District of Philadelphia's per-pupil expenditure dropped from $97.09 in 1931 to $90.77 in 1935.[22] School administrators had to do more with less public funding, which had a dire effect inside the schools. Classroom size surged as schools had fewer teachers, but more students. Principals slashed expenditures on essential resources, such as textbooks and other classroom materials, and canceled extracurricular activities and programs.[23] In 1934, Edwin C. Broome, the superintendent of Philadelphia's public schools, told taxpayers that the board had cut expenditures for school resources to "an irreducible minimum."[24]

School district officials faced another challenge. As more parents lost their jobs and homes, childhood poverty increased. In 1933, Broome noted "a considerable percentage" of students in the city's public schools who were living in "poverty, resulting from their own incapacity to succeed, from improvidence, or from conditions beyond their control."[25] Rather than pressure the state to provide more support, school officials relied on philanthropy to provide poor relief inside the city's schools. The Committee on Unemployment Relief (CUR), a citywide fundraising initiative that raised $14 million in private donations from 1930 to 1932, provided funds for the city's school breakfast and afterschool programs.[26] The Red Cross and the Philadelphia County Relief Board established relief centers in public schools to collect and distribute more than 400,000 essential items, such as clothing and shoes, to Philadelphia youth.[27] A few years after the market crashed, these charities had run out of funds. In Philadelphia, elected officials refused to provide the public funds necessary to match the city's needs, as one journalist noted, "the poor are taking care of the poor."[28]

Worried about its ability to care for its youth, the school board hired Dr. George A. Works, a professor at the University of Chicago, to study the school district's finances and curriculum. After a year of intensive study, Works issued a searing report about the school district's future. Works argued that Philadelphia ranked high among cities for its capacity to fund its schools due to its wealth and size, but its reliance on low property taxes and insufficient state support had generated a fiscal disaster. In other words, Works believed that Philadelphia had the funds it needed to operate its schools effectively, but city officials refused to tax residents at a rate to do so. When the Depression hit, the city's meager, and ever-shrinking, local tax base, combined with insufficient state support and dwindling private philanthropy, had dire effects on its public schools.[29] Between 1931 and 1937, as school enrollment rose dramatically, the school district lost about $9 million in tax revenues. Works argued that state officials had neglected their duty to fund Philadelphia's public schools. Compared to other cities, Philadelphia relied heavily on local taxes to fund its schools because the city had one of the smallest state and federal funding streams in the nation.[30] State and federal funding accounted for 8.5% of Philadelphia's annual school budget, compared with 36.1% of Detroit's school budget.[31] As a result, Philadelphia had one of the lowest per-pupil expenditures among cities in the nation. Works and his colleagues told the board that it had a choice: increase local and state funding streams or eliminate public school programs and staff.[32]

In addition to this fiscal analysis, Works also evaluated the curricular programs in Philadelphia's high schools. Echoing national critiques of American high schools in vogue at the time, Works argued that the academic curriculum in many of the city's high schools did not match the needs of lower-middle- and working-class youth who had flooded the schools during the Great Depression. Rather than emphasize academic learning, Works urged school administrators to implement additional vocational programs for youth who in ordinary economic times would never have attended high school. He encouraged school officials to provide teachers with professional development programs to help them understand how to support the "intellectually and vocationally low-grade pupils who are now entering secondary schools in large numbers."[33] While he never mentioned race and class in his remarks, the publication of his study coincided with the influx of more low-income Black and white youth in Philadelphia's public high schools.[34]

In response to his findings, Philadelphia school administrators replaced several academic programs with new vocational programs. The implementation of these programs reflected widely held, but misguided, assumptions about the academic capabilities and vocational trajectories of students based on their race, class, and gender—assumptions that educators "validated" with racially and culturally biased intelligence tests.[35] Moreover, evidence suggests that school officials were more likely to increase vocational programs in high schools that had the highest concentrations of Black youth. In 1940, school officials increased the vocational programs at Simon Gratz

High School, a school that served a growing number of Black youth. The curricular changes that the board implemented were yet another way to differentiate Philadelphia's high schools from one another based on race.[36]

In 1937, Broome, Philadelphia's school superintendent, proposed a slight increase to the school tax rate to generate additional revenues to hire more teachers and pay for these new curricular programs.[37] Mayor Samuel Davis Wilson criticized Broome and filed a lawsuit as a private citizen to block his proposal. The court sided with the mayor and ruled that the school board, an appointed body, did not have the power or authority to raise taxes.[38] The board appealed.[39] On November 16, 1937, Pennsylvania Supreme Court Chief Justice John W. Kephart upheld the court's decision, arguing that the board's "expensive innovations" and decision to build "elaborate and ornate buildings" over the past several years clashed with its "fundamental duty to maintain an economical and adequate system of schools."[40] Broome and his allies criticized the court's ruling, but their criticisms did nothing. As the nation seemed to be recovering from the financial turmoil of the 1930s, Philadelphia's inadequately funded public schools limited educational opportunities and generated educational inequality based on class, race, and space.[41]

A Generation of "Lost Youth" Emerges
from the Depression's Dust

In the fall of 1937, social scientists, educational leaders, and prominent journalists raised concerns about the prospects of youth who had come of age during the Great Depression. They attacked the American high school for failing to respond to global economic changes and demanded that educators replace the high school's traditional academic curriculum with more vocational programs. However, the challenges that these youth faced were related to the decimation of the youth labor market, not the high school curriculum. In 1937, American youth ages 16–24 represented one-third of the nation's unemployed workers. Nearly 40% of youth who were eligible for employment could not find work.[42] The Great Depression created a "lost generation" who were, compared to their predecessors, more likely to graduate from high school but less likely to have secure employment.[43] American youth had witnessed their families struggle to maintain their economic security and now had little hope that they would find a decent job and a comfortable home.[44]

Even though Germantown had a much lower unemployment rate than most parts of the city, the challenges of the "lost generation" affected the high school. On March 9, 1937, Principal Leslie Seely gave a lecture to the Germantown Lions Club in which he noted that the high school's composition and size had changed dramatically since its founding, and a new youth problem was "confounding educators and filling the courts." Many students, he said, "do not have the desire or the ability to progress with the normal members of their age." These students, Seely added, rarely reached a fifth or sixth grade reading level and were often the oldest students in their classrooms. Seely contended that neither he nor his faculty had control over these challenges because they stemmed from the students' home conditions. According to him, these lost youth lived in homes that were "not homes but places where the boys and girls merely stop to eat and hurry out on the streets in search of some pastime that will offer a thrill."[45]

The so-called new youth problem stemmed from the changes on the city's labor market, which pushed hundreds of young people into the city's high schools for the first time, and from a drop in per-pupil expenditures. During the Great Depression, Germantown High School's enrollment surged by 40% as its per-pupil expenditure dropped by 30%.[46] Student mischief rose as classrooms and corridors overflowed with new students who would not have attended high school in ordinary economic times. In response, Germantown faculty and its student-led senate instituted rules to curb school tardiness, hallway loitering, and cigarette smoking inside the school. Marion Garrison, who transferred to Germantown in 1932, resented these rules and recalled that she often had to push through large crowds of students who refused to go to class on time or had to walk around the building to find an appropriate staircase to get from one class to another. Garrison and others felt that the school senate members "thought that they were the policemen" and that they created a hostile feeling inside the school.[47]

After the stock market crashed, Germantown administrators and faculty urged students to enroll in the school's prestigious academic program to prepare them for postsecondary schooling, professional careers, and bourgeois marriages. School administrators encouraged students to meet regularly with their guidance counselors to plan their course selections; local clubs and organizations sponsored scholarships to defray college tuition for Germantown graduates. Students published articles in the school newspaper that detailed the accomplishments of recent alumni/ae who had completed college degrees.[48] Germantown educators understood the connections between

the school's academic program and the community's and school's reputations, and thus, they worked diligently to promote and preserve the academic program. Initially, these tactics worked. In the early 1920s, thousands
of upper- and upper-middle-class families remained or moved to Germantown to take advantage of the community's reputable public schools, including its young high school.[49] In 1929, 47% of Germantown graduates indicated
that they planned to attend college after graduation. One year later, the academic program remained the most popular option; 57% of graduates earned
an academic diploma. Upper-class youth were significantly more likely to
earn an academic degree than a commercial degree (table 5; see appendix
for statistical details).

Less than 5% of Germantown High School's 1930 graduates were Black.
Like their predecessors, most were the sons and daughters of southern mi-
grants who had moved north to provide their families with a better future.
And like the Black graduates in the 1920 cohort, most (64%) enrolled in the

Table 5. Course Enrollment by Gender, Race, Nativity, and Class, Germantown
High School, 1930

	Academic	Commercial	Vocational
All Graduates ($n = 367$)	57%	24%	19%
Gender			
Female	58%	30%	12%
Male	56%	17%	27%
Race			
Black	64%	21%	15%
White	57%	24%	19%
Nativity			
Immigrant[1]	49%	37%	14%
Native Born	61%	19%	20%
Class			
Upper Class	70%	13%	17%
Upper Middle Class	56%	29%	15%
Lower Middle Class	35%	37%	28%
Working Class	37%	42%	21%

[1] The immigrant category includes foreign-born youth and youth with foreign-born parents.
SOURCE: GHS Yearbooks, January and June 1930; United States Census, Philadelphia County,
1930.

academic program. A few years later, in 1936, Marion Campbell, whose father worked as a laborer in the local steel mills and whose mother stayed at home to raise her children, was one of a handful of Black youth who graduated from Germantown High School. When Marion registered for high school, she spoke with a school counselor, who never looked at her academic record, to finalize her course selection. The counselor urged Marion to enroll in the commercial course. Marion disregarded this advice and demanded to be placed in the academic program.

As a Black student in the academic program, Marion experienced racism throughout her schooling experience. She recalled that her teachers seated students alphabetically, with all the white students in the front of the classroom and all the Black students in the back. A few weeks before graduation, Marion's calculus teacher gave her an F minus for the course. When Marion complained about this to her peers, she learned that the teacher had given this grade to all the Black students in her class. The students knew that this teacher was racist but could not publicly challenge the teacher's assessments. Marion and her peers registered for another calculus class and graduated the following semester with their academic diplomas.[50]

The racism that Marion experienced extended beyond the classroom. A few weeks before the annual senior trip to Washington, faculty advisors told the Black students that they had to find their own accommodations because the hotel that their class had selected did not allow Black guests. The faculty encouraged them to find a private home in the area so that they could stay overnight and participate in the festivities. Marion recalled feeling outraged and confused when she heard this. Like many of her Black peers, she did not know anyone in Washington and did not feel that she should have to pay an additional fee to stay in a private home. Marion and her Black peers protested. School administrators canceled the trip. Even though she felt pride that Black students voiced their concerns, Marion never forgot the racism she experienced inside Germantown High School.[51]

Oral history evidence suggests that race and racism also shaped the postsecondary and career trajectories of Black and white academic graduates. In 1930, upper-class graduates were still significantly more likely to earn an academic diploma than a commercial one (table 5; see appendix for statistical details). Berthold Levy, a white Jewish man who graduated from Germantown in 1930 with an academic diploma, experienced greater financial security than most during the Great Depression. Even though his father never graduated from high school, Berthold's father held a lucrative position in a local insurance agency. Berthold's family lived in a large, upper-middle-class home and vacationed in Europe during the summer. One of the top students in Germantown's academic program, Berthold earned a Mayor's Scholarship, which covered four years of tuition at the University of Pennsylvania. When he received the news of his scholarship, Berthold's parents praised him, and then urged their son to relinquish his prestigious award. His father had the financial resources to pay for college, and in the middle of the Great Depression, he wanted the scholarship to be redirected to a child who might need it more than his son. Berthold followed his father's advice and returned his scholarship to the committee. With academic skills honed at Germantown High School and his family's financial resources, Berthold earned a bachelor's and a law degree at the University of Pennsylvania, married his summer vacation sweetheart, and moved to Elkins Park, an upscale white suburb a few miles from his childhood home, where he practiced law for several decades.[52]

Even though the high school remained a majority upper- and upper-middle-class white institution, many Germantown students struggled to finance their college education during the Depression. Race and class often shaped their options. Marion Garrison, the white 1936 Germantown graduate whose father lost his family's fortune in the stock market, enrolled in the academic program to prepare for college and a career as a public school teacher. When she graduated, she knew that her family did not have the resources to finance her college education. One night, she shared her concerns with her cousin, who in turn contacted a colleague who worked at Beaver College, a local woman's college with a reputable education program. Her cousin's colleague spoke to Marion and urged her to apply for a special scholarship that covered four years of tuition. She immediately applied and received the scholarship. After graduating from college, Marion taught elementary school in Philadelphia's suburbs, lived with her family in their modest apartment, and contributed her salary to help maintain their new middle-class lifestyle. Even though Marion lacked the financial resources that her family had once enjoyed, her social networks, which were tied to her white bourgeois status, helped her secure a scholarship and earn her teaching degree.[53]

Savannah Holman, a working-class Black woman, graduated from Germantown High School with Marion Garrison in 1936. Savannah had always hoped to be the first person in her family to graduate from college. Like many Black women with an academic diploma, Savannah wanted to work as a nurse in one of the city's segregated hospitals. She and Marion shared many things. They both earned academic credentials from Germantown High School. They both lacked the financial resources to attend college. Yet, their futures were vastly different. When Savannah graduated, she had to forgo her college dreams and find work. Her mother, who had been a widow for almost two decades, needed her young daughter to contribute to the family wage. After graduation, Savannah found a position as a nursing assistant in a local hospital to provide her mother with additional income. As the daughter of working-class Black parents, Savannah had to give up her dream of attending college and accept any position she could find. Savannah's race and class barred her from the social networks and educational opportunities that Marion Garrison could access.[54]

Challenges to the School's Overreliance on Philanthropy and Emphasis on Academics

Even though Germantown fared better than other neighborhoods during the Great Depression, the high school experienced a significant reduction in funding as the school district struggled to balance its budget. From 1929 to 1934, the annual per-pupil expenditure at Germantown High School dropped from $176 to $124.[55] To subsidize inadequate public aid, the school, once again, asked faculty, families, and students to donate private money to their public school. Despite the economic hardship, Germantown High School remained a doubly advantaged school. In the 1920s and 1930s, Germantown High School students pressured their peers to pay their poll taxes, class dues, and club fees to raise funds for school programs. Students had to pay fees to vote in school elections, to participate in class activities, and to enroll in afterschool programs.[56] The Germantown High School mothers' association raised money for the school's students assistance fund, which provided essential financial support to help low-income youth pay for school expenses, including school lunch fees, trolley fares, and club dues.[57] Dozens of Germantown teachers defied the school board orders to refrain from poor relief and donated money to these efforts and their students.[58] Germantown faculty even spoke to the local press about the escalation of poverty in the school and urged wealthy residents to donate to relief for poor students.[59]

The community also contributed funding to community-based organizations that offered additional resources and programs to low-income families. Throughout the Great Depression, community-based organizations, such as the local YMCA and YWCA and Boys Clubs, relied on private donations from the Committee on Unemployment Relief and local fundraising drives to operate afterschool and summer programs for local youth.[60] These organizations sponsored employment bureaus and urged wealthy residents to hire their members for short-term employment opportunities, such as raking leaves and shoveling snow.[61] The Germantown YMCA and YWCA relied on private donations to purchase coal, clothing, and food for those in need.[62]

Although many community members donated money and time to their local public schools and community-based organizations, as unemployment and poverty rose, the community struggled to raise the funds to meet the needs of the poor.[63] In 1931, the Germantown High School senate, which generated private money to provide "necessary things not furnished by the Board of Education," raised less money than in earlier years even though student enrollment had risen.[64] To encourage more students to give, the senate lowered the tax rates, ran collection campaigns in each homeroom, and urged their peers to remember that these voluntary contributions helped their high school maintain its cultural traditions, extracurricular activities, and school clubs. Students instituted rules that their peers had to pay these fees to participate in these activities.[65] These campaigns and rules had little impact. The funds that students raised never reached pre-Depression levels. Many of the students who attended Germantown High School during the Depression did not donate private money to their public school because they did not have disposable income to give. In 1930, working-class youth represented 6% of Germantown High School's graduating class. By 1940, that figure had risen to 40% (see tables 3 and 4).[66] As poverty escalated in the community and the demographics of the school shifted, white working-class youth challenged the legitimacy of the high school's reliance on philanthropy and eventually its academic program and postsecondary focus.[67]

Even though the majority of 1940 graduates earned an academic degree, yearbook data suggests that Germantown graduates were much less likely to be interested in college than the generation that graduated before the 1929 crash. In fact, the percentage of graduates who wanted to attend college after graduation dropped from 47% in 1929 to 18% in 1939.[68] Class and gender

Table 6. Course Enrollment by Gender, Race, Nativity, and Class, Germantown
High School, 1940

	Academic	Commercial	Vocational
All Graduates ($n = 638$)	52%	33%	15%
Gender			
Female	45%	48%	7%
Male	61%	16%	23%
Race			
Black	58%	34%	8%
White	52%	33%	15%
Nativity			
Immigrant[1]	42%	36%	22%
Native Born	54%	33%	13%
Class			
Upper Class	66%	23%	11%
Upper Middle Class	55%	29%	16%
Lower Middle Class	37%	40%	23%
Working Class	36%	56%	8%

[1] The immigrant category includes foreign-born youth and youth with foreign-born parents.
SOURCE: GHS Yearbooks, January and June 1940; United States Census, Philadelphia County,
1940.

shaped these shifts. In 1940, upper-class youth were still significantly more
likely to graduate with an academic diploma than with a commercial diploma
(table 6; see appendix for statistical details). For the first time in the high
school's history, female youth were significantly more likely to graduate
with a commercial diploma than an academic diploma (table 6; see appendix for statistical details).

Even though most white working-class youth graduated with a commercial degree, some defied the odds, graduated with an academic diploma, and
received a postsecondary degree. Many of these youth recalled that one
person, usually a teacher in their high school, helped them carve this path.
David Alcorn, a 1940 Germantown graduate and the son of two Irish immigrants, recalled that his high school seemed like "the perfect society." For
David, in many ways, it was. His father, David Sr., left school after third
grade to help his widowed mother tend the family farm in Ireland; he im-
migrated to the United States in 1910 and worked as a gardener and trolley

conductor. David's mother, Emily, finished sixth grade in Ireland, came to America in 1910, and worked as a domestic before she had children. Even though his parents never finished high school, David's stellar academic record made him a perfect candidate for Germantown's academic program.

David recalled that one of his teachers, Dr. Anna Mullikin, challenged him to delve deeply into his studies and develop skills for his future.[69] He routinely went to Mullikin's home a few blocks from the high school to study advanced mathematics, and he occasionally worked for her. One afternoon, Mullikin told David that her brother had earned a degree in chemical engineering and had accepted a lucrative position in a local firm. David recalled that he had never heard of a career in chemical engineering, but he thought about what she said. He enjoyed math and science, and engineering had one clear appeal: engineers earned a lot of money. He graduated from Germantown High School in 1940 with the Mayor's Scholarship. Four years later, Alcorn became the first member of his family to graduate from college. His degree in chemical engineering—and the educational experiences and opportunities that he enjoyed at Germantown and later at the University of Pennsylvania—provided him with the credentials and skills to secure a rewarding professional career.[70]

Marilyn "Monie" M. Engle, a white woman who graduated in 1940 with a degree in vocational arts, a program for college-bound art students, echoed David Alcorn's sentiments about their high school. Born in Philadelphia, Monie lived in her grandparents' house in the mixed-income Logan community. Monie's father, Albert, graduated from high school and worked as a chauffeur for a private family. Her mother, Alverna, left school in eighth grade and stayed home to raise her only child. When Monie was almost school-aged, her family purchased a home in an "upscale, but not top of the line" neighborhood so that she could walk to and from Germantown High School. She described her high school experience as one of the best times of her life. A naturally social person and talented artist, she participated in extracurricular activities and earned a G-pin, an award reserved for a small group of students to recognize their commitment to the school community. Monie also excelled in her coursework. During the fall of her senior year, one of her teachers encouraged her to apply for a merit-based scholarship to attend the Moore College of Art, one of the city's premier art schools. Monie had never heard of Moore or the scholarship. She recalled that this teacher changed her life—she applied to Moore, earned the scholarship, and became the first person in her family to earn a college degree.[71]

In contrast to these white youth, Black academic youth, due to the racism that they experienced in their schools and community, usually credited their families and educators in community-based organizations for their decision to pursue a postsecondary degree. Although they only made up 4% of the 1940 graduating class, most Black youth (58%) who graduated in 1940 earned an academic diploma. William T. Coleman Jr., a Black man who graduated from the high school in 1939, enrolled in Germantown's academic program to prepare him for college and an esteemed career.[72] He was the eldest son of William T. Coleman Sr., who managed the all-Black Wissahickon Boys Club and attended Hampton University and the University of Pennsylvania, and Laura Beatrice Mason Coleman, who taught in Baltimore's segregated school system after earning her degree from the Baltimore Coplin Normal School. William Coleman Jr.'s family taught him about the importance of education from an early age, despite the racism that he encountered as a student in Germantown's public schools. He attended the all-Black Meehan Elementary School, where his teachers noticed that he had a stuttering problem and enrolled him in special speech classes held at the nearby all-white Fitler Elementary School. Even though he was quite young, William noticed that the Fitler School had much better facilities and resources than the Meehan School. A few years later, he transferred to the all-Black Hill Elementary School, which drew its students from a larger and more economically diverse geographic area. There, he was exposed "to a different kind of discrimination, one based on poverty, class, and envy rather than [solely] race." His teachers at the Hill School reinforced and broadened his understanding of Black history and culture. After Hill, he attended Roosevelt Junior High School, where for the first time, he attended an integrated school.

Even with his impeccable academic record, like the generations of Black graduates who came before him, William encountered racist educators who publicly questioned his aspirations and abilities. After he gave a presentation in his English class, his teacher, Miss Egge, told him that he would make a fine chauffeur one day. When he responded that he wanted to be a lawyer, Egge reprimanded him for disrespecting her and sent him home. The next morning, his college-educated, middle-class parents accompanied him to school and spoke to Germantown's Principal Seely and Miss Egge. According to William, Miss Egge apologized for her remarks the moment she noticed his parents' respectable dress. The racism he experienced extended beyond his classroom. In the 1930s, William had developed a reputation as

one of the best swimmers at the all-Black Wissahickon Boys Club. When he
started high school, he asked if he could join Germantown's interscholastic
swim team. The coach said he could not participate because the Germantown YMCA only permitted whites to use its facilities. His parents met with
the coach and urged him to reconsider. To avoid a public debate, the coach
canceled the swim team while William was a student.[73]

But even though he recognized the racism in the high school, William
also asserted that Germantown High School provided him with a first-rate
academic education and gave him access to opportunities and networks that
few Black youth enjoyed at the time. He matriculated to the University of
Pennsylvania, where he encountered more racism. According to Coleman,
his academic peers from Germantown High School helped him focus on his
goals and cope with his frustrations at Penn. After college, he earned his law
degree from Harvard, became the first Black man to serve as a Supreme
Court law clerk, and promoted civil rights throughout his lifetime. William T. Coleman Jr. credits his family and his teachers at his father's all-
Black Wissahickon Boys Club for pushing him to recognize the importance
of education and for encouraging him to pursue a path available to a small
percentage of Black graduates.[74]

The End of the Great Depression Reveals Cracks
in Germantown's Foundation

The Great Depression strained the fiscal capacities of public school districts
across America. As families struggled to keep their homes and jobs, Philadelphia continued to rely on philanthropy even though it never made up for
the shortfall of public funding. As the city struggled to fund its programs
and schools, the Great Depression decimated the youth labor market and
pushed lower-middle- and working-class individuals to attend high school.
The Great Depression created the perfect storm: more students, more need,
less money. These challenges coincided with a dramatic shift in the social
composition of Philadelphia's high schools—shifts that slowly but surely began to differentiate these schools based on the racial and class status of the
students who attended them. By 1940, Simon Gratz High School, which
opened in 1925 to serve the northwest region, served many more low-income
Black and immigrant youth than Germantown High School. The racial
composition of these schools, in turn, affected the decisions school officials

made about their curricular programs. Faced with mounting concerns about the academic nature of the high school, officials expanded vocational programs in the city's high schools. This expansion was more evident at schools like Gratz that served less wealthy students of color who officials assumed were destined for vocational positions. Germantown High School's location in an affluent white neighborhood protected it from many, but not all of the changes that occurred during the Depression. The high school remained doubly advantaged. It enrolled a majority-affluent, majority-white student body that donated private money to subsidize Philadelphia's inadequate public school budgets. These advantages made it possible for school administrators to sustain Germantown's academic and extracurricular programs. During the Depression, the school's private funding streams also provided essential relief and additional resources to low-income students who attended Germantown High School.

Nonetheless, the Great Depression ushered in a wave of changes inside Germantown High School. The percentage of white working-class graduates surged during the Great Depression. These youth challenged the legitimacy of its academic programs. By the end of the 1930s, the first signs of the transformation of Germantown High School had emerged. The school had shifted from an institution reserved for Philadelphia's elites to an institution that served an ever-increasing number of lower-middle- and working-class white youth. As poverty grew and the social composition of the neighborhood and high school began to change, Germantown High School faculty, students, and families sometimes failed to raise the funds needed to make up for public budget shortfalls. The foundation that had sustained the school for nearly two decades had already begun to crack as the nation prepared for a war to save democracy abroad.

CHAPTER 4

Philadelphia Mobilizes for War, Inequality
on the Homefront Escalates, 1941–1957

Robert Tresville Jr., one of eight Black students to graduate from Germantown High School in February 1938, frequently received accolades for his
impressive high school academic and athletic record, including his admission to West Point.[1] To celebrate his acceptance by the famed military
academy, Germantown's student-run newspaper described him as a leader
"among the colored boys in the community" and often focused more on his
athletic rather than academic achievements.[2] The racism that he experienced
at Germantown High School persisted at West Point. From the moment he
arrived on campus, Robert was treated as a second-class citizen. Robert lived
alone because the other white cadets refused to live with a Black man. When
Robert and his peers lined up to receive a handshake from upperclassmen to
commemorate the end of their first year, Robert stood silently as every white
upperclassman silently walked past him, refusing to shake his Black hand.[3]
After graduation, Robert enlisted in the Air Force, deployed to Europe, and
eventually died in combat.[4] After his death, Robert's wife, Vivien, raised their
daughter, Barbara, and continued Robert's fight for racial equity.[5] Robert's
short life exemplified the hypocrisy of a nation that engaged in wars to end
tyranny and oppression abroad but often remained steadfast in its commitment to maintain the color line at home.

World War II revitalized Philadelphia's sluggish economy and drew thousands of new residents to the city. The influx of these newcomers altered the
city's racial landscape and strained its housing markets. As wartime labor
demands increased, high school–aged youth enrolled in accelerated programs or simply dropped out of high school to secure lucrative positions in
the wartime economy. When the war ended, Philadelphia, like other north-

ern cities, lost thousands of jobs as wartime production ceased and firms moved production to nonunion, business-friendly areas in the South and Southwest.[6] As the jobs moved, white families used their GI benefits to move their families and find work in the city's periphery or adjacent suburbs. Most Black families found that racial discrimination made this exodus impossible, and thus, they remained concentrated in the city's center and other communities that had historically welcomed them: West Philadelphia, Southwest Philadelphia, and Germantown. The in-migration of Blacks to and out-migration of whites from these communities increased segregation and inequality in Philadelphia's neighborhoods and schools.

As the nation emerged from the Great Depression, Germantown High School retained its reputation as a doubly advantaged school and, as a result, continued to attract families to the area. However, during the war, the school diverted the private money that it had relied on for decades to support the school to support the war efforts at home and abroad. When the war ended, the school experienced a significant decline in private funding. School administrators had to find a way to support the school and its programs with fewer private dollars. In addition, Philadelphia's postwar economic challenges once again raised questions about the traditional academic curriculum in most American high schools. In response to these critiques and labor-market shifts, Philadelphia's public school officials expanded the vocational programs in the city's high schools, including Germantown. These programs might have met the city's short-term needs, but the expansion of these programs increased curricular tracking based on class, gender, and race.

The Advent of War Alters the City's Racial Landscape

The advent of war in the late 1930s and early 1940s spurred Philadelphia's economic and population growth as thousands moved to the "City of Brotherly Love" to secure lucrative jobs in the city's growing wartime economy. Between 1940 and 1950, Philadelphia's population increased by 7%. The white population remained relatively stable while the Black population increased by 50%.[7] Thousands made their way to Philadelphia to work in the city's wartime factories and firms, though economic gains were not evenly distributed. While white workers enjoyed tremendous gains, in 1940, nearly one in three Black men and more than one in two young workers (ages 16–19) remained unemployed.[8] Moreover, the influx of new residents placed a tremendous strain on the city's already inadequate and racially segregated housing stock.[9] During the war, Philadelphia revitalized its public housing program to provide housing for wartime workers and their families. However, of the nearly 12,000 housing units that the Philadelphia Housing Authority (PHA) constructed, only 2,300 were available to Black residents.[10]

The housing options in the racially biased, private housing market were not much better. In Philadelphia and other northern cities, such as Chicago, Cleveland, and Detroit, many homeowners either refused to rent to Black residents or charged them more.[11] As a result, many Black families had to settle for substandard, overcrowded housing. During World War II, 10% of Black residents lived in overcrowded housing compared to 2% of white residents. While 75% of Philadelphia's white residents lived in homes that met the PHA's minimum standards, which meant that the homes had indoor plumbing, safe structures, etc., only 46% of Black residents lived in homes that met this standard.[12] The census tracts with the highest density of Black residents remained concentrated in historically Black communities: Germantown, North Philadelphia, West Philadelphia, and Southwest Philadelphia. Over time, Black families expanded their presence on the boundaries of these communities, but white racism barred them from neighborhoods on the city's periphery, such as Chestnut Hill (on the northern tip of Germantown) and Northeast Philadelphia. The increase in Black residents, coupled with discriminatory practices in the city's public and private housing markets, intensified racial segregation between Philadelphia's neighborhoods. During the war, the number of census tracts where Black residents made up 70% of the total population increased significantly from 10 in 1940 to 26 in 1950. Black migrants in Philadelphia and other cities moved to secure a better life for their families but found once again that racism limited their access to the most desirable jobs, homes, and schools.[13]

Throughout the Great Depression, Germantown's business community and housing activists worried about the dilapidated and outdated housing in the working- and lower-middle-class communities that surrounded Germantown High School. Many of these row homes lacked indoor plumbing and adequate heat and thus failed to meet the PHA's minimum standards.[14] In the late 1930s, the federal Home Owners' Loan Corporation surveyors classified the area around the high school as hazardous, the lowest grade on its scale, which raised significant concerns among Germantown's civic and business leaders.[15] On April 17, 1939, B. W. Frazier, the chairman of the Germantown Community Council (GCC), an advocacy group comprised of local churches, schools, business associations, and social service agencies, sent a letter to PHA officials. Frazier asked the PHA to consider using Germantown as a site for the city's public housing program.[16]

A few months later, PHA officials announced that they had allocated $6 million to build public housing units on "the scene of dilapidated homes and squalid living conditions" that bordered Germantown High School. Roland R. Randall, the PHA's vice chairman, told reporters the decision was made "after exhausting surveys disclosed that this vast blighted area was endangering a high-class residential area and tending to become a permanent liability on the community."[17] The Germantown Realty Board, the Germantown Businessmen's Association, and the Germantown and Chestnut Hill Improvement Association immediately announced their support for the plan. William H. Emhart, a member of the GCHIA, said: "The section in question is a low rental district, and the people who live there will be unable to pay higher rents which the government must of necessity charge. . . . The entrance of a class of people who have the money asked for rent . . . will raise the standards of the neighborhood and improve the district in a number of ways."[18] Emhart's statement suggests that these housing activists had two aims: to improve the quality of housing in lower Germantown and to attract "a class of people" who could uphold and promote Germantown's bourgeois reputation, private homes, and desirable schools.

Even though Germantown's housing activists and business leaders supported the plan, many white middle- and working-class Italian residents who lived on or near the proposed site opposed it. Practicing what sociologist Margaret Weir called "defensive localism," these white residents engaged in a racist campaign to block a public housing project that they feared might attract more Black residents to their community.[19] They organized local marches with placards that said, "Don't Make Beautiful Germantown a Hall of Horror" and "Germantown is Not Glenwood Cemetery." Glenwood Cemetery was the site of the city's first all-Black public housing project, and thus, the residents' signs clearly illustrated the racist motivations behind their opposition.[20] The protests worked. In response, PHA officials assured them the authority had no intention of building on a site that residents opposed.[21] Philadelphia mayor Robert E. Lamberton abruptly withdrew funding for new public housing projects including the one in Germantown.[22] The white residents who had opposed the plan paraded through the streets and hung American flags in their windows to show their gratitude and support of their mayor, a man who had blocked a public housing project in their backyard.[23]

While these white residents in Germantown opposed public housing, thousands of other white residents in Philadelphia began the slow but steady retreat out of the public school system. Even though the total number of white residents in the city rose between World War I and World War II, the public school system lost 40,000 white students between 1925 and 1945. Many of these children still lived in the city but enrolled in parochial and private schools rather than their local public schools.[24] The percentage of white children in the city that attended parochial and private schools rose from 27% and 3% in 1925 to 35% and 5% in 1945 respectively.[25] As white families pulled their children out of the public schools, Black children filled these empty seats. The movement of white children out of the public school system and Black children into it altered the racial demographics of the city's public schools. In 1940, Black children represented 20% of the city's public school population. By 1950, that figure had risen to 30%.[26]

Wartime Labor Demands Pull High School–Aged Youth Out of the School House and Push Them Back into the Factory

Across the nation, thousands of high school–aged youth left school to find work in America's lucrative, and short-lived, wartime economy. To facilitate the movement of high school–aged youth from the schoolhouse to the factory, school administrators implemented accelerated curricula, part-time programs, and job placement supports. President Roosevelt and national school leaders urged administrators to create programs that maintained the academic standards of the traditional high school program to prepare youth for the war and postwar economy.[27] Philadelphia school officials did not always heed this advice. In 1943, Philadelphia's school board implemented a policy that permitted nonacademic students to expedite graduation to work in local wartime production firms. Under this policy, school district Junior Employment Service (JES) counselors helped students who wanted to secure jobs in the wartime economy by designing customized course schedules that included accelerated curricular programs.[28] Between 1941 and 1945, JES counselors matched 161,595 Philadelphia students with local employers and granted them permits to let them work during the school day. The overwhelming majority of the youth who used these programs (83%–97%) were

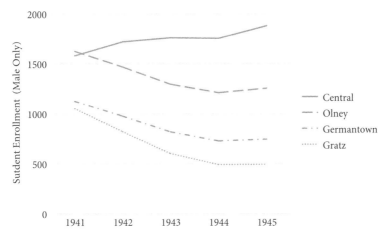

Figure 12. Male Enrollment in Central, Germantown, Gratz, and Olney High Schools, 1941–1945. Source: *ARBPE-P*, 1941–1945.

white. Initially, most of the work permits went to males (69% in 1941), but eventually many permits went to female youth (58% in 1945).[29]

Although thousands of young people secured part-time employment through the JES, thousands more simply dropped out of high school. Data suggest that youth in the city's neighborhood high schools were much more likely to drop out of high school during the war than youth in the city's two elite exam high schools. In fact, during the war, high school enrollment remained relatively consistent at the all-female Philadelphia High School for Girls and increased at the all-male Central High School. In contrast, the three neighborhood high schools in the city's northwest region—Germantown, Gratz, and Olney—experienced a significant drop in male enrollment (see figure 12). This finding suggests that male youth in these neighborhood high schools were willing to forgo or delay their high school education to work in the city's wartime factories. The largest drop in enrollment occurred at Simon Gratz High School, which in 1940 and 1950, had a larger percentage of Black graduates compared to Germantown or Olney High School (see table 7). This finding suggests that Black youth were more likely to leave school than white youth.

As thousands of young people across many communities dropped out of high school to find work, Bruce L. Melvin, a researcher in the Works Progress Administration, argued that wartime employment only offered temporary relief. Melvin predicted that when the war ended and production

Table 7. Percentage Black Graduates, Philadelphia, Citywide Exam and Northwest
High Schools, 1940 and 1950

Black Graduates	1940	1950
Central High School	11%	6%
Germantown High School	4%	13%
Gratz High School	6%	44%
The Philadelphia High School for Girls	14%	22%
Olney High School	0%	0%
School District of Philadelphia	Unknown	30%

SOURCE: GHS Yearbooks, January and June 1940, January and June 1950; Central High
School Yearbooks, January and June 1940, January and June 1950; Philadelphia for Girls
Yearbooks, January and June 1940, January and June 1950; Simon Gratz High School
Yearbooks, June 1940, January and June 1950; Olney High School Yearbooks, January and
June 1940, June 1950; United States Census, Philadelphia County, 1940; Levenstein, *Movement
Without Marches*, 127.

returned to normal levels, these youth would remain either under- or unemployed in the postwar economy.[30] Gladys Palmer, who had studied the Philadelphia economy for decades, echoed Melvin's predictions.[31] These predictions
came to fruition. When the war ended, the young men and women who
dropped out of school to secure work on the wartime economy faced a difficult situation. They lost their lucrative wartime positions and then largely
had to settle for low-wage, nonunion work in the postwar economy because
they lacked a high school diploma. Facing labor market discrimination and
lacking social networks, low-income and Black youth found postwar labor
options even more limited than their white and more affluent peers. The
economy lured low-income and youth of color seeking a better life out of
school during the war, but when the war ended it left them scrambling for
employment.[32]

Philadelphia's Increasingly Separate and Unequal System
of Neighborhoods and Schools

As more Black families moved to the city during and after the war, they
found racist housing policies and practices that barred them from the city's
best housing stock. In the postwar period, white GIs in Philadelphia and
other northern cities used federal housing benefits to purchase new homes

in majority-white communities on the city's periphery, in Mt. Airy, Chestnut Hill, and Northeast Philadelphia and in suburbs such as Levittown. Racism barred Black residents from these communities, and thus Black residents remained largely concentrated in the urban areas that had traditionally welcomed them: Lower Germantown, which was near the high school, and North, Southwest, and West Philadelphia. A 1953 Commission on Human Relations study of Philadelphia's new private housing made this point quite clear. In the postwar period, more than 144,000 private housing units were built in Philadelphia's metropolitan area. Only 1,044 of these units (less than 1%) were available to Black homeowners. Limited housing supply and increased demand forced Black families to pay more for less.[33]

Even though Germantown prided itself on its abolitionist past and progressive approach to race relations, its housing market exemplified this racism. Between 1948 and 1952, local civic leaders conducted a community audit of race relations in the area. The audit indicated that "the most urgent human relations problem in Germantown at the present time is that of housing." The report continued, "where ever a minority family moves into a city block, some of the older residents are inclined either to move out as soon as possible, selling their house at a reduced rate, or remain in the neighborhood as a focal point for interracial and inter-faith irritation and friction."[34] In the postwar period, Germantown experienced a surge in new Black and Jewish families who had moved out of older neighborhoods in the city's inner core to take advantage of Germantown's amenities—a thriving commercial center, public transportation, and public schools. The Black population of Germantown increased from 10% to 15% between 1950 and 1956.[35] In response to the influx of Black families, many lower- and middle-class white ethnics left their row homes near Germantown High School for more modern, spacious homes in the white communities of Mt. Airy, Chestnut Hill, and nearby suburbs. Most white homeowners sold their homes as soon as they could. Other white families retained their homes and then rented them to the incoming Black families, charging them exorbitant rents and often providing poor maintenance.[36] Like most American communities, white flight occurred block by block in Germantown—first in the most southern part of the community and eventually further north.[37]

In the 1950s, housing activists, community leaders, and local businesspeople sponsored a community-wide campaign to pressure these landlords to upkeep their homes.[38] Despite widespread local support, most white landlords dodged the pressure. The homes that they owned and rented to Black families near Germantown High School and its commercial district continued to deteriorate.[39] To counter the racism and neglect of the community's private housing market, Black families and their allies pressured city officials to construct new public housing in the area, but white residents once again blocked this idea.[40] Years later, Germantown's white business community convinced city officials to demolish 40 Black homes to build shoddy public housing units tucked neatly away on Queen Lane, an increasingly low-income Black community located near Germantown High School.[41]

While some Black and white families in Germantown and Mt. Airy challenged these discriminatory practices, racism in the city's public and private housing markets made it nearly impossible for Black families to secure the housing, and in turn, the public schools that they desired.[42] Racial segregation in Philadelphia's neighborhoods and schools intensified in the postwar period. In 1950, nearly 85% of Philadelphia's Black elementary-aged youth attended majority-Black elementary schools; 63.2% of these children attended schools where Black youth made up 90% or more of the total enrollment.[43]

Add B. Anderson Makes His Mark

From 1936 to 1962, Add B. Anderson served as the school district's business manager. The school board's unusual governance structure, which until 1965 consisted of appointed members, gave Anderson the power to pass budgets with little to no public oversight. To keep taxes as low as possible, Anderson implemented budgets that barely covered essential resources in the city's schools.[44] Moreover, Anderson, whose racist views were well-known throughout the city, routinely allocated more money to white schools. For example, in 1959, 9 schools in West Philadelphia's District 4 received more than $250 in per-pupil expenditures. Seven of these public schools had a majority-white student population. The 15 schools in the district that received less than $250 in per-pupil expenditures were all majority-Black.[45] These funding inequities affected educational experiences. Black schools had higher teacher-pupil ratios, more overcrowded classrooms, fewer guidance counselors, and fewer curricular resources. Due to overcrowding, Black youth were more likely to attend schools that operated on shift schedules that assigned each student to either a morning or afternoon session, giving them less instructional and extracurricular time.[46] As a result, Black youth bore the brunt of Anderson's reckless and racist budgetary decisions.[47]

In Philadelphia and other American cities, school district construction policies further exacerbated educational inequities based on race.[48] In the postwar period, Philadelphia school officials embarked on an $80 million campaign to build and renovate its outdated public school buildings, 20% of which had been built before 1907. After the war, school officials built dozens of new schools to address decades of neglect and postwar population shifts. Decisions about where to build these new schools maintained, and in some cases intensified, racial segregation. School officials built 19 of the 22 new public schools in racially segregated communities.[49] The new white schools had better facilities, more windows, and more attractive grounds than the district's new Black schools. The district's racially motivated construction policies promoted separate and unequal schools, even though the 1954 *Brown v. Board of Education* decision had declared them unconstitutional.[50]

Throughout the postwar period, Black residents and civil rights advocates pursued a multipronged approach to alleviate school segregation and resource inequities between Black and white schools.[51] Inside the schools, civil rights activists and their allies promoted intercultural education to increase awareness about racial and religious diversity.[52] Outside the schools, activists, such as Floyd Logan, the founder of the Educational Equality League (EEL), challenged racial discrimination in the city's housing and labor markets and demanded more equitable distribution of resources among the city's public schools. The Pennsylvania NAACP and EEL hosted conferences to discuss the "alarming growth of predominantly colored schools in Philadelphia."[53] In the spring of 1949, after careful investigation, state officials announced that nearly one-third of Pennsylvania school districts "maintained some form of formal segregation based on race."[54] In response, the Philadelphia NAACP wrote a letter to the governor demanding that he outlaw segregation in the state's public schools, arguing that in Philadelphia, Black children were "being cheated of a proper education because of the way they are herded into [overcrowded] classrooms like cattle into pens."[55]

In the 1950s, the board of education in Philadelphia stopped reporting racial demographics, which made it increasingly difficult for Logan and his allies to document and fight escalating school segregation.[56] To make their case, civil rights activists collected their own data and relied on findings from external evaluations to bolster the claims that Philadelphia's public schools were increasingly segregated and unequal.[57] In 1952, the Middle States Association of Schools and Colleges published a report that provided an evaluation of Benjamin Franklin High School and highlighted challenges in the city's racially segregated school system. Franklin had a nearly all-Black student enrollment (95%). The school had some of the lowest graduation and attendance rates in the city. Given these shortcomings, the association argued, Franklin "deserves all the help the Board of Education can give it— in fact, more help and more generous support than any other school unit in the city."[58] The association also noted that the deplorable physical condition of the school had "a deleterious effect on the mental health of the students, the teachers, and the entire school community." In order to repair the school to meet the conditions necessary for academic learning, the association recommended that the board close the school and transfer its students to more modern high schools in the city.

Even though the report focused on Benjamin Franklin High School, the association also pointed out that the school district's open-enrollment policy promoted "Jim Crow" schools. Under this policy, students could request transfers from their neighborhood high school to another high school outside their catchment zone. In practice, these policies and practices often generated more school segregation. The committee urged the board to end these policies immediately, stating, "the educational injuries being perpetuated on the Benjamin Franklin pupils by this complete segregation and by the anti-democratic implications of the discriminatory practices . . . is wholly out of line with progressive tendencies through the country and replete with perilous implications for racial amity in the entire city."[59] Civil rights activists used the findings from this report to educate Philadelphia families about the negative effects of segregation and to pressure school district officials to end their racially biased practices and policies that effectively maintained or intensified neighborhood and school segregation.[60]

In Germantown, these debates focused on two elementary schools: Eleanor Cope Emlen, built in 1925, and Anna Blakiston Day, built in 1952. In the late 1940s and early 1950s, white residents asked school officials to build a new elementary school in their neighborhood. These residents argued that they were worried about their children who had to cross busy streets and railroad tracks to attend Emlen. Civil rights activists charged that the residents' grossly overstated their concerns about the railroad to mask their anxieties about the racial changes in the neighborhood. The white children, these Black activists and their allies argued, could easily use one of the many railroad underpasses in the area to walk safely to and from school. Race—not railroads—motivated the white parents' demands to build a new school in the area. The white parents opposed putting the school on the other side of the railroad tracks because that community had a much higher percentage of Black residents and children. Eventually, school officials granted the white parents' request, and in 1952 they used the railroad tracks to delineate the Day and Emlen School boundary. When the Emlen and Day schools opened, 27 years apart, each school had a majority-white student body.[61] Over time, residential segregation, combined with the district's racially biased, gerrymandered zoning practices, contributed to a shift in the racial composition of several Germantown elementary schools, including Emlen. In the postwar period, the Emlen School became a majority-Black school while the Day School remained a majority-white school. School officials could have easily prevented this shift by drawing the school boundaries differently, but instead, these officials privileged the needs of white parents who demanded that their children attend racially segregated publicly funded schools.[62]

Frustrated with the school district's "muddied" zoning and enrollment policies, the Westside Neighborhood Council asked the Germantown Human Relations Committee to investigate racial segregation in the community's elementary schools.[63] The committee promised to gather statistics on the racial composition of the school and information on the process for approving or refusing student transfers.[64] It also invited Dr. Harry Giles, the director of New York University's Human Relations Study Center, to speak at a community-wide meeting about racial segregation on April 19, 1956.[65] Before his lecture, Dr. Edward T. Myers, Germantown's regional superintendent, sent Giles a letter that described the community. Myers told Giles, in the past Germantown had been regarded as a "high class residential area," but, "changes are taking place. Many colored families have moved in and continue to move in." He noted there had been "some wonderful examples of acceptance and fine co-existence," but as more Black families moved into the area many "old families" moved to the suburbs. Rather than acknowledge that school district policies had contributed to this segregation, Myers told Giles, "some schools are becoming Negro by geography."[66] During his lecture, Giles urged the community to collect data to understand the nature and extent of racial segregation, to sponsor community-wide events to promote open dialogue about the situation, and to plan for short- and long-term goals to integrate their schools. Even though the organizers promised an open and transparent dialogue, they censored the residents' pre-submitted questions, permitting only those that celebrated the community as racially progressive.[67]

Several months later, representatives from over 20 neighborhood associations, civic organizations, and religious groups drafted a resolution to end racial segregation in their local public schools. Refusing to attribute school segregation to residential segregation alone, they asserted that they knew children living in the same area, sometimes the same block, who walked in one direction to school if they were white and in another direction if they were Black. The residents argued that school officials had purposely drawn the Emlen and Day School boundary to segregate Black and white youth. They provided evidence that school officials had privileged student transfer requests based on race—white families were more likely to file and receive student transfers out of predominantly Black schools. The representatives submitted their plans to school district officials and urged them to comply with the *Brown v. Board of Education* decision by integrating the schools immediately.[68]

Myers acknowledged these concerns but defended the district's policies. First, he asserted that the makeup of the neighborhood schools reflected an increasingly segregated city and community. Second, he noted that hundreds of Black students had used the transfer policy to attend schools in Germantown, including the high school. Many of these students, Myers pointed out, lived in majority- or increasingly Black communities and came to Germantown to attend Roosevelt Junior High School, which Myers said felt like "heaven on earth" compared to their neighborhood schools.[69] He worried that abolishing the transfer policy might intensify segregation in Germantown's schools.[70] Myers had a point. By the late 1950s and early 1960s, Black families used the school district's open-enrollment policy to move their children out of under-resourced schools that relied solely on inadequate, often racially biased, public aid in North and West Philadelphia and into better-resourced and privately subsidized public schools such as Germantown High School. The movement of Black families from other schools into Germantown's schools actually increased local school integration. While this movement might have benefited the children who moved, it further eroded public support for the city's most vulnerable, and under Anderson's policies, most under-resourced public schools.

As segregation intensified in Germantown's elementary schools, the demographic shifts in the city's northwest region reflected the hardening of racial lines that was slowly, but surely occurring inside the city's public high schools. In 1950, Black youth were significantly more likely to graduate from Germantown than Olney or the all-male Central High School (table 7). And they were significantly less likely to graduate from Germantown compared to Gratz or the all-female Philadelphia High School for Girls (table 7). These graduation rates correspond to the spatial distribution of race in these school communities. In 1939, school district officials moved Central High School from its original Center City location to the Olney neighborhood. In 1950, the Olney neighborhood had a higher concentration of white residents than did the Germantown neighborhood. In contrast, the Gratz and Girls communities had a lower concentration of white residents than Germantown did. As a result, Black youth were more likely to graduate from Girls and Gratz and less likely to graduate from Central and Olney than from Germantown (see figure 13).

While the spatial distribution of race shaped student enrollment in these high schools, the school district's open-enrollment policy also had a significant effect on their racial composition. The open-enrollment policy permitted families to file a voluntary transfer to move their children from their local high school to any high school in the city if the receiving school had space for them. In 1940, data suggest that white families were more likely than Black families to use this policy to move their children from majority-Black schools to majority-white Germantown High School. In 1950, however, data suggest that Black families were more likely than white families to use this policy for that same purpose. In fact, as figure 14 shows, most of Germantown High School's 1950 Black graduates (52%) lived more than two miles from the school. Most lived near majority- or near-majority-Black high schools, such as Gratz, Franklin, and West Philadelphia High School. Many of these students likely used the school district's open-enrollment policy to move out of these schools and into Germantown High School—a majority-white, doubly advantaged institution. While these transfer decisions might have benefited children who moved out of Black high schools, the movement of Black youth out of their neighborhood high schools contributed to the erosion of public support for public schools in low-income Black communities.[71]

World War II Strains Germantown High School

On December 8, 1941, the day after the Japanese bombed Pearl Harbor, hundreds of Germantown High School students gathered in the auditorium to

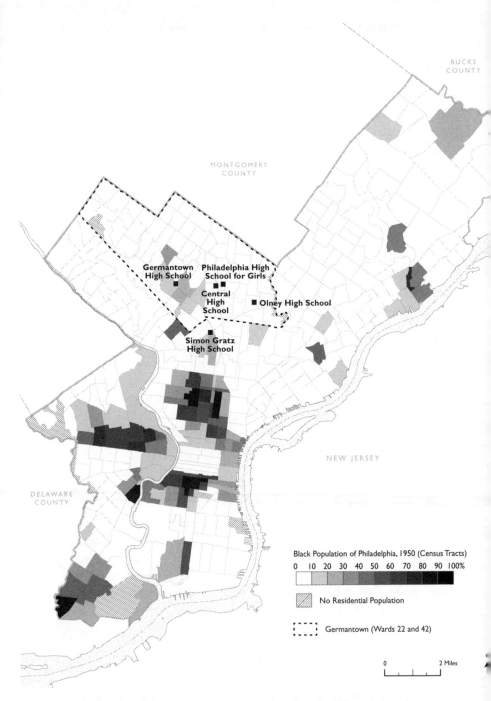

Figure 13. Location of Citywide Exam and Northwest High Schools and
Percentage of Black Residents by Census Tract, 1950. Source: United States
Census, 1950.

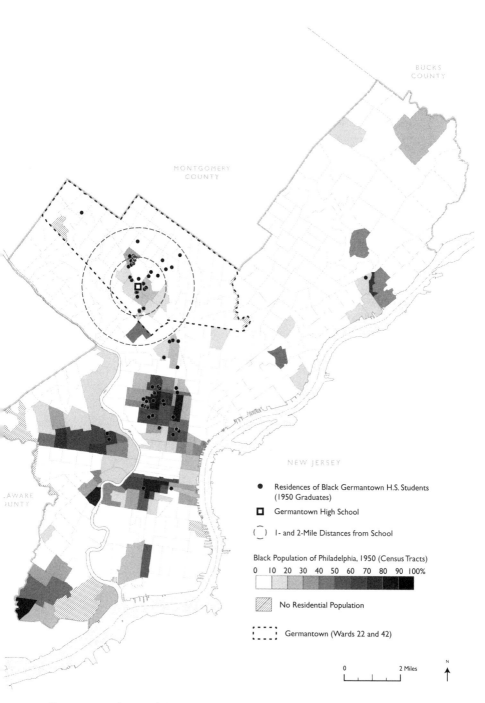

BUCKS
COUNTY

MONTGOMERY
COUNTY

NEW JERSEY

● Residences of Black Germantown H.S. Students
(1950 Graduates)

□ Germantown High School

⟨ ⟩ 1- and 2-Mile Distances from School

Black Population of Philadelphia, 1950 (Census Tracts)

0   10   20   30   40   50   60   70   80   90   100%

▨ No Residential Population

⌐ ¬ Germantown (Wards 22 and 42)
└ ┘

0   2 Miles

N

Figure 14. Residences of Black Germantown High School Graduates and
Percentage of Black Residents by Census Tract, 1950. Source: Germantown
High School Yearbooks, January and June 1950; United States Census, 1950.

listen to President Roosevelt address the nation and declare war on Japan and its allies. When the radio broadcast finished, the students burst into applause and sang the national anthem.[72] The decision to officially enter the war had a profound effect on the high school's curriculum, programs, and philanthropy. Germantown High School administrators leveraged wartime federal funding to expand the school's vocational programs and institute a series of afterschool and weekend courses to train youth and adults for wartime production.[73] Like others across the nation, Germantown administrators doubled physical education courses to better prepare male youth for military service and female youth for wartime factories.[74] High school administrators across Philadelphia banned traditional extra-curricular activities and established Victory Corps, which supported wartime military service and conservation efforts; the Junior Salvage Army, which collected scrap metal and other goods for the war; and the American Junior Red Cross, which offered youth and residents emergency medical training.[75]

After the United States officially entered the war, Germantown High School faculty and students redirected the philanthropy that had supported the school for decades to instead support the war effort. Students knitted blankets for American soldiers, collected keys and scrap metal, and sent over 200 care packages with novels, cigarettes, games, and toiletries to wounded soldiers stationed at nearby Valley Forge.[76] Germantown High School students also organized war bond campaigns to raise money for the war effort. The first campaign, which ran from January to May 1942, raised $10,000.[77] In October 1942, the school senate announced a campaign to raise $150,000 to purchase an army bomber for the US Air Force. To encourage giving and competition among the students, the school senate placed caricatures of Hitler, Mussolini, and Hirohito in the school lobby. When one of the home-rooms reached a certain campaign goal, senate members "blacked out" a body part on "one of these menaces"—"an arm . . . for $300, a leg for $700, the body for $10,000, and the head for $13,000."[78] A year later, Germantown High School students had raised enough money to purchase a bomber. The student-run newspaper published a photograph of the plane with the school's name etched on its side, and the school senate later displayed in the lobby the certificate of thanks that the Treasury Department sent to the faculty and students.[79] In response to student demand, the school senate sponsored a second bomber campaign, which raised over $145,000 for the war effort (see figure 15).[80]

Figure 15. Germantown High School War Fundraising Campaign.
Source: "Bond and Stamp Booth," *CC*, November 3, 1942.

The movement of private funding toward the war effort affected the school community's ability to generate private funding for the school once the war ended. After the war, administrators reinstituted school programs and activities. Students urged their peers to pay their poll taxes and purchase athletic tickets to offset these program costs. However, despite the encouragement from administrators and students, the high school's increasingly diverse student body refused to donate money to the school. Black and female youth did not want contribute funds to support the many clubs and activities that still barred them—both formally and informally.[81] Further, working-class youth often had part-time jobs after school, which limited their ability to participate in these programs. Thus, they refused to donate funds to the school.[82] Due to this decreased private philanthropy, educators had to rely increasingly on inadequate public school budgets, which limited their ability to provide the resources and programs that Germantown High School students had once enjoyed.[83]

As Germantown High School struggled to finance its programs and activities, low-income youth increasingly depended on programs and activities at the community's social service agencies. One story illustrates the importance of these organizations for local youth. During his childhood, Charles A. Shirley Jr. lived a few blocks away from the all-Black Wissahickon Boys Club. His father, Charles, served as a caretaker for several apartment buildings in the area; his mother worked as a domestic for local families. After school Charles routinely attended activities at the Wissahickon while his parents worked. During his senior year at Simon Gratz High School, Jim Smith, a Wissahickon staff member, asked about Charles's postsecondary plans and encouraged him to consider college. Before this meeting, Charles had never thought about applying to college—neither of his parents had gone to college and no one at his school had ever encouraged him to consider a postsecondary degree. With Jim Smith's support, Charles earned a senatorial scholarship at Lincoln University, a historically Black college outside of Philadelphia. When he registered for courses, Lincoln administrators told Charles that he needed to take additional coursework to meet the school's admissions requirements. Charles was not sure he wanted to go to college that fall and had hoped that this news meant that he had a "way out of college." Smith persisted. The next day, Smith told Charles that he had an idea to ensure that he went to college that fall. Smith called a colleague who worked at St. Paul's Polytechnic Institute in Lawrenceville, Virginia, and told him he had a terrific basketball player who needed a scholarship. Based on this conversation, the school awarded Charles a scholarship. Smith failed to tell him that Charles—at five feet, five inches—hardly looked like a star basketball player. Charles boarded a bus the following week for Lawrenceville, Virginia, worked at the Wissahickon Boys Club every summer, earned his college degree, and eventually spent over three decades as a teacher, at the R. W. Brown Boys Club and at Dobbins Technical School.

When Charles Shirley recalled his experiences at the all-Black Wissahickon Boys Club, he referred to it as "my family's savior." His access to free afterschool activities at the club enhanced his educational and recreational experiences and gave his working-class parents free afterschool care for Charles and his siblings. Club mentors helped him attend college, gave him work every summer, and provided experiences that prepared him for a professional career. For Charles Shirley and countless other low-income and Black youth who attended segregated and unequal public schools, the Wissahickon Boys Club and other organizations like it provided the institutional and personal supports that they might not otherwise have received.[84] The resources that these institutions provided made a significant difference in the lives of low-income and Black youth, but in the postwar period many of these organizations struggled to finance their programs due to decreased philanthropy. The funding shortages were exacerbated by postwar economic anxieties and the exodus of Germantown's "monied families" who had contributed generously to these organizations since their founding.[85] As a result, these organizations had to cut and streamline their youth programs, leaving low-income and Black youth without the support that their families had depended on for decades.[86]

Expansion of Curricular Offerings Spurs
Differentiation and Segregation

The dramatic labor shifts that occurred in the postwar period forced many American youth in Philadelphia and other communities to swap their lucrative wartime manufacturing positions for nonunion, low-wage work in the nation's expanding service and retail sectors. Between 1953 and 1954, Philadelphia's unemployment rate rose from 2.7% to 7.0%. Philadelphia's movement from manufacturing to service employment outpaced the rest of the country.[87] Thousands of youth who had dropped out of high school to accept work in the wartime economy lost their positions when the GIs came home. As these labor market shifts, once again, forced more youth to remain in high school, officials raised newfound concerns about the nation's high school dropout rate.[88] Reports released a few years after the war ended indicated that 70% of high school–aged youth attended high school, but 60% of those who attended high school failed to graduate.[89] Social scientists, educational leaders, and prominent journalists argued that these failures stemmed from the irrelevant academic high school curriculum.[90] In the summer of 1945, educators gathered in the nation's capital to discuss concerns about the academic nature of American high schools and to develop a solution to change it. Near the end of the conference, Dr. Charles A. Prosser, a highly regarded vocational education expert, proposed a plan. High schools, Prosser argued, should train 20% of high school–aged youth for postsecondary schooling, another 20% for skilled trades, and the remaining 60% should have "life adjustment training." Prosser and his allies defined life adjustment training as a combination of vocational and social training for clerical, service, and unskilled labor positions.[91] Prosser's proposal gave educators a mechanism to split America's high school–aged youth into distinct groups: those that the school deemed "worthy" and destined for postsecondary schooling and professional employment and those that the school placed in life adjustment training where they earned a watered-down high school degree.[92]

Philadelphia school officials embraced Prosser's visions and expanded the curriculum in the city's comprehensive high schools, including Germantown, to include more vocational and life training programs. In 1950, Germantown High School offered students a choice of eight curricular programs: the school's established academic and commercial programs as well as several vocationally oriented programs—distributive education, industrial, mechanical arts, music, agriculture, and vocational arts.[93] In addition to these programs, the school offered new elective courses in retail sales, clerical work, and nursing care. These courses reflected the ideals of Prosser's life adjustment training and prepared students to enter nonprofessional positions after high school.[94] School administrators urged students to meet with their guidance counselors and select courses that matched their personal dispositions and career aims.[95] To differentiate students, administrators split the counseling staff into separate groups that focused exclusively either on vocational or academic students. Counselors only provided college counseling to academic youth. This change effectively separated Germantown youth into two future pathways: college and noncollege-bound youth.[96]

Despite these changes, in 1950, the academic program remained the most popular option among Germantown graduates, followed by the commercial program and then the school's six vocational tracks. Female graduates were significantly more likely to select the commercial program than the academic or vocational track (table 8).[97] The movement of women out of the academic program and into the commercial program followed the growth in clerical positions after the war as well as reflected increased anxieties about the impact of academic learning on young women. Many families routinely encouraged their daughters to select Germantown's commercial program, secure clerical work, find a husband, and eventually stay home to raise their children.[98]

Oral history evidence suggests that class, gender, and race shaped the decisions students made about their high school courses and, ultimately, their postsecondary lives. Rosalie August, a white Jewish woman who graduated from Germantown in 1949, moved to West Mt. Airy, a middle-class, majority-white Germantown community, in 1939. Rosalie recalled that her family moved out of their ethnic neighborhood in the city's center to take

Table 8. Course Enrollment by Race and Gender, Germantown High School, 1950

	Academic	Commercial	Vocational
All Graduates ($n = 581$)	46%	35%	19%
Gender			
Female	40%	52%	8%
Male	56%	5%	39%
Race			
Black	49%	25%	26%
White	46%	34%	20%

SOURCE: GHS Yearbooks, January and June 1950.

advantage of Germantown's reputable public schools. Rosalie recalled that her West Mt. Airy neighborhood consisted of row homes with a mixture of middle-class Jewish and Catholic families "who had moved from the old neighborhood to the new ones." According to her, the Catholic children attended Catholic high school, the "top Jewish boys" attended Central High School. Rosalie's family sent both of their daughters to Germantown High School because, she reported, "we were too lazy to go to Girls' High."

Rosalie described Germantown High School as a "highly integrated institution" where administrators "very carefully tracked" students into distinct curricular tracks. Rosalie's family expected her to attend college, and so, she enrolled in Germantown's academic program, where she received a "very good education from excellent teachers." In her interview, Rosalie acknowledged that her decision to select the academic program limited her interactions with Black students inside the high school. She said, "I did have some Black friends, but they must have been from homeroom because I don't remember any Black students in the advanced classes, which is of course what happened a lot in those days." When she graduated, Rosalie attended Temple University, earned an English degree, and taught in Philadelphia's public schools, including Germantown High School from 1957 to 1961.[99]

Rosalie described Germantown High School's commercial program as a place for "smart girls whose parents did not want to send them to college." Vincenza Iannuzzi Cerrato was one of these girls. Born to Italian immigrant parents, Vincenza lived in a modest lower-middle-class home several blocks from the high school. Her father, Gennaro, worked as a stonemason and built many of the homes in Rosalie's West Mt. Airy neighborhood; Vincenza's mother, Assunta, managed a small store, and later, stayed home to raise her seven children while mending clothing to augment the family income. Vincenza attended Catholic elementary school and eventually transferred to public school. Her parents, who never completed high school, encouraged their daughter to enroll in Germantown's commercial track. Vincenza never questioned this advice because, as she said, "Italian people didn't educate a girl. They thought it was useless. You know, it wasn't important because a girl was going to get married." After she graduated from Germantown High School in 1949, Vincenza married her childhood sweetheart, Sam Cerrato, an Italian man who grew up in her neighborhood. Within a few years, she moved out of Germantown to raise her children in a nearby suburb.[100] Vincenza's decision to enroll in the commercial course fulfilled her parents' expectations: she graduated from high school, married an Italian man, and stayed home to raise her children.

Although Germantown faculty still routinely discouraged Black youth from enrolling in the academic course, 49% of Germantown's Black 1950 graduates earned an academic credential (table 8). Adrianne Valentine Morrison, a Black woman who graduated from Germantown with an academic degree in 1951, grew up in a middle-class home in Germantown's increasingly integrated Mt. Airy neighborhood. Adrianne's father, Irad, held a position with the post office; her mother, Josephine, was a housewife. Adrianne attended Emlen Elementary School, which she described as an "excellent school." From an early age, her teachers noticed Adrianne's academic proclivities and, like her parents, encouraged her to excel in school. Even though she had fond memories of elementary school, she also experienced racism there. Her second-grade teacher sponsored a story time every Friday afternoon during which students shared their favorite books. At the end of one story time, Adrianne's teacher read *Little Black Sambo*, a book with overtly racist overtures. Adrianne recalled that white students in her classroom often referenced the overtly racist ideas in the book to harass her and the other Black youth in her classroom.

The racism that Adrianne experienced in elementary school persisted at Germantown High School. Adrianne's stellar academic record made her eligible for membership in the National Honor Society, but when she attended her first meeting, she remembered being the only Black student in the club—documented in figure 16. Adrianne recalled that the society's faculty sponsor "looked at me as if I were a pane of glass." Several weeks later, the society sponsored an annual dinner. Adrianne told her mother that she did not want

Figure 16. National Honor Society, Germantown High School.
Source: Germantown High School Yearbook, January 1950.

to attend because she did not want to see the racist teacher. Her mother told her to get dressed, saying, "You earned the honor. You are going to the dinner." The dinner took place at Pelham Manor, which, Adrianne said, was a "very, very exclusive" place for Philadelphia's white elite. Her mother escorted her daughter to the entrance. Adrianne remembered that when she reached the top of the staircase, she turned around, hoping to escape. She glanced down the stairs and saw her mother patiently waiting for her to enter the dining room and sit with her peers. At the entrance, a white student came to the door and greeted her, saying, "Adrianne, I'm so glad that you are here." Adrianne turned toward the staircase to wave goodbye to her mother who had already left. Adrianne took her seat at the dinner table—she was the only Black student in the room. Despite her academic achievements, as a Black woman, Adrianne was often alone.

Even though she often felt isolated inside her high school, Adrianne recalled that one person, the high school counselor, Virginia Raacke, helped her cope with the racism that she experienced at Germantown. When Adrianne entered high school, Raacke recognized Adrianne's stellar academic record and placed her in Germantown's elite academic program. Her teachers knew that Adrianne was "Raacke's girl," which she believed protected her from the racism that many Black students experienced. She recalled that most faculty acted differently around her because they did not want to "mess up Dr. Raacke's student." Adrianne recalled that Raacke "found out very quickly" that Adrianne "loved a challenge." She urged Adrianne to participate in a variety of school clubs and activities and provided her with opportunities that most students never had. Raacke handpicked Adrianne to represent the school in the American Friends Workweek, a citywide community development program in North Philadelphia.[101] Participants painted and plastered low-income homes, visited a homeless shelter, and observed Philadelphia court hearings. Adrianne recalled that this experience exposed her to "the real world" of poverty and racism—something that middle-class Black youth like her rarely saw—and shaped her decisions about her future. After graduation, she earned a scholarship to attend Temple University and earned a master's degree in Social Work from Bryn Mawr College, Dr. Raacke's alma mater. With her family and Raacke's support, Adrianne graduated with an academic diploma and secured a professional career as a social worker, despite the racism that existed in her school and nation.[102]

In the postwar period, school administrators, faculty, and students promoted school-wide assemblies and programs to cultivate friendship and understanding among students from different racial, ethnic, and religious backgrounds. The high school administrators and faculty sponsored an annual friendship week that highlighted the contributions of African American and other ethnic and racial groups to the nation. The faculty hosted a linguistic and international club that focused on foreign languages and travel abroad. Finally, Germantown faculty encouraged students to participate in interracial and intercultural programs and activities at the Philadelphia Fellowship House.[103] In 1957, a Germantown student published "The Germantown Way," an article that celebrated the racial harmony at the high school. The author asserted that Germantown faculty had always permitted students to participate in school activities and programs regardless of their racial or religious background. According to the author, if a segregationist from the South visited Germantown High School, he or she would probably be "amazed to see Negro and white students laughing and learning together." Racism had never existed at the high school, the author suggested, and interracial friendships and cooperation represented "the Germantown Way."[104]

Germantown administrators, faculty, and some students—both Black and white—routinely promoted the school as an integrated, harmonious institution where faculty treated Black and white youth equally and everyone got along in perfect harmony.[105]

Yet, many Black students and their allies pointed out the ways that Germantown administrators, faculty, and students maintained and perpetuated racist practices and policies. In the spring of 1949, members of Germantown Community Council's Committee on Human Relations, an interracial group that met monthly in the community center, met with Germantown High School's principal to discuss the school's practice of sitting students at racially segregated tables during their senior luncheon. The principal acknowledged the practice and agreed to work with the committee to end it.[106] A few months later, rumors surfaced that the prom organizations had planned to segregate students during dinner. Again, after Black students protested, the prom organizers abandoned the idea.[107]

Oral history evidence reveals the painful effects of the school's racist policies and practices on low-income, Black youth. Born in Philadelphia at the height of the Great Depression, Ernest "Ernie" Cuff, a lower-middle-class Black man who attended Germantown High School, never felt that his teachers supported low-income, Black youth like him. His father, Arkie, worked in a local bakery; his mother, Esther, raised her children at home. During his childhood, Ernie lived in an older home a few blocks from the high school. Like many of the homes in the area, the Cuff residence lacked indoor plumbing, and the family used an "outhouse that someone had enclosed on the back porch." Eventually, his family moved into a "much bigger home" a few streets away and enrolled Ernie in Emlen Elementary School, where he never felt challenged. Frustrated with his schooling experience from a young age, Ernie routinely "skipped it [school]." Instead, he recalled, "I went off into the woods and goofed around, sometimes, I got into trouble. I wasn't a school person."

Despite a spotty academic record, Ernie enrolled in Germantown High School. His school counselor placed him in the school's industrial course with many of the other Black male students from his neighborhood. Ernie recalled that he did not ask to be placed in the school's academic program "because that was more for whites. I knew I could do it, but the incentive was not there." Even though he never enjoyed the rote learning that dominated his schooling, Ernie remembered one teacher, Ms. Duffy, who encouraged her students to excel. Duffy defied school practice and taught trigonometry to her all-Black industrial math class, even though many of her students had never taken algebra. Ernie described Duffy as a patient teacher who had a commitment to give her students the academic skills she thought they needed to be successful after high school. To Ernie's delight, he excelled at trigonometry and even tutored his peers. A few weeks after she started teaching her students trigonometry, Duffy abruptly stopped. To this day, Ernie thinks that Germantown administrators reprimanded Duffy and demanded that she stop. After she told her students she had to stop teaching them trigonometry "she was never the same." Asked whether he had other teachers like Duffy who taught him subjects traditionally reserved for academic students, he said with a touch of bitterness and anger, "No. She was the only one, male or female."

Ernie recalled that many of his teachers deliberately failed to provide him and the other Black students in his classes with the skills to secure decent employment. For example, he described a class in which the teacher handed him a steel block and instructed him to use a hand-held file to carve angles on its four sides. Ernie knew that postwar factories had machines to do this work, and thus, he immediately recognized this lesson as "stupid and pointless." The longer he stayed at Germantown, the more he realized that Black youth rarely had access to the educational opportunities of white youth, and even when they did, the faculty made it virtually impossible for them to succeed. A few months before graduation, an administrator told Ernie that he lacked the academic credentials for a traditional diploma and urged him to leave school with a certificate of completion. Ernie knew that a certificate of completion "meant nothing . . . it was just a piece of paper to keep you quiet . . . to pacify you." Although his parents repeatedly reminded him to remain patient and "wait" for racism to end rather than "fight the system on his own," he understood the school's racist policies and practices. Rather than endure more racism only to earn a certificate that had little value on the labor market, Ernie dropped out of high school, enlisted in the army, earned his GED, and worked a variety of odd jobs throughout his lifetime. Sixty years later, he did not regret his decision. He had just wanted the trauma that he had experienced inside his high school as a Black man to end.[108]

Germantown High School: An Institution Full of Paradoxes

Throughout the postwar period, Germantown High School remained an institution full of paradoxes, a place where doors of opportunity opened for some students and closed for others. Despite their racial differences, Rosalie August and Adrianne Valentine Morrison received a first-rate academic education that prepared them for a four-year college and professional careers. When Adrianne attended Germantown High School, most upper- and middle-class Black students enrolled in the academic program. In 1950, Black youth made up 13% of the graduating class. Despite their small numbers and the racism that they experienced, 49% of these Black graduates earned an academic diploma. As Adrianne recalled, many of these Black students felt isolated and alone in their overwhelmingly white academic classrooms. Adrianne and her Black peers fought to be recognized in an institution where many individuals refused to accept them. Dr. Raacke and a few other faculty like her tried to protect Black students like Adrianne from racism, but Black students remained vulnerable to the faculty and students who did not think that they belonged in the school's prestigious, and predominately white, academic track. Others, like Vincenza Iannuzzi Cerrato and Ernie Cuff, found that their gender or race barred them from the academic programs and instead opted into the commercial and vocational tracks. Vincenza graduated, married, and moved to the suburbs with thousands of other white women like her. Racist faculty and students pushed Ernie Cuff to leave high school early. Given the scarcity of school archives, it is impossible to know how many other Black men and women who entered Germantown High School shared his experience or how many Black men and women left the school early because of the racism that they experienced. But, we know, based on what he told us, that Ernie was not alone. Racism limited educational opportunities for Black students at Germantown High School from its founding, but the lines that determined opportunity based on race and class hardened in the postwar period as the number of Black and low-income students who entered the high school slowly continued to climb. Like the generations of Black students who came before them, Adrianne, Ernie, and their Black peers experienced and challenged racism in their Germantown classrooms, school activities, and community organizations. They resisted to change the institution and to showcase the hypocrisy in the nation's commitment to save the world from tyranny abroad while refusing to acknowledge racism at home. Their resistance set the stage for the turbulent decade that followed.

CHAPTER 5

Urban Renewal, Urban Unrest, and the Threat of a "Poverty-Stricken Negro Ghetto," 1958–1967

Born in Philadelphia on May 6, 1931, Gilbert Fuller Sr. grew up in a modest home in the heart of North Philadelphia's Black community. His mother, Mercedes, worked as a domestic until her husband secured a lucrative wartime position as a laborer in the Philadelphia Naval Yard. Gilbert attended Philadelphia's segregated majority-Black public schools—Dunbar Elementary, a few blocks from his home, and eventually, Benjamin Franklin High School, an under-resourced, majority-Black high school located in the city's center. In high school, Gilbert worked as a student aide in his school counseling office. One day, his counselor asked him if he wanted to go to college. He told his counselor he did, but that he was not sure that his parents, southern migrants with an elementary school education, understood the benefits of a college education. The counselor offered to meet with Gilbert's father to discuss the college application process and tuition costs. Following that meeting, Gilbert's father told his young son that the family could not afford to send him to college. Reflecting on this experience more than 60 years later, Gilbert said that he wished the guidance counselor had explained that he could have worked to pay for college, "I did not know that. And I don't think [my father] knew." Even though she told him that he was "qualified and capable" of attending college, he never had the opportunity to prove it.

As Gilbert recalled, despite this disappointment, when he earned his high school diploma, he, "framed it, put it under my arm, and went for employment.... [Y]ou couldn't tell me anything. I thought I had the ticket ... to open the door of opportunity, to get the job." He quickly learned that a high school diploma from North Philadelphia's majority-Black Benjamin Franklin High School had little value on Philadelphia's racially biased labor market. While he waited in the employment lines, he talked to white men who told him that they lacked the qualifications for the positions that they were applying to. Even though Gilbert had the necessary qualifications, employment officers routinely hired the white men and told Gilbert and other Black men that they "needed a little bit more." He did not need a bit more. These employment officers simply refused to hire Black men. Frustrated with Philadelphia's racially biased labor market, he enrolled in trade school and opened a shoe-repair business near his uncle's Germantown home. In 1953, he moved his family from North Philadelphia to a modest row house a few blocks from Germantown High School to take advantage of what Gilbert called Germantown's "quality of life": its suburban-style housing, its bustling commercial district, and its reputable public schools. When he turned the key to his new Germantown home, Gilbert Fuller was full of hope—hope that his children might have access to the educational opportunities that he never had.[1]

However, between 1953 and the time that his children eventually entered Germantown High School in the mid-1960s, white flight, coupled with racist school district policies and practices, intensified segregation in the city's neighborhoods and public high schools. As residential and school segregation increased, Black families remained divided on how to address this problem: some families demanded that school officials integrate the city's public schools; others demanded that school officials equalize resources between majority-Black and majority-white schools.[2] Rather than respond to these demands, school officials hired university experts to study segregation and offer recommendations. Meanwhile, Germantown's many white and some Black middle-class families increasingly questioned the value of their local public high school. They either moved their families to the suburbs or transferred their children to other public, parochial, and private high schools in the city. In 1956, white students made up 67% of Germantown High School's enrollment; by 1965, that figure had dropped to 37%.[3] As middle-class families—both Black and white—opted out of Germantown, the high school continued to lose the private funding that had sustained its doubly advantaged institution since its founding. For the first time in Germantown's history, administrators had to rely solely on inadequate public funding to support the school. The movement of middle-class families and their funds occurred at the very moment that Germantown High School transformed from a majority-white to a majority-Black institution, which reinforced the idea that majority-Black public schools were less desirable and less resourced than majority-white public schools. As these ideas circulated in the community, Black community and youth activists demanded that administrators respond to their calls for recognition and justice through the implementation of an Afro-centric curriculum and equitably funded public schools.

Urban Renewal Sets the Stage for Center City's 21st-Century Gentrification

The election of reform-oriented Democratic mayors and escalation of white flight spurred a citywide urban renewal program that attracted over $2 billion in private, city, state, and federal funding.[4] Beginning with the 1947 Better Philadelphia exhibit, city planners, under the direction of Edmund Bacon, sought to engage the public in discussions about their vision for their communities and to incorporate these ideas into their plans.[5] In contrast to federal guidelines that encouraged wholesale demolition and displacement, Bacon and his colleagues initially relied on selective demolition to improve housing options in the city. After the passage of the 1954 federal housing act, Bacon and his colleagues shifted their approach and focused their urban renewal efforts on economic development and urban renewal projects in the city's center.[6] The transformation of Philadelphia's Center City in the 1960s ushered in a wave of private investment and altered the area's racial demographics. The historically Black neighborhood witnessed a significant influx of white residents.[7]

While Bacon focused on the city's center, Henry S. Churchill and Henry Magaziner, two city planners who lived in Germantown, proposed plans to use federal funds to demolish substandard housing, curb white flight, and revitalize local commerce in the area near Germantown High School.[8] For nearly two years, civic leaders and city planners hosted community meetings to listen to residents' ideas about these plans.[9] Residents largely agreed that Germantown's commercial district, which had lost several businesses in the past decade, needed support. Residents urged planners to consider the needs of young families, who craved updated recreational facilities and well-resourced public schools. Even though residents agreed on many initiatives, the conversations revealed both class and racial tensions and different ideas about the purpose of urban renewal. Lower Germantown's increasingly Black and working/lower-middle-class residents who lived near the high school wanted to use urban renewal funds to generate more low-income housing and integrated public schools. Upper Germantown's racially integrated upper- and middle-class residents who lived in Mt. Airy and pockets of Chestnut Hill wanted to use these funds to demolish substandard homes, to broaden streets to ease traffic to and from the city's center, and to create a historic shopping mall with suburban-style amenities along Germantown Avenue. The community deliberated for years but was unable to reach a consensus on how to move forward with either one of these plans. While Bacon concentrated on the revitalization of the city's center, communities on the city's periphery, including Germantown, lost middle-class families and jobs. The movement of these families and jobs to the suburbs intensified inequality in the community between the majority-Black and lower-income families who lived near Germantown High School and the majority-white and upper-income families who did not.[10]

Race Shapes Educational Inequality in the Postwar Period

In the postwar period, Black activists and families demanded that school officials pursue policies and practices to address racial segregation and inequity in the city's public schools. The racial demographics of the city changed significantly between 1940 and 1960. In 1940, Black residents represented about 13% of the city's population. By 1960, that figure had reached 26%.[11] And as figure 17 shows, Black residents remained concentrated in the communities that had historically welcomed them: Germantown and North, West, and Southwest Philadelphia. In 1950, Black youth accounted for 30% of the city's public school enrollment. In 1960, however, even though they comprised only 26% of the city's residents, Black youth accounted for 47% of the city's public school students. As Black youth made up a larger percentage of public school enrollment, racial segregation increased in the schools. In the postwar period, 85% of Black students and 93% of Black teachers attended and worked in schools where at least 80% of the students were Black.[12]

The choices that Philadelphia families—both Black and white—made about their children's education had a profound effect on racial segregation inside the schools. First, white children were much less likely to attend public school than Black children. In 1962, 92% of Black children and 48% of white children attended public schools.[13] In the 1950s and 1960s, thousands

Black Population of Philadelphia, 1960 (Census Tracts)

0 10 20 30 40 50 60 70 80 90 100%

No Residential Population

Germantown (Wards 22 and 42)

0   2 Miles

Figure 17. Percentage of Black Residents by Census Tract, 1960.
Source: United States Census, 1960.

Table 9. Percentage Black Graduates, Philadelphia, Citywide Exam and Northwest High Schools, 1950 and 1960

Black Graduates	1950	1960
Central High School	6%	4%
Germantown High School	13%	27%
Gratz High School	44%	98%
Philadelphia High School for Girls	22%	18%
Olney High School	0%	0%
School District of Philadelphia	30%	47%

SOURCE: GHS Yearbooks, January and June 1950, January and June 1960; Central High School Yearbooks, January and June 1950, January and June 1960; Philadelphia High School for Girls Yearbooks, January and June 1950, June 1960; Olney High School Yearbooks, June 1950, June 1960; Simon Gratz High School Yearbooks, January and June 1950, June 1960; Levenstein, *Movement Without Marches*, 127.

of white families who lived in the city opted out of their local public schools for other options. Many sent their children to the city's extensive network of parochial and private schools. Hundreds of families moved their children into Philadelphia's elite, exam-based public high schools—the all-male Central High School and the all-female Philadelphia High School for Girls— which still required prospective students to take an exam for admission. White and affluent families, like those in Germantown's Mt. Airy and Chestnut Hill communities, were more likely to send their children to the exam-based public schools, private, and parochial schools.[14] The movement of white children into exam, parochial, and private schools pushed Black children out of these schools. In 1960, Black youth were significantly less likely to be among the graduates of Central and, for the first time in history, the Philadelphia High School for Girls than from the neighborhood-based Germantown High School (see table 9 and the appendix for statistical details).[15]

School district policies actively shaped school enrollment patterns. In the postwar period, thousands of Philadelphia families used the school district's open-enrollment policy to move their children from their neighborhood public schools to other public schools in the city. In 1961, over 15,000 families—10,000 Black and 5,000 white—did so. Most Black and white families who used this policy moved their children from majority-Black neighborhood schools to majority-white schools outside their neighborhood.[16] In 1960, residents in Philadelphia's northwest region still had three public school options: the majority-white Germantown High School, the majority-Black Simon Gratz High School, and the majority-white Olney High School. Black youth were significantly more likely to be among the graduates of Germantown than from Olney High School but were significantly less likely to be among the graduates of Germantown than from Gratz High School (table 9; see appendix for statistical details). While the Black student population had increased significantly at Germantown and Gratz, Gratz had the largest percentage of Black graduates among these three schools (table 9). The outmigration of white families from the area near Gratz played a role, but yearbook data suggest that reliance on the school district's open-enrollment policy among white families who remained in the area also played a role in this transformation. In 1960, nearly 40% of white graduates and only about 7% of Black graduates lived more than two miles from Germantown High School (see figures 18 and 19). Many of the white graduates who lived outside the two-mile radius were zoned for majority-Black neighborhood high schools: Benjamin Franklin (91% Black), Gratz (95% Black), and West Philadelphia (92% Black).

White families made up the majority of families who relied on the school district's open enrollment policy to move children out of majority-Black high schools near their home and into the still majority-white Germantown High School (35% Black).[17] In the 1940s, '50s, and '60s, white families did not necessarily need to vocally resist integration to preserve the color line, rather they could use the school district's open-enrollment policy to silently transfer their children out of their majority-Black neighborhood schools and into majority-white schools, including Germantown. The quiet movement of white children from majority-Black to majority-white schools intensified racial segregation in the city's public high schools. School district officials ended Philadelphia's open enrollment policy in the 1960s. As the data in table 10 illustrate, the end of the school district's open-enrollment policy curbed school choice and escalated white flight from Philadelphia's neighborhood high schools (see table 10, Racial Demographics, Philadelphia High Schools).

Civil Rights Activists Demand School Integration

On June 7, 1961, the Philadelphia NAACP filed a lawsuit, *Chisholm v. Board of Education*, against the School District of Philadelphia. Built on landmark rulings in New Rochelle and Rochester, New York, the lawsuit claimed that school district officials had violated the 14th Amendment. The NAACP accused

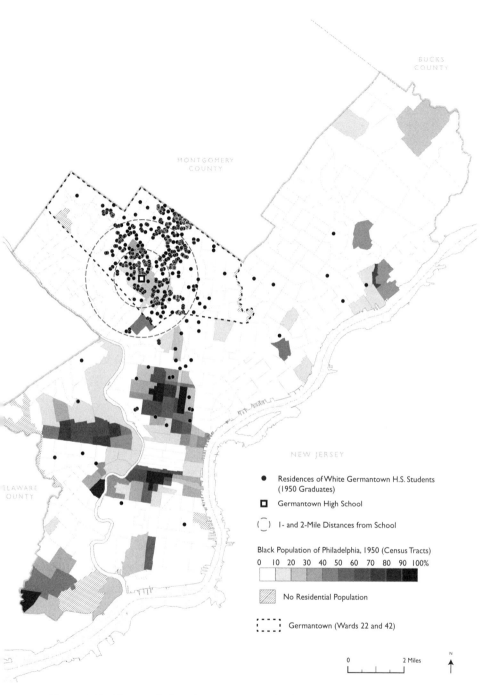

BUCKS
COUNTY

MONTGOMERY
COUNTY

NEW JERSEY

DELAWARE
COUNTY

●   Residences of White Germantown H.S. Students
     (1950 Graduates)

◻   Germantown High School

(◌) 1- and 2-Mile Distances from School

Black Population of Philadelphia, 1950 (Census Tracts)
0   10 20 30 40 50 60 70 80 90 100%

▨   No Residential Population

▭   Germantown (Wards 22 and 42)

0   2 Miles

N

Figure 18. Residences of White Germantown High School Graduates and
Percentage of Black Residents by Census Tract, 1960. Source: Germantown
High School Yearbook, January and June 1960; United States Census, 1960;
NHGIS.

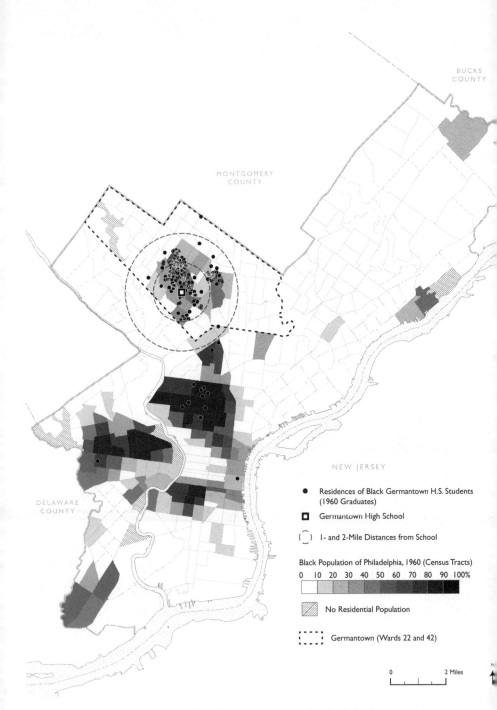

Figure 19. Residences of Black Germantown High School Graduates and
Percentage Black Residents by Census Tract, 1960. Source: Germantown High
School Yearbook, January and June 1960; United States Census, 1960; NHGIS.

Table 10. Percentage Black Graduates, Philadelphia, High Schools, 1956–1965

	1956	1957	1958	1959	1960	1961	1962	1963	1964	1965
District 1										
Bartram	27%	30%	32%	35%	41%	45%	48%	48%	49%	56%
West Philadelphia	68%	73%	79%	85%	92%	97%	98%	97%	99%	99%
District 2										
Benjamin Franklin	90%	91%	93%	91%	91%	91%	93%	96%	94%	96%
Philadelphia High School for Girls	26%	22%	19%	16%	16%	18%	18%	18%	20%	22%
William Penn	91%	93%	95%	95%	96%	95%	97%	95%	96%	97%
District 3										
South Philadelphia	15%	16%	17%	15%	16%	17%	19%	24%	31%	40%
Bok Vocational-Technical	66%	66%	71%	71%	75%	78%	81%	83%	86%	89%
District 4										
Gratz	84%	86%	93%	96%	95%	99%	99%	99%	100%	99%
Overbrook	52%	48%	46%	48%	50%	54%	54%	57%	62%	73%
Dobbins Vocational-Technical	30%	31%	35%	39%	41%	45%	43%	44%	45%	46%
District 5										
Edison	48%	52%	54%	56%	52%	58%	54%	61%	67%	72%
Kensington	39%	43%	42%	45%	46%	42%	40%	43%	47%	50%
Mastbaum Vocational-Technical	3%	3%	3%	3%	4%	4%	4%	5%	5%	6%
District 6										
Central	5%	5%	6%	6%	6%	6%	7%	7%	8%	10%
Germantown	33%	33%	32%	32%	35%	41%	41%	44%	50%	63%
Roxborough	4%	4%	4%	4%	5%	4%	4%	4%	6%	11%
Wissahickon Farm	9%	12%	13%	19%	13%	17%	14%	15%	19%	32%
District 7										
Frankford	3%	3%	3%	3%	3%	3%	3%	3%	3%	5%
Olney	0%	1%	1%	1%	2%	3%	4%	7%	10%	20%
District 8										
Lincoln	1%	1%	1%	1%	1%	1%	1%	1%	1%	2%
Northeast	NA	1%	1%	1%	1%	1%	1%	1%	1%	1%
TOTAL	30%	30%	30%	39%	32%	34%	34%	36%	39%	48%

SOURCE: Philadelphia Board of Education, Division of Research, "A Ten-Year Summary of the Distribution of Negro Pupils in the Philadelphia Public Schools, 1957–1966," December 23, 1966, box 23, folder 6, Floyd Logan Collection; "Number of Negro Teachers and Percentage of Negro Students in Philadelphia Senior High Schools, 1956–1957 [n.d.]," box 14, folder 10, Floyd Logan Collection, cited in Delmont, *Nicest Kids in Town*, 93–94.

school district officials of deliberately creating, perpetrating, and intensifying racial segregation through racially biased student assignments and gerrymandered public school boundaries.[18] The case focused on two elementary schools in Germantown: the majority-Black Emlen School and the majority-white Day School. NAACP lawyers argued that school officials had deliberately drawn the Emlen and Day school boundaries from east to west to create racially segregated schools rather than from north to south, which would have created racially integrated schools.[19] Even though evidence supported their claim, the case was mired in problems from the beginning. First, northern courts rarely, if ever, required northern school districts to desegregate their schools. The courts generally ruled that school segregation stemmed from residential segregation, and thus, according to the courts, school officials were not responsible for the level of segregation in the public schools.[20] Second, the board of education had stopped reporting racial statistics to the public and the NAACP lacked the funds to conduct an independent assessment about the level of racial segregation in the city's public schools. They needed this assessment to prove their point in court. Rather than craft a case that he might lose, Isaiah Crippens, the NAACP's lead counsel, agreed to collaborate with the school board to develop an integration plan. He told the court: "We think that integration is a positive education factor. Now, what we are after is the best educational opportunity for each and every child. The Board officially changed its policy from this so-called non-discrimination [policy] to . . . state that now they are going to foster integration. We felt that in an atmosphere of friendliness we might make use of the studies and discussions by citizens' groups and at last come up with an amicable solution."[21]

In response to this agreement, Richardson Dilworth, Philadelphia's former mayor and new school board president, held nearly 100 community meetings to gather input on the level of segregation and on ways to alleviate it. Busing Black and white students represented the most effective approach, but vocal white residents in the city's overwhelmingly white northeast region opposed any plan to bus their children, stating they "feared that their children will be attacked by black [children]." Many Black families also opposed busing, arguing, "their children are already being bused too much already."[22] In some cases, Black families and activists were less focused on integration and more focused on forcing school officials to equalize resources between majority-Black and majority-white schools.[23]

On September 26, 1963, the court approved a plan to integrate schools and equalize school resources. The plan required school board members to revise feeder patterns and school boundaries to increase integration, to end part-time attendance and overcrowding with busing, and to allocate resources to the most under-resourced schools first. School district officials purchased books and instructional materials that highlighted the contributions of Black leaders and implemented reading programs to strengthen instruction in the most challenging institutions. Officials promised to revise teacher transfer and placement policies to create a more integrated teaching staff. This never happened. A month after the plan's passage, Crippens, the NAACP's lead counsel, filed a motion for Judge Wood, who oversaw the case, to order compliance with the plan. In the hearing, Crippens presented two concerns. First, school officials refused to transfer students to underutilized white schools to reduce overcrowding and instead created makeshift classrooms for these students in already overcrowded Black schools. Second, school officials dodged their promises about teacher staffing. Judge Wood responded that the board had acted in good faith and dismissed the charges. For the next two years, the court protected white school officials, who remained reluctant to foster meaningful integration, over Black residents, who demanded racial justice and equity in their schools. Black residents picketed school buildings and organized citywide protests to demonstrate their outrage and anger with the courts and schools.[24]

School Board Studies Racial Segregation
in the City's Public Schools

To mitigate unrest and assuage demands from civil rights activists, school board members initiated two studies to survey the level of segregation in Philadelphia's public schools: a special committee, under the direction of school board vice president Ada Lewis, and an independent committee, under the direction of Stanford University's William R. Odell.[25] Less than a month after President Johnson passed the 1964 Civil Rights Act, the Lewis committee, which consisted of over 100 administrators, officials, and residents, released its findings about the nature and level of school segregation in the city. The report asserted that the school board remained committed to "a positive policy of fostering integration in the public schools," but it also confirmed that Philadelphia's public schools were segregated and unequal.[26] The report noted that the city had 102 schools with 70% or more Black student enrollment and that these schools were "definitely inferior in all major categories."[27] Despite clear evidence to suggest otherwise, the committee insisted that the level of racial segregation, and in turn the obvious inequities that this segregation generated, stemmed from residential segregation and individual choices, not past school district policies or practices. Drawing on ideas about the culture of poverty, the committee argued that Black youth were underrepresented in academic programs because Black youth understand that "no effort on their part could lead to success in the highly competitive white world which deliberately shut them out."[28] The committee asserted that school officials had not intentionally dissuaded Black youth from the academic program, but instead Black youth had independently chosen to avoid the academic program because they did not see the value of an academic degree on Philadelphia's racially biased labor market. The committee had no evidence to support these claims.

Despite the report's obvious shortcomings and racially biased conclusions, the committee urged the school board to consider policies to integrate and equalize Philadelphia's public schools by creating K-4-4-4 plans and educational parks, which were large school campuses with multiple schools to foster cross-neighborhood schools, and in turn, racial integration. The committee also recommended that the board evaluate the distribution of funding and resources across the city. Finally, the committee suggested that the board revise its curricular programs "to include instructional materials, readers, texts, and literature which give adequate and dignified treatment to the contributions and lives of Negroes and other minority group members in American life and history."[29] Even if the school board had wanted to implement these recommendations, however, neither the city nor the school district had the political will or the public funds to do so. The committee knew this. In the report, the committee noted that Philadelphia still had one of the lowest per-pupil expenditure rates among the nation's largest cities. But instead of advocating higher taxes, which might encourage more white flight from the city, the committee urged the board to secure federal and philanthropic funds to cover the costs of these policies and programs.[30] Once again, Philadelphia's civic leaders urged school officials to rely on philanthropy to fund its public school system.

Nearly one year later, Odell released a 389-page report on the conditions in Philadelphia's public schools. Conducted over an 18-month period with a team of over 20 educational researchers, Odell's study indicated that Black youth were more likely than white youth to attend overcrowded and older schools, less likely to participate in extracurricular activities, and more likely to drop out of high school.[31] These findings, Odell argued, were related to the school district's fiscal challenges. He noted that Philadelphia's public schools were grossly underfunded compared to those of other urban areas. Philadelphia's funding shortage had a negative impact on school staff, instructional practices, and extracurricular opportunities. The city had one of the highest student-teacher ratios, which created overcrowded classrooms in many schools and made it difficult for teachers to provide students with personalized instruction for deep learning and understanding.[32] Finally, Odell asserted that the school district's reliance on student fees to cover the costs of extracurricular activities presented a significant hardship to low-income and Black youth. His study revealed that nearly half of high school–aged students did not participate in extracurricular activities due to the cost of these activities.[33]

Odell's survey contained only five pages of recommendations—none of which addressed the racial segregation in the school district. Instead, he reiterated that Philadelphia public school students remained "approximately one-half year below achievement levels for other comparable pupils in other school systems." He blamed these results on the haphazard organization and structure of the school day—a school day that allowed for too much recreation in the elementary schools and too little instruction in the high schools—and then outlined a plan to improve instruction for all youth. Odell urged the school board to address these issues by raising per-pupil expenditures, increasing teacher salaries, reducing class size, lengthening the school day, expanding achievement testing, and developing a master plan to improve facilities. Odell projected that his plan would cost the district $125 million and another $38 million annually and encouraged the board to find government funds to do this work.[34] In his concluding remarks, he wrote:

Any final solution to genuine improvement of the public-school program in Philadelphia depends upon broad community acceptance of the fact that past educational programs and financial support levels are not adequate to meet the accumulated tasks of the local public schools. If problems that exist are to be solved, additional funding equal to or greater in amount than those spent in surrounding suburban school systems (where in many ways school problems are simpler) must be made available. This is a problem for the local community of Philadelphia, the state of Pennsylvania, and the Federal government to solve together.[35]

Civil rights leaders lambasted Odell's report for ignoring the racial segregation in the city's public schools, relying on racially biased intelligence tests
to advance his claims, and proposing a plan that would have cost the city
millions to implement.[36]

Despite these critiques, board members praised the findings in Odell's
report and moved forward with incremental measures to give the impression
that they remained committed to school integration. On March 26, 1965,
the board announced a plan to bus 3,000–7,000 Black children from overcrowded majority-Black schools in North and West Philadelphia to underutilized majority-white schools in Philadelphia's Northeast. School officials
limited the number of Black student transfers "to avoid flooding the receiving schools with underprivileged slum children."[37] The following day, the
superintendent created a 52-member (18 Black and 34 white) Citizens Advisory Committee on Integration and Intergroup Education to advise him on
plans to integrate the city's public schools.[38] Four days later, frustrated with
the school district's refusal to expedite integration, the NAACP filed papers
in federal court that argued that the school district's most recent integration
report, which cited the Odell report and an educational park plan in Germantown as the most notable moves to integrate the city's public schools,
was "an insult to our intelligence." Isaiah Crippens, the NAACP's lead counsel, contended that the report ruined the progress that had been made in the
past few months and demanded an immediate conference with school officials to devise a detailed integration plan within 90 days.[39] In response, C.
Taylor Whittier, Philadelphia's superintendent of schools, appointed Robert L. Poindexter, a Black educator with 29 years of experience, as his deputy
superintendent, making him the nation's highest-ranked Black educator.
Poindexter promised to collaborate with school officials and local residents
to "do everything in [his] power to speed up the integration of both pupils
and staff in the school system."[40] A few weeks later, after only two years in
the position, Whittier abruptly resigned as the superintendent of Philadelphia's public schools due to the city's inadequate public school funding
streams and mounting white resistance to his integration plans.[41]

On December 1, 1966, school district officials announced that they had
hired Mark Shedd, a progressive white reformer with a doctorate from the
Harvard Graduate School of Education and several years of experience as
superintendent of the public schools in Englewood, New Jersey, as superintendent of Philadelphia's public school system.[42] Heralded for his work on
racial equity, Shedd came to Philadelphia poised for radical reform. He

strongly believed that any effort to reform the Philadelphia school system had to start with Black empowerment.[43] Shedd supported Black students' demands for a culturally responsive and relevant curriculum and representation in school and district governance. He implemented a Black studies curriculum in the city's high schools and praised Black youth for establishing Black student unions. At the same time, Shedd consistently advocated for teachers and principals to have more control and power over their schools and to promote curricula and programs that, in his words, "turned kids on." Shedd understood that Black resistance to the current school curriculum and structures reflected, at least in part, their desires to have more control and autonomy over their schools. Being responsive to student needs remained central to Shedd's leadership throughout his tenure. He told teachers, "It should be perfectly clear to anyone who reads the daily roster of violence, hatred and despair which fill the newspapers that this country needs a social revolution—a revolution in human values and human relationships. If this does not occur, I see no reason for bothering to educate our children. And if this is to occur, the schools must be the cauldron, whether we like it or consider it our traditional role or not."[44] To show his support for this public school revolution, Shedd enrolled his four white children in his majority-Black neighborhood public schools, Roosevelt Junior and Germantown High School.[45]

Germantown High School's Expansion
Spatially Segregates Youth

On January 6, 1957, the Germantown Community Council's school committee, a community-wide organization focused on improving the quality of Germantown's public schools, sponsored a meeting to discuss the overcrowding at Germantown High School. Speaking to a nearly all-white audience, Charles Nichols, the school's principal, asserted that student enrollment had surged 18% between 1950 and 1957. The school, built to accommodate 2,300 students, was attended by 2,864 students. Nichols noted that administrators had opened makeshift classrooms in the school's cafeteria, library, and hallways to accommodate the overflow of students. Rosalie August, who graduated from Germantown in 1949 and returned to teach there a few years later, recalled teaching English in the school's fourth-floor hallway with 40 desks and a rolling chalkboard. Rosalie noted that this arrangement hardly met families' expectations regarding suitable conditions for academic learning inside the school.[46]

After Nichols concluded his remarks, Edward T. Myers, the regional superintendent for Philadelphia's northwest schools, told the audience that the overcrowded conditions stemmed from an influx of families who used the school district's open-enrollment policy to move their children out of their neighborhood high schools and into Germantown High School. Myers shared a map of the district with an outline that indicated Germantown High School's catchment area. The data indicated that 1,887 students who attended Germantown High School lived in the school catchment area (see figure 20). These students enrolled in Germantown High School because it was their zoned neighborhood school. The data on the map also indicated that nearly 800 students used the school district's open-enrollment policy to transfer out of their zoned neighborhood schools and into Germantown High School. Many of these youth lived in Nicetown (204 students) and parts of North Philadelphia (374 students). Their zoned schools were either the nearly all-Black Simon Gratz High School or the nearly all-Black Benjamin Franklin High School.

Even though Myers and Nichols argued that these conditions stemmed from an enrollment surge, evidence suggests otherwise. In fact, Germantown High School enrolled more students in 1941 than in 1957.[47] But there was one clear difference. In 1957, the school had fewer teachers than it did in 1941. The school was not more crowded, but its classrooms were. In September 1957, Germantown had 826 classroom sections with more than 35 students. The school's overcrowded classrooms stemmed from Philadelphia's inadequate school budgets—budgets that forced public schools to operate with overcrowded classrooms because they lacked the teachers to staff the school properly.[48] After Nichols and Myers spoke, audience members expressed their concerns that overcrowded conditions threatened the school's academic program and the community's desirable public schools. They demanded that school officials secure funding to build "a modern cosmopolitan high school which would adequately serve the needs of the Germantown community."[49]

Once again, school officials gave Germantown's white residents what they wanted. In 1958, the board announced the construction of a new wing of classrooms on the west side of Germantown High School.[50] This new high school fit neatly with the ideas of a modern comprehensive school—where students of all backgrounds and abilities could be served in one building—pushed by

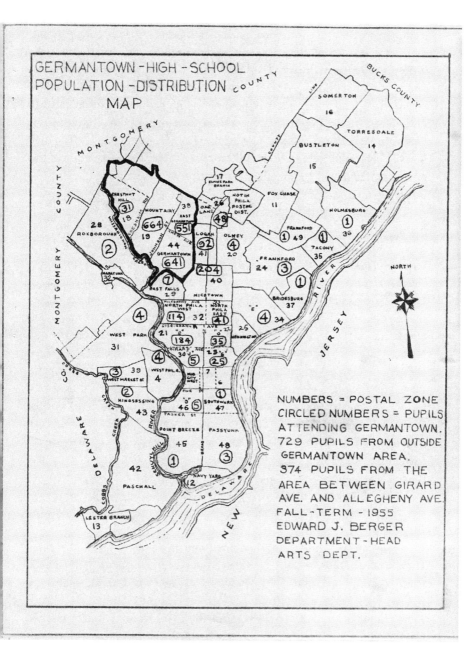

Figure 20. Number of Pupils Attending Germantown High School by Postal Zone, Fall Term 1955. Source: Germantown High School Population Distribution Map, Germantown High School Archives.

leading theorists and educational reformers.[51] Germantown's white residents rejoiced. Even though they pinned the expansion on the overcrowded conditions inside the high school, it seems that racial shifts in the community and high school influenced their demands. In the postwar period, the number of Black students inside Germantown High had risen significantly. In 1940, Black students represented less than 4% of the school's graduates. By 1965, Black youth represented 63% of the student body (table 11). The high school's expansion coincided with these racial shifts. The completion of this new wing facilitated the physical segregation of Black and white students inside Germantown High School.

On February 28, 1961, after three years of disruptive construction, Germantown High School opened its new west wing. Dubbed the '50s wing, this new area had 37 modern high school classrooms designed and reserved for commercial and vocational students. Once the wing opened, Germantown administrators put the majority-white academic students in the original 1914 building and the majority-Black commercial and vocational students in the new wing. The decision to separate the academic and commercial-vocational programs into two distinct wings of the building physically segregated students by race and class. In 1960, Germantown High School offered eight curricular programs: academic, commercial, general, trade preparatory, industrial arts, mechanical arts, home economics, and vocational arts. In 1960, the majority of graduates earned an academic diploma (53%). For the first time in history, Black graduates were significantly more likely to earn a commercial diploma than an academic one. In 1940, 58% of Black youth earned an academic diploma; by 1960, that figure had dropped to 33% (table 11; see appendix for statistical details). The physical separation of majority-white academic students and majority-Black commercial/vocational youth limited interracial socialization and fueled racial inequality inside the high school.

Cathy Spears Schuler, a white woman who graduated from Germantown High School in 1964, felt that she received a first-rate education at the school. Cathy's family had "old Germantown roots" and lived comfortably in a middle-class, white Mt. Airy home. Her father, Carl J. Spears, a Germantown High School alumnus, worked for the city government. Her mother, Catherine Cooker Spears, assembled circuit boards for a local firm near her Price Street home. Cathy always felt that she "wasn't the best student," because she "went to school earlier than [she] should have." On the advice of her junior high school counselor, Cathy enrolled in summer school to take

Table 11. Course Enrollment by Race and Gender, Germantown High School, 1940–1960

	1940 (n = 638)			1950 (n = 581)			1960 (n = 776)		
	Academic	Commercial	Vocational	Academic	Commercial	Vocational	Academic	Commercial	Vocational
All Graduates	52%	33%	15%	46%	35%	19%	53%	30%	17%
Gender									
Female	45%	47%	7%	40%	52%	8%	54%	40%	6%
Male	61%	16%	23%	56%	5%	39%	51%	14%	35%
Race									
Black	58%	33%	8%	49%	25%	26%	33%	43%	24%
White	52%	33%	15%	46%	34%	20%	60%	25%	15%

SOURCE: GHS Yearbooks, January and June 1940, January and June 1950, January and June 1960; United States Census, 1940.

the prerequisites she needed to enroll in Germantown's majority-white academic program. Cathy recalled that her academic courses at Germantown were quite challenging, and even though she remembered many fine teachers, she said, "there weren't a whole lot of supports at Germantown High School . . . if you needed support, you went out and got a tutor." Like many of her upper- and middle-class white peers, Cathy had private tutors to help her with school work. The private tutors helped, but she said that her personal relationship with her school counselor most strongly influenced her future. During high school, Cathy babysat her school counselor's children and had many informal conversations with her counselor about her future. Based on her counselor's recommendations, Cathy applied to and enrolled in Penn State-Altoona, where she earned a degree in art education. Fifty years after graduation, she credits her Germantown teachers and counselor with preparing her for college and her career as an art teacher. Even though she always thought of her high school as an integrated high school, both she and her husband and Germantown High School alumnus, George Schuler, recalled that they did not know many Black students in the high school because most of the Black students were enrolled in commercial and vocational programs, and thus, took their classes in the new '50s wing.[52]

Michelle "Shelley" Deal Winfield, a Black woman who graduated with Cathy Spears in 1964, earned an academic diploma at Germantown. Her parents, Ponsie Barclay Hillman and Alphonso Deal, who served as the president of the Philadelphia NAACP's action branch, modeled racial activism for their children from a very early age. When Shelley entered Germantown High School, she selected the academic course, which she said was "predominantly Jewish." Shelley never thought much about the racial segregation in the various curricular programs during high school. However, after she graduated, she remembered looking at her yearbook and counting the number of Black graduates in her class. To her surprise, like Cathy and George Schuler, she hardly knew any of them. Most of the Black students in Shelley's class enrolled in commercial and vocational courses housed in the '50s wing. She did not know them because she did not see them during the school day.

Even though she excelled academically, unlike Cathy Schuler, Shelley recalled that she did not receive much advice from Germantown faculty or her school counselors. She remembered that "there were so many stories coming out of the [school counselors'] office that if you went in there they would tell the young men of color to apply to go into the armed services," and thus, Black students routinely avoided the office. In her academic courses, Shelley felt that many of her high school teachers held her and the other Black youth in the academic program to lower standards than their white peers. Even though she lacked faculty support, Shelley's mother insisted that her children were going to college, and thus, Shelley relied on her family to help achieve her postsecondary school aims. Her mother encouraged her to leave Philadelphia to meet new people and learn new ideas. Shelley followed her older sister to Howard University, saying, "Howard University was top of the food chain Black college, and so, that's where we went." Shelley recalled that she did not feel prepared for Howard's academic rigor, noting, "I've always been very honest about that. I was not prepared. . . . I actually thought my skills were up to par, and when I got to college and realized that they were not, I was quite disappointed." She struggled academically. She recalled that her Howard professors "were really tough. They had a certain scale of what you had to do, and they made no bones about it, you either met their criteria or you've got some skills to make up, or you are not going to make it here, and they'd tell you that." Despite the tough standards, her Howard professors taught her the academic skills that she did not learn in high school. After college, Shelley accepted a position as a fashion designer, and after a short stint in Philadelphia, she became a teacher in the New York City public school system.[53] Shelley's tenacity and persistence, coupled with her family's support, made this journey possible. Shelley dedicated her life to giving Black children the chance to learn academic skills that many white faculty refused to provide to her.

Other Black students recalled similar experiences with racist faculty in Germantown's academic program. Born in Poughkeepsie, New York, Linda Singleton, a Black woman who graduated from Germantown High School in 1963, had always enjoyed a comfortable middle-class lifestyle. Her father, Arnold Winslow Gallimore, enlisted in the Air Force and completed his training as a Tuskegee airman. Her mother, Thelma Mae West, worked as a seamstress in a factory, stayed home to raise her daughter, and eventually opened a beauty salon. In the mid-1950s, Linda's mother remarried and moved to Germantown to be closer to her in-laws, who lived in "one of the huge single-family homes" on Pelham Road. Her grandfather worked as a tool and die maker for the Budweiser beer company, and her grandmother, who had inherited money from her family, worked as a nurse. Linda remembered that many residents considered Pelham Road as an enclave for rich white residents; her grandparents were the only Black residents on the block. Linda's family lived in a middle-class Black neighborhood that she described as "very good . . . there was excellent transportation . . . with well-established residences around us."

In the late 1950s, Linda attended Roosevelt Junior High School. Even though the school felt integrated, Linda remembered, her academic classes were not. "Most of the Blacks were in the vocational [track], Black and white in the business [commercial track], and the academic [track] was mostly white," she said. She was often the only Black student in her academic classes. Linda later attended the Philadelphia High School for Girls, which she regarded as a "great opportunity" for her future. But Girls High, she said, stressed "rote learning and a lot of memorization, a lot of spitting back, and for me, the creativity was very low. [The faculty] just wanted me to tell them what I had read . . . that did not seem like a challenge or interesting experience, so I was becoming very despondent about education and what it meant." In addition to her schoolwork, Linda had been working part time in her mother's beauty salon and increasingly felt that she wanted to own her own business rather than focus on what she referred to as "the academic world."

During her junior year, Linda transferred to Germantown High School, where she felt like she "had gone to heaven." "I was still in classes with Girls High and Central transfers," she reported, "but there wasn't this rote memorization. There was more discussion. There was more thinking about the why instead of just the what." As an academic student, she felt, the "academic stimulation was there, the satisfaction that I was learning something was there, the sense of achievement was there, but the social isolation was intense because I was the only Black person in my class and I experienced racism from my teachers." One day in class, the teacher asked a question. Linda raised her hand. After several seconds, Linda was still the only student with her hand raised. Eventually, Linda's teacher said, "Well, if no one knows the answer, we will go on." One of Linda's classmates, a young white man, raised his hand, and the teacher said, "Yes, Jerry?" He said, "Linda raised her hand. She wants to answer." The teacher turned to her and said, "Yes, Linda." Linda answered the question correctly, and then the teacher said, "Now, we can go on." Linda recalled that the teacher never offered "any recognition or approval" of what she had said. In her words, "it was like, if you are going to force me to [listen to a Black student], then I'll do it." After that, Linda "reached a point where [she] just felt discouraged."

Class divisions within the Black student community made her life even more difficult. Linda remembered that Black students expected their peers to sit together in the cafeteria, but as an academic student, Linda did not know many Black students. Her preppy clothes—Peter Pan collar shirts, long pleated skirts, socks with ruffled trim, and polished saddle shoes—made her feel like an outcast. Despite these challenges, as the daughter of a Tuskegee airman, Linda knew that her family expected her to go to college. Her mother, who had strong connections to Philadelphia's educated Black upper class, told her that she had to apply to at least one college. Linda enrolled in her father's alma mater, Tuskegee University, when she was only 16 years old. She eventually earned her doctorate in educational counseling and, many years later, returned to Germantown High School to provide high school youth with the academic and social support she never received.[54]

Like Linda, Walter Ballard was one of the Black students who earned an academic degree at Germantown. Born in South Philadelphia on February 3, 1942, his father, Allen, was Philadelphia's first Black inspector; his mother worked at home and raised her children. When Allen entered elementary school, his family moved to Germantown to take advantage of the reputable public schools. He attended Houston Elementary School, a predominately white institution, Leeds Junior High School, where he was one of four Black students in his class, and finally, Germantown High School, which according to him "was 48% Black, 48% Jewish, and 4% which didn't really matter." Ballard recalled that "For the most part, we [Black and white youth] all got along fine. . . . [T]he teaching staff was a great teaching staff." The summer before he entered Germantown, he met with the school counselor, shared his academic record with her, and told her that he wanted to be an engineer. She told him, "if you want to be an engineer, you should go into an industrial arts course." Ballard knew that the industrial arts course "consisted of wood shop, metal shop, these [courses] are like nine hours a week, six to nine hours a week." Because students spent a lot of time in these shop courses, they "could only take, I think, up to geometry, you could take one year of a language, no chemistry, no physics. This is where the counselor directed me to, so I went into industrial arts. About midway through my tenth grade, it didn't feel right to me. All of my [white] friends coming out of Leeds were in the academic courses, and I'm in industrial arts."

During his sophomore year, Ballard wrote a letter to an administrator at the Massachusetts Institute of Technology. In the letter, he listed his courses that he had taken and that he planned to take and asked if these courses would "get me into MIT? Is this what I should be doing in high school if I want to be an engineer? Are these the courses I should be taking?" Two weeks later, he received a letter from the MIT admissions office. The letter stated that he needed additional coursework, three years of a foreign language and advanced sciences. Ballard took the letter to his counselor and said, "this is what MIT says I need to be an engineer. That's what I want." This time the counselor did not question him. Together, they revamped his course schedule so that he had the coursework that the MIT admissions counselor said he needed. In his senior year, he served as the class president and graduated fifth in his class. Ballard recalled that his role as class president "meant a lot for Black kids at that high school, at a moment when they were becoming the majority, that a Black student could be the president" of the senior class. He earned a full scholarship to attend Lehigh University, where he was one of four Black students on campus, and eventually had a lucrative career as an engineer. Ballard challenged the racist practices in the high school and earned the academic diploma that he knew he needed. At the same time, he credits his family, several Germantown teachers, and his Black and white classmates for the support that he needed to achieve his goals.[55]

These three youth were not alone. The frustrations that Germantown High School's Black youth had with the racist practices inside the high school were well-founded. In the 1960s, the percentage of Black youth in the academic course reached a historic low. For years, Germantown High School faculty and counselors had routinely directed Black students into the commercial and vocational programs. For years, Black youth defied these directives, but as more Black youth entered the high school in the late 1950s and 1960s, they made up the majority of students in Germantown's commercial and vocational programs.

Residents Question Germantown High School's Reputation as Black Enrollment Increases

As more Black students enrolled in the high school, white residents began to question its quality, privately and publicly.[56] In the spring of 1964, Mother

Francis Joseph, a white Germantown High School alumna and Catholic-school administrator, told an audience at a community-wide meeting that Germantown High School had been a "good school" when she attended the majority-white institution, but that she was worried that it had fallen into disarray.[57] Even though she never mentioned race, her comments implied that the school was "good" when it was majority-white, but not after it transformed into a majority-Black institution. A few days later, Mary Ellen Brown, a new teacher at Germantown High School, responded to Joseph's claims. Brown acknowledged that due to a "lack of money and public support" Germantown "cannot provide the attractive physical surroundings and the number of up-to-date books and other aids that its students deserve." However, Brown noted that Germantown faculty and students were still "amazingly effective in some important areas." Germantown students graduated from college at much higher rates than the national average, and the school had one of the city's lowest dropout rates. Finally, Brown asserted that the Germantown High School community reflected progressive race relations. Brown wrote, "the spirit of friendship and cooperation among Negro and white students and teachers [at Germantown High School] is exciting . . . [and] anticipates . . . a future when different groups can live together peacefully and fruitfully."[58]

School administrators and teachers like Mary Ellen Brown promoted the idea that Germantown High School represented a racially harmonious school where Black and white youth socialized "peacefully and fruitfully," but the escalation of racial unrest and violent incidents challenged this belief.[59] In the early 1950s and mid-1960s, several students—both Black and white—were seriously injured or killed in or near Philadelphia high schools, including Benjamin Franklin, Germantown, Simon Gratz, and South Philadelphia High School.[60] On October 27, 1962, the unrest reached Germantown High School. On that day, three Black young men assaulted a Black Germantown High School student outside the school for refusing to give them money. Police arrested the perpetrators and vowed to institute measures to end the unrest, but the violence persisted.[61] On December 8, 1964, police arrested a student for stabbing his classmate inside the high school.[62] Nearly three years later, 15 youth invaded the high school and wounded 2 students.[63]

To assuage fears, Dominick Abbruzzese, a former police lieutenant and head of nonteaching assistants for the school district, promised at least 20 security guards would be on duty the next day. Police arrested eight adolescent boys; seven of them attended Germantown High School.[64] In response, the school board implemented stricter disciplinary policies and gave administrators the power to expel "incorrigibles and serious trouble makers."[65] They also expanded the use of nonteaching assistants to patrol the hallways, lunchrooms, and bathrooms for any deviant behavior.[66] Finally, in the late 1960s, the school board hired police officers, including several at Germantown High School, to quell the unrest.[67] Citywide, the new policies increased the number of students expelled from their neighborhood high schools and established what individuals later called the school-to-prison pipeline—a pipeline that disproportionately affected Black and Latinx youth even as early as the late 1950s and early 1960s.[68]

Germantown activists argued that this unrest and violence was related to the escalation of poverty and the shortage of afterschool activities for local youth.[69] In 1950, 7% of Germantown residents were considered poor; by 1960, that figure had risen to 11.5%. Many of these poor families lived in the nearly all-Black census tracts near the high school.[70] For nearly a century, low-income families had relied on the community's local service agencies, such as the YMCAs, YWCAs, and the Boys Clubs, to provide afterschool recreational opportunities for their children. However, in the postwar period, as poverty escalated, these organizations faced several challenges. First, many of the elite families who had donated and sustained these organizations in the early 20th century no longer lived in the community. The movement of these families and their support led to a significant funding shortage. To save revenues, these organizations cut programs, including their free summer camps.[71] Second, in 1946, the national YWCA passed an interracial charter, which required local chapter to integrate. Germantown YWCA leaders encouraged white members to use the all-Black YWCA, which had a central location and better facilities. Most white residents refused. Eventually, local leaders closed the all-Black YWCA and merged its membership with the all-white YWCA. Clarice Herbert, who lived in the area and belonged to the YWCA, recalled, many Black residents felt that local Y leaders "took our building away from us!"[72] Frustrated with the loss of their own institution, many Black residents canceled their YWCA memberships and private donations.[73] The loss of membership, coupled with the loss of funds, forced these organizations to curtail the programs that had once sustained afterschool and recreational activities for low-income youth.[74]

The unrest in the community also stemmed from the fact that by the mid-1960s most Germantown High School students attended school on shift schedules due to overcrowded conditions and teacher shortages. In 1964,

4,000 students attended a high school built to hold 2,500 students. Half of the students enrolled in the high school attended in the morning and the other half attended school in the afternoon.[75] The shift schedule created a situation where students either slept long hours, worked part-time jobs, or roamed the streets with little to occupy their time while they were not in school. Residents charged that the shift schedules short-changed student learning and created chaos in the community. They demanded that school officials find a solution to end the shift schedules and, perhaps, address racial segregation in the community's elementary, junior, and high schools.[76]

In 1964, city officials proposed a plan to build a centralized education park, which was a multischool campus to promote desegregation in Germantown's public schools. School district officials planned to use federal urban renewal funding to purchase and renovate historical buildings in Germantown's commercial corridor and to convert these buildings and the high school into a mixed-aged school facility for the entire community. The proposal required busing students from 14 different and segregated elementary, junior, and high school buildings to one centralized, racially integrated educational campus. Under the proposal, elementary-aged students would remain in their zoned neighborhood schools for core instruction but then travel to the educational campus for racially balanced, mixed-school elective courses, such as arts, music, and language. The proposal, which was one of the first of its kind in the nation, had unanimous support from the Philadelphia school board's Committee on Nondiscrimination and the Committee on Sites, Buildings, and Facilities and strong support from civil rights leaders.[77]

Philanthropy sustained the idea. In 1964, the Ford Foundation donated money to hire a consultant, Ray Donner, to design the park.[78] Donner hosted a series of town halls to gather feedback on the idea. In these meetings, Donner told residents that the park aimed to strengthen the community and its schools and to attract "new people who believe Germantown is a nice place to live and find it exciting to send their children to school here."[79] White residents immediately opposed the plan, arguing that it was too dangerous to bus their elementary-aged children to the park. As white opposition mounted, school officials withdrew their plans. Donner told the press that school officials had abandoned the plan because they feared that it might accelerate white flight and "the conversion of Germantown into a poverty-stricken Negro ghetto."[80] In lieu of the park, school officials allocated $5 million to build new classrooms on Germantown High School's east side.

They promised to explore the idea of building a new high school in the northern part of the community in the near future. White resistance, once again, thwarted the possibility of meaningful school integration in Germantown.

Frustrated with racism in their communities and schools, Black activists and youth mobilized to pressure school officials to implement Black studies in their schools. The movement to include Black studies in the city's schools began outside the high school, and then it moved inside the institution. These youth activists and their allies demanded that school officials recognize their power and autonomy to control their school curriculum and structures. Many of the individuals had grown tired of waiting for integration to happen and frustrated with the liberal state.[81] They wanted school officials to respond to their demands and appealed to Shedd and other school leaders in a variety of ways. Youth activists in Philadelphia and Germantown formed and participated in the Philadelphia Students for a Free Society. The society sponsored an annual Freedom Day with local Black clergy that featured lectures and arts events about Black history and culture.[82] On November 3, 1967, Cecil B. Moore, the head of the Philadelphia NAACP, and Dick Gregory, a civil rights activist and comedian, held rallies at several local high schools, including Germantown High School, to encourage students to pressure school officials to add Black history courses and increase the number of Black students in academic programs.[83] Youth activists, including the young David Richardson, a 1965 Germantown High School graduate and soon-to-be elected state congressperson, joined the Black People's Unity Movement (BPUM). BPUM organized a citywide education committee that aimed to expand Black history education and to dismantle disciplinary codes that prohibited African clothing and names inside the city's public schools. These youth worked closely with Black Power activists in the city and beyond to expand BPUM's membership and impact.[84]

The Germantown Community Council's schools committee also urged administrators to expand course offerings "to convince the community of the safety of the environment and the soundness of the educational content."[85] Frustrated that educators pushed Black students into nonacademic tracks, school committee members met with school district leaders and local administrators. They testified at board of education meetings about the scarcity of basic resources, such as textbooks and elective courses. They encouraged residents to call elected officials and to meet with school district leaders to express their frustrations with funding shortages and the conditions inside their children's schools.[86] Germantown residents wrote letters, issued statements, and conducted studies demanding increased funding, more resources, and better integration policies.[87] These residents hoped that their actions might generate radical reforms and racial equity inside their local public schools. While many hoped for racial integration in the city's schools, they wanted immediate change and influence over their children's curriculum and school structures. As historian Elizabeth Todd-Breland suggests, their demands were part of a broader policy of Black achievement that sought to implement a model of Black education "grounded in the Black Power era ideals of self-determination."[88]

On Friday, November 17, 1967, during their 10 a.m. lunch period, more than 200 Black students walked out of Germantown High School and marched toward the board of education administration building in the city's center. Wearing skullcaps with Germantown's green and white school colors and gold Black Power buttons, these students met up with students who had walked out of Simon Gratz High School. Students from Bok Vocational, South Philadelphia, William Penn, Benjamin Franklin, Kensington, West Philadelphia, Bartram, Overbrook, West Catholic, and the Philadelphia High School for Girls stormed out of their schools and boarded trolleys or walked miles to meet others who had already converged on the Parkway outside the school board's headquarters. Within two hours, more than 3,500 students had gathered outside the school board's administration building. Newspaper articles described the event as a "picnic," but the students had a clear agenda: to meet with Mark Shedd, the city's school superintendent; Richardson Dilworth, school board president; and Reverend Henry Nichols, board vice-president.[89] Student activists asked the board to expand Black history courses, hire additional Black teachers and administrators, appoint more Black representatives on the school board, remove the requirement that students salute the American flag, and remove police and nonteaching security assistants from their schools. These activists also demanded that Black students have access to the academic programs in their high schools, including those at Germantown High.[90]

While their leaders met with school officials, hundreds of students marched around the building chanting "beep, beep, bang, bang, boom, boom, Black Power" and carrying signs advocating "more Black Power in the school system." Congress of Racial Equality (CORE) activists circulated, handing out flyers urging community control of public schools. Hopeful about promoting open dialogue, Dilworth asked plainclothes police officers to monitor the situation as the crowd continued to grow. Police commissioner Frank Rizzo, who had developed a reputation for his racist beliefs, refused to comply and instead ordered hundreds of police to converge on the demonstrators. Local television news footage captured Rizzo telling those under his command to "get their Black asses."[91]

With little warning, Philadelphia police started swinging their billy clubs, injuring hundreds of youth and bystanders. By the end of the afternoon, police had arrested 57 individuals for participating in the demonstration. The demonstration brought newfound attention to the frustrations of Black youth in the city's two-tiered, racially segregated public school system.[92] The brutal police response drew a national spotlight to these youth's frustrations, their demands for change, and the realities of their lives. Philadelphia's elected officials and school leaders had a choice: respond to the students' demands and end the racial disparities in the schools or support a system that privileged the shrinking white populace and relegated Black youth to overcrowded and under-resourced public schools.

White Flight, Inadequate Funds, and Segregated Schools

The late 1950s and 1960s brought significant changes to the city's landscape and its public schools. Between 1958 and 1967, urban planners transformed the city's center to convince upper- and middle-class white professionals to return to or remain in the city. The urban renewal process altered racial demographics, particularly in the city's center, but these policies did little to improve housing conditions in communities on the city's periphery. In particular, the neighborhoods of Germantown, South Philadelphia, and North Philadelphia never received the federal urban renewal funds that many civic leaders demanded. Worried about the level of racial change in the community, thousands of white residents left the city for the majority-white suburbs. These events, coupled with the school district's racist policies and practices, drained critical resources and intensified racial segregation across the city's public schools.

Germantown High School was a microcosm of the broader changes that occurred in Philadelphia and other cities. As white families continued their exodus to the suburbs and as more Black families entered the community, Germantown High School shifted from a majority-white to a majority-Black school. Civil rights activists demanded better resources and integrated institutions: an educational park, Black studies courses, and more racially inclusive educational practices. Youth activists brought these demands into the schoolhouse, but school officials lacked the political and financial resources to address their demands. By the end of the 1960s, Germantown High School had transformed into a majority-Black high school that had to rely on inadequate public aid, and thus, lacked the resources it needed for its students to thrive.

CHAPTER 6

The Emergence of an "Urban" School System

Fiscal Shortages, Labor Strikes, and Stalled Desegregation, 1968–1981

On September 8, 1970, reports surfaced that talks between the Philadelphia Board of Public Education and the Philadelphia Federation of Teachers (PFT), AFL-CIO, had reached a stalemate. For weeks, the school board and PFT had been negotiating a new contract, and there were two remaining sticking points: the length of the school day and teacher compensation. At the time, most students in the state attended high school for six hours a day; in Philadelphia, they attended school for four and a half hours. School board members worried that students lost valuable instructional time and demanded that teachers work an additional hour and a half to meet state standards. PFT leaders agreed to extend the school day but refused to have its members work longer hours. Instead, they wanted the school board to hire additional teachers to fill in these hours. The PFT also demanded that the school district increase teacher compensation, which lagged behind most school districts in the state and nation. The board declined. According to board calculations, these measures would cost an additional $38 million annually. School board president and former Philadelphia mayor Richardson Dilworth refused to accede to the PFT demands and ordered administrators to close the city's public schools. In response, the PFT fired back, telling residents that Dilworth had created a school lockout and told its members to cast their votes for the union's first strike.[1]

For approximately two weeks, thousands of teachers marched outside of their schools demanding higher wages and better working conditions. At the same time, hundreds of other Philadelphia teachers defied union orders and reported to work. Most of the teachers who refused to strike were members of the Black Education Forum (BEF). BEF teachers worked with volunteers—public school parents, religious leaders, and community activists— to staff makeshift schools so that Philadelphia's majority-Black student body did not lose critical instructional time, and so that working families had a place to send their children during the strike. Most of these makeshift schools were located in Black communities to serve Black children.[2]

On September 14, the PFT and the board agreed on a 30-day truce and reopened the public schools.[3] The truce did not last: PFT members violated a court injunction to end the strike and returned to the picket lines. Once again, thousands of white teachers marched; thousands of Black teachers staffed makeshift classrooms in 238 of Philadelphia's 275 public schools.[4] On October 20, 1970, the strike finally ended. The PFT agreed to extend the high school day; the board agreed to increase teacher compensation.[5] Even though many teachers welcomed these victories, the strike fractured teachers along racial lines. White teachers who participated in the strikes resented the Black teachers who reported to work; Black teachers who staffed the makeshift schools resented white teachers who stood on the picket lines.[6]

The 1970 teachers strike occurred at a moment of white flight, fiscal instability, and racial unrest in the city and school district. From 1940 to 1980, Philadelphia's white population declined by more than 40%.[7] The loss of white residents drained the city's postwar tax base. Those white residents who remained in the city actively resisted the movement of Black residents into their neighborhoods and schools, which in turn, intensified racial segregation and unrest. White residents protested in their neighborhoods and schools to block school integration and racial equity.[8] Philadelphia politics exacerbated these tensions. In 1972, Philadelphia residents elected Frank Rizzo, the racist police chief who ordered police to silence Black protesters in 1967, as their mayor. Rizzo pledged to maintain the city's low tax rate and restore law and order through the expansion of police presence and mass incarceration.[9] Rizzo's policies, coupled with white flight and labor instability, created a fiscal disaster at the very moment that the School District of Philadelphia moved from a majority-white to a majority-Black school district. Urban residents, including those in Philadelphia, began to associate public school shortcomings and challenges with the school's racial composition, rather than with the public policies that contributed to the disinvestment in urban schools and communities. The school district's challenges fueled disillusionment with the public school system and catalyzed middle-class flight—both Black and white—from the city and its schools.[10] The "urban" school system—an underfunded, majority-low-income, and majority-Black system—emerged as Philadelphia tried to cope with misguided government policies, contentious teacher strikes, and rising school segregation.[11]

The Rizzo Administration Keeps Its Promise

In the spring of 1971, Philadelphia school officials announced that they had exhausted their operating revenues. Fearing that he might have to close the schools early, Superintendent Mark Shedd negotiated several low-interest loans to keep the schools open. In addition, he cut extracurricular programs at hundreds of schools, laid off 2,000 school district employees, and asked the PFT to defer its new salary scale. On September 22, 1971, Shedd testified before the United State Senate's Select Committee on Equal Education Opportunity and told them that Philadelphia was "dying from financial strangulation." Shedd argued that the task "of rescuing the nation's urban public schools from disaster has become too big for the limited resources of the state and local governments." He asked the Senate committee to make education "a new national priority" and urged the federal government to take over the 25 largest school districts in the nation to save them from financial ruin. The Senate committee rejected Shedd's proposal; Philadelphia had to find another way to save its schools.[12]

As the School District of Philadelphia teetered on the edge of bankruptcy, voters elected Frank Rizzo, the brazen police chief, as their next mayor. Rizzo had campaigned on a promise to maintain the city's low tax rate, to restore law and order, to tighten school board control, and to fire Mark Shedd.[13] Even though Shedd had received national acclaim for his leadership, city officials started negotiations to terminate Shedd's contract shortly after Rizzo won the election.[14] On December 9, 1971, Shedd resigned.[15] A few weeks later, Rizzo appointed Matthew W. Costanzo, a veteran of the city's public schools and fellow Italian American, as Philadelphia's new superintendent of schools.[16]

The school district's fiscal challenges persisted under Costanzo. Shortly after he took office, Costanzo appealed to federal officials to release emergency funding to the city's public schools. They refused.[17] To keep the schools open through the end of the school year, Costanzo instituted a series of massive program cuts that left educators scrambling to support Philadelphia youth with less and less.[18] He met with state officials and requested that the state implement a weighted per-pupil subsidy "that more realistically recognize[d] the devastating effects of urban poverty on a school system."[19] In 1970, Black residents made up 8.6% of Pennsylvania's population, but 33.6% of Philadelphia's population. In Pennsylvania, 7.9% of families lived below the federal poverty line; in Philadelphia, the rate was 11.2%.[20] Costanzo wanted state officials to recognize that the School District of Philadelphia, which had the highest concentration of Black and poor children, needed more money to operate.

As Costanzo worried about the fiscal stability of the school district, the PFT announced another strike three days before the schools were set to open for the 1972–73 school year. The teachers' union and the school board, once again, disagreed on two key points: lengthening high school instruction time and increasing teacher compensation.[21] The strike, once again, pitted teachers along racial lines. Thousands of white PFT members picketed while thousands of Black teachers defied PFT orders and reported to their schools. Black teachers argued that the strike robbed Black children of essential instructional time, and thus, many Black teachers refused to strike.[22] With the second strike underway, public school families and youth marched through the streets, and stormed city hall. They even picketed outside Richard Nixon's reelection headquarters to demonstrate their frustrations with elected officials, school board members, and PFT leaders. The protesters, mothers and youth, publicly called these leaders racist for promoting policies to increase police presence and mass incarceration rather than funding public schools that served poor Black youth.[23] Fearing more unrest and resistance, Rizzo met with congressional officials and asked them to allocate federal funding to Philadelphia's public schools. Rizzo refused to increase taxes to fund the schools, but he also recognized that the city needed additional funding to meet the PFT's salary demands.[24]

To pressure the PFT to return to work, a local nonprofit organization and an independent lawyer filed separate lawsuits arguing that the strike had caused "irreparable harm to the city's low-income children" and jeopardized the livelihood of thousands of Philadelphia families.[25] PFT leaders fired back stating that Philadelphia teachers had a legal right to strike.[26] The court disagreed. Judge D. Donald Jamieson negotiated a memorandum of understanding between the PFT and school board to end the strike and settle a new contract. The 18-day strike—one of the longest teacher strikes in the nation—ended.[27] However, the détente did not last. After weeks of failed negotiations, the PFT prepared for another strike. As the PFT mobilized, school board members begged the court to block the strike.[28] Rizzo blasted the PFT for "not thinking of the school children or of the taxpayers who are paying their salaries" and asked teachers who were "truly professional and dedicated to children" to report to work.[29] On January 11, 1973, 11,291 of the 13,000 PFT members went on strike. Rizzo publicly blamed Philadelphia public school teachers for shutting "down the system in their foolish strike."[30]

Judge Jamieson recognized that the strike created hardships for working families and limited opportunities for Philadelphia youth, and thus, four days later, he ordered the PFT to end the strike. The PFT refused.[31] Frustrated that their children's schools were once again closed, hundreds of mothers and their children marched outside their local public schools with signs that read "After all is said and done, tell me who has really won" and "Teachers unfair to children."[32] To quell the unrest, Philadelphia school officials hired hundreds of substitute teachers to reopen Philadelphia's public schools. They broadcast courses on the local television stations for students who were still stuck at home.[33]

The chaos continued. Judge Jamieson fined the union $160,000 and sentenced PFT president Frank Sullivan and chief negotiator John Ryan for violating his injunction to end the strike.[34] Philadelphia police arrested hundreds of picketing PFT members for blocking school entrances and other minor misdemeanors.[35] William Ross, the school board president, condemned the police actions and announced his resignation. Rizzo vowed to fight the PFT's "power-hungry blackmailers" who planned to "sell out the city" with their lavish demands.[36] As unrest intensified and negotiations stalled, AFL-CIO president George Meany asked President Nixon to send William J. Usery Jr., the assistant secretary of labor and head of the Federal Mediation and Conciliation Service, to help settle the dispute. After meeting with Usery, the PFT and board agreed on a significant salary increase, a reduction in maximum class size from 35 to 33 students, and additional prep time during the school day.[37]

The 1972–73 PFT strike highlighted Philadelphia's racial and fiscal challenges to a national audience, and yet its settlement resolved none of the city's or school district's most pressing problems. First, neither the district nor the city had the political will or financial capacity to finance the teachers' new salaries. Second, it seemed unlikely that city officials in Philadelphia, a still majority-white city, had the will to raise taxes to support a majority-Black, financially troubled public school system.[38] Finally, it was not clear if the families of children in the public schools would keep their children in those schools amid the chaos and instability. James Lytle, a school administrator and parent of two school-aged children in the Germantown High School catchment zone, recalled that the 1972–73 strikes pushed many upper- and middle-class families—both Black and white—to reconsider their commitment to public schools. Worried that the latest PFT settlement might be short-lived or that it could force the district to cut educational programs to meet the new labor costs, many of these families made a pragmatic choice: they pulled their children out of the public school system and either moved to the suburbs or enrolled their children in private or parochial schools. Even those families who had vowed to remain in the public system began to move their children out as the strikes continued.[39]

On July 7, 1975, only a few years after he assumed his role, Matthew Costanzo resigned as Philadelphia's superintendent of schools. Citing differences with the Rizzo administration, Costanzo accepted a new position as the superintendent of schools in Haddonfield, New Jersey, a white suburb a few miles from Philadelphia.[40] Less than a month later, the board of education appointed Michael P. Marcase, Rizzo's handpicked choice, as the new superintendent of Philadelphia's public schools. The chaos and instability that had already driven thousands of middle-class residents out of the city's public schools continued under Marcase's leadership.

Rizzo's Handpicked Superintendent Struggles to Manage Philadelphia's School District

Less than a year after he assumed office, Marcase asked the city council to provide the school district with "funds for survival" to close a projected $75 million budget deficit. The city council argued that it had its own fiscal challenges and that it could only release the funds if Rizzo promised to raise taxes. Rizzo refused.[41] In response, Marcase slashed educational programs and eliminated critical staff to cut millions in operating expenses from what many regarded as an already bare-bones budget.[42] While Marcase tried to balance his budget, in the summer of 1976, the PFT prepared to strike, again.[43] Worried about the effects of a strike on academic learning and working families, the Parents' Union for Public Schools (PUPS) and Black Educational Forum (BEF) hosted workshops to train hundreds of concerned parents and civic leaders to run emergency schools that offered "more than a babysitting service" during the strike.[44] Public school parents criticized the mayor and council for refusing to allocate more funds and lambasted the board for delaying labor negotiations.[45] The strike never happened. In a midnight decision, the board approved a new contract with better salaries and benefits. The new contract averted the strike, but it cost the school district money that it could not afford to spend.[46]

In the spring of 1977, about nine months after the board approved the new PFT contract, Marcase threatened to shut down the school system. The school district needed $68 million to keep its schools open and an additional $146 million for the upcoming school year. Marcase proposed radical program cuts to save costs: eliminating almost 10,000 staff positions, including school counselors and teachers in the city's museums; slashing kindergarten and early childhood programs; reducing special education programs for struggling readers and the mentally gifted; terminating extracurricular programs; and closing the city's alternative schools.[47] On August 21, 1977, the school district received $50 million in state aid and $10 million in city aid to reinstate kindergarten classes, some alternative programs, partial counseling services, and to rehire the 10,000 staff members laid off in June. Still, the district needed another $84 million to retain its other programs and services.[48]

To avert a shutdown, Marcase met with Philadelphia bankers about a $50 million school loan. John R. Bunting Jr., the chairman of the First Pennsylvania Bank, offered Marcase a loan with several contingencies: Marcase had to secure an additional $10 million from the city to support the schools and labor concessions from the PFT. The board eliminated teachers to save costs, which drove the school district's average class size from 33 to 35 students. The loan had another stipulation: school officials had to pass a balanced budget with no more than a 7% funding increase over the next five years. For the next five years, Marcase's budgets left little room for innovation in the city's classrooms; rather, he cobbled together funds to keep the school doors open as long as he could. Marcase had enough money to fund higher teacher salaries, but Philadelphia's public schools lacked basic educational resources.[49]

The Movement to Desegregate Philadelphia's Public Schools "Lags Behind the Ku Klux Klan"

On February 2, 1968, the Pennsylvania Human Relations Commission (PHRC), a state body charged with monitoring and addressing discrimination, sent a letter to the 17 Pennsylvania school districts with the highest rates of school segregation. The letter demanded that these districts submit a plan and timeline to eliminate racial imbalance in their schools by July 1, 1968. Philadelphia was one of the 17 school districts on this list. For the next four decades, Philadelphia school officials effectively dodged the PHRC's mandate. Between July 1, 1968, and July 1, 1969, Philadelphia school officials filed and received four extensions on their desegregation plan. But then, in 1971, the PHRC sued the School District of Philadelphia for refusing to comply with its mandate and ordered officials to eliminate racial imbalance by 1974. It was a daunting task. In 1971, 69% of Philadelphia public school students attended schools that were either 80% Black or 80% white.[50]

Rather than implement a desegregation plan in an increasingly segregated and racially polarized city, in 1971, Dilworth, the school board president, and Shedd, the superintendent, proposed legislation to cut the School District of Philadelphia into smaller geographical units and then merge these smaller units with suburban school districts that bordered the city. Philadelphia's suburban school districts had a majority-white student enrollment, more resources, and less poverty. Philadelphia's urban school district had a majority-Black student enrollment, fewer resources, and more poverty. Their proposal promised to increase racial and financial equity across the metropolis's poor, Black, urban district and its affluent, white, suburban districts.[51] Opposition to the plan mounted almost immediately. White suburban residents refused to open their schools to Black urban children. White urban residents rejected the proposal's reliance on busing. Rizzo and his white supporters had no interest in cooperating with the PHRC to desegregate Philadelphia's public schools. Black urban residents resented the idea that their children might have to attend predominantly white schools with racist youth and teachers. These families urged Shedd to focus less on metropolitan desegregation and more on eliminating and preventing racist attitudes inside their children's public schools.[52] After Shedd resigned, the idea never resurfaced again.

Instead, for the next decade, superintendents Costanzo and Marcase, Rizzo's handpicked successors to Shedd, followed Rizzo's orders and refused to comply with the PHRC's 1968 mandate. Under Costanzo's and Marcase's leadership, Philadelphia school officials established a citywide committee to study enrollment patterns and design desegregation plans, which the PHRC repeatedly rejected for, as one committee said, "lagging behind the Ku Klux Klan."[53] The desegregation committee faced myriad challenges. First, even though some committee members felt an urgency to desegregate the city's public schools, they could not agree on the best approach to desegregate schools in a deeply segregated city with a small and shrinking white population concentrated mainly in Northeast Philadelphia, far from majority-Black Philadelphia communities. Second, white residents, motivated by racism, resisted any plans to bus students from one part of the city to another. On January 19, 1974, the school board hosted a community meeting to gather feedback on a plan to bus a small number of public school children. Worried about white resistance and violence, the school board implemented makeshift barricades and elaborate security measures to screen families before they entered the board's headquarters. Inside, the board gave 50 individuals permission to speak—48 white individuals who opposed the plan and 2 Black individuals who supported it. The testimony revealed the racist motivations behind white opposition. One white parent told the school board, "my child wants to be a lawyer, if bused to a Black school she may very well end up a cosmetologist. I will not send my child into gang territories in Black neighborhoods."[54] Hundreds of other white residents, who could not gain access to the public hearing, stood outside the board's headquarters chanting "We won't bus!"[55] White resistance rested on racist assumptions about Black children and majority-Black schools.

Frustrated with Philadelphia school officials' outright defiance, in 1974 the court appointed Dr. David H. Kurtzman, the chancellor of the University of Pittsburgh and a former state secretary of education, to draft a desegregation plan "without massive busing and at minimal expense."[56] As Kurtzman worked on his plans, the US Supreme Court released its landmark *Milliken v. Bradley* decision that decided the fate of school segregation in Detroit. The case rested on the differences between de jure and de facto segregation, with the court ruling that school segregation was illegal if and only if the school district had implemented explicit policies to segregate students based on race. The court argued that Detroit's school segregation resulted from de facto segregation that occurred naturally and stemmed largely from the city's housing patterns, not de jure segregation, which occurred through a legal process or school district policies. The court ordered the city to implement a Detroit-only busing plan, which basically closed the door on the possibility of a metropolitan desegregation plan. Despite pleas from civil rights activists, the court strengthened the case for local control over public schools and asserted that desegregation did not require "any particular racial balance in each school, grade or classroom."[57]

Philadelphia school officials understood that state and federal courts in the North usually sided with school districts on matters of de facto rather than de jure segregation. Even though civil rights lawyers argued that de facto segregation in Philadelphia and other cities stemmed from housing and school laws and policies, after the 1974 *Milliken* ruling, most courts in the North refused to listen to this argument and instead sided with school officials in Detroit, Cleveland, Chicago, Milwaukee, and Philadelphia who insisted that school segregation stemmed from residential segregation rather than their policies or actions.[58]

A month after the Supreme Court released its *Milliken* ruling, David Kurtzman submitted a 37-page desegregation plan that called for a major busing program. Kurtzman's plan excluded two sections of the city: the majority-white Northeast and the majority-Black West Philadelphia. Black residents called the report yet another excuse to avoid integration; white residents vowed to fight any plan to bus their children.[59] At a citywide community meeting about the proposed plan, over 900 white residents marched carrying signs reading, "I'll be bused to jail before my child gets bused." Philadelphia's school board president promised to join the angry white residents in jail if the busing plan passed.[60] After the meeting, Superintendent Costanzo told the press, "It's obvious our parents have told us to defy the court order."[61]

For nearly four decades, Philadelphia school officials effectively dodged the PHRC 1968 mandate. Every time that officials refused to comply, PHRC officials sued the school district. Every time that the PHRC sued the school district, Philadelphia school officials argued that racial segregation in the city's public schools stemmed from racial segregation in the city's neighborhoods. Philadelphia school officials actively defied the PHRC's 1968 mandate because they recognized that most white residents hated the PHRC and that most white judges often sided with local school officials over state governance bodies. As one desegregation committee member noted, when school officials refused to comply with the 1968 mandate, no one threw "thunderbolts from heaven. In fact, nothing happen[ed] at all."[62]

The Effects of Fiscal Instability, Labor Strikes, and Racial Unrest

On May 23, 1970, the Germantown Community Council released a report about the rise of gang violence in the city and community. Lillie Everett,

who worked with Germantown's Neighborhood Renewal Project, titled the
report "A Community in Crisis." The report, which was based on interviews
with local youth, some of whom belonged to local gangs, examined the
causes of gang violence, the role of youth workers, and details about the
educational, cultural, and recreational needs of Germantown's Black youth.
Everett wrote: "The Black youth in the community have lost faith and confidence in the will of the community to try and put its house in order. They have
stopped believing that their community will do anything about the recreation crisis, the education crisis, the job crisis, the poverty and racism of the
community, there is a general feeling of defeat and frustration among Black
youth." Even though Everett acknowledged that the recent spike in violence
represented a significant community challenge, she asserted: "every act of
self-inflicted violence is a cry for help. . . . The Black gang has been saying
this to society for a long time—look at me—something is wrong with the
way that things are." Everett told the council that many of the recreational
programs that had existed in the past had closed their doors and that the
community's two remaining Boys Clubs—the majority-Black Wissahickon
and the majority-white Germantown Club—were doing what they could,
with their limited funding, to provide Germantown youth with programs
and activities. Everett's message was clear: if the community wanted the
violence to stop, they had to fix the multiple crises that Black youth faced.[63]

The community tried to respond. Germantown residents used city and
private funds to support summer camp programs in the Poconos and the
local Ys for hundreds of low-income youth.[64] The community created a nonprofit organization, Germantown Homes, Inc., to provide low-income families with modern homes near the high school.[65] Even with these efforts,
however, unrest, poverty, and blight persisted, particularly in Germantown's
now majority-poor and majority-Black communities near the high school.[66]
Germantown's—and Philadelphia's—crisis stemmed from the same racial
conflict, white flight, and economic dislocation that plagued other American cities during this period.[67] Frustrated and defeated, Germantown residents eventually realized that they could not fix "the crisis in the community"
that Everett described with more recreational and nonprofit programs. Fix-
ing this "crisis" required the creation of more jobs, better housing, and of
course, a system of adequately resourced and racially integrated public
schools.[68] In other words, it required addressing the structural roots of racism
and poverty—something that even Germantown residents, with all their
private resources, networks, and funds, had never done.

In an effort to curb unrest in the community and retain middle-class Black and white school enrollment, school officials approved a multi-million-dollar school construction project to modernize and expand Germantown High School. This expansion made it possible for the entire student body to attend school together rather than on the shift schedules—one morning and one afternoon—that existed in the 1960s. School officials also created and promoted the Lankenau Motivation School, a small and separate special-admit school for academically oriented youth located inside Germantown High School, to attract and retain Black and white middle-class families who often opted out of the local neighborhood high school. Finally, Germantown administrators responded to Black demands and implemented innovative courses on Black history and literature and a Black student union, which hosted events and workshops for Black youth and families. The school district also hired a Black principal, Samuel Beard, to reflect the majority-Black student body. Although many residents publicly expressed their gratitude and support to school officials who implemented these changes, white flight and racial conflict persisted in the community and its high school.

Residents argued that the construction project to expand the high school's footprint, while necessary, generated chaos and unrest inside the high school. In the late 1960s, Germantown administrators barricaded and closed several classrooms to protect students and staff during the construction process. These classroom closures created a challenge: administrators did not have enough classroom space to accommodate the number of students enrolled. To address this challenge, school administrators established a make-shift, overflow school annex for incoming 10th grade students and built temporary classrooms using underutilized space in the school library, gymnasium, and basement. The temporary classrooms lacked adequate heat, decent lighting, and proper classroom walls or ceilings.[69] To reduce the noise level between the classrooms, faculty often limited lectures and discussions; students routinely sat silently doing independent work in these classrooms. Students quickly realized that they could toss objects from one classroom to another because the classrooms lacked ceilings. Germantown administrators put chicken wire across the tops of the classrooms to end this mischief. But while the chicken wire might have stopped this behavior, it generated frustration among Germantown families. Mary Howe, the president of Germantown High School's home and school association, told the press that many families had expressed their shock and outrage about the "hazardous and unhealthy conditions" inside Germantown's "chicken coop" classrooms.[70]

In the middle of the construction hysteria, Germantown's Black Student Union invited Jeremiah X. Shabazz, a Black Power activist, to speak at a school-wide National Negro History Week assembly. Shabazz denounced the story of Adam and Eve from the Judeo-Christian Bible and argued that the Black race was superior to the white race. Upon hearing this, 50 white students stormed out of the school auditorium. Later that afternoon, several white families called the school board demanding that Shabazz retract his statements and that event organizers apologize. Mark Shedd, Philadelphia's school superintendent, reiterated his commitment to free speech in the city's public schools, but said that Shabazz had crossed the "usual limits and bounds of good taste." Samuel Beard, Germantown High School's Black principal, denounced Shabazz's speech, telling the press that it represented a "carefully arranged and neatly timed trick" to fracture Germantown High School's community along racial lines.[71] In response to the Shabazz talk and earlier incidents, the Citizens Committee on Public Education, a white-led citywide school-improvement organization, reported that it had found "evidence that separatists in the Black Power movement" existed inside the school and that gang activity threatened student safety outside the school.[72] Two weeks later, over 200 Germantown students staged an afterschool melee a few blocks from the high school. The incident involved two serious assaults—a gunshot to a student's chest and a stabbing of a student's neck—as well as a takeover of a public bus. Germantown High School's principal called it an isolated incident.[73] In a city where gang-related violence led to an average of one death a week, Beard's comment did not exactly assuage concerns about the unrest in the city, community, or high school.[74]

While school administrators tried to placate anxieties, reports surfaced that 22 white families had filed voluntary transfers to move their white daughters from the majority-Black Germantown High School and place them into majority-white public schools in Northeast Philadelphia. These white families argued that their daughters had expressed concerns about their safety, specifically that young Black men looked up their skirts as they walked into school. Principal Beard denied their claims. Germantown High School's home and school association president told the press that these families filed these transfers not because their daughters feared for their safety, but because they were "anti-Negro." A few weeks later, school officials revoked 12 of the 22 transfer requests because these families who had filed these transfer requests had falsified their home addresses on their transfer applications.[75] Though these families failed to move their daughters, they used a similar argument that the founders of Germantown High School had used six decades earlier in their demand that school officials honor their requests to protect their white middle-class daughters from young Black men.

School officials responded to the unrest and tension by hosting community-wide meetings and hiring additional school staff. Richardson Dilworth, the former mayor and school board president, led these meetings to listen to residents' ideas and grievances. Samuel Beard hired Barbara Thompson, a Germantown mother who sent three of her sons to the high school, to "build a better image and reputation" for the school and to improve the "sense of self-worth" among its students. She publicly challenged the idea that low-income, Black families did not care about their children's education and worked tirelessly to improve the experiences of Black children inside the high school.[76] To pacify middle-class fears, Beard expanded the school's security apparatus and hired several new nonteaching assistants, security guards, and school police. In February 1969, 28 security guards worked in Philadelphia's public schools—10 of them worked inside Germantown High School.[77]

Black families and students resented these policies, arguing that the increased security measures made the high school feel like a "prison." The rise in security measures inside the city's public schools coincided with a rise in incarceration nationally.[78] The Black families and youth that challenged the high school's new security measures recognized that school officials put these practices in place to protect white bodies, including those 22 young women who claimed that they were unsafe in a majority-Black school. These new security measures fed into a national movement to create a school-to-prison pipeline—a pipeline that disproportionately moved Black and Brown bodies from their public schools to state-run prisons.[79]

Eventually, Beard resigned as principal of Germantown High School. On January 6, 1970, school officials hired a new principal, Santee C. Ruffin, a 37-year-old Black educator who lived in Germantown's Mt. Airy community and graduated from Gratz High School.[80] A few months after he assumed his role, Ruffin closed the school cafeteria following a student stabbing in that space. After that, school officials dismissed students at lunchtime.[81] The citywide teacher strikes also created chaos and unrest inside the school. Each time the PFT went on strike, Germantown administrators scrambled to keep their school open. Sometimes, Germantown High School served as a special educational center to educate seniors from an array of high schools. For example, during the 1972–73 strike, Germantown hosted seniors from the all-male, elite Central High School and two comprehensive neighborhood high schools, Germantown and Roxborough. The school staffed its classrooms with teachers who refused to strike and community members who volunteered their time. School ran from 8:30 to 12:30 daily.[82]

Operating a school with students from multiple high schools and limited staff created confusion and instability inside the school. Students had to adjust to new teachers. Michele Hewitt, a Black Germantown senior, recalled, "I resented . . . having to adjust to new schedules and new teachers, some of whom were administrators and hadn't taught for years." When asked about her feelings about the strike, Hewitt told reporters, "most students seem to sympathize with the teachers, but at the same time we're the ones being pushed in the middle."[83] Hewitt and others like her wanted administrators to treat their teachers fairly, but at the same time, she felt frustrated and angry that the strike altered, and perhaps even shortchanged, her educational experience at Germantown High School. However, Michele remained one of the fortunate ones in the community. She could attend school because she was a senior. Most Germantown students sat at home during the strike because the school did not have enough educators to teach them. These idle youth created problems in the community and lost valuable instructional time throughout the 1970s.[84] As the strikes lingered on, middle-class families pulled their children out of Philadelphia's public school system to give their children a more stable and consistent educational experience in the city's suburban, private, or parochial schools.[85]

The challenges inside the school, coupled with the school district's fiscal shortages and teacher strikes, pushed many middle-class residents—mostly white, but also some Black—to question their commitment to the city's local high schools, including Germantown High. Middle-class residents used a variety of mechanisms to opt out of majority-Black schools. First, thousands of middle-class residents left the city between 1960 and 1980 to take advantage of lower tax rates, racially homogenous white communities, and better-resourced schools in Philadelphia's suburbs.[86] The decisions to flee the city pulled millions of dollars in tax revenues out of the city and drained Philadelphia's public schools of essential public and private funding at the very moment that the PFT demanded higher wages for its teachers. Second, thousands of white residents moved from older homes in predominantly Black neighborhoods, such as Germantown, West Philadelphia, and South Philadelphia, to postwar communities located predominantly in Northeast Philadelphia.[87] Finally, thousands of middle-class white residents pulled their children out of their local public high schools and sent them to private, parochial, and special-admit public high schools.[88]

School-level data suggest that white families' decisions to move their children from their neighborhood majority-Black public high school intensified racial segregation at Germantown High School. In 1970, Black students made up about 55% of the city's high school enrollment but represented about 85% of Germantown High School's enrollment. Black enrollment was much lower at the all-male, elite Central High School (about 20%) and the all-female, elite Philadelphia High School for Girls (about 30%). White families only represented 45% of the city's high school enrollment, and yet, they made up the vast majority of students enrolled in the city's prestigious exam high schools (see table 13 and the appendix). The spatial patterns of class and race that existed when Germantown High School was founded had completely reversed. In 1970, the majority of students who enrolled in the community's overcrowded neighborhood high school, Germantown High School, were Black, while white students traveled miles from home to attend the city's two prestigious exam schools.[89]

School Officials Build a New School in Germantown

In the spring of 1970, school officials began construction on a new high school to address segregation, overcrowding, and unrest at Germantown High School. Located about two miles northeast of Germantown, Martin Luther King Jr. High School represented a beacon of hope when it opened in 1973. Instead of moving students from Germantown to King, school officials paired the two high schools—students attended King for 9th and 10th grade and then transferred to Germantown for 11th and 12th grade. School officials divided King students into several smaller schools, each with its own thematic curriculum and designated lunchroom. When the school finally opened on February 8, 1972, residents praised the school district's innovative approach and urged families to stay in Germantown and consider these schooling options.[90] Despite this optimism, the King-Germantown pairing had problems from the beginning. School officials failed to consider territorial neighborhood boundaries when they made student assignments. Students often had to walk through rival gang territories to and from school; gang violence spiked in the community and eventually seeped into the schools.[91]

Residents argued that the unrest stemmed from the disinvestment in social service agencies, such as the YMCA, YWCA, and Boys Clubs that had provided afterschool recreation to low-income youth for close to a century. Civic leaders urged elected officials to allocate public funds for these programs. They also asked their friends and neighbors to donate to these organizations.[92] Germantown residents hosted annual fundraising campaigns, but many of the Germantown elite who had financially supported these institutions had left the community. The loss of these families generated fiscal shortages for these social service agencies in the postwar period. Though the city and residents continued to provide funding to these institutions, the money never matched the need. With limited funding and support, these organizations curtailed their youth programs at the very time that poverty and unrest escalated in the city and community.[93]

Frustrated and exhausted with the unrest and instability, residents demanded that school officials end the King-Germantown partnership and create two separate high schools. School officials finally agreed, and in 1976, they ended the partnership. Even though many residents had hoped that ending the King-Germantown partnership might end the challenges in the community and its schools, the problems persisted. In the spring of 1978, educators, families, and youth testified that Germantown and King classrooms had insufficient classroom resources, faulty school facilities, overcrowded classrooms with inexperienced teachers, and unrest and chaos in the schools' corridors and cafeterias.[94] The schools' shortcomings stemmed from a decrease in public and private revenues and an increase in poverty and segregation in the community. While national educational expenditures rose in the 1970s, the expenditures often went directly to teachers, who had been underpaid for decades in Philadelphia and other cities. And with the decline in private funding, school administrators did not have access to the same discretionary funds they had enjoyed in the past. As a result, they did not have the financial resources to purchase new textbooks, hire enough teachers, lower class sizes, or finance extracurricular activities. In other words, overall educational revenues might have increased, but schools often lacked what they needed at the very moment that middle-class families left the city, taking their tax dollars and private subsidies with them. The challenges in Philadelphia's public high schools stemmed from inadequate public budgets—the same challenge that existed when residents fought and won the right to build Germantown High School at the turn of the 20th century.

The Shame of the Schools

On April 10, 1981, school officials announced a $223 million budget deficit and begged city council and Philadelphia's new mayor, William Green III, to allocate more money to Philadelphia's public schools.[95] The school board eventually passed a budget that required shorter school days, 3,400 staff layoffs, and 12 school closures. PFT leaders blasted elected officials for refusing to provide adequate public school funding.[96] A few weeks later, city and state officials released a report that suggested that the School District of Philadelphia's fiscal challenges stemmed from "extravagant teacher contracts and a weak, top-heavy administration," not insufficient public aid. Green asserted that the report "confirms our worst fears" and demanded that the school board revise the PFT contract, close underutilized schools, and lay off administrators.[97] The PFT refuted the report's findings and prepared for its sixth strike in 11 years.[98]

On September 8, 1981, 21,000 PFT members picketed in front of their schools. Police arrested hundreds of teachers for defying the court's no-strike mandate and transported them to temporary, makeshift jails throughout the city. After weeks of failed negotiations, the common pleas court ordered the PFT to end its strike.[99] The PFT refused. Nearly 1,000 PFT members marched down Broad Street, the city's main thoroughfare, to City Hall chanting, "Mayor Green, we're no fools. You got the money, so open the schools." Bystanders who had gathered to watch the march expressed their outrage with PFT leaders who ordered the strike and city officials who refused to allocate adequate public aid to the city's schools.[100] Angered by these actions, school officials planned to open more schools, arrest more teachers, and fine PFT leaders for defying the court's no-strike mandate. The court rejected the first two proposals but ruled that the PFT was guilty of civil contempt and fined the union $10,000 for each day of the strike. Negotiations eventually reached a standstill. Fearing that the strike might last many more months, the court forced the board and PFT to negotiate. On October 29, the board and the PFT reached an agreement to end the city's 50-day strike. Frustrated and exhausted, Marcase resigned as Philadelphia's superintendent of schools a few weeks after the strike ended.

The strike ended, but the experience of six strikes in 11 years, coupled with the school district's fiscal instability and racial segregation, left Philadelphia residents and educators disenchanted and disillusioned with the city and its public schools. Public school families felt frustrated that Philadelphia teachers enjoyed some of the highest wages in the country, but that their children still lacked adequate classroom resources and updated school facilities.[101] Middle-class families left the public system and enrolled their children in private, parochial, and suburban schools. The white families that remained fought any movement to desegregate their neighborhood public schools. As thousands of white families left the city and thousands more resisted desegregation, racial segregation continued to escalate. Educators felt exhausted with the cycle of layoffs and strikes that they had endured over the past decade. Hundreds of teachers left the city for more stability and better resources in other schools. As one principal told the press, Philadelphia's public schools "suffered an insufferable loss."[102]

In the middle of the strike, reporters released a year-long study of the city's public schools that described the system as an organization "that neglects the most basic needs of its 224,000 students." The reporters attributed the district's shortcomings to weak administrative leaders, dominant labor unions, lavish teacher salaries, and inadequate school funding. Data indicated that among the 10 largest school districts in the nation, Philadelphia ranked first in spending for teacher pay and fringe benefits and second to last in spending for basic classroom supplies. Fully 75% of residents admitted that the school district faced "deep and serious financial trouble," but they refused to pay more taxes to support the city's public schools. Most Philadelphians did not have children enrolled in the city's public schools, and thus, were not invested in the system. The reporters noted that Black families and the small but growing number of Latinx families that "had a stake [in the public school system] tend to have relatively little power."[103] The white families that held the political power refused to support a public school system that they did not use; the Black and Latinx families that used the public school system did not have the political power to press elected officials to give their children an adequately funded system of public schools.

The escalation of childhood poverty and racial segregation in the city and its public schools compounded the district's fiscal shortcomings. By 1981, half of the city's public school children's families received welfare benefits (compared with 20% of children citywide); 70% of the city's public school children were students of color (compared with 42% of children citywide). The reporters wrote, "even if the district were magically relieved of its money problems, enjoyed the full support of taxpayers and city leaders, and were managed and staffed by hosts of angels, serious troubles would remain. For it is no easy task to educate so many poor children."[104] As the city searched for a new superintendent to lead its schools, city leaders knew that they had to find an individual willing to lead an "urban" school system—a majority-Black and majority-low-income system struggling to meet the essential needs of its youth due to decades of local disinvestment, widespread unrest, and white flight.

CHAPTER 7

Philadelphia School Leaders Fight to Restore and Control Philadelphia's Public Schools, 1982–2000

On October 5, 1982, the School District of Philadelphia hired Dr. Constance Clayton as the first Black and the first female superintendent. Born in Philadelphia in 1933 to Levi and Willabell (Harris) Clayton, Clayton attended the all-Black Paul L. Dunbar School and Jay Cooke Junior High School and graduated from the Philadelphia High School for Girls, the city's most prestigious special-admit school for girls. She began her teaching career in 1955 as a fourth and fifth grade teacher at the all-Black William Harrison Elementary School in North Philadelphia and then as a social studies curriculum designer and the head of the African and Afro-American studies program. In 1973, she entered school administration as the first director and then the associate superintendent of the Early Childhood Program for the School District of Philadelphia.[1] Throughout her career, Clayton held onto her belief that "the mission of education is to educate all kids and not just the middle class and the mainstream." "We must educate the kids born into poverty and despair," she declared, "we must value all kids and not just a select few."[2] Clayton made it clear from the beginning that she intended to lead a district that cared for all its youth.

Clayton promised to restore order and stability in the city's schools and to create an ethos and culture, as she always said, where "children come first."[3] She led a crusade to improve educational standards, options, and outcomes and to attract and retain middle-class families in the city's public schools. With the support of funding from philanthropic foundations, government agencies, local businesses, and Philadelphia families, Clayton passed balanced budgets with innovative curricular programs and afterschool activities. Clayton retained cordial relationships with the leaders of the teachers union and Philadelphia educators who admired Clayton's commitment, as an educator and leader, in her city and its public schools. As the first Black, female superintendent, Clayton faced enormous pressure to comply with the Pennsylvania Human Relations Commission's 1968 school desegregation mandate. In 1983, she implemented a modified desegregation plan that created new innovative school options as well as expanded opportunities for Black children to transfer to majority-white schools and for white children to transfer to majority-Black schools. Her modified desegregation plan generated a more desegregated school district, but the fact that it rested on increased school choice also replicated and reinforced educational inequality based on class, race, and space.

As Clayton worked to restore faith in the city's public schools, state officials slowly created the conditions to seize power and control over the School District of Philadelphia. State officials argued that Clayton's modified desegregation plan had failed and threatened to implement a mandatory busing plan. Around the same time, state officials passed a new public school funding formula that had dire effects on Pennsylvania's poorest school districts, including Philadelphia. The School of District of Philadelphia had always been dependent on state funds to operate its schools, but the collision of job losses, white flight, and escalating poverty intensified its dependency at the very moment that the state slashed funding. This dependency on the state made the School District of Philadelphia vulnerable to changes and shifts in state legislation and educational policy. Philadelphia lost millions of dollars in state school funding that it depended on for its survival. For the first time in nearly a decade, the School District of Philadelphia faced a multi-million-dollar budget deficit. Frustrated with the state's threat of a mandatory busing program and its decision to slash educational funding, Clayton retired with 38 years of service in Philadelphia's public schools.

David Hornbeck, an ordained minister and educational administrator, took over the School District of Philadelphia in 1994, one year after the state's new inequitable school funding formula took effect. To address the district's budget shortages and fund his reform, Hornbeck secured a $50 million grant from the Annenberg Foundation. The gift, however, rested on Hornbeck's ability to secure matching public and private funds. Despite several appeals to city and state officials, Hornbeck failed to secure the funds he needed. As a result, he curtailed his reforms and entered a contentious multiyear battle with the state over its school funding formula. This fight distracted him from the needs of Philadelphia's local public schools, including Germantown High School. After six years in office, he resigned, leaving Philadelphia educators, families, officials, and youth on their own to stave off a state takeover of the city's schools.

Clayton's and Hornbeck's leadership had a significant effect on Germantown High School. Clayton used her modified desegregation program to expand public school options for white families who lived near the majority-Black Germantown High School. Her policies exacerbated inequities between middle-class Black and white families and poor Black families in the community. White families often had better access to the public school options under the modified desegregation plan than did low-income families of color. Germantown High School educators recalled that Clayton's modified desegregation program intensified the challenges associated with childhood poverty, insufficient funding, racial segregation, and urban disinvestment. The state's new school funding formula drained essential financial resources and forced school administrators to slash operating expenditures. By the turn of the 21st century, Germantown High School had become an underfunded, neglected, hyper-segregated school that served poor Black youth who often lacked other educational options.[4]

City's First Black Female Superintendent Brings Hope and Stability

Clayton assumed her role as superintendent as the city's public schools were emerging from the chaos of 1970s budget cuts and teacher strikes and as the city faced new challenges associated with escalating childhood poverty, income inequality, job loss, racial segregation, and white flight. Between 1970 and 1980, the city lost 260,000 residents—most of them white—and 40% of its manufacturing jobs. The mass exodus of jobs and middle-class families, coupled with wage stagnation and rising living costs, had a dire effect on family incomes. Philadelphia's median family income, per-capita income, and overall education levels lagged behind national averages. Half of Philadelphia families made less in 1980 than families had in 1970. These inequities led to an increase in poverty. In 1970, approximately one in seven Philadelphia residents lived below the poverty line; by 1980, that figure had risen to one in five. Half of Philadelphia public school children lived with families who received some form of government assistance.[5] Data from the 1980 census suggested that the deepest pockets of poverty occurred in Philadelphia's hyper-segregated Black communities, including Germantown.[6]

In her first month, Clayton conducted a series of unannounced visits to assess the conditions inside the city's public schools. These visits revealed that many schools did not have the resources or facilities to promote effective teaching and learning.[7] Using data from these visits as leverage, Clayton asked federal and state officials to allocate additional funding to Philadelphia's public schools. State officials appropriated modest funding increases earmarked to support tighter graduation requirements, more testing programs, and targeted desegregation measures. State officials refused to give Clayton flexible funding to implement her ideas to enhance classroom instruction and resources across the district. Echoing refrains from the 1970s, state officials argued that the School District of Philadelphia's fiscal problems resulted from the city's lavish teacher contract, not insufficient state aid. The state's refusal to allocate the funds that Clayton actually needed, coupled with President Ronald Reagan's decision to slash educational and welfare programs, had a devastating effect on Clayton's ability to effectively provide services and resources to the city's public schools.[8]

To raise revenues, Clayton cultivated philanthropic relationships with local foundations, philanthropies, businesses, and families. Clayton received millions to fund innovative curricular programs and extracurricular activities.[9] Local businesses participated in an adopt-a-school program and agreed to provide resources directly to their adopted schools.[10] Public school home and school associations raised thousands of dollars to cover capital improvements, subsidize class trips, school-wide assemblies, extracurricular activities, and essential resources.[11] While these alternative revenue streams provided essential funds and resources to enhance curricular programs and educational outcomes, the influx of philanthropic funds masked the school district's long-term fiscal problems and intensified educational inequality based on class, race, and space. Philadelphia's majority-white, middle-class schools often received more private money than majority-Black, poor schools. The families that sent their children to majority-white, middle-class schools had more financial and social capital to support their schools than did the families who sent their children to majority-Black poor schools. Philadelphia's majority-white, middle-class schools were doubly advantaged. Class, race, and space still shaped educational opportunities and outcomes among Philadelphia's public school youth.[12]

White families enjoyed other privileges and benefits under Clayton's leadership. Clayton recognized that the school district's long-term financial stability and compliance with the state's desegregation mandate rested on her ability to retain and attract middle-class white families in the city and its public schools. In 1960, white residents made up 73% of Philadelphia; by 1980, that figure had dropped to 58%.[13] White flight destroyed Philadelphia's tax base, and in turn, its public school revenues. White flight also made it more difficult for Clayton to comply with the Pennsylvania Human Relations Commission's (PHRC) 1968 desegregation mandate. Even though Philadelphia remained a majority-white city when Clayton became superintendent, white students made up only 27% of Philadelphia public school enrollment. The white families who remained in the city often sent their children to parochial and private schools in lieu of their local public schools. Clayton wanted to change this.[14]

Six months into her new position, Clayton unveiled a plan to comply with the PHRC's 1968 school desegregation order and entice white families back to the city's public schools. Clayton refused to entertain any plan that included mandatory busing because she feared that busing might accelerate white flight and cost the school district millions of dollars that it could not afford to lose.[15] Instead, Clayton proposed a modified desegregation plan that focused on "education rather than transportation" and aimed to move the relationship between the school district and the PHRC from "confrontation to . . . cooperation."[16] She planned to increase resources to Philadelphia's 116 racially isolated schools—schools that had either a 90% "minority" or 90% "non-minority" enrollment. In addition, she aimed to increase *public* school choice to entice "minority" families to enroll their children in majority-white schools and white families to enroll their children in majority-minority schools.[17]

Using a combination of public and private funding, Clayton created and sustained about 20 magnet schools, a dozen magnet programs, and about 50 school-based desegregation programs, known locally as desegregation schools, to increase integration across the school district. While both of these schools had citywide admissions policies, Clayton opened the desegregation programs in schools where enrollment was at least 60% white and urged Black families to file transfers to send their children to these schools. She also opened desegregation programs in majority-Black schools located in communities that had a significant white school-aged population and encouraged white families to enroll their children in these schools. For example, Clayton designated Lincoln High School in the city's majority-white Northeast as a desegregation school and urged Black families to file transfers so that their children could attend this school. She also designated the Charles Houston School, a majority-Black school (83%), in Germantown's majority-white (57%) West Mt. Airy community as a desegregation school. Clayton encouraged white families to file transfers so that their children could attend this majority-Black school.[18]

The PHRC approved Clayton's modified desegregation plan, but it did not mandate full integration across the district. Rather, the commission required school officials to make a concerted effort to make the schools less segregated, which it referred to as "maximum feasible desegregation." The PHRC defined maximum feasible desegregation as a school system where white students represented 25–60% and Black students represented 40–75% of enrollment in each of the schools across the district. This definition provided wide flexibility for school leaders and reflected the fact that Philadelphia's school system had a majority-Black student enrollment with a small but growing white student population. If Clayton failed to achieve maximum feasible desegregation within three years, the commission reserved the right to petition the court and implement mandatory busing.[19] After the plan passed, Clayton assured the commission and the city about her commitment to desegregation, saying, "I did not accept this job . . . to preside over a segregated school system. And I will not do so."[20]

When Clayton unveiled her plan, hundreds of Black families filed school transfers to move their children out of their majority-Black neighborhood schools. Less than half of these Black families who filed transfers received them. One story illustrates the challenges with the plan. When Charlene Ranton, a Black single mother who lived in the majority-Black North Philadelphia neighborhood, learned about the voluntary transfers, she thought it seemed like a perfect program for her seven-year-old daughter, Andrea. Ranton hand delivered her daughter's voluntary transfer application to school district officials on the first day that the applications opened. Ranton requested a spot in the Meredith School, an integrated, middle-class school near Philadelphia's gentrified and increasingly white Queen Village neighborhood.[21]

Ranton made several follow-up phone calls and inquiries about her daughter's application, but at the end of the school year, Ranton learned that her daughter did not receive a spot in any of the city's desegregated school programs. Ranton called Meredith's principal to ask why her daughter had been denied a spot at the school. He told her that he did not have space for any more students in the school's second-grade classroom. Ranton refused to send her daughter to her under-resourced public school. Instead, she enrolled her in private school. Ranton was one of hundreds of Black families who sought better educational opportunities for their children but who found that school district policies and practices routinely prevented them from accessing the city's most reputable, and oftentimes doubly advantaged, public schools.[22]

Black parents, like Charlene Ranton, tried to leverage Clayton's desegregation plan to provide their children with the educational resources and facilities that white families often enjoyed in their city. But many Black families had their requests denied. Meredith did not have space, at least in part, because the middle-class families in Queen Village eagerly sent their children to their local public school, a doubly advantaged school, an institution that served an affluent and white student body and that historically relied on private donations to subsidize public aid. Space in these schools, itself, did not bar Black families from desegregation spots in schools like Meredith. The School District of Philadelphia was a majority-Black school district with many more majority-Black schools than majority-white schools. When Clayton implemented her modified desegregation plan, the number of spots for Black children to transfer to majority-white schools was numerically smaller than the number of spots for white children to transfer to majority-Black schools. As a result, Clayton's modified desegregation plan privileged white families in middle-class communities, who had more schooling options available to them.

The plan had other shortcomings. In the spring of 1986, 18 Black families filed complaints with the PHRC that white educators discriminated against Black children who transferred from majority-Black to majority-white public schools. To bolster their claims, Parents United for Better Schools, a citywide public school advocacy organization, studied the experiences of 350 Black students who transferred to majority-white schools. The study found striking differences in the educational opportunities and resources that white and Black students received in these schools.[23] Veronica Joyner, a former public school educator and Germantown Black mother who led the study, understood the effects of this racism on Black youth personally. When her son reached high school, Joyner filed a voluntary transfer to move her son from Germantown High School, his local, majority-Black neighborhood high school, to Northeast High School, one of the city's only majority-white neighborhood high schools. Joyner told the press that she had decided to move her son to Northeast High School because her son seemed different from most of "the children that I see going" to Germantown High School. At one point in the interview, she compared sending her son to Germantown to putting him inside "the lion's mouth." Even though she successfully transferred her son to the majority-white Northeast High School, she pulled him out after a few months and homeschooled him due to the racism that he experienced inside his new school.[24] Joyner's experience and the Parents United for Better Schools survey suggest that the Black families that successfully received a transfer under Clayton's modified desegregation plan faced racism inside the city's majority-white schools, making it difficult, if not impossible, for them to thrive. Clayton's emphasis on choice under the modified desegregation plan was an insufficient remedy for the deeper structural problems that generated educational inequity between Philadelphia's Black and white youth.

Finally, as the plan continued, Black families and Philadelphia educators raised concerns that Clayton's magnet and desegregation schools disproportionately benefited white families and their children. School district enrollment data supported these claims. In 1990, less than 10 years after Clayton implemented her modified desegregation plan, white students made up a disproportionate share of magnet and desegregation school enrollment: 45% of students enrolled in these schools were white, while white students made up only about 23% of total school district enrollment. Clayton's modified desegregation plan disproportionately benefited white families and their children who had better access to the city's most reputable public school options.[25] Clayton's plan led to a more desegregated school district, but it also privileged the needs of middle-class white families, who district officials relied on for school revenues, over the needs of poor, Black, and Latinx families who also called Philadelphia home.

A Plan to Reform Philadelphia's
Comprehensive High Schools

Clayton recognized these critiques of her modified desegregation program. In response, she implemented programs to strengthen instructional practice and educational experience in the city's public schools, especially its hyper-segregated, nearly all-Black high schools. In 1989, Clayton unveiled a multi-million-dollar plan, funded by the Pew Foundation, to transform Philadelphia's large comprehensive high schools into small learning communities (SLCs) under the auspices of the Philadelphia Schools Collaborative (PSC). The SLCs were smaller schools with less than 400 students; each school had a distinct theme and curriculum. PSC represented an innovative consortium of educational researchers and practitioners committed to improving educational opportunities and outcomes among high school youth.[26] Led by Michelle Fine, a University of Pennsylvania professor, and Janis Somerville, a school district employee, the collaborative engaged educators, families, and researchers in a collective movement that gave these stakeholders the power to manage and shape their new, small schools.[27]

Philadelphia's SLCs promoted more intimate, personalized learning experiences and improved student engagement and educational outcomes.[28] Compared to large comprehensive high schools, SLCs had fewer disciplinary problems and better attendance rates. Students in the SLCs felt a stronger sense of belonging and trust with administrators and teachers. Teachers appreciated the autonomy that they had in their classrooms and the opportunity to collaborate with colleagues to create a school that reflected their ideas and student needs.[29] Dina Portnoy, a Germantown resident and Philadelphia public school teacher, recalled, the collaborative "felt like Camelot. . . . [I]t gave teachers a chance to dream about what we could do inside our schools and do it."[30]

Even though the collaborative created a culture that encouraged teachers to reimagine the American high school, union practices and structural racism undermined its impact. From the moment the collaborative started, union leaders resisted the hiring practices that many of the educators in these SLCs relied on. The Philadelphia Federation of Teachers, the city's teachers union, created and sustained a hiring process that gave teachers with the most seniority the right to select positions before teachers with less experience. In Philadelphia, most public school teachers never interviewed with school administrators during the hiring process. Rather, at the end of every year, Philadelphia public school teachers gathered and, by seniority, picked positions from a list of districtwide teaching vacancies maintained by district officials. The PSC argued that schools functioned more effectively when school leaders can interview the teachers before they hire them, and thus, urged the union to amend this policy. Union leaders resisted the PSC's challenges to the seniority process and ultimately stymied the reform.[31] And while the PSC's approach clearly improved the schooling experience for

Philadelphia youth and educators, the reform did not address the hyper-segregation of Philadelphia's public schools. In 1990, Philadelphia had 25 comprehensive high schools. In 13 schools, Black students represented 90% or more of the student enrollment. In 12 of these schools, more than half of the students qualified for free and reduced lunch. Even with the collaborative's vision, Philadelphia's neighborhood high schools remained racially segregated institutions serving mostly poor, Black youth.[32]

One School Becomes Many Under Clayton

By the time that Clayton assumed the superintendency, Germantown consisted of three racially distinct neighborhoods: majority-white Chestnut Hill, racially integrated Mt. Airy, and majority-Black Germantown. The neighborhood's class composition often mirrored its racial composition: the wealthiest residents tended to live in Chestnut Hill, middle-class families lived in Mt. Airy, and poor residents concentrated in Germantown. School enrollment patterns reflected the community's class and racial differences. For the most part, Chestnut Hill families sent their children to elite private schools. Mt. Airy families often sent their children to parochial, private, and special-admit public schools. Germantown's middle-class Black and white families usually sent their children to local public elementary schools and then parochial, private, and special-admit public high schools. That left Germantown's working-class Black residents as the only families likely to send their children to Germantown High School.[33] Clayton understood these patterns and used her modified desegregation plan to disrupt them.

Clayton's desegregation plan rested on the voluntary movement of Black students to majority-white public schools and white students to majority-Black public schools. To facilitate the movement of white students to majority-Black public schools, Clayton strengthened and expanded public school choice with a series of special desegregated and special-admit magnet public schools. When Clayton assumed office, the School District of Philadelphia operated eight special-admit "motivation" schools. Motivation schools provided a rigorous college-preparatory curriculum for students who met the school admissions criteria. In the mid-1960s, school officials opened one of these schools, Lankenau Motivation, inside Germantown High School's basement. The school's location facilitated relatively easy movement between Lankenau and Germantown and gave Germantown residents the impression that the two schools operated as a collective unit. Eventually, perhaps due to the unrest and violence inside Germantown High School, school district officials moved Lankenau to an empty building located a few blocks from the high school. In 1981, school district officials purchased the Lankenau School for Girls, a private school campus located in the woods, to house Lankenau Motivation and double its capacity.[34]

When the new campus opened, school district officials implemented racially biased admissions policies and practices that privileged white families who wanted to send their children to Lankenau. Black youth had to live in the school's catchment zone to apply to the school, while white youth only had to live in the city. Lankenau students visited public elementary schools in predominately white communities to provide students with an overview of the school and its admissions process. The school district's modified desegregation program expanded public school choice particularly for white middle-class families who had left the city's public schools in hopes that with new school options, they might return.[35]

These policies and practices frustrated Germantown High School teachers. Kathy Bagley, a white Mt. Airy resident who taught at Germantown High School, felt that the decision to move Lankenau created two separate and unequal public schools—a special-admit high school that served middle-class Black and white youth and a neighborhood high school that served poor Black youth. Bagley recognized that most middle-class families did not send their children to Germantown High School. After all, she made the same decision for her own family. She sent her two biracial sons to local elementary schools and then to Central High School, the city's most prestigious special-admit high school. However, as a teacher, she worried about the concentration of the city's most vulnerable Black youth in the city's neighborhood high schools. As she recalled, Clayton's policies were an "attempt to keep it [the school system] integrated, but no white kid ever came to Germantown."[36] Bagley had a point. The expansion of public school options under Clayton's modified desegregation program, coupled with white flight and urban disinvestment, had a profound effect on the school's demographics. In 1990, the school enrolled 1,180 students; just 15 were white. Black youth represented 98% of the school enrollment; nearly half of Germantown students qualified for free and reduced lunch.[37] Clayton's modified desegregation program led to a more integrated school district, but it also concentrated the city's most vulnerable youth in the comprehensive neighborhood high schools, including Germantown High.[38]

The emphasis on choice under Clayton's modified desegregation program had a profound effect on Germantown's majority-Black high school. In majority-Black high schools like Germantown, the success of desegregation rested on the movement of Black families out of majority-Black high schools and the movement of white families into them. As Kathy Bagley and others point out, Black families leveraged Clayton's modified desegregation plan to transfer their children out of Germantown High School and into special-admit programs, such as Lankenau, and majority-white high schools, such as Northeast High School. Most of the families that filed these transfers were middle-class Black families. As these families moved out of Germantown, the school served a higher concentration of poor, Black youth at the very moment that state officials decimated funding.

While many middle-class Philadelphia families—both Black and white—sent their children to their local neighborhood public elementary schools, these families often refused to send their children to their local neighborhood high school, Germantown High. As middle-class families used choice to move their children, Germantown High School teachers recalled that the school served an increasingly poor, Black student population. The emphasis on choice as a means of desegregating Philadelphia's public schools concentrated poverty in the city's neighborhood high schools. Moreover, increased school choice never adequately addressed the deeper structural problems related to racism and poverty that existed in the community and its schools. The state legislature's decision to cut essential public funding and to expand school choice—in the form of charter school reform—only compounded the challenges inside the school. This is why one Germantown teacher referred to the movement of Lankenau out of the school building as "Germantown's death knell."[39] The combination of expanded school choice, which often privileged middle-class Black and white families, and state policies that cut funding and increased privatization eviscerated teacher morale and the community's hope for their once prestigious neighborhood public high school.

Even though Germantown educators and families recognized the shortcomings of Clayton's modified desegregation plan, they seized the opportunity to work with the Philadelphia Schools Collaborative to reimagine the school. With the collaborative's support, Germantown faculty broke up their large, comprehensive high school into four SLCs with distinct themes and curricula. They worked closely with local businesses and nonprofit organizations that provided additional funding and resources to support innovative teaching, student internships, and afterschool programs.[40] Caroline Maxwell, a white woman who began her teaching career at Germantown in the 1990s, said that the SLC structure "helped us [teachers] focus on the students." Maxwell recalled that these SLCs "had funding from outside sources," which enhanced teaching and learning. For example, Germantown High School had "extra Title I money," which provided revenues to subsidize school resources and compensate teachers for curriculum planning and student support. Maxwell remembered that administrators used this funding to pay teachers to "meet after school and talk about the kids. . . . [I]t was really terrific. . . . [A]s an SLC, we were able to focus on student needs more than student issues and talk to each other, which is really key, being able to talk to one another."[41]

However, the funding that these SLCs relied on did not last. The implementation of the state's new educational funding formula, coupled with federal education cuts, stymied Clayton's and, later, Hornbeck's ability to provide these funds. As a result, Germantown High School lacked the funding it needed to operate these SLCs effectively. These SLCs were more costly to staff than traditional large comprehensive high schools.[42] Dennis Barnaby, a teacher who served as Germantown High School's union leader, recalled that Germantown High School's SLCs did not always have the staff they needed to function. "The problem was that we didn't really have the personnel to make it possible for kids to really be in their SLC," he remembered. "Where did they go to gym? Where is the science lab that they go to? To make an SLC work, you should really be able to be an independent school. It became impossible. [Another] problem was that all ninth-grade students are not all ninth graders, many of them were repeating, some don't need to take English, some don't need to take social studies, but where do they go? Out of the SLC? It was constant difficulty."[43]

The school district's budget deficits made a difficult situation even worse. In 1992, reports surfaced that there were 60 students in some Germantown High School classrooms due to funding and staff shortages. Eloise Goldenberg, a Germantown High School teacher, told the press, "It's very unfair to the students to put them in classes where they're lining the walls. It's also pedagogically unsound to have to get used to one teacher for two months, and then have to get used to another."[44] Germantown teachers did not have enough textbooks or desks to accommodate the influx of new youth to the school. Dennis Barnaby recalled that the situation had a dire effect on student engagement: "if a kid comes to school and there's no desk and no book for him, the message is clear: 'Nobody wants me.'"[45] Latrese Wynn, a Black student who transferred to Germantown from the nearby suburbs, told the press that the crowded conditions and insufficient resources made it impossible for her "to get the education that I should."[46] As the state continued to starve Philadelphia's public schools of the funding they needed to survive, Germantown High School administrators, educators, families, and youth had to educate the city's most vulnerable Black youth with fewer and fewer financial resources.

State Officials Pass a New Educational Funding Formula and Press Mandatory Busing

As Clayton neared the end of her tenure as superintendent of schools, most Philadelphia residents praised her for passing balanced budgets that promoted innovative reforms, like the Philadelphia Schools Collaborative, that enhanced teaching and learning in the city's public schools.[47] However, state action undermined her ability to sustain a balanced budget. In 1991, state legislators passed Act 25, which had a devastating effect on the state's poorest school districts, including Philadelphia. Pennsylvania's new funding formula did not account for changes and shifts in school district demographics, such as increases in the number of poor students, special education students, or English language learners, all of whom cost more than other students to educate and support. In the 1990s, the School District of Philadelphia lost millions of dollars in state funds that it would have received under the old funding formula. The funding decrease occurred at the very moment that the school district needed additional revenue to serve these vulnerable student populations and operate its public school system.[48] In 1993, the first year the new funding formula took effect, the school district faced a $60 million budget deficit.[49] To keep the schools open, Clayton slashed staff, including librarians, music and art teachers, reading specialists, and classroom aides. The budget cuts disproportionately affected majority-Black and majority-poor schools.[50]

As Clayton tried to balance her budget on insufficient state funding, a court-appointed commission ruled that her modified desegregation plan failed to achieve maximum feasible desegregation. In February 1994, the PHRC filed a lawsuit that required Philadelphia to develop another desegregation plan and strengthen outcomes for Black youth.[51] Clayton fired back arguing that her plan had worked. In 1983, when Clayton instituted her plan, only 20% of Philadelphia students attended a desegregated school. Four years later, that figure had risen to 31%.[52] The commission refused to acknowledge the progress that Clayton had made and pressed forward with recommendations for a new desegregation plan with a mandatory busing program. Clayton, once again, asserted that a mandatory busing plan might increase white flight and cost the school district millions of dollars that it needed to operate its schools.[53] Rather than oversee a mandatory busing plan that she did not support in a school district with insufficient state funding, Clayton retired after 38 years of service to Philadelphia's public schools.[54]

Hornbeck Brings His Vision
of "Radical Change" to Philadelphia

One year after Clayton left the school district, the school board hired David Hornbeck as the next superintendent of the School District of Philadelphia. Hornbeck, an ordained minister and experienced educator, had worked as an educational consultant in Kentucky and as the superintendent of Maryland's public schools. He brought a critical view about the historical failures of urban school reform and a deep faith that he could rewrite the future of Philadelphia's public schools.[55] However, from the moment that Hornbeck assumed his role as superintendent, state officials continued to advance policies that consolidated their power over the management and governance of the city's public schools.

A few weeks after Hornbeck assumed his position, a court-appointed state panel released a 138-page report detailing its plan to improve Philadelphia's educational outcomes and comply with the spirit of the 1968 desegregation mandate and its 1994 lawsuit against the school district. The report asserted that the School District of Philadelphia had failed Philadelphia youth for decades. The panel argued that the failure of public education in Philadelphia stemmed from "a lack of will on the part of policymakers, educators and the wider public to implement change."[56] The panel asserted that Philadelphia's system-wide failure started early and permeated the entire system. Data indicated that 25% of first-grade students were not promoted, 70% of elementary students were reading below grade level, and at least 30% of high school students dropped out of school. The panel blamed school district officials, who in their words, historically evoked "an overall attitude of helplessness and resignation."[57] To improve educational outcomes, the panel issued 40 recommendations, including smaller class sizes, longer school years, full-day kindergarten, and a school funding formula based on student need rather than enrollment. The panel also encouraged the expansion of magnet programs and the conversion of large schools into small ones and advocated the creation of school-based councils to increase local control over school budgets, policies, and practices. The panel calculated that these reforms would cost the school district an additional $300 million but did not indicate who should pay for them.[58]

A few weeks later, Hornbeck unveiled his own recommendations. Known as Children Achieving, Hornbeck's systemic reform model had several goals: to secure fair and equitable city and state funding; set high standards to articulate learning goals; create accountability systems to assess school performance; improve resource coordination and school leadership; and increase civic capacity and parent engagement.[59] Under the plan, Hornbeck proposed splitting the school district's centralized administration system into 22 smaller clusters of elementary, middle, and high schools. He planned to move resources from the central office to these clusters and to raise funds for full-day kindergarten and additional professional development programs. The reform also gave parents, teachers, and community members the opportunity to develop curricular and assessment standards and issue rewards or sanctions based on district-wide school performance measures.[60] In many ways, Hornbeck's plan reflected the state panel's recommendations.

After Hornbeck and the state released their ideas, Commonwealth Court Judge Doris Smith heard testimony from state and school district officials about these various plans and recommendations. Hornbeck told the court that he viewed PHRC's February 1994 lawsuit and court-ordered panel recommendations "as a great opportunity" that "could provide the conditions and context in which we could get this done." He continued, "if we have the resources, the [school] board is resolved to pass the policies. We're not looking for a cure to some incurable disease. We are dealing with will, resolve and politics here." He pleaded with Smith to be his partner and force the state to allocate more educational funding to Philadelphia. Hornbeck made it clear to Smith that he could improve the conditions inside Philadelphia's public schools, but the School District of Philadelphia needed more money.[61]

On November 28, 1994, Judge Smith ordered school district officials to develop a plan to implement most of the state panel's recommendations with Hornbeck's Children Achieving plan. Smith's 26-page report included one short paragraph about funding. She urged school district officials to use local, state, and federal monies to fund the reforms. In this paragraph, Smith sidestepped the most critical question in Philadelphia: how could school officials in the state's largest and poorest school district convince Pennsylvania's Republican-controlled legislature to adequately fund its public schools?[62] School district officials begged Smith to include the state and city as defendants, which they argued, would have forced state legislators to provide additional revenues to the city's public schools. Smith refused. Hornbeck had to find a way to pay for the reforms with inadequate public funds. It was an impossible task.[63]

Hornbeck Relies on Philanthropy to Kickstart His Reforms

Like so many Philadelphia school leaders before him, Hornbeck turned to philanthropy to fund his reforms. On January 27, 1995, news leaked that Hornbeck had received a $50 million gift from the Annenberg Foundation to fund Children Achieving. The foundation donated the funds as a challenge grant, and thus, Hornbeck had to secure public and private matching funds to support his reform. Since he enjoyed strong support from the city's elected officials, Hornbeck first reached out to them.[64] Mayor Edward Rendell told Hornbeck that his administration had done as much as he could for the school district given Philadelphia's current revenue and tax structure.[65] When Rendell became mayor, Philadelphia had one of the heaviest tax burdens and some of the weakest services in the nation. Rendell feared that another tax increase might drive middle-class flight, and in turn, adversely affect the city's tax revenues. Given the city's shrinking revenues and burdensome taxes, Rendell felt it was a risk he could not take.[66] After the mayor refused, Hornbeck appealed to the state. The state refused and asserted that the School District of Philadelphia did not need more school funding, but rather Philadelphia families needed more school choice.[67]

Hornbeck then turned to the court. He argued that Children Achieving fulfilled the PHRC's 1968 mandate to desegregate Philadelphia's public schools and asked Judge Smith to force state officials to allocate more funds.[68] A few weeks later, state officials filed a motion with the Pennsylvania Supreme Court to remove Judge Doris Smith from the desegregation lawsuit. State officials asserted that Smith had served on the PHRC, and thus, could not objectively rule on the case. School district lawyers fired back, stating that the state's actions represented "a move to get rid of a judge who has been a strong advocate of children's rights."[69] Smith argued that the state had a "constitutional requirement and responsibility to maintain and support a system of public education on equal terms to all public-school children." She ordered state legislators to increase funding to Philadelphia's public schools. City officials praised Smith's decision and stated that it was the first time that the court had affirmed "the state's constitutional responsibility to equalize funding." State officials condemned the ruling, arguing that Smith's orders violated the separation of powers—the court, state officials contended, had no right to force the state to act.[70] On September 10, 1996, exactly three weeks after Smith issued her ruling, the Pennsylvania Supreme Court overturned Smith's ruling and assumed the case.[71]

With Smith gone, state officials introduced measures to expand school choice. On June 19, 1997, legislators passed a bill to permit charter schools, publicly funded but privately managed schools that are often free from the state regulations and oversight that govern traditional public schools. The legislation represented one of the only educational reforms that received bipartisan support across geographical and racial lines in the state legislature. Black Democratic politicians from Philadelphia, such as Dwight Evans, a representative who taught in Philadelphia's public schools and graduated from Germantown High School, joined forces with white Republican politicians from rural Pennsylvania to expand choice and charter schools.[72] That fall, four charter schools opened in Philadelphia. It was the beginning of a movement to privatize schools that would radically alter the School District of Philadelphia's landscape.[73]

Rendell and Hornbeck Sue the State
to Provide More School Funding

On January 27, 1998, Philadelphia's Mayor Edward Rendell filed a lawsuit against the state to avert a district-wide shutdown. The lawsuit claimed that state officials violated federal civil rights legislation. The state had failed to provide adequate educational funding to the School District of Philadelphia—the school district with the most Black and Latinx students in the state.[74] When the court hearings opened, Hornbeck asserted that if the state did not provide additional funding, the school district "would cease to exist as we know it." The state's attorney disagreed and argued that the school district had enough money to fund its schools.[75] Outside the courthouse, the friction between the state and city intensified. In the middle of the hearings, Republican governor Tom Ridge passed a budget with a $400 million surplus that included a 6% increase for the state's prison system and only a 2% increase for the state's public schools. In response, Hornbeck threated to shut down the school system, while Philadelphia activists took to the streets to protest the state's decision to fund its state prisons more than its public schools.[76]

In a five-one decision, the Pennsylvania Supreme Court ruled that state officials had fulfilled their constitutional duty. According to the court, school funding rested with local authorities, and thus, state officials did not need to allocate more money to Philadelphia's public schools.[77] The city appealed, arguing that the state's funding formula violated Title VI of the 1964 Civil Rights Act. In 1991, Philadelphia received 17.2% less in state aid than predominantly white districts with similar levels of poverty. In the 1995–1996 school year, that figure had risen to 33.1%. City officials attributed this shift to the state's inequitable school funding formula.[78] US District Judge Herbert J. Hutton rejected the city's claims, calling the lawsuit "merely a 'we need more money' allegation." City officials appealed one more time and argued that between 1992 and 1996 per-pupil state aid to majority-white school districts increased by $498; in Philadelphia, a majority-Black school district, it only increased by $361. The federal judge refused the appeal. The court, once again, failed to bring educational equity and justice to Philadelphia public school educators, families, and youth. The state did not need to allocate more funding to the city's public schools.[79]

After the court released its decision, Hornbeck intensified his attacks. In a national speech, Hornbeck lashed out against state officials, saying, "The observation that the state [of Pennsylvania] discriminates against children of color and youngsters whose first language is not English is characterized by many as being impolitic. . . . [W]hat ought to be impolitic is a system that results in children of color, non-native English speakers, disabled kids and poor children in general having larger classes and no access to prekindergarten programs, lousy libraries, and fewer textbooks."[80] Republican state legislators from the Philadelphia suburbs demanded an apology from Hornbeck for "basically calling us racists" and threatened to force Hornbeck out.[81]

For months, the state had been laying the groundwork to remove Hornback and take over the School District of Philadelphia. On April 27, 1998,

State legislators passed Act 46, which gave them the power and authority to remove the superintendent, replace the school board, and assume management of the School District of Philadelphia. Republican officials said that they did not want to run the school district, but that the district's fiscal problems forced this action.[82] Philadelphia residents took to the streets, arguing that the state's inequitable funding formula generated these fiscal problems. Philadelphia's public schools needed more funding, not state oversight.[83] On March 31, 2000, Philadelphia's school board approved a $1.6 billion budget that contained a $205 million deficit to push the state to increase funding. State officials refused and moved forward with the state takeover of the School District of Philadelphia.[84] Hornbeck slashed millions from his budget to save the district from fiscal ruin and state intervention.[85] This tactic worked at least for the moment. State officials promised nearly $70 million in aid if the school district dropped its lawsuit against the state. Philadelphia officials, desperate for school funding, agreed.[86] Frustrated and outraged with these actions, David Hornbeck resigned as the superintendent of Philadelphia's public schools on June 5, 2000. With Hornbeck gone, Philadelphia residents and officials had to convince the state to withdraw its threatened takeover, pressure the state to increase aid to Philadelphia's public schools, and find a new superintendent willing to manage one of the poorest, majority-Black school districts in the nation.[87]

Germantown High School Suffers as Hornbeck Battles the State for Funds

As Hornbeck battled in the courts to force the state to allocate more funding to the School District of Philadelphia, Germantown High School administrators and educators struggled to operate a nearly 100-year-old building on limited public aid. Germantown administrators, educators, families, and youth complained about the deterioration of the school's physical plant and the shortage of essential classroom resources. Educators and youth coped with moldy and antiquated bathrooms, dirty and dingy stairways, and mice-ridden classrooms that lacked adequate heat, light, and desks. Mindy Noble, who taught math at Germantown High School in the 1990s, recalled that these conditions "took a huge toll on the kids and the teachers." Germantown families filmed the abysmal school conditions. These families took the film to the school board and threated to release it to the press if the school board did not act. The board responded and promised to renovate the school.[88]

While families and educators initially welcomed the school board's pledge, the renovations ultimately created more chaos and confusion inside the school. Dennis Barnaby recalled that the projects that school district officials promised rarely happened. When they did, they were often rushed and incomplete. Barnaby spent hours in meetings with school district officials and engineers. When he complained about some of the renovations, school district officials often blamed students for the shortcomings. Officials told Barnaby that Germantown students broke the materials and damaged the renovations. Barnaby denied these claims and insisted that school district officials used inexpensive materials to save costs. The materials were not well-suited for industrial use and thus broke easily. Barnaby said, "we spent a year in hell and when the district finished it wasn't much better than it was before they started. . . . It was awful. It made me question if anyone [at the school district level] wanted the school to work. We did. We were trying. . . . [Germantown teachers] had so much frustration about what could be. We could do this, we knew we could do it, but we could not do it under these physical conditions and without the resources." According to him, the frustrations created a "combative modus operandi" among Germantown teachers. Barnaby continued, "we felt that we always had to fight for anything that we needed. . . . [N]obody ever asked us what we needed."[89] And the top-down nature of reform under Hornbeck, coupled with the shortage of funds for essential resources, generated animosity and anger among Germantown staff that undermined their ability to survive and thrive in a school with a crumbling infrastructure and dwindling resources.

As Hornbeck continued to battle the state for more funds, Germantown High School's problems persisted. George Schuler, a Germantown High School alumnus and experienced administrator, became the sixth principal to lead Germantown in six years. When he visited the high school to assess school conditions, he recalled, "I almost died." Weeds concealed the school's iron fence. Graffiti covered the school's ornate doorway. The marble that lined the school lobby walls was damaged or missing. Schuler said that when the marble is intact the lobby is "wonderful, but when every nineteenth piece is missing and you just see a dark colored background of some sort where marble used to be, it's not so great." Inside the school, the problems continued. Schuler remembered that his office looked more like a warehouse than a school building. He had peeling plaster and moth-eaten rugs. The school walls, which in Schuler's time had displayed several pieces of original artwork by famous Germantown artists, were painted white with splotches of dark beige paint to hide graffiti. Even though he did not have much time, he knew he had to act. Schuler remembered thinking, "I can't allow parents . . . I can't have students seeing a school like this." Schuler called his friends and colleagues in the school district's central office and begged them to help him find the supplies and resources he needed to restore some semblance of the school that he had attended in the mid-1960s. He begged them for staff, more desks, and of course, more marble. Within a few days, he had more staff and more desks, but no marble. Schuler used his own funds to buy marble at a local hardware store and asked a school facilities worker to "find a way to get it on the walls before school started." When he walked into the school the next morning, the marble was on the wall.[90]

These efforts enhanced Germantown's physical condition, but Schuler never had the time or resources to address the school's significant staffing shortages. When Schuler assumed his position, Germantown High School still had several teaching and staffing vacancies including a position for the person who created and managed the school schedule. Five days before the school year officially began, school district officials finalized the hiring process for these positions. It was too late. When school opened, Schuler distributed temporary schedules to teachers and students because the new hire did not have time to create and finalize the school's master schedule. For weeks, Germantown High School students attended classes that they did not need to graduate and teachers taught students who should not have been in their classes. Frustrated with the chaos and instability, Germantown teachers began a campaign to close the school and reopen it when the schedules were finalized. Schuler begged the teachers to stay; they did. At the beginning of October, Schuler distributed new and final schedules to students and teachers. The new schedules presented other problems. Many high school seniors had been attending the wrong classes for weeks. When they received their new schedules, some of them realized that they did not have enough credits or the appropriate classes to apply to college. Students expressed their own frustrations and anger about the situation and its effects on their future aims. As one Germantown High School student remarked, "all schools make mistakes, but it seems that Germantown makes big mistakes that can really affect your future."[91]

The school district's funding shortages and the high school's dysfunctional ethos limited educational opportunity and outcomes for Germantown

High School youth. Renee Connor, a Black graduate of Germantown's communications SLC, had the grades and records to attend any high school in the city. She chose Germantown, her parents' alma mater, and felt "proud going to Germantown . . . where my roots were." When she was 10 years old, Renee's father passed away, leaving her mother, a factory worker, to raise her two young daughters on her own. Renee said that her mother wanted her children to excel in school, but that by the time they reached high school, her mother often lacked the knowledge and experience to help her children with their plans for the future. While she clearly appreciated what her mother did for her, Renee credits her teachers in the communications SLC and in her after-school programs at the First United Methodist Church of Germantown with her decision to attend college after high school. In particular, Renee recalled that one person, Dr. Mitchell, a First United Methodist volunteer, emphasized the importance of postsecondary schooling. When Mitchell met Renee, she immediately asked if Renee had any plans to apply to college. "She is the one who talked to me about college," Renee said. "My mom wasn't going to talk to me about college. I am a first-generation person; she [Dr. Mitchell] had a PhD. I remember her telling me everything about her life and everything about her own education." Renee recalled that she also received support from several Germantown teachers. Frank Burd, a math teacher, invited Renee on a school-sponsored visit to Delaware State University, a historically Black college located near Philadelphia. After her visit, she applied to the school, received a substantial scholarship, and eventually, became the first person in her family to graduate with a four-year college degree.

When I interviewed her, Renee worked as a teacher's aide in a low-income Philadelphia public school. Renee has realized that the School District of Philadelphia, which she attended and works in, rarely provides low- and middle-income youth of color like herself with the educational opportunities that most American children—particularly those in wealthier and whiter suburban communities—receive. Renee and her husband, a Black man who attended schools in suburban Delaware, have talked extensively about the differences in their high school experiences. According to Renee, her husband experienced "a lot of stuff that I never had [in high school], and now when I hear about this, I think, 'Wow, I didn't have that.'" Her husband read Shakespearean plays, participated in extensive extracurricular activities, and went on several field trips as a high school student. She felt cheated by a system that never gave her and her peers the opportunities to do this in school. And she is angry about the reputation that her high school has in her city. Renee told me that her work colleagues, both Black and white, are often surprised when she tells them that she graduated from Germantown High School. When I asked her why, she explained, "People in my school look very highly at me. I went to college. They think I am well-spoken. If people know anything about [Germantown] high school, they are kind of shocked that I went there. The school's reputation is that bad."[92] Renee knew that most Germantown High School students never had the opportunities that she had, and even those who did, still lacked the educational experiences of individuals, like her husband, who attended more affluent, better-resourced public schools.

Threat of State Takeover Looms in Philadelphia

As the United States moved into the 21st century, urban communities struggled under the weight of escalating poverty, population loss, shrinking wages, structural racism, and urban disinvestment. Philadelphia and its majority-Black public school system reflected these challenges. From 1982 to 2000, Constance Clayton and David Hornbeck tried to restore public confidence and trust in Philadelphia's system of public schools. Clayton implemented tighter academic standards, innovative school curricula, modified desegregation programs, and a radical vision to break large comprehensive high schools into smaller learning communities. Hornbeck pushed for racial equity and justice and argued that all children could, in fact, achieve if the Philadelphia's public schools had the funds they needed to operate effectively. As leaders in a state and city with limited educational funding, Clayton and Hornbeck relied on philanthropy to subsidize insufficient public funding for the city's public schools. Clayton's and Hornbeck's reforms opened up space for families, faculty, and community members to voice their concerns and ideas about how to improve school curriculum, governance practices, and district-wide assessments. Clayton's Philadelphia Schools Collaborative and Hornbeck's Children Achieving had positive effects on the educational experiences and outcomes of Philadelphia youth, but neither Clayton nor Hornbeck had the private or public funds to sustain their reforms. Philanthropy had, once again, failed to make up for Philadelphia's insufficient public school funding.

As Clayton and Hornbeck tried to operate a school system on inadequate public aid, state officials slowly but surely instituted measures to erode the power and autonomy that Philadelphia's school leaders and their constituents had over their public schools. State officials dismissed Clayton's modified desegregation plan and threatened to force the city to adopt a mandatory busing plan to increase desegregation. Clayton resisted and insisted that a mandatory busing plan might increase white flight from the city and cost the school district millions of dollars that it could not afford to lose. As the court deliberated these plans, state officials instituted a new inequitable school funding formula that drained millions of dollars from the state's poorest, majority-Black and Brown public school districts, including Philadelphia. Under this new formula, Clayton and Hornbeck faced multimillion-dollar budget shortages that limited educational resources and opportunities in Philadelphia's public schools. Hornbeck begged the courts to leverage the PHRC's 1968 mandate to force the state to allocate more funds. This tactic never worked, but Hornbeck continued his fight. As he escalated his rhetoric against the state, state officials pushed forward with plans to expand school choice and take over the governance and management of Philadelphia's public schools.

The challenges associated with escalating poverty, population loss, shrinking wages, structural racism, and urban disinvestment affected Germantown High School, but local and state policies and practices exacerbated the school's challenges. Germantown High School had been a majority-Black high school since the 1960s, but the school district's decision to purchase a private school campus and Clayton's decision to expand Lankenau's student enrollment had a significant effect on Germantown High School. Germantown educators and residents felt that these decisions further fractured school enrollment by class and race. Lankenau, a special-admit school on a beautiful private school campus, served a more affluent and racially integrated student body while Germantown High School, a large comprehensive school in the community's once-thriving commercial district, served some of the city's poorest Black youth. Even though these educators welcomed the opportunity to transform Germantown High School into smaller learning communities, they never had the power or the resources under Clayton or Hornbeck to address the effects of childhood poverty and structural racism inside their school. The decimation of school funding and the threat of a state takeover generated a new feeling of hopelessness and defeat among Germantown High School educators, families, and youth.

CHAPTER 8

Philadelphia Implements the "Largest and Boldest Experiment" in Urban Public Education, 2002–2011

After Hornbeck resigned as the superintendent of one of the nation's poorest school districts, Philadelphia ignited. Fed up with months of contentious labor negotiations, the Philadelphia Federation of Teachers prepared to strike.[1] Philadelphia families and youth staged a series of citywide marches and school walkouts to protest stark budget cuts, harsh disciplinary policies, and inadequate public funds.[2] And as families and youth marched, city officials prepared to hire new leaders to oversee their beleaguered district, while state officials hired outside consultants to study the School District of Philadelphia's fiscal affairs and performance measures.[3] In the midst of all of this, Philadelphia educators, families, and youth testified at school board meetings, staged citywide protests, and mobilized in their communities to protest state officials who threatened to take over the city's schools. Their actions only stalled the inevitable: at precisely 12:01 am on December 21, 2001, the state assumed control over Pennsylvania's largest school district.[4]

The takeover gave state officials unprecedented powers. Pennsylvania's governor replaced Philadelphia's school board with a school reform commission (SRC). State officials appointed three SRC members; Philadelphia's mayor appointed two. Under the direction of the school district's new CEO, Paul Vallas, the state unveiled plans to implement the "largest and boldest experiment in the history of urban public education"—an experiment that rested on outsourcing the city's lowest-performing public schools to private managers, who bid on the right to operate them.[5] Vallas's market-driven reforms, which relied on privatization to expand choice, dovetailed neatly with the 2001 federal No Child Left Behind (NCLB) Act. The local and federal reforms insisted that public school shortcomings resulted from inefficiency, not poverty, and often scapegoated educators for the challenges that public schools faced.[6] Vallas and his successor, Arlene Ackerman, spent millions to expand school choice, standardized curricula, and zero-tolerance policies. Philadelphia's majority-Black public schools, including Germantown, bore the brunt of these deficit-oriented, punitive educational policies and practices. These policies often downplayed the assets in low-income, Black, and Latinx communities, and instead, started with the assumption that public schools had deficits that needed to be "fixed" often times by outsiders who pushed market-based reforms without addressing the history of disinvestment and neglect that had contributed to the challenges in the city's public school system. And if the school did not change quickly, these individuals implemented punitive measures that eroded teacher morale and student engagement.[7]

The history of Germantown High School illustrates the significant mismatch between the reforms that these CEOs implemented and the challenges inside the school. For more than a decade, Germantown educators had begged city and school officials to recognize the effects of childhood poverty, chronic underfunding, racial segregation, and urban disinvestment on their school. The market-based, NCLB-driven reforms that Vallas and Ackerman implemented failed in places like Germantown because the reforms demanded improvements on an impossible timescale and because they never addressed the effects of childhood poverty, insufficient school funding, structural racism, and urban disinvestment.

Vallas's Reforms Fracture the City's Schools by Class, Race, and Space

On December 18, 2001, just two days before the state officially took over the School District of Philadelphia, Congress passed the federal No Child Left Behind (NCLB) Act. Written by a bipartisan committee that included Senator Edward Kennedy (D-MA) and Representative John Boehner (R-OH), the act expanded the role of the federal government in public education. It required states and schools to implement standards-based assessments, address safety and security measures, and raise teacher certification requirements. NCLB mandated that schools meet annual benchmarks, known as Annual Yearly Progress, to qualify for federal aid. Schools that did not meet these benchmarks were labeled as failing and subject to punitive measures, including privatization or closure. Legislators hoped that NCLB might spur competition, and in turn, raise school standards and/or expand school choice. Urban school officials, including those in Philadelphia, felt pressure to comply with NCLB mandates because they relied heavily on federal funding to operate their schools.[8]

Shortly after the passage of the federal 2001 NCLB Act, Philadelphia school leaders implemented a diverse provider model that allowed multiple organizations to manage its public schools. The model promised to expand market-based school choice and competition, which state officials believed would make the fiscally distressed school system more efficient and effective. Under the diverse provider model, Philadelphia families had an array of options, including, traditionally managed public schools, district-managed public schools, and privately managed public and charter schools.[9] In April 2002, the SRC selected seven organizations to bid on the right to manage the city's 46 lowest-performing schools. A few months later, the SRC appointed Paul Vallas, who had led a similar reform effort in Chicago, as the School District of Philadelphia's first Chief Executive Officer (CEO). Vallas's title signaled that Philadelphia finally had a school leader with strong business acumen and unprecedented power to oversee the SRC's reforms.[10]

Vallas wasted no time implementing his vision for Philadelphia's public schools. A few weeks after he took office, the SRC announced that it had granted multiyear contracts to seven organizations—three for-profits, two nonprofits, and two universities—to manage the city's lowest-performing public schools. The diverse provider reform affected more than 80 elementary and middle schools.[11] In the remaining schools, Vallas implemented a series of top-down, rapid-pace interventions to improve NCLB outcomes. He expanded early childhood programs, created K-8 schools, and opened small high schools. Finally, Vallas instituted a Campaign for Humans to hire and retain Philadelphia public school teachers.[12]

Inside the schools, Vallas implemented a multi-million-dollar district-wide curriculum that included a system of benchmark assessments. Vallas expected teachers to follow the standardized curriculum with absolute fidelity. Every six weeks, educators suspended classroom instruction and administered test-driven assessments. School administrators shared the results of these classroom-level assessments and other school-level NCLB metrics, such as school attendance and disciplinary infractions, with district officials who tracked and assessed progress.[13] To improve NCLB security metrics, Vallas instituted zero-tolerance disciplinary policies. He increased police presence in the schools and purchased additional security measures, such as surveillance cameras and metal detectors. Vallas implemented policies to move disruptive students from neighborhood public schools to an expanded network of privately managed disciplinary schools.[14]

Even though some residents welcomed these changes, thousands of Philadelphia educators, families, and youth critiqued and resisted these reforms. Educators argued that Vallas's standardized curriculum moved too quickly for students to master skills and knowledge. They felt that it promoted narrow ideas about teaching and learning that eroded their professional judgment and autonomy. One Germantown High School teacher recalled that Vallas's curriculum created a situation where teachers had "much less time to meet individual needs. . . . [T]here were fewer kids that had their problems identified. And even if you could do that as a teacher, there wasn't much that you could do about it."[15] Families worried that Vallas's reforms promoted test-taking skills over authentic learning.[16] Educational advocates critiqued the curriculum for neglecting to include Black, Latinx, and LGBTQ+ voices and perspectives.[17]

Youth activists spoke out about the prison-like atmosphere in their schools—in the city's charter and disciplinary schools, students routinely had to walk in silent lines with their hands clasped together behind their backs, like prisoners.[18] These activists also spoke out about the connections between Philadelphia's zero-tolerance policies and the school-to-prison pipeline. On March 17, 2004, Philadelphia youth attended the SRC meeting clad in bright orange T-shirts reading "School District Correctional Facility." Philip Pearce, a West Philadelphia High School student, told the SRC, "there is a problem of violence in our schools, but putting cops in our schools will not solve it." The educators, families, and youth who challenged Vallas's approach recognized the challenges in their communities and schools, but they refused to support punitive, deficit-oriented reforms that had a disproportionate effect on Black youth.[19]

Perhaps most importantly, these individuals resented the fact that Black families and youth, once again, bore the brunt of school privatization, standardized curricula, and zero-tolerance policies under Philadelphia's NCLB-driven reforms. Vallas insisted that school officials use objective measures to identify public schools to outsource to private providers, but in fact school privatization disproportionately affected schools that served Black youth.

White students made up 17% of the school district's enrollment, but only 2% of the enrollment in the schools targeted by privatization under the diverse provider reform model.[20] State officials made these matters worse. In 2003, they announced the names of 28 "persistently dangerous schools." Most were majority-Black; 27 of the 28 schools were located in Philadelphia. Patricia Mazzuca, the principal of Roberto Clemente Middle School, which was on the list, called it "a ridiculous way to classify schools."[21] The decision to label the schools had ramifications for what happened inside of them. After the state labeled a school as a persistently dangerous institution, officials often increased police presence and surveillance. Philadelphia public school families and advocates resented the fact that school district officials, once again, had to fund more police and security instead of more counselors and mental health specialists.[22] To make their case that Vallas's policies disproportionately affected majority-Black and majority-Latinx schools, Philadelphia public school families and educational activists often pointed to the vastly different school reforms that Vallas instituted in Philadelphia's increasingly gentrified, white Center City District.

When Vallas assumed his role, Philadelphia's Center City District, which included hundreds of blocks around City Hall, was home to the city's largest concentration of affluent, white residents.[23] Data indicated that Center City residents appreciated the neighborhood amenities, but that they often left the city when their children reached school age, taking their families and tax dollars with them to the suburbs. Elected officials and school leaders felt that the city's prosperity and its school district depended on the robust tax base that Center City residents provided. From 2004 to 2008, business and school leaders created a new initiative, the Center City Schools Initiative (CCSI), to entice Center City's middle- and upper-class families to stay in Philadelphia and invest in their local public schools. CCSI represented a public-private partnership between business and education partners to increase educational resources and outcomes in the public schools that served the Center City region.[24]

With support from the CCSI and other local and national organizations, Vallas opened several small, boutique magnet public high schools in the area, such as Constitution High School and Science Leadership Academy. These small schools had more autonomy and freedom to select their students and teachers than most other Philadelphia high schools. These magnet schools maintained citywide admissions policies, and thus, they often had more affluent and more white students compared to other neighborhood

public high schools.[25] Finally, these schools had another advantage: they received private funding from businesses, corporations, and families to subsidize inadequate public funding.[26] Like Germantown residents 100 years earlier,
Center City families poured thousands of dollars and other resources into
their public schools. These funds and resources guaranteed advantages to their
children, such as beautiful playgrounds, well-resourced libraries, and additional staff.[27] The reforms achieved their aim: the number of affluent, white
Center City residents who decided to stay in the city and send their children
to their doubly advantaged public schools increased significantly.[28]

Vallas's reforms limited educational opportunity and intensified educational inequities based on class, race, and space. The creation of the Center
City District, which was spearheaded by civic, elected, and school officials,
generated a protected space of white affluence and privilege in one of the nation's poorest, majority-Black cities. In some ways, the patterns of opportunity and inequity reflected the past. Philadelphia's affluent, white youth
attended doubly advantaged public and charter schools, such as the ones in
Center City, with thematic curricula and significant private funding. Philadelphia's poor, Black, and Latinx youth often attended neighborhood public
and charter schools or prison-like disciplinary schools that had narrow
test-based curricula, zero-tolerance disciplinary policies, and inadequate
public funding.

However, there was one clear difference that resulted from Vallas's reforms: the spatial distribution of Philadelphia's doubly advantaged schools
had moved from the city's periphery to the city's center. At the turn of the
20th century, Philadelphia's doubly advantaged public schools had been located on the city's periphery in predominately bourgeois and white communities like Germantown. A century later, Philadelphia's doubly advantaged
public schools moved to the city's center, to increasingly gentrified and
white communities such as Center City, mirroring a trend that also occurred in other American cities. The distribution of Philadelphia's doubly
advantaged public schools represented an inversion of the past.[29]

Costly Reforms and Inequitable Funding
Generate Fiscal Disaster

On February 2, 2006, Vallas announced that the school district had an unanticipated $20 million budget deficit. Vallas instituted a hiring freeze and

ordered principals to cut discretionary spending—the funds that covered extracurricular activities and other miscellaneous expenditures—by 30%.[30] He said these cuts seemed like "a small price to pay."[31] Thousands of Philadelphians disagreed. Aissia Richardson, the president of Powel Elementary Home and School Association, argued, "In the past two years, [our schools] have gone from cutting the fat to cutting the meat, to starvation, to outright cannibalism."[32] After years of funding cuts and urban disinvestment, Philadelphia residents and elected officials publicly demanded to know how this deficit happened.

The unanticipated budget shortfall stemmed from a variety of factors. First, the state's inequitable funding formula, which it passed in 1991, drained millions in educational funding—funding that Vallas desperately needed to fund his reforms and operate Philadelphia's schools.[33] Second, the state's charter school laws made it difficult for Vallas to project and track his budgets. Even though charter school supporters and critics had many differences, most agreed that Pennsylvania had one of the nation's most flawed charter school funding mechanisms. In Pennsylvania, school districts paid charter school expenditures, and then, later, the state reimbursed them. In practice, however, state reimbursements did not always cover Philadelphia's charter school expenditures. In 2006–2007, Philadelphia spent $240 million in charter school expenditures; the state reimbursed $78 million.[34] Because of this gap between the real and reimbursed charges, many Philadelphians, including some SRC members, opposed the expansion of charter schools. But Vallas refused to listen and instead expanded the city's charter school network.[35] In 1997, Philadelphia had 4 charter schools. In 2009, it had 60.[36]

On October 11, 2006, the School District of Philadelphia faced a $21 million deficit due to a budget miscalculation.[37] A week later, school district officials announced that the district actually had to slash $70 million—three times what it had initially predicted—due to budgetary miscalculations including underestimating the costs of charter schools and teacher retirement payments and overestimating the reserve fund from money that the schools did not spend. Vallas promised to avoid cuts that directly impacted classroom instruction, but he could not keep that promise.[38] On November 8, 2006, Vallas announced the elimination of hundreds of administrators, the closure of several school offices, the reduction of executive benefits, and the elimination of essential school staff: school counselors, social workers, school librarians, art/music teachers, and athletic coaches.[39]

Angry residents, youth activists, and frustrated officials, including the city's mayor, grilled Vallas and the SRC about the deficit and these decisions.[40] Vallas understood that these events might end his tenure in Philadelphia; "in May or June we'll know if we have [resolved SDP's financial problems], and if we don't, it'll be my head on the chopping block," he predicted in December 2006.[41]

Vallas's problems escalated. A few weeks later, a national study by the RAND Corporation and Research for Action revealed the shortcomings of Philadelphia's school privatization movement. The study indicated that test scores in the privately managed schools that received additional funding were on par with the district-managed schools that had survived on the city's limited funding.[42] Henry M. Levin, director of Columbia University's National Center for the Study of Privatization in Education, said the study's results suggested that the private reform experiment was like "a romance that just hasn't worked. It's not that they're [Philadelphia's privately managed schools] doing worse, but they don't seem to be doing better, and they cost more. That's a serious challenge, particularly for a district that is facing a deficit."[43] A few days later, the SRC announced a projected $140 million budget deficit. The failures of the diverse provider model, coupled with a massive, and mounting, revenue shortage signaled the end of Vallas's power as CEO.[44] Within a few months, Vallas resigned. The policies and practices that he put into place exacerbated educational inequality and generated fiscal instability in Philadelphia's two-tiered, racially segregated, quasi-public system of schools.[45]

New CEO Promises to Expand School Choice and Privatization

On February 18, 2008, news leaked that the SRC had entered contract negotiations to hire Arlene Ackerman as the next CEO of the School District of Philadelphia.[46] In her first public meeting, Arlene Ackerman, the second Black woman to lead Philadelphia's schools, blasted the racial disparities in the city's school system. She promised to collaborate with officials, educators, families, and youth to end the opportunity and resource gap in Philadelphia's schools.[47] Ackerman's own educational experiences as a woman who attended racially segregated schools in St. Louis, and her professional trajectory as a public school teacher, principal, and superintendent, gave many residents hope and confidence that their new CEO might indeed strengthen Philadelphia's public schools.[48]

Their hope and confidence were short-lived. Ackerman continued Vallas's push for school choice and privatization. She turned dozens of traditionally managed public schools over to privately controlled charter organizations. She instituted a multi-million-dollar, top-down reform to rapidly improve NCLB metrics in district-managed public schools. And, following her predecessor's policies, Black schools, once again, bore the brunt of Ackerman's drive to privatize public schools, expand school choice, and implement NCLB-driven reforms, which, as Germantown High School's history illustrates, destroyed teacher morale and student engagement. And like Vallas's plans, Ackerman's reforms drained millions of public dollars that the fiscally under-resourced school district could not afford to lose.

About a year after she assumed office, Ackerman unveiled Imagine 2014, a five-year plan to improve the city's schools. Based loosely on Chicago's Renaissance 2010 and President Barack Obama's Race to the Top market-based educational initiatives, the plan once again identified and outsourced Philadelphia's lowest-performing schools to a privately managed charter school or a publicly managed community group. School officials recruited families, youth, and community members to serve on School Advisory Councils at every Renaissance School. These councils were responsible for evaluating school management organizations—either the school district or private charter organizations—that had applied to operate the school. They then made recommendations to the SRC about which turnaround team best met the needs of the school community. As a result, some schools remained under district control; school officials outsourced that management of other schools to private charter school organizations. These reforms represented yet another mechanism to increase school privatization in Philadelphia. In the district-managed schools, Ackerman stipulated strict and often punitive hiring policies. Teachers in the district-managed Renaissance schools had to reapply for their positions. In schools remaining under district control, administrators could rehire no more than 50% of the original staff. Ackerman structured the reform in a way that suggested that public school teachers and their union was the main impediment to improving the schools slated for Renaissance reform. Ackerman and her allies downplayed the effects of escalating childhood poverty, chronic underfunding, racial segregation, and urban disinvestment on Philadelphia's schools and communities.[49]

   While some residents praised Ackerman's vision for sparking change in
Philadelphia's public schools, thousands of Philadelphia educators, families,
and youth resisted the reforms. Union leaders argued that these reforms had
already failed under Vallas. Philadelphia youth activists resisted Ackerman's
vision and asserted that the reforms disproportionately targeted schools that
served poor, Black, and Latinx youth. On February 25, 2009, protests erupted
outside of Ackerman's office, with protesters shouting "It's not a choice if we
have no voice. They say it's innovation, we say it's segregation."[50] In response,
Ackerman met with educators, families, and youth and promised to "work in
conjunction with the affected parents and families in each school to choose
ONLY instructional models with a proven track record of success that best fit
the needs and desires of that particular community."[51] Finally, educational
advocates and local journalists in Philadelphia worried that school officials
did not actually have the state and local funds to cover Ackerman's five-year
reform plan.[52] School officials confirmed these fears and asserted that inadequate state funding threatened the city's ability to pay for these reforms.[53]
Ackerman dismissed these critiques, saying, "I'm not worried about the
money; it's so basic. Everything in this plan, I got in my high school 40 years
ago. So why is it we can't do it for children in Philadelphia in 2009?"[54] Undeterred, the SRC approved a $3.2 billion budget including over $100 million to
fund Ackerman's controversial Renaissance School reforms.[55]
   On September 14, 2010, President Obama visited Philadelphia to celebrate Ackerman's vision. The celebration made sense: Ackerman's reforms
reflected Obama's own commitment to competition, choice, and charters.[56]
School officials asserted that they had created an objective school performance index to identify these schools. But in practice, the index was a com-
plicated measure that included racially biased data from state-mandated
tests and NCLB metrics such as attendance and discipline.[57] While most
Philadelphia voters supported Obama in 2008, they did not necessarily
share his admiration of Ackerman's reforms. Philadelphia educators, families, and youth argued that these reforms, once again, disproportionately
affected Black communities and schools. Figure 21 confirms this point. Most
of Ackerman's Renaissance schools were in Black communities. Residents
critiqued the opaque and secretive nature of the reform, which they felt represented an erosion of public accountability and democratic governance.
Ava Reeves, a junior who attended a school on the Renaissance list, pushed
school officials at a community meeting and asked, "Whatever happened to
democracy, for the people by the people? If this is a democracy and not a

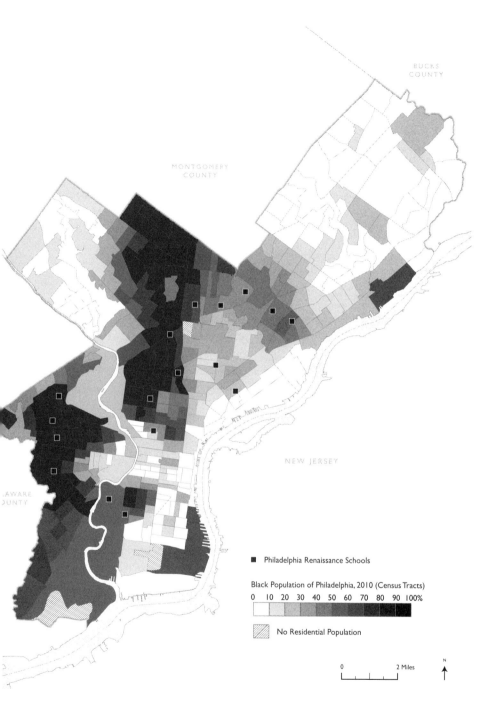

Figure 21, Location of Renaissance Schools, 2017, and Percentage of Black
Residents by Census Tract, 2010. Source: Benjamin Herold, "Where Charters
Run the Neighborhood Schools," *PPSN*, October 17, 2012, http://thenotebook
.org/articles/2012/10/17/where-charters-run-the-neighborhood-school.

dictatorship and you claim that 'parents are our partners' and 'children come first,' why didn't any community members have a say so in which educational provider they wanted for their children?"[58] When Ackerman had unveiled her reform, she had promised "to work in conjunction with affected parents and families."[59] These youth and families did not feel that she had kept this promise.[60]

While educators, families, and youth resisted these reforms, problems mounted inside Ackerman's Renaissance schools. Ackerman's decision to replace more than half of the teachers at Renaissance schools meant that they would have the least experienced teaching staff because they were generally replaced with teachers who had less than five years of experience. Educators felt that the city's lowest-performing schools deserved the most, not the least, experienced teachers.[61] Ackerman's reforms further limited teaching and learning. She required these schools to use a lock-step, test-based curriculum called Corrective Reading and Corrective Math. In this curriculum, teachers read a prewritten script while students tapped their pencils to indicate understanding. The curriculum advanced a deficit-oriented, high-stakes-accountability, remedial approach to teaching and learning that destroyed teacher morale and student engagement. Philadelphia educators later testified in SRC meetings that this curriculum left little time for students, even young children, to ask questions or master critical skills.[62] Philadelphia families resented that their children were, in the words of one parent, "only being taught what's on the next test."[63]

Vallas's and Ackerman's Reforms Focus on Policy Metrics, Not Actual Needs

In the 2000–2001 school year, Black youth represented 65% of the city's school enrollment, followed by white (16%), Hispanic (13%), and Asian (5%) youth, and slightly more than one-third of Philadelphia school children lived below the poverty line. Germantown High School enrolled 1,475 students. Black youth made up 97% of the student body. Nearly one-third of Germantown students lived below the federal poverty line. By 2000, Germantown High School was a hyper-segregated Black school with a significant population of poor youth who struggled to meet NCLB standards.[64] In the 2002–2003 school year only 21.5% and 5.3% of Germantown students scored at or above proficient on the state-mandated tests in reading and math, respectively. In Philadelphia, 27.5% and 21.6% of students scored at proficient or better on state-mandated tests in reading and math, respectively. These test scores were substantially lower than those for the state of Pennsylvania as a whole, where 60.3% and 52.3% of students showed proficiency in reading and math, respectively.[65] These data showed a clear opportunity gap between Philadelphia schools as well as between city schools and schools in the rest of the state.[66]

To improve the performance of Germantown's state-mandated NCLB tests, Vallas replaced Germantown's popular and effective SLCs with a centralized, large, comprehensive high school structure complete with his signature standardized curriculum and assessments. Vallas also implemented zero-tolerance disciplinary policies, purchased metal detectors, and increased police presence in the school. Vallas and his allies instituted these policies and practices with one goal in mind: to quickly and efficiently bolster his schools' performance on critical NCLB measures, including test scores, attendance, and disciplinary infractions.[67]

Germantown teachers acknowledged the school's challenges, but they resented and resisted Vallas's reforms and power under the state takeover.[68] Like many Philadelphia teachers, Germantown teachers felt that the state takeover was yet another way for Republican, nonurban legislators to dictate policies and procedures to officials in Philadelphia, a majority-Black, Democratic city. They were outraged that the state takeover simultaneously blamed teachers for the school's challenges and limited the power of these teachers to shape its future.[69] They had many reasons to believe this. The state takeover made it illegal for teachers to strike and coincided with contentious contract negotiations between union teachers and elected officials. Daniel Campbell, who had taught at Germantown since the late 1990s, felt that state officials had seized control of the city's public schools to curtail the power of teachers during these and future negotiations. Campbell said, "I'm not a big union know-it-all person, but when they [state officials] came in and said that we could not strike, it just really changed everything. It gave us the feeling that you [teachers] really have no say in what we are doing."[70] Educators felt that the state officials used the takeover to blame teachers for the school's shortcomings.[71] These reforms and the takeover ignored the effects of childhood poverty, chronic underfunding, racial segregation, and urban disinvestment on the school and its community.[72]

Educators argued that Vallas's mandates and reforms forced them to adopt a narrow version of teaching and learning that seem counterproductive to what they believed promoted student achievement and engagement.[73] Caroline Maxwell, a white female educator who had taught at Germantown since the early 1990s, recalled that "kids were really learning" in the SLCs. Teachers felt that the SLCs allowed them to focus on a small group of students, collaborate with one another on curriculum, and develop relational trust with their colleagues and students.[74] Under the SLCs, teachers said that they had felt like professionals, with autonomy over their classrooms, which they lost under the reforms of NCLB and Vallas.[75] Caroline Maxwell asserted that NCLB mandates and Vallas's policies forced teachers to focus on test-taking skills rather than authentic student engagement.

The reforms contributed to disengagement and frustration among Germantown youth. Maxwell recalled that "many of our kids were bored because they were given worksheets [that emphasized test-taking skills] and when they [the students] had to take the state tests, there was just so much depression, the expectations for them was ridiculous."[76] The depression that Maxwell described about the reforms was evident in the school. During the 2007–2008 school year, dozens, if not hundreds, of Germantown High School youth refused to take the state mandated bimonthly benchmark exams and annual tests. They did not want a test company to define their worth. In protest, many Germantown students pushed the tests aside and placed their heads on the table for the duration of the testing period. Their acts of resistance, while perhaps warranted, had a negative effect on the school's aggregate test scores.[77]

Germantown teachers also resented and rejected the deficit-oriented assumptions about teachers and youth that these policies and practices promoted. These reforms did not match their own ideas about the optimal conditions for teaching and learning for students to thrive. NCLB's policy mandates and Vallas's standardized curriculum rested on the assumption that teachers must be masters of content knowledge and should adhere to research-based, test-driven teaching techniques. These policies and practices emphasized a narrow, one-size-fits-all approach to teaching and learning enforced by threatening punitive measures for schools, like Germantown, that "failed" to meet the rigid definition of academic achievement though annual yearly progress defined by school outcomes, such as attendance levels, suspension rates, and state-mandated standardized test scores. Germantown teachers resisted NCLB mandates and Vallas's reforms because these approaches limited teacher autonomy in the classroom and were counter to their ideas about teaching and learning. Educational theorists and researchers shared the teachers' sentiments; for decades they had repudiated the theories that were the foundation of NCLB policies and Vallas's reforms.[78]

In addition to these instructional challenges, the pressure to improve student outcomes using NCLB metrics exacerbated the leadership churn that had plagued Germantown High School since the 1970s. Between 2001 and 2009, Germantown had eight different principals. This turnover created an unpredictable and chaotic environment for teachers and students.[79] Deborah Grill, who spent nearly four decades teaching in Philadelphia's public schools, said that the leadership upheaval made her feel like Germantown High School "was the stepchild of the district. I really felt that . . . that the district was out to screw Germantown, I really felt that. I felt that it was a neglected school. . . . I mean look at Germantown. When I was there [from 2005 to 2009] the school went through seven principals in a span of four years."[80] Other Germantown teachers shared Grill's frustrations. Many of them believed that school officials had deliberately placed weak principals at Germantown High School so that they could later brand the school as "failing."[81]

The 2006–2007 school year represented, as one teacher said, the "lowest of the lows."[82] In the summer of 2006, school district officials appointed Rose Ford, an administrator with no high school experience, to lead Germantown High School. Ford was Germantown's fourth principal in three years. Teachers recalled that she often pitted teachers against their students, which created animosity and distrust. Ford routinely blamed and berated teachers for the school's challenges. Teachers asserted that Ford and the other administrators never set clear consequences or school norms. Teachers felt that a small, but powerful, group of disobedient students controlled the school.[83] Germantown teachers and youth feared for their safety. Annie Phillips, a Black female Germantown student, recalled that when teachers tried to reprimand students for inappropriate behavior such as swearing in class, using electronic devices, or roaming the hallways, rather than adjust their behavior, some students threatened their teachers, telling them "they were going to jump them or hit them."[84] The chaos and instability made it difficult for teachers to teach and for students to learn.

On February 23, 2007, the chaos culminated in an event that raised national attention. Frank Burd, who had taught math in Philadelphia for over 20 years, stood at his chalkboard teaching his Algebra II class at Germantown

High School. As Burd recalled, several students entered his classroom late, after the bell rang. Latecomers were routine in his classroom and the school. One of the late students, Donte Boykin, went to the back of the classroom and took his seat. A few minutes later, Burd heard loud music coming from the back of the room from a student's iPod. He asked Donte to turn the music down. He did not comply. Burd repeated his request. Finally, Burd walked to the back of the classroom and asked Donte to turn the music off. Eventually, Donte put the iPod on the desk. Burd picked up the iPod and confiscated it. Burd said, "that was the last thing I remembered."[85] According to school surveillance video footage and eyewitness testimonies, Burd walked out of the classroom and into the hallway. Donte followed him. He shoved Burd into another student, James Footman. The two students pushed Burd to the ground, punched him in the face, and pushed his head into a locker and onto the floor. Burd sustained several injuries: a broken neck, cracked vertebrae, and a brain injury. Several Germantown students came to Burd's aid after the attack. One student grabbed Burd's cell phone from his pocket, called 9-1-1, and stayed with him until help arrived. Burd left the school with broken bones, damaged vertebrae, and brain damage.[86]

Philadelphia police charged Donte Boykin and James Footman with aggravated assault and turned their case over to the court. On April 26, 2007, Donte Boykin and James Footman pled guilty. During the court proceeding, both men apologized for their behavior. Burd accepted these apologies. Boykin, who was 18, served time at a lower-security facility in Grove City, located several hours from his home, where he could finish his high school education; Footman, who turned 15 the day after the attack, served time at the state's maximum-security facility for juveniles because he had assaulted another teacher in middle school. The judge believed that this facility "would provide Footman with the remedial education, structure and intensive emotional and behavioral support that the records showed Footman needs."[87] These events illustrated the instability at Germantown High School as well as intersections between urban public schools and the carceral state.[88] The incident launched a national conversation about the level of violence inside Philadelphia's public schools.[89]

Several days after the incident occurred, school district officials held an afterschool meeting to discuss the incident and reiterate the district's zero-tolerance policy with Germantown teachers. In the meeting, teachers complained that no one had notified them of the incident when it had occurred.

Then, they cited a recent report, compiled by school district officials, that showed the haphazard disciplinary policies and practices in the city's public schools.[90] Several teachers argued that the school had failed to provide students, like James Footman, with their legally entitled supports. They had a point. Court records showed that Footman had been in and out of public and disciplinary schools throughout middle and high school. These records also showed that Germantown administrators had to provide Footman with 30 hours of help each week, including 10 hours of group counseling. They never did this.[91] To help overcome these challenges, Germantown teachers begged district officials to replace Principal Ford as soon as possible. Officials complied with these demands and opened a search for a new principal to lead the bruised and battered school.[92]

Two months after Burd's assault, school district officials appointed Michael Silverman, a Germantown resident with nearly three decades of experience in the city's public schools, as Germantown High School's new principal. Silverman inherited a school that many believed broken beyond repair. He took the position because he lived two blocks from the high school. He had grown exhausted with his liberal, mostly white, neighbors constantly complaining about the climate at Germantown High School, and then, according to him, refusing to do anything to improve it. He felt that "this job was an opening to do something about it, you know, improve the school, help the kids, and make the school better for everybody in the community because schools shouldn't be these islands in the community. They should be places where the community comes together and it's successful." He felt it was time for Germantown residents to "stop complaining [about the school] and do something about it." Finally, he said that he applied for the position because he believed that the most "experienced people need to take the hard jobs. . . . I'm really tired in the district that they send the youngest and least experienced people to places like Germantown, they come to the school they get eaten alive, and they get burned out and that's the end of them."[93]

Silverman leveraged his connections and decades of school district experience to prepare the school for the upcoming year. Silverman focused on hiring more than a dozen new teachers who were willing, and hopefully even eager, to come to a school known for its violent climate. Second, he took inventory of the school's resources. He spent weeks in the sweltering Philadelphia summer heat organizing and cataloging textbooks. He walked around the building assessing the physical plant and classroom resources. He worked closely with his building engineers to fix moldy and chipped plaster, to repair the heating unit, and to purchase new window shades. Silverman leveraged his school district connections and contacts to secure resources to improve teaching and learning inside the school. A week before the 2007–2008 school year began, Silverman called a colleague in the school district's central office, who he had known for years, to request additional desks for classrooms that needed them. The next morning, the desks arrived. For the first time in years, Germantown classrooms finally had the appropriate number of desks.[94]

A New School Leader Attempts to Rewrite
Germantown High School's Future

On September 4, 2007, Germantown faculty reported for their first day of school under Silverman's leadership. Michael Silverman told them he was happy to see them. He told them that it had been a lonely summer, but that he had spent every day preparing for the start of the school year. He wanted the school to be ready for them and their students. Silverman looked at his staff and said, "next Monday will be the most critical first day [of school] that I've ever had. To make [Germantown] successful, we need to work together." He continued, "You see, we have the chance to do something special, to show people that Germantown High School can be an effective place for kids to learn, to silence the people who want to make us something other than a public school." He finished by telling them, "there will be struggles, but we have the chance to quiet a lot of naysayers—it's in everybody's hands and hearts to make it happen." He urged them to be focused and passionate about their work, and he promised to support them. Then, he rhetorically asked, "Did you hear that? I'm here to support you. It is not last year. It is not five years ago." Silverman then encouraged them "to start making the story of Germantown High School ours and not someone else's story." He acknowledged that "right now the narrative is being dictated to us." In a short five-minute speech, Silverman acknowledged the fears and frustrations that many teachers had about the upcoming year. He encouraged them to remember they had a fresh start. It was a new school year. He assured them that he took the position to support them and to change the school's narrative. He did not need to say what he meant by "the school's narrative." Most teachers knew that Silverman was referring to a local movement among residents and leaders to take over Germantown High School and turn it into a privately managed charter school. Silverman urged teachers to realize that they had the power to stop that if they worked collectively to alter the climate and improve instruction.[95]

Even though this might have felt like an insurmountable task, many teachers believed that together they could rewrite the school's narrative. Bonnie Uditsky, who served as an assistant principal at Germantown under Ford and Silverman, recalled that Silverman felt like a "breath of fresh air."[96] Silverman allocated discretionary funds to hire four teacher coaches— experienced and respected teachers who had worked at Germantown—to mentor their peers. He used other funds to reinvigorate the school's extra-curricular programs and pay teachers to start clubs and activities inside the school. He collaborated with external partners, such as the Germantown Clergy Initiative, a consortium of religious leaders with a vested interest and commitment to the school. He courted leaders of Philadelphia Academies, Inc., a Philadelphia nonprofit, to create and implement new small learning communities focused on academic and career outcomes.[97]

Silverman's leadership improved the relationship between Germantown's teachers and its administration. Daniel Campbell, who had taught at the school for nearly a decade, recalled that the 2007–2008 school year felt like "the first year that I actually wanted to stay at Germantown." "In the past," he reported, "I stayed for the kids, but now I have a leader who makes it easier for me to want to stay." Campbell said, Silverman was the first principal "that actually came in here with a vision and he says, I'm going to be here [at Germantown] for six years . . . he's not bouncing around from here to there. He wants to do something with the school, we've never had that."[98] Other teachers shared these sentiments. John Grayford, a white male first-year teacher, said that Silverman "definitely has a goal and vision for the school." Silverman created an inclusive environment where "everyone in the school is included" in planning for the school's future.[99] Similarly, Tim Hopkins, who had taught at the school for four years, felt that Silverman supported teachers in their classroom. In an interview, Hopkins said, "Mr. Silverman has a much better idea of what it feels like to be in a classroom with 33 or 35 students." Hopkins noted that Silverman was the first administrator who wanted to support teachers in the classroom. Hopkins felt that he could meet with Silverman and openly discuss any problems or questions he had about his teaching practice.[100]

Germantown students also felt that Silverman's leadership improved the relationship that they had with their school and, ultimately, strengthened their educational experience. During virtually every class transition, Silverman walked the hallways with other administrators and Germantown High School's 13 police officers. He urged his colleagues to greet students and interact with them. He collaborated with community volunteers, including local clergy, to greet students and monitor the streets before and after school. Silverman said that creating a new culture around discipline was his primary aim when he came to the school. He said, "I run all over this building . . . to interact with people, to show them that you *talk* to people, to show them that you are *interested* in learning more about their job." Over the summer, he worked with school administrators, teachers, and police to develop clear disciplinary processes and school norms. He articulated these processes and norms to students on the first day of school. He implemented a proactive approach to discipline so that administrators could "figure out where the problems are going to start and be there before they do."[101]

Germantown educators and youth asserted that Silverman's care and visibility changed their relationship with school administrators. Emily Sanders, a white woman who had taught at the school since the late 1990s, recalled that Silverman "supported a lot of people, he was outside every morning, shaking the kids' hands, saying good morning to each of them . . . that was huge." Sanders said that Silverman made himself accessible to teachers and students, "he was always willing to discuss anything."[102] Annie Phillips, a Black female student, said "I see Mr. Silverman all the time. He is always speaking to the students, helping people out and everything, he comes in our classes and talks to us about school and why it's important to finish."[103] James Downing, a Black male student, agreed and said that Silverman "isn't just walking the hallways, he cares about you and asks how you are doing in class and stuff like that."[104] Germantown educators and youth asserted that Silverman created a caring environment where teachers and youth felt seen and heard. His leadership generated a sense of relational trust among administrators, educators, and youth that had not existed in earlier years.[105]

Even though many people felt a renewed sense of hope, low teacher morale stymied school-wide change. As one teacher said, some of her colleagues felt, "the new principal is great, but we can't save this place." Some of her colleagues refused to engage with the new administrators and would rather "kick up their heels" than do the work that the school reform required them to do.[106] These teachers' sentiments stemmed from decades of disinvestment and neglect in the community and school, which left them feeling demoralized and devalued as teachers in a system that never had the public resources to support its schools, but that now under NCLB had the power to use teachers as scapegoats for its systemic shortcomings. These teachers refused to believe that together they could change the structural challenges that affected their daily lives as teachers in an institution that city and school officials had abandoned for decades. They resented being blamed for the challenges that Germantown High School faced due to this disinvestment and neglect, and thus, some teachers refused to exert their energy on Silverman's vision for the school and, ultimately, undermined the reform that Silverman and others tried to implement.[107]

Germantown teachers recognized the changes under Silverman's leadership, but they remained frustrated with the other school district officials. Teachers asserted that district officials mandated policies and programs but then routinely refused to give Germantown teachers the resources needed to implement them. For example, district officials mandated Read 180, a new district-wide reading program, to bolster the district's NCLB state-mandated test scores. When school district officials visited Germantown to evaluate the program, they reprimanded teachers for implementing the program incorrectly. The program required small classrooms, no more than 15 students, with one computer for each student. Germantown High School did not have any classes with 15 students because the school did not have enough teachers to create these small classes. Likewise, they did not have enough computers to institute the one-to-one policy that the program required. Deborah Grill recalled that the program "was never set up to run well. Never. . . . It was as if [Germantown High School teachers] were set up to fail. We never had the resources that we needed to succeed."[108] The mismatch between the demands that school district officials placed on teachers and the realities that teachers faced inside Germantown generated animosity and anger between officials and teachers like Grill who remained deeply committed to improving classroom instruction and school outcomes. Under Vallas and Ackerman, school officials were much more concerned with meeting federal and state mandates than the school and community's needs and demands.

While students recognized that Silverman created a more welcoming school environment, Silverman's reforms could not eradicate the adverse effects of poverty and racism. During high school, Angela Foster, a poor Black

female student, moved frequently. In 9th and 11th grade, she lived with
her mother in North Carolina. In 10th and 12th grade, Angela lived with her
grandmother in Philadelphia. Angela recalled that moving every other year
made it difficult to develop relationships with her teachers and peers. Poverty compounded these challenges. Angela's grandmother had Alzheimer's
disease and could not work. Angela served as her grandmother's primary
caregiver and worked several afterschool jobs as the sole income earner in
the home. Even though her mother tried to help her financially, Angela said
that her grandmother's debilitating illness and financial insecurity strained
her ability to concentrate on school.[109]

Angela was not alone. During her senior year, Maggie Johnson, another
poor, Black female student, left her family's chaotic home. Johnson recalled
that she initially moved from "house to house" sleeping in her friends' spare
bedrooms or on family room couches and then eventually lived in a North
Philadelphia homeless shelter. Maggie missed the first two months of the
2007–2008 school year. When she tried to reregister for school, administrators told her that school district policy required that a parent or legal guardian register her. Maggie explained that she did not have a parent or legal
guardian to do this. Administrators refused to bend the rules. Maggie was
only 17 years old. A parent or guardian had to sign the paperwork. After
weeks of frustration and delay, Maggie convinced her estranged mother to
sign the paperwork for her to attend her old high school, Germantown High.
Maggie filled out the paperwork; her mother signed it. Maggie met with
school counselors to finalize her schedule later that afternoon. The school
counselors informed Maggie that she had to retake several courses that she
had either missed or failed.

In her interview, Maggie said, "starting school two months late was
really hard. Just trying to focus on the work, not knowing [what I missed],
because I wasn't [t]here. . . . [Teachers] were giving me work and telling me
what to do. I had no idea what it was." She struggled academically in her
courses because she had missed two full months of instruction. She also
described the challenges that she faced socially and emotionally. Even
though she should have been a senior, she had to take classes that she had
failed with sophomores and juniors. She resented being in classes with students that she did not know, saying, "I'm 17 years old and I'm in class with
15-year-olds. I won't graduate until 2009, and everything that I was sup-
posed to do this year, my senior trip, my senior prom, I won't be able to do.
I'll be doing it next year with people I don't even know. People I'm not even

friends with." Despite these setbacks, Maggie expressed her desire to complete her high school education: "only two people, my brother and my cousin, have graduated from high school [in my family], for me, I want to be the third person. School is my life." She continued, saying, "My brother is my role model . . . he always says time will pass, he always says, school is important. Without an education, what else do you have?"[110] She had a vision for her future: she wanted to graduate from high school, attend college, and become a writer. Maggie understood that the odds were against her. She wanted to defy those odds.

Even though they could not eradicate youth poverty or structural racism, Germantown administrators, faculty, and staff did what they could to help poor Black youth. They offered to take their students' clothes home and wash them. They gave them money to buy food and to commute to school. They allowed students to use their cell phones to speak to their families and secure housing. But there was a fundamental difference between these efforts to alleviate poverty among Germantown students compared to those in the early 20th century. In the past, teachers often relied on the community's privately funded social service agencies to provide youth resources and supports. In the early 21st century, organizations that had sustained and supported poor youth—the YMCAs, YWCAs, Boys Clubs, and settlements—had either closed or curtailed their services.[111] At the turn of the 21st century, Germantown teachers had to do this work on their own. School district officials implemented reforms to improve NCLB metrics, not alleviate poverty. The reforms did not match what the students needed. Faculty did what they could, but the absence of these institutions, the mismatch between school reforms and student needs, and the rise in childhood poverty made this an impossible task.

Less than a year after he assumed his role as principal of Germantown High School, Michael Silverman accepted a new position as a regional superintendent. He accepted the position hoping that he could implement systemic change in the school district where he had worked for nearly three decades. When she heard the news, Emily Sanders recalled feeling "thrilled for him, but devastated for Germantown." School district officials appointed two interim principals to oversee the school during the 2008–2009 school year. Sanders described the interim principals as individuals "who did their job, but . . . were there to tread water." According to her, neither of these principals "made any changes." She felt that the appointment of these interim principals marked the "beginning of the end."[112] Germantown High

School, once again, had a leadership vacuum. Teachers felt defeated and exhausted. Eventually, in the 2009–2010 school year, school district officials appointed Margaret Mullen principal—the fifth principal in four years. For the next two years, Mullen tried to build on the vision that Silverman had started, but Ackerman's top-down, rapid-fire reforms undermined this work.

Germantown High School Is Slated for Ackerman's Promise Academy Reform

On January 25, 2011, school district officials announced plans to turn Germantown into a Promise Academy, a traditional public school with longer school days, Saturday-morning classes, and heavily scripted curricula, under school district control and management. Teacher hiring was another key feature of this reform: school district officials planned to rehire no more than half of Germantown's current teachers. Once again, Ackerman blamed Germantown teachers for the school's shortcomings. Officials promised to retain Mullen as the school principal since she had been at the school for less than two years.[113]

On February 17, 2011, school district officials hosted a community meeting at Germantown High School to outline the Promise Academy reform. In her opening, Margaret Mullen told the 50 or so Germantown families, alumni, teachers, and students gathered that when she took her job she "had a lot of cleaning up to do." Mullen said that the Promise Academy reform reflected the vision that she had tried to implement over the past two years. She viewed the reform as a way for the school, which had 9 principals in 10 years, to have consistent leadership. School district officials explained that the reform required longer school days and Saturday-morning classes. Officials assured listeners that they would provide additional funds and programs to increase educational supports and outcomes despite the news about district-wide budget shortfalls. Vera Primus, the head of the Germantown alumni association, praised Mullen. She told listeners that under Mullen's leadership the school's attendance rate has increased from about 70% to 80%, that suspensions had dropped from nearly 600 the previous year to about 350, and that for the first time in eight years, Germantown had been taken off the state's "persistently dangerous" schools list. Primus acknowledged that the school's test scores remained low, but she argued that the Promise Academy reform aimed to change that. Next, Danielle Dixon and her son, Simone, who transferred to Germantown, spoke about the school's strengths. The speakers seemed optimistic and hopeful about the proposed reform. No one mentioned the effects of urban disinvestment, racial segregation, or childhood poverty on the school and its youth.[114]

While some residents focused on the Promise Academy reform, others worried that school officials might close Germantown High School. A few days before the community meeting took place, Dale Mezzacappa, an experienced educational journalist, published a piece entitled "Finally, It's Closing Time," in which she discussed the school district's plans to assess and close dozens of Philadelphia public schools due to low enrollment and shrinking funds. Enrollment in the district hovered around 160,000 students, slightly more than half of what it was at its peak of nearly 300,000 in 1970. District officials attributed the decline in enrollment to urban flight and charter school expansion. In 2011, Philadelphia's charter schools educated more than 40,000 students. Germantown felt these pains. In 1970, the school enrolled over 4,000 students. By 2011, that number had shrunk to about 800 students. The dramatic decrease in enrollment stemmed from the larger structural and institutional forces that eroded support for the school. For decades, middle-class residents—both Black and white—left the city's schools for neighboring suburbs or opted for other high school options—private, parochial, and special-admit schools, and now, in the 21st century, charter schools. Ackerman and her deputies had already begun an internal design to close schools in an effort to "right size" its physical plant. At the time, school district officials refused to provide details on the process or a timeline for when closures might begin, but it was clear that Germantown might not survive.[115]

Even though many educators recognized that the Promise Academy might be the last chance to save Germantown from closure, they did not share the speakers' hope and optimism about the reform. Caroline Maxwell noted that from the beginning the staff felt that the Promise Academy reforms were yet another way for school officials "to get rid of teachers." Maxwell described the reform as "a takeover where you automatically get rid of staff which is kind of crazy." "Maybe some were not good," she said, "but they got rid of a lot of good teachers. That was really sad to me." Maxwell explained that between March and April, Germantown staff had an opportunity to reapply for their positions. Many teachers resented that Ackerman and her allies blamed them for the school's shortcomings, and when the interviews opened, they refused to reapply. Many teachers used their seniority to secure new positions in more reputable and traditionally managed public schools.

Mullen refused to rehire some of the teachers who did reapply. Emily Sanders said that the whole process felt like "a nightmare. It was demeaning to the staff because you had to reapply. It generated bad feelings toward the administration and set staff member against staff member."[116] Maxwell and Sanders reapplied for their positions and stayed. Still, Maxwell recalled that when the school opened as Promise Academy, she felt somewhat "like a refugee . . . , kicked out of your own home, you might find a place to go, but they took a part of you. They made you feel bad about yourself."[117] The collective depression of the returning staff made it difficult to restart the school year; the fact that most of the teachers were new to the school made the task even more difficult.[118]

The School District of Philadelphia Faces
Yet Another Fiscal Crisis

On March 30, 2011, the SRC announced that it faced an unprecedented $629 million budget deficit, which stemmed from the end of federal stimulus funds, the costs of Ackerman's reforms, the expansion of charter schools, and the decision by a new, Republican governor, Tom Corbett, to slash education funding. Fearing cuts to essential programs and resources, educators, families, and youth testified at SRC meetings and staged citywide rallies decrying Corbett's decision to cut $550 million in basic education funding while at the same time allocating $650 million to build three new prisons. As the SRC detailed the grim budget forecast, nearly 1,500 individuals marched on Broad Street, chanting "close down the jail house, open up the school house." Like others across the nation, Philadelphia youth and other educational advocates protested the expansion of the school-to-prison pipeline, which now threatened to shift millions of dollars from basic education to Pennsylvania's prisons.[119] While these advocates marched, school officials outlined their proposals to address the deficit: eliminating full-day kindergarten, laying off almost 4,000 educators, and closing dozens of public schools.[120]

Philadelphia public school families criticized these proposals and urged state officials to provide additional school funding. Affluent white families admitted that the budget cuts challenged their commitment to the city's public schools because these cuts affected their children's schools. Many of these families had, perhaps, never experienced this because their class and racial privileges had shielded them from the realities that many poor, Black, and Latinx families had experienced for decades: insufficient public school funding.[121] Upper- and middle-class white families threatened to leave the city and its public schools if the budget cuts continued.[122] The arguments that these families made sounded vaguely familiar to the ones that George Darrow and others had made nearly a century earlier during the campaign to secure funds for Germantown High School: bourgeois white families threatened to leave the city if they did not have access to the educational resources and opportunities that they felt *their* children deserved.

A few days later, Philadelphia's SRC passed a budget that slashed basic educational services. In response, Mayor Michael Nutter passed an educational accountability agreement, which required Ackerman and the SRC to share "all documents, material, and briefings" with the mayor or his deputy.[123] The agreement went into effect on June 9, 2011. On June 25, 2011, reports surfaced that school officials had previously drafted a document detailing a comprehensive strategy to close and consolidate dozens of public schools. School officials violated the city's educational accountability agreement because they had not disclosed the document to the mayor.[124] On August 22, Mayor Nutter announced that he was working with the SRC to end Ackerman's contract, a decision that the SRC and Ackerman had mutually agreed to almost two months earlier. Nutter assured his constituents that he had negotiated terms to minimize the buyout costs to the taxpayers, with $405,000 of the total $905,000 funded with private money to appease taxpayers who were outraged that she received any buyout given the school district's fiscal conditions. Later that afternoon, Nutter and the SRC chair appointed Leroy Nunery as Ackerman's temporary replacement. Nutter and Nunery acknowledged in a joint statement "that recent events have made some key stakeholders question the leadership and direction of the School District of Philadelphia. We know we have work to do to earn their trust once again. We are committed to doing so."[125] These words carried little weight among Philadelphians who had been asking elected officials and school leaders to listen and respond to their concerns for decades.

A School System Transformed
by Privatization and Standardization

The narrow, standardized reforms that Vallas and Ackerman instituted first under President George W. Bush's No Child Left Behind Act and then under

President Obama's Race to the Top generated a narrow and often punitive version of teaching and learning that did little to address childhood poverty, racial inequities, and urban disinvestment. These reforms shattered teacher morale and student engagement, particularly in Philadelphia's hypersegregated, majority-poor, majority-Black, and majority-Latinx neighborhood schools. The state takeover catalyzed school privatization. Under Vallas and Ackerman, the School District of Philadelphia transformed from a system of public schools into a system of private charter organizations, some of which had little accountability to the families and city that they served. Vallas and Ackerman, desperate to improve standardized test scores and eager to provide new schooling options, supported the privatization movement that state officials pushed through. And yet, when the dust cleared from the destruction of the city's public school system, results showed that the city's charter schools drained millions of dollars from the city's public schools and did little to improve the educational outcomes of the youth that attended them. The reforms never addressed the sources of inequities—childhood poverty, racial segregation, and urban disinvestment.

When one takes a closer look inside Germantown High School, the top-down, market-based reforms that Vallas and Ackerman implemented failed to provide the kind of changes that the school actually needed and, thus, stymied educational improvements. At the same time, the mismatch between school district policies and practices and the school's actual needs reflected the long arc of the school's history. When the school district opened Germantown High School at the turn of the 20th century, there was a mismatch between the public revenues that school officials had at their disposal and the funds that public schools needed to provide a robust education to their youth. Germantown's affluent white families donated private funding and resources to alleviate this shortcoming. After *Brown v. Board of Education*, there was a mismatch between school district rhetoric and its actions to desegregate Philadelphia's public schools. School officials repeatedly assured residents that they did not discriminate on the basis of race. And yet, officials passed policies and implemented practices that perpetuated and often exacerbated racial inequities. In the 21st century, there was a mismatch between the push to meet federal and state policy mandates and the demands of Germantown educators, families, and youth. Germantown educators felt that reform required additional funding and professional autonomy not scripted curricula and zero-tolerance policies.

While the structural constraints that the school faced clearly shaped its story, its history also illuminates the possibility of change—when the school had committed leadership, when the teachers had a chance to dream, and when students felt visible and cared for. School administrators and teachers, particularly under Silverman's short time at the school, argued that they needed time to show that their ideas had merit and that they could determine Germantown High School's future. Neither Vallas nor Ackerman gave them the time that they felt that they needed to improve educational outcomes. Families and youth shared these views, but they also argued that they needed programs and policies to address poverty, homelessness, and racism in their city, community, and school. Vallas's and Ackerman's top-down mandates never did that. And as the Philadelphia's SRC searched for yet another person willing to take over the school district, many Germantown educators and families seriously worried that their school, which had suffered decades of neglect and disinvestment, might be one of Philadelphia's public schools slated for closure.

CHAPTER 9

_____

School Officials Close Schools to "Save"
Philadelphia's Public School System

On December 13, 2012, William Hite, Philadelphia's newly appointed superintendent of schools, announced that the School District of Philadelphia planned to close 37 schools—22 elementary, 4 middle, and 11 high schools—to save revenues and increase efficiencies. Germantown High School was one of the schools slated for closure. Hite promised to use the millions of dollars saved through these closures to implement innovative educational programs and remodel Philadelphia's outdated schools and facilities. Hite asserted:

> As we navigate this journey, we are guided by the belief that all students in The School District of Philadelphia can and will be successful, and that public education is an institution worth saving. For years, the number of buildings that we maintained has not reflected our enrollment. In this harsh financial climate, we must use our resources wisely to provide students with quality academic programs, increased access to opportunities and more chances to learn and thrive in safe, modernized schools. . . . As an educator and parent, I realize these recommendations will be shocking, painful and disruptive for many communities, not least of all our students, staff and families. However, we believe that at the end of this process, our school system will be better run, safer and higher performing. Ultimately, this is an opportunity for us to evaluate the overall state of public education in Philadelphia. It is a chance for us to consider the kind of school district that we want not only for our current students, but those to come.[1]

According to Hite, some public schools had to close to protect the future of the public school system.

When school officials announced these planned closures, they noted the school district's dire fiscal situation, including the projected $218-million-dollar budget shortfall. In 2011, Governor Tom Corbett, Pennsylvania's new Republican governor, had slashed education funding by over $1 billion. Corbett's education cuts had a disproportionate effect on Philadelphia—the state's largest, poorest, and most racially diverse city. Philadelphia endured 30% of the state's funding cuts even though it educated 12% of the state's schoolchildren. Under Corbett's new budget proposal, Philadelphia lost 13% of its state educational funds while the state's 499 other school districts received a 3% increase.[2] The expansion of charter schools in the city over the past few decades had intensified the school district's financial problems. Between 2000 and 2010, the district lost 50,000 public school students due to the expansion of the city's charter schools—an expansion that many state legislators, including some from Philadelphia, enthusiastically supported.[3] The exodus of 50,000 students generated a loss of over $500 million in public funds. To cope with these cuts, the School District of Philadelphia slashed its workforce by 17% and argued that school closures were necessary to stave off a fiscal disaster.[4]

From December 2012 to February 2013, Superintendent Hite and his colleagues hosted community meetings throughout the city for Philadelphians to voice their ideas, perspectives, and concerns about the proposed school closures. In every meeting, school officials reiterated the fact that the school district had lost tens of thousands of students and now had empty seats in many public schools. Closing these schools, school officials argued, saved the school district millions of dollars in operational costs. These savings made it possible to invest more resources in the public schools that remained open. In a meeting hosted at Martin Luther King Jr. High School, Superintendent Hite told his constituents, "It should have been done years ago. . . . We have [empty] seats available for 53,000 students in our schools and the money that it has cost us to maintain those seats can be better utilized for different resources for students, different programs, different facilities . . . better professional development." School officials tried to reassure families that they were studying the landscape of the proposed school closures to ensure that children would be safe during the closure and transfer process. Officials promised that every child affected by these school closures would be able to choose from a variety of alternative schooling options.[5] In each of these meetings, school district officials created a narrative of inevitability about these closures, a narrative that used technocratic and fiscal rationales to justify the necessity and urgency of these closures.[6]

After they presented their case, school officials gave Philadelphia youth, families, educators, and activists three minutes to voice their concerns about the school closures and the effects that they might have on their children and communities. In their three-minute remarks, homeowners worried that their properties might lose their value if the district closed schools in their communities. Others raised concerns about gentrification once the district officials sold their shuttered schools to private developers. Still others voiced fears about violence. Closing schools would force youth to travel further to school, which might threaten their safety. Families worried about young children crossing busy streets and older children crossing neighborhood boundaries. Others felt that school officials had targeted their schools for closure without understanding the progress that educators had made in these schools. Vera Primus, the head of the Germantown High School alumni association, criticized school officials for placing her alma mater on the school closure list. Primus argued that the school had made significant progress in the past few years and invited school officials to "come and visit our school to see what we are all about."[7] To show their frustration and opposition to the threat of closure, Germantown High School educators placed a banner at the entrance of the school that read "Open Schools Create Open Minds, Closed Schools Breed Closed Minds" (figure 22).

On March 7, 2013, nearly 700 people gathered outside of the school district's Broad Street headquarters to protest the SRC's upcoming vote about the school closures. American Federation of Teachers (AFT) president Randi Weingarten told the crowd that studies showed that school closures do not improve academic outcomes. Students from activist groups such as Philadelphia Student Union and Youth United for Change testified about the effects of school closure on their lives and the lives of their teachers. Others held signs that said, "THIS IS ABOUT RACISM + Greed." These signs reminded residents in Philadelphia that, as figure 23 illustrates, the school district's proposed school closures disproportionately impacted low-income communities of color. Students put duct tape across their mouths to illustrate that the SRC had silenced their voices. More than a dozen protesters tried to block the doors to prevent the SRC from entering the building and starting the meeting. Police arrested 19 individuals, including Weingarten. Inside the SRC's meeting room, activists, educators, and parents voiced their

Figure 22. "Open Schools Create Open Minds, Closed Schools Breed Closed Minds" Banner, Germantown High School, 2012–2013. Photo by Erika Kitzmiller.

dismay. One individual told officials that closing the schools in Germantown represented "an empty reminder of how the district and the city abandoned the children of Germantown."[8] Representative Stephen Kinsey, Representative Cindy Bass, and Germantown principal Margaret Mullen testified at the SRC to keep Germantown High School open. Despite the appeals, on March 7, 2013, the SRC voted to close 23 public schools, including the 99-year-old Germantown High School.[9]

After they learned that district officials intended to close the school, Germantown High School teachers expressed their frustrations with a system that they felt had neglected poor, Black youth for decades and forced educators to adopt reforms, such as the Promise Academy, that set them up to fail. These feelings were rooted in frustration that their colleagues, many of whom had been dedicated to the institution for decades, needed to find new positions in schools and communities and that their students, who often struggled with the challenges associated with urban poverty, had to attend new schools in neighborhoods where they might not be welcomed. One teacher said, "the school had been deprived of resources for years, the student body had been siphoned off by magnet and charter schools, and staff

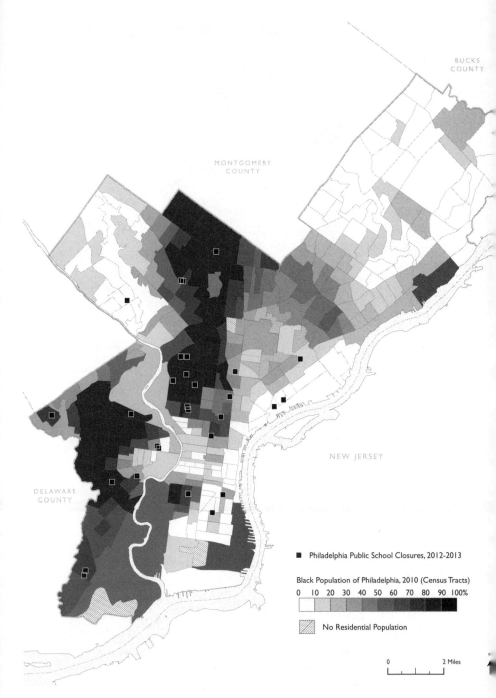

Figure 23. Philadelphia Public School Closures, 2012–2013, and Percentage of Black Residents by Census Tract, 2010. Source: United States Census, 2010.

were driven off by district initiatives, such as Promise Academies and administrative changes. [The SRC's decision to close the school] felt like a set up."[10]

Germantown teachers and students were also angry that school officials had not adequately thought about the transition process and the effects of these school closures on Germantown High School youth.[11] Shortly after the SRC announced its decision to close Germantown High School, many students refused to come to school. Teachers tried to remind students that they needed to pass their classes and that their grades affected their future. But, as one teacher said, many of the students were outraged at the district's decision; "for some of them, [Germantown High School] was the only family they had; it was their only security."[12] Fearful that her students would have less support or be lost in their new schools, one special education teacher called the closure a "death sentence" for her students.[13]

On June 17, 2013, the community gathered to celebrate Germantown High School's 99-year history. During the ceremony, Germantown High School seniors paraded around the school building in their graduation caps and gowns while teachers, parents, and residents applauded the students' achievements. Margaret Mullen, the school's retired principal, praised the students for supporting her efforts to "turn this school around and bring it back to the way that everyone remembered it . . . as the best school in the northwest" part of Philadelphia. The crowd roared. Mullen asked the graduates to "continue the fight and remember always Germantown High School, the school that turned everything around for you in your life and turned a school around for this community." Former administrators, teachers, and alumni spoke about their "excellent school" and "magnificent institution" and vowed to fight to keep the school open for future generations.[14] Two days later, Germantown High School hosted its final commencement ceremony. On June 21, 2013, teachers removed their belongings from the building and shut the doors to Germantown High School for the very last time.[15]

From the moment that news broke that the school district planned to close Germantown High School, concerned alumni, elected officials, and local residents banded together to perpetuate a narrative of the school as having a glorious history as a safe and caring institution that supported everyone who walked through its magnificent entranceway. In the final months of the 2012–2013 school year, Germantown High School alumni initiated discussions about the future of the school building and continued to pressure the SRC to reconsider its plans.[16] Newspaper reporters interviewed prominent alumni, including Kevin Eubanks, Patricia Newton, and Ralph Roberts, to illustrate the school's legacy.[17] Although many alumni voiced their concerns about Germantown High School's closure, reporter Benjamin Herold pointed out that their actions pitted their own sentiments and nostalgia against data and reality. Many of the alumni who advocated to keep Germantown High School open already lived outside the city, where they enjoyed lower taxes and better-resourced public schools. The small percentage of Germantown alumni who remained in the area rarely sent their children to Germantown High School.[18] William Hite understood this tension between the residents' sentiments and the school's data. Hite told constituents that he wanted to make district-managed schools "an option when parents are making their decisions about where to send their children. Right now, unfortunately, the district becomes a default option for individuals who do not get to choose something else."[19] Closing these schools, he argued, represented the first step in this process because it would free up millions of dollars that could be used to strengthen other schools.

In the fall of 2013, Germantown High School teachers who had enough seniority to retain their positions found themselves scattered in new schools. Most students transferred to Germantown High School's long-time rival, Martin Luther King Jr. High School.[20] Facing even larger fiscal problems due to another round of state cuts to education, Mayor Michael Nutter and Superintendent Hite announced the creation of a new fund, the Philadelphia Education Supplies Fund, to raise philanthropic contributions "to purchase supplemental classroom supplies, including workbooks, paper, pens and pencils."[21] The funds that Hite and Nutter solicited never met the school district's actual needs, and to save costs, the school district laid off 3,783 employees—including all its school librarians, most of its school nurses, and hundreds of school counselors. These cuts forced many educators and activists to question whether Philadelphia's public schools were schools or just custodial buildings for its youth.[22]

The Rhetoric of the "Failing" American High School Often Downplays the Institution's Bourgeois Origins and Its Shaky Fiscal Foundation

Today, numerous reform efforts assert that American high schools are broken, that they worked well in the past but now fail to meet 21st-century needs. This argument obscures the history of urban high schools in this country and promotes a false sense of hope that high school reform, alone, can change the inequities that we witness in society today.[23] As the Germantown High School story illustrates, even though these institutions clearly helped some youth, high schools at the turn of the 20th century were not the social engines that many had hoped that they might be or that many of us remember them as.[24] Rather, many American high schools were institutions that were largely reserved for white elite youth who were destined for a bourgeois life as professionals and wives. A high school education did not guarantee social mobility. Instead, the expansion of American high schools in the late 19th and early 20th centuries often reproduced and perpetuated inequality based on race and class.[25] As journalist and MacArthur Fellow Nikole Hannah-Jones said, "Our public schools are not broken, but are operating as designed. Our public schools were set up to provide unequal, inadequate education for Black children . . . that's what they do."[26]

To understand the magnitude of the challenges that urban schools face, scholars, educators, and activists need to push the story back and consider how the fiscal structures in place at the turn of the 20th century set the stage for the challenges that urban schools currently face. There is no question that poverty in Philadelphia, the poorest of the nation's 10 largest cities, escalated to a point that the leaders of the Germantown High School campaign might not have been able to anticipate. In 2018, nearly 1 in 4 Philadelphia residents live below the federal poverty level; more than 1 in 10 lived in deep poverty. In 2018, the poverty line for a household of four was $25,100 and the deep poverty line was $12,550 in annual income. This rate has remained consistent for the past 10 years. The rates are even higher for children.[27] In 2016, 37% of Philadelphia children under the age of 18 lived below the federal poverty line of $19,337 in annual income for an adult living with two children.[28] As David Volkman, Pennsylvania's executive assistant secretary of education, said: "we really don't have an education crisis in this country, we have a child poverty crisis, which not only impacts education . . . it also impacts a child's ability to become everything he or she was born to be."[29] The COVID-19 pandemic has intensified these challenges.[30]

The shortage of public funds for Philadelphia's public schools exacerbated the challenges that the city has faced as it tries to take care of and educate its youth. A January 2018 report published by the United States Commission on Civil Rights argues that fiscal inequities and school resegregation have contributed to educational inequities based on class, race, and

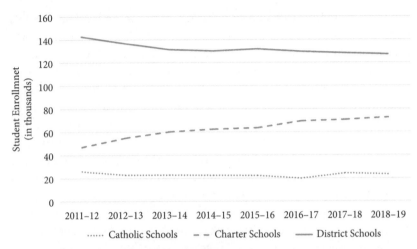

Figure 24. K-12 School Enrollment, 2011–2019.
Source: "The State of Education in Philadelphia," https://www.pewtrusts.org/-
/media/assets/2019/03/state_of_education.pdf.

space throughout the nation. The report noted that Pennsylvania, perhaps
more than any other state, exemplifies the problems of funding inequities
between low-income and high-income communities. High-income communities spend approximately 30% more per pupil than low-income communities. In 2012, Pennsylvania school districts' expenditures per pupil varied
about $2,500 from the state's average or by a factor of 16.8%. The state's
poorest rural districts spent about $8,700 per pupil while Philadelphia, the
county with the largest number of poor and youth of color, spent about
$13,000 per pupil. Affluent suburban districts, most of which border the city
of Philadelphia, spent up to $26,600 per pupil. These funding inequities
have a significant impact on the schooling experiences of children in each of
these jurisdictions. As one Pennsylvania parent noted in her testimony to
the commission, schools with lower per-pupil expenditures often have "larger
class sizes, fewer academic options, older buildings, less technology, and
fewer art, music, and gym classes." The report acknowledges that teachers in
low-income schools purchase supplies for their classrooms with their own
funds, however, the report does not acknowledge the way that private philanthropy has contributed and sustained resource inequities between and
within school districts.[31] Moreover, it pays scant attention to the ways that the
expansion of charter schools in Philadelphia has drained thousands of students and millions of dollars from the city's public schools (see figure 24).

Even though the funding inequities and school resegregation that have taken place in the post-*Brown* era have had a significant effect on the ability of the nation's public schools to provide an equitable educational experience to all youth, the Germantown story highlights the ways that class, race, and space interacted to generate longstanding educational inequalities and fiscal inequities in urban schools since their founding at the turn of the 20th century. Germantown High School never had the public funds it needed to operate. Private residents supplemented inadequate public budgets with private aid to give their white bourgeois youth who attended Germantown's prestigious school more resources and money, and ultimately, an educational advantage over low-income immigrant and Black youth who attended less-resourced schools near their homes in the city's center. When it was founded, Germantown High School represented a doubly advantaged school.

When Germantown High School opened in 1914, the community's bourgeois residents recognized the importance of having a first-rate academic high school tucked away neatly in their "suburb in the city."[32] The school community—its faculty, families, residents, and youth—donated funds to subsidize the city's insufficient public budgets. The influx of private money guaranteed that Germantown's new high school had the resources to provide upper- and upper-middle-class white youth with the educational experiences that their families demanded. From its founding, Germantown High School served as a community anchor and attracted other upper- and upper-middle-class families to the area, in large part because of the reputation of Germantown's public schools. However, while Germantown's bourgeois white elite benefited from the influx of this private funding, Black and immigrant youth in the city's center attended underfunded and overcrowded schools because their families could not afford to provide private funding to their schools. These resource inequities generated inequality based on class, race, and space as schools in the city's periphery, which served primarily white upper- and upper-class youth, enjoyed many more resources than those schools that served primarily Black and immigrant working-class youth in the city's center.

This private funding structure extended beyond the high school. Throughout the first half of the 20th century, Germantown residents donated to an array of social service agencies that offered additional educational and recreational experiences to community youth. As this story demonstrates, these agencies provided critical supports to middle- and low-income youth and their families and protected the community's reputation as a safe place for young families to raise their children. The high school community raised funds to help low-income youth defray school-related expenses. Low-income Black youth participated in programs and activities at the community's YMCAs, Boys Clubs, and settlement organizations under the guidance of highly skilled educators. These youth learned nonacademic skills, such as conscientiousness, perseverance, and sociability, soft skills that have been associated with long-term gains in economic and social mobility, particularly among low-income youth.[33]

Over time, the upper-class white patrons who donated thousands of dollars to support the public schools and these social service organizations moved out of the city, forcing many of these agencies to cut programs and staff at the very moment that poverty in the community skyrocketed. Educational policymakers have overlooked the importance of such institutions and the skills that they promote. Most educational reforms have focused instead on increasing academic achievement measured by narrowly conceived standardized tests.[34] With the exception of a handful of schools that served Philadelphia's elite and receive private funds from their families, in 2013, the city's public schools cut virtually all extracurricular activities— arts, music, sports, and other programs—because the school district did not have the funding to support what many considered nonessential programs. Research suggests that extracurricular programs are critical sites for social and emotional development and supporting long-term educational outcomes. These programs should be restored to Philadelphia's public schools.[35]

The story of this one city and high school pushes us, as scholars, taxpayers, educators, and activists, to understand how class, race, and space generated inequality in the past and to think about how this inequality impacts individuals today, in Philadelphia and other cities. Rhetoric about the national- or district-level failures of our public schools desensitize us to the individuals behind Philadelphia's 2013 $218 million budget shortfall, its 3,787 staff layoffs, and its 24 public school closures. Situating the story of this high school in the context of its city allows us to examine how the city's changes affected the public school system and to acknowledge the ways that racism limited opportunities for Black youth inside this one high school. This ground-level view forces us to grapple with the factors that contributed to educational inequality and how this inequality shaped the lives of youth based on race and class well before white flight, failed desegregation, and neoliberal reforms.

There is no question that overall school funding has expanded dramatically in the United States since 1965.[36] Even though the nation now spends more on public schools than it did in 1965, the loss of middle-class taxpayers, the escalation of poverty, and the erosion of social welfare programs has strained the School District of Philadelphia for decades. In Philadelphia, elected officials, local educators, and committed activists have framed Philadelphia's current budget challenges as natural consequences that stemmed from the state's decision to alter its funding formula in 1991, or even worse, they blame youth they characterize as beyond reach and teachers they view as lazy and overpaid and with costly pensions as the root causes of the challenges that the city's public schools face. It is true that the state's decisions have had a significant impact on the city's ability to fund its schools. But the budget crisis that the school district faces in the early 21st century also existed in the past. Philadelphia has never had the public funds needed to operate its public schools.

Beginning at the turn of the 20th century, the city's reliance on philanthropy often masked its budgetary shortfalls and created doubly advantaged public schools in wealthy, majority-white communities, including Germantown. The dependence on philanthropy in Philadelphia and other places such as Cleveland and Detroit exacerbated fiscal inequities and educational inequality between bourgeois, white communities who could afford such donations and poor, Black communities who could not. However, inequality is not static. It, too, is shaped by history. The history of this one city and school demonstrates that the structure of inequality in Philadelphia's public schools in the early 21st century is a complete spatial inversion of its past. At the turn of the 20th century, Philadelphia's periphery, which included Germantown, West Philadelphia, and Frankford, was home to the city's white elite. One hundred years later, white elites had moved into Philadelphia's gentrified inner core and pushed lower-income Black and Latinx families to the city's periphery. White families in the city's center, like their predecessors, subsidize the city's inadequate public budgets with their own money to ensure that their children's schools have resources—resources that all children should have. Low-income Black and Latinx families who now primarily live on the city's periphery do not have the same financial resources or social capital as those who send their children to schools in the gentrified white inner core. They cannot always donate their own money to make up for inadequate public school budgets. As a result, the public schools that serve Philadelphia's poor, Black, and Latinx youth in the city's periphery have far fewer resources than the doubly advantaged Center City schools, which serve a disproportionate number of the city's white bourgeois youth.[37]

A growing body of scholarship analyzes the current importance of philanthropy in public education. However, the reliance on philanthropy to support public schools is not a late 20th- or early 21st-century phenomenon. Germantown's story illustrates that philanthropy has long financed public schools in this country and has promoted a community-wide approach to supporting youth and alleviating poverty—though it does neither today in disadvantaged communities like Germantown. The current dependence on philanthropy to support public goods such as education both resembles and differs significantly from past patterns at Germantown High School.[38] In the 2010s, philanthropies including the Gates and Broad Foundations gave millions of dollars to support education reform. Often, these foundations earmarked funds for market-based initiatives, charter school expansions, and increased performance measures, even though these reforms have not always lived up to their promise that they would advance academic achievement, particularly in urban schools that serve low-income youth of color.[39] As Germantown's story suggests, such efforts have cost urban school districts billions of dollars previously spent on classroom resources and have driven out some of the most creative and experienced educators.[40]

Another kind of philanthropy, seldom acknowledged, has also fueled inequality in our nation's public schools. Glaring funding disparities in Philadelphia go beyond the typical divides between suburban and urban schools or between charter and public schools. In the city's most affluent and increasingly white neighborhoods, influential school administrators and powerful home and school associations have courted local institutions (philanthropies, businesses, and universities) and pressured middle- and upper-income families to donate to their neighborhood public schools. The William M. Meredith Elementary School, whose catchment boundaries include most of Philadelphia's Queen Village community, with its appealing historical row homes and thriving independent eateries, attracts middle- and upper-income families deeply committed to their neighborhood public school. Meredith has a much less racially and economically diverse student body than the School District of Philadelphia. In the 2013–2014 school year, 61.5% of the 530 students who attended Meredith were white (compared to the district's 14.4%); 15.5% were Black (compared to the district's 52.8%); 9.6% were Asian (compared to the district's 8.1%); and 49% of the student body was classified as economically disadvantaged (compared to the district's 84.9%).[41]

For decades, Meredith administrators, engaged teachers, and bourgeois families have raised hundreds of thousands of dollars to preserve its long-standing reputation as one of the finest elementary schools in the city. During the 2013 budget crisis, the home and school association asked each Meredith family to contribute several hundred dollars per student to boost the school's operating budget. The association has sponsored community fundraisers. At the beginning of each year, teachers ask families to provide specified supplies and to donate money for additional classroom expenses.[42] Today, Meredith is one of the only public schools in Philadelphia with an art and music program, a full-time school nurse, and a school counselor, due largely to these private funds and local resources. In other words, Meredith is a doubly advantaged school.

Other Philadelphia public schools have also leveraged private funds. When Greenfield Elementary School faced a $355,470 budget shortfall in 2013, Daniel Lazar, the principal, asked parents to donate $613 dollars per student to cover essential resources that the school district could not afford. He told them, "As a school, we're fortunate enough to be in a neighborhood that has a higher level of income than other parts of the city. There are people who have means who've decided that they are making a commitment to public education. They don't want to move to the suburbs. They don't want to send their kids to private school. They believe in public schools." Lazar recognized that the requested donation might be a hardship for some families but urged those who could contribute to do so to allow him to re-hire employees, such as school counselors and teachers' aides, who he had to cut because of the budget shortfall. One parent told reporters that she was stunned by the request, saying it was difficult to believe "that a public school was charging tuition."[43]

Other doubly advantaged schools—Science Leadership Academy, Penn Alexander, the Philadelphia High School for Girls, and Central High School—have also appealed to parents to donate. Like Greenfield and Meredith, the student enrollment in these schools was often wealthier and whiter than the average Philadelphia public school. On November 29, 2017, school officials reported that Central High School received a $10 million gift from Joseph Field, a 1949 Central High School graduate, for the school's $42 million campaign to expand the school's facilities.[44] The public schools that serve Philadelphia's elite rely on these donations to preserve the programs and resources that attract upper- and middle-class families. Without these funds, these schools might lose the upper- and middle-income families who have the financial means to move their children to the city's more prestigious private and suburban public schools.[45] In other words, private funds benefit the schools with parents who can afford to donate their time and money—those parents who often have the financial and social capital to move or opt out of the city's public schools. In the city's poorest neighborhoods, where the majority of Philadelphia's low-income youth of color live, schools have only pitiful government aid and, in most cases, are barely functioning.

The influx of this philanthropy has not been limited to Philadelphia. Alane Salierno Mason recalled the changes she witnessed after her first-born child began attending public school in New York City. At first, she received a letter asking for "a modest contribution to the PTA" and a request to purchase supplies for her children's classrooms. Since then, she has participated in extensive school fundraising activities to cover teachers' professional development and in-school "enhancement" programs and other extracurricular activities. The school relied on these funds to pay for an art teacher, a science teacher for younger children, middle school language programs, and high school admissions test prep for eighth graders. In the 2012–2013 school year, parents raised $185,000 to retain programs cut due to city budget shortfalls—an impossible feat in the city's poorest schools.[46] Mayor Michael Bloomberg raised millions of private dollars for the city's public schools through the Mayor's Fund to Advance New York City and the Fund for Public Schools, but the Fund for Public Schools has shrunk and struggled to attract wealthy donors under the administration of Mayor Bill de Blasio.[47] Public school teachers have used their social networks to raise personal funds for their classrooms through platforms such as donorschoose.org. In 2021, there were over 25,000 projects across the nation, ranging from arts projects, field trips, to extracurricular programs, which individuals could fund based on their own preferences and geographies.[48]

Suburban school districts have also used philanthropic efforts to bolster their revenues and keep tax dollars low. In 2012, private contributions to the Hillsborough, California, public school foundation amounted to $3.45 million, or $2,300 per pupil.[49] At the beginning of the 2013–2014 school year, the district asked parents to match that amount and donate $2,300 per child to the foundation. In one of the best school districts in the state and one of the wealthiest communities in the San Francisco Bay area, with a median income of about $250,000 at the time, parents did so, supplementing the already high $13,500 per-pupil expenditures. These donations financed smaller class sizes, librarians, art and music teachers, and smart technology in every classroom. Other wealthy school districts in Wayland, Massachusetts; Palo Alto, California; and Menlo Park, California, have private foundations that funnel millions of dollars of charitable funding into the public schools annually.[50]

Private contributions to public schools do have several advantages. Philanthropy provides a critical revenue stream for programs, including extracurricular and afterschool programs that once were government supported in low-income communities. Philanthropy supports innovative programs, such as the Harlem Children's Zone, that government cannot fund on its own. Principals can use flexible philanthropic funding on immediate school needs. If a principal wants to fund a reading program, she can use parental donations to do so. If later she wants to fund an arts program, she can do that as well. In other words, unlike government funding, such donations are not earmarked for specific programs.

Public school families donate because they want to support their public schools. Many of these families donate because they are saving hundreds of thousands of dollars over their children's lifetime by sending their daughters and sons to public rather than private schools. They also donate because donations to public schools are tax-deductible charitable gifts. However, unlike charitable giving to social welfare organizations, as Rob Reich notes, "private giving to public schools widens the gap between rich and poor. It exacerbates inequalities in financing. It is philanthropy in the service of conferring advantage on the already well-off."[51] Moreover, when philanthropists donate money to support charter schools or privately run foundations, they threaten the democratic processes that govern public goods, including schools. Funding private alternatives may provide better options to a few hundred students, but it does little to address the root causes of inequality among low-income urban youth, which stems from inadequate public support for the schools that serve America's low-income and youth of color.

In 2020 and 2021, the COVID-19 pandemic, once again, illustrated the ways that private funding for public education confers advantages for public school students who are generally already advantaged. Throughout the spring and summer of 2020, scholars raised questions and concerns about the ways that affluent, white families leveraged their own social networks and private resources to form pandemic pods, hire private tutors, and leave COVID hot spots. Public schools relied on private money and philanthropy to hire additional staff, such as assistant teachers, and essential resources, such as iPads and Chromebooks, to facilitate in-person and online learning.[52] While some families argue that these practices were necessary given the horrific federal response, no one can deny the fact that these practices exacerbated educational inequality based on class, race, and space.[53]

The story of Germantown High School shows that private funding for public schools and the inequality that funding generates are not new. This funding mechanism has long privileged the communities and schools that need the least support—those institutions that primarily serve white upper- and middle-class Americans. Germantown's story also shows that the fragility of this mechanism is an aspect of urban school failure often overlooked in explanations that pin the current challenges in urban schools to white flight or failed desegregation. It is clear that these factors contributed to the challenges that urban schools face, but the reliance on philanthropy, which has existed since the beginning of the 20th century, generated inequities that predate the postwar period, and at least in part, set the stage for white flight, white resistance, and ultimately, failed desegregation. As this story illustrates, the roots of racial segregation, fiscal instability, and dependence on private funding sources was woven into the foundation of America's public schools, including Germantown High School.

When I asked Germantown teachers what the school district could have done to help them in the years before its ultimate closure, they offered a variety of ideas. Rather than spend money on educational reforms that stressed test results and school restructuring, they wanted the school district to spend more money on programs to attract, retain, and develop the city's best teachers. While they understood the need for an accountability system, they urged school officials to end performance systems that punished schools, teachers, and students and replace them with opportunities for teachers to reflect on and talk about their practice and its effects. They felt that the school district should loosen its reins and bureaucracy and let teachers do what they know how to do best: teach. Germantown alumni/ae, educators, families, and youth wished that school officials had visited their school before they closed it and that they had created meaningful ways for them to participate in the decisions that affected everyone in the school community. Many individuals agreed that schools had to close, but they questioned the rapid pace and process around these decisions.[54] The school needed many things that government and school officials had failed to provide. As one teacher said, the school had: "Nothing without strings attached . . . we needed more of that. We needed more of teachers being valued . . . we were not treated like resources.

We were treated like criminals. At Germantown at the end, it was completely demoralizing. We weren't meeting student needs because we didn't have the resources that we needed to do it right."[55] From its founding, Germantown High School never had the resources it "needed to do it right." It never had the public dollars it needed to serve all of its youth.

Many public school advocates consider Philadelphia a harbinger for what our nation's public schools could become—a grossly underfunded skeleton public school system with a vast, privately funded charter school network. The reliance on philanthropy to fund public goods and the educational inequities that this relationship has produced has a long history. History also reminds us that there have always been alternatives—paths that political leaders, school officials, and local educators could have taken to improve the educational outcomes for American youth. This story illustrates that sometimes educators challenged inequities and sometimes they did not. The challenges that our schools face are structural ones with a long history, and they require sustained efforts and government funds to ensure that all children have access to the educational opportunities and resources that they all so richly deserve.

APPENDIX

The appendix describes the statistical analyses that I used to characterize the demographics of the students who graduated from Germantown High School. These analyses compare demographic data from Germantown High School graduates to the demographics of students who graduated from the two elite exam schools, the all-male Central High School and the all-female Philadelphia High School for Girls, and from the two neighborhood high schools in the city's northwest section, Gratz and Olney.

I constructed several school data sets using high school yearbooks that listed the first and last name, street address, and course of study of youth who graduated from these five schools. The 1920 data sets include Central, Germantown, and Girls; the 1930 data sets include Central, Germantown, Girls, and Gratz (which opened in 1925), and the 1940, 1950, and 1960 data sets include Central, Germantown, Girls, Gratz, and Olney (which opened in 1932). To increase the sample size due to the small graduating classes in the early 20th century, the 1920 dataset includes data from the 1919, 1920, and 1921 school yearbooks. For example, the June 1919 yearbook listed Jane Hill, who lived at 3602 Queen Lane, as one of Germantown's graduates.

After I pulled the names and addresses from the high school yearbooks, I then searched the names in US census records on ancestry.com. If the census and yearbook name and addressed matched, I kept the graduate in my sample and used the census information on ancestry.com to pull the graduate's race, gender, nativity, and the occupation of the head of household. I listed this information on my yearbook spreadsheets. For example, I found a high school aged–girl, Jane Hill, who lived at 3602 Queen Lane. Since the census address matched her yearbook address, I listed her demographic information on my spreadsheet. The census states that Jane is a white female who was born in Pennsylvania. Her father was a letter carrier. I repeated this for the remaining graduates in the 1920, 1930, and 1940 cohorts. I list sample size and return rates in the descriptions of the data that follow.

Since census data are not available for the 1950 and 1960 cohorts, I had to rely on yearbook photographs to tally the number of Black and White students in the graduating class. While this method is imperfect, the results closely matched data that Floyd Logan, the president of Philadelphia's Educational Equality League, collected on the racial composition of the city's high schools in 1960. I have included these data on table 10 for reference.

To ease the analysis, I coded nativity first as either native born or immigrant. In my study, "native-born" graduates refers to native-born youth with native-born parents; "immigrant" youth refers to graduates who are either foreign born or have one or more foreign-born parents.

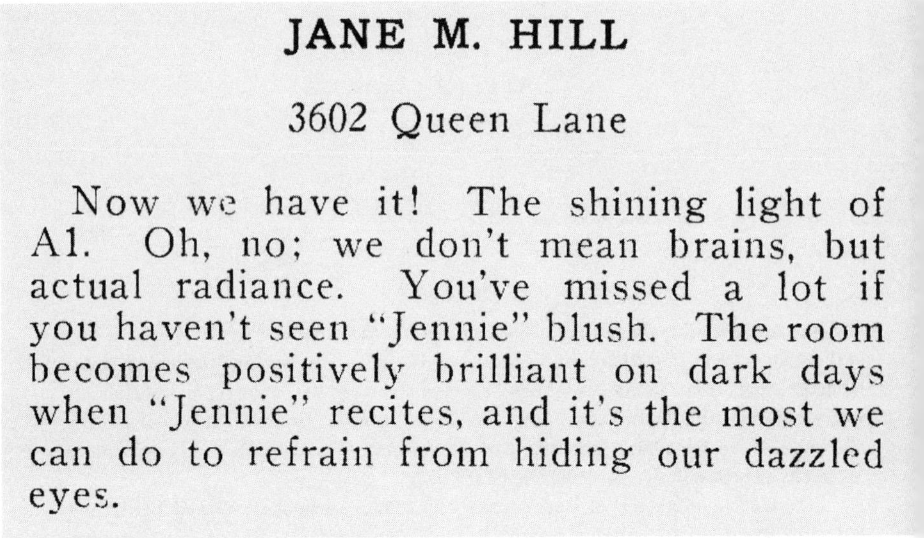

JANE M. HILL

3602 Queen Lane

Now we have it! The shining light of A1. Oh, no; we don't mean brains, but actual radiance. You've missed a lot if you haven't seen "Jennie" blush. The room becomes positively brilliant on dark days when "Jennie" recites, and it's the most we can do to refrain from hiding our dazzled eyes.

Figure 25. Jane Hill, Yearbook Entry. Source: GHS Yearbook, June 2019.

Table 12. Head of Household Codes

IPUMS Occ 1950 Codes	Final Codes
Professional Technical 0–99 Managers, Officials, and Proprietors 200–290	Upper Class
Clerical and Kindred Workers 300–390 Sales workers 400–490	Upper Middle Class
Craftspeople 500–595 Operatives 600–690	Lower Middle Class
Service Workers and Laborers 700–970	Working Class

Class can be a difficult concept to define and to track over time. To alleviate many of the problems associated with this concept, I relied on the Integrated Public Use Microdata Series (IPUMS) coding scheme for 1950 occupations. This coding scheme allowed me to give each occupation a numerical value, which I used as a proxy for class status for the 1920, 1930, and 1940 graduates.[1] Using the census information on occupations, I created seven class categories, which I eventually collapsed into four categories for the purposes of analysis (table 12).[2]

I performed a binomial multivariate regression analysis of these data to determine if there were demographic differences between the youth who graduated from Germantown High School and the other city's elite exam schools and the two neighborhood high schools located in the city's northwest. The regression was set up to test if the following factors—race, nativity, and head of household occupation (class)—predicted whether an individual graduated from Germantown High School or not. This equation describes the regression:

High School $= \beta_0 + \beta_1 \text{race} + \beta_2 \text{nativity} + \beta_3 \text{head of household occupation (class)}$

When I ran this regression for the all-male Central and the all-female Philadelphia High School, I created a single-sex sample for Germantown (all-male for the Central analysis and all-female for the Philadelphia High School for Girls analysis).

For the 1950 and 1960 cohorts where I did not have the full data set to perform this regression, I instead used a chi-square test of significance to determine if there was a statistical difference in the racial composition of Germantown High School and the four comparative schools, the all-male Central High School, the all-female Philadelphia High School for Girls, Olney High School, and Simon Gratz High School.

1920 Binomial Regression Findings

The return rates for the 1920 yearbook data are as follows: Central High School, $n = 330$, return rate 63%; Germantown High School, $n = 428$, return rate 90%; Philadelphia High School for Girls, $n = 148$, return rate 72%. The return rate refers to the percentage of graduates that matched demographic data on the United States census. These samples only include the demographic information for the graduates who had a matched address in their school yearbook and the census.

CENTRAL HIGH SCHOOL AND GERMANTOWN HIGH SCHOOL

Two factors—class and nativity—significantly affected whether a given person was likely to be a graduate from Germantown High School or Central High School. Immigrant male youth were significantly more likely to be found among the graduating class of the elite all-male Central High School than from Germantown High School ($p < 0.001$). Class status was also of interest. The model indicates that upper-class and upper-middle-class male youth were significantly more likely to be found among the graduating class at Germantown High School than from Central High School ($p < 0.03$ and $p < 0.05$, respectively).

THE PHILADELPHIA HIGH SCHOOL FOR GIRLS AND GERMANTOWN HIGH SCHOOL

Three factors—nativity, race, and class—significantly affected whether a youth was likely to be found among the graduating class at Germantown High School or the Philadelphia High School for Girls. Immigrant female youth were significantly more likely to appear in the graduating class from Philadelphia High School for Girls than from Germantown High School ($p < 0.005$). In addition, Black female youth were significantly more often among the graduating class of Philadelphia High School for Girls than from Germantown High School ($p < 0.02$). Finally, working-class female youth were significantly more likely to appear in the graduating class from Germantown High School than from Philadelphia High School for Girls ($p < 0.04$).

1930 Binomial Regression Findings

The return rates for the 1930 yearbook data are as follows: Central High School, $n = 302$, return rate 59%; Germantown High School, $n = 449$, return rate 87%; Gratz High School, $n = 356$, return rate 87%, Philadelphia High School for Girls, $n = 242$, return rate 71%.

CENTRAL HIGH SCHOOL AND GERMANTOWN HIGH SCHOOL

Nativity significantly differed between the graduates of Germantown High School and Central High School. Immigrant male youth were significantly more likely to be in the graduating class of Central High School than Germantown High School ($p < 0.001$).

THE PHILADELPHIA HIGH SCHOOL FOR GIRLS AND GERMANTOWN HIGH SCHOOL

Two variables—nativity and race—significantly differed between the graduates of Germantown High School and the Philadelphia High School for Girls. Immigrant female youth were significantly more likely to be among the graduates of Philadelphia High School for Girls than Germantown High School ($p < 0.001$). Black female youth were also significantly more likely to be among the graduates of Philadelphia High School for Girls than Germantown High School ($p < 0.003$).

SIMON GRATZ HIGH SCHOOL AND GERMANTOWN HIGH SCHOOL

Nativity significantly differed between the graduates of Germantown High School and Simon Gratz High School. Immigrant youth were significantly more likely to be among the graduates of Simon Gratz than Germantown High School ($p < 0.001$).

1940 Binomial Regression Findings

The return rates for the 1940 yearbook data are as follows: Central High School, $n = 275$, return rate 60%; Germantown High School, $n = 638$, return rate 58%; Gratz High School, $n = 315$, return rate 56%, Philadelphia High School for Girls, $n = 325$, return rate 54%, Olney High School, $n = 608$, return rate 65%.

CENTRAL HIGH SCHOOL AND GERMANTOWN HIGH SCHOOL

Race, nativity, and class significantly differed between the graduates of the elite, all-male Central High School compared to Germantown High School. Black, immigrant, and upper-class male youth were significantly more likely to be among the graduates of Central High School than Germantown High School ($p < 0.001$, $p < 0.001$, and $p < 0.002$, respectively). Working-class male youth were significantly more likely to be a graduate of Germantown High School than Central ($p < 0.001$).

THE PHILADELPHIA HIGH SCHOOL FOR GIRLS AND GERMANTOWN HIGH SCHOOL

Race, nativity, and class significantly differed between the graduates of Germantown High School and the Philadelphia High School for Girls. Black, immigrant, upper-middle-class, and lower-middle-class female youth were significantly more likely to be among the graduates of the Philadelphia High School for Girls than Germantown High School ($p < 0.001$, $p < 0.001$, $p < 0.02$, $p < 0.05$, respectively). Working-class female youth were significantly more likely to be among the graduates of Philadelphia High School for Girls than Germantown High School ($p < 0.001$).

Nativity and class significantly differed between the graduates of Germantown High School and Olney High School. Immigrant, upper-middle-class, and lower-middle-class youth were significantly more likely to be among the graduates of Olney than Germantown High School ($p < 0.001$, $p < 0.05$, and $p < 0.004$, respectively). Working-class youth were significantly more likely to be among the graduates of Germantown than Olney High School ($p < 0.006$).

Race, nativity, and class significantly differed between the graduates of Germantown High School and Simon Gratz High School. Black, immigrant, upper-middle-class, and lower-middle-class youth were significantly more likely to be among the graduates of Gratz than Germantown ($p < 0.06$, $p < 0.001$, $p < 0.04$, $p < 0.002$, respectively). Working-class youth were significantly more likely to be among the graduates of Germantown than Gratz ($p < 0.001$).

1950 Chi-Square Findings

In 1950, Black youth were significantly more likely to be among the graduates of Germantown than the elite, all-male Central High School ($p < 0.001$) and Olney High School ($p < 0.001$). Black youth were less likely to be in the graduating class of Germantown than the elite all-female Philadelphia High School for Girls ($p < 0.001$) and Gratz High School ($p < 0.001$).

1960 Chi-Square Findings

In 1960, Black youth were significantly more likely to be in the graduating class of Germantown than the elite, all-male Central High School ($p < 0.0001$), the elite, all-female Philadelphia High School for Girls ($p < 0.01$), and Olney High School ($p < 0.0001$). Black youth were significantly less likely to be among the graduates of Germantown than from Gratz High School ($p < 0.0001$).

In addition, I secured data from the School District of Philadelphia to examine the racial demographics of these high schools from 1990–2010. Data were not available in 1980. See table 13, Percent Black Student Enrollment, Northwest High Schools, 1920–2010.

Graduate Demographics and Curricular Tracks

The final question I examined is whether there were demographic differences between the graduates of Germantown High School's academic, commercial, and vocational (home economics and manual arts) programs. I used a regression to conduct this analysis. The regression was set up to test if gender, race, nativity, and class predicted a graduate's curricular track. This equation describes the regression:

Curricular Track $= \beta_0 + \beta_1$gender $+ \beta_2$race $+ \beta_3$nativity $+ \beta_4$head of household occupation (class)

For the 1950 and 1960 samples, I ran a regression to determine if a student's race and/or gender affected their curricular placement.

Curricular Track $= \beta_0 + \beta_1$gender $+ \beta_2$race

Table 13. Percent Black Student Enrollment, Philadelphia, Citywide Exam and Northwest High Schools, 1920–2010

High Schools, Black Graduates	1920	1930	1940	1950	1960	1970	1980	1990	2000	2010
Central High School	2%	4%	11%	6%	4%	20%		37%	33%	31%
Germantown High School	2%	4%	4%	13%	27%	85%		98%	98%	97%
Gratz High School		1%	6%	44%	98%	100%		99%	98%	97%
Philadelphia High School for Girls	9%	12%	14%	22%	18%	31%		46%	57%	65%
Olney High School			0%	0%	0%	39%		52%	55%	51%
School District of Philadelphia				30%	47%	60%		63%	65%	58%

SOURCE: GHS Yearbooks, 1919–21, January and June 1930, January and June 1940, January and June 1950, January and June 1960; Central High School Yearbooks, 1919–21, February and June 1930, January and June 1940, January and June 1950, January and June 1960; Philadelphia for Girls Yearbooks, 1919–21, February and June 1930, January and June 1940, January and June 1950, June 1960; Simon Gratz High School Yearbooks, June 1930, June 1940, January and June 1950, June 1960; Olney High School Yearbooks, January and June 1940, June 1950, June 1960; United States Census, 1940, ancestry.com; School District of Philadelphia, Open Record Officer, e-mail, author has data; Levenstein, *Movement Without Marches*, 127; John T. Gillepsie, "Negro School Enrollment," *EB*, June 12, 1970, EBC-TUUA.

1920 Regression Findings

Race and class significantly differed between the graduates of the academic and commercial tracks. Black youth were significantly more likely to be among the graduates of the academic track than white youth ($p < 0.05$). In addition, upper- and upper-middle-class youth were more likely to be among the graduates of the academic track than the commercial track ($p < 0.01$ and $p < 0.04$).

1930 Regression Findings

Nativity and class significantly differed between the graduates of the academic, commercial, and vocational tracks. Immigrant youth were significantly less likely to be among the graduates of the academic track than the commercial track ($p < 0.002$) and upper-class youth were significantly more likely to be among the graduates of the academic track than the commercial track ($p < 0.01$). In addition, female and immigrant youth were significantly less likely to be among the graduates of the vocational track than the commercial track ($p < 0.0001$ and $p < 0.01$, respectively).

1940 Regression Findings

Gender and class significantly differed between the graduates of the academic, commercial, and vocational tracks. Female youth were less likely to be among the graduates of the academic track than the commercial track ($p < 0.001$) and upper-class youth were more likely to be among the graduates of the academic track than the commercial track ($p < 0.001$). In addition, female youth were less likely to be among the graduates of the vocational track than the commercial track ($p < 0.001$) and upper-middle- and lower-middle-class youth were more likely to be among the graduates of the vocational track than the commercial track ($p < 0.05$).

1950 Regression Findings

Gender significantly differed between the graduates of the academic, commercial, or vocational tracks. Female youth were significantly more likely to be among the graduates of the commercial track than the academic or vocational tracks ($p < 0.01$).

1960 Regression Findings

Gender and race significantly differed between the graduates of the academic, commercial, or vocational tracks. Female youth were significantly more likely to be among the graduates of the commercial track than the academic or vocational tracks ($p < 0.01$). Black youth were significantly more likely to be among the graduates of the commercial track than the academic track ($p < 0.001$).

NOTES

Prologue

1. Joseph Gambardello and Robert Moran, "Teacher Assaulted in School Hallway," *PI*, February 24, 2007; "High School Teacher Assaulted After Confiscating iPod," *AP*, February 24, 2007; Lesli A. Maxwell, "Phila. Cracks Down on Assaults by Students," *EW*, March 20, 2007; Burd, "Philadelphia Teacher Frank Burd," *Radio Times*, July 16, 2008; Martha Woodall and Susan Snyder, "City Special-ed Lapses Increase School Violence," *PI*, May 20, 2007.

Introduction

1. Bartlow and Zitarelli, "Who Was Miss Mullikin?"
2. Brainerd, GHS Yearbook, June 1920; Manley, GHS Yearbook, June 1918.
3. "Got High School by 11 Years' Work," November 12, 1915, folder, Germantown High School—History, Public School Papers.
4. Brian Hickey, "Sources Say Germantown High School Targeted for Closure," December 12, 2012, WHYY website, https://whyy.org/articles/uncertainty-about-germantown-highs-future-swirl-amid-pending-school-district-announcement/.
5. "Philly School-Closings Vote Marked by Protests, Arrests, and Raw Emotion," March 8, 2013, WHYY website, https://whyy.org/articles/philly-school-closings-vote-marked-by-protests-arrests-and-raw-emotion/.
6. Kevin McCorry, "Philly School Principals Appeal Directly to Parents for Cash," August 9, 2013, WHYY website, https://whyy.org/articles/philly-school-principals-appealing-directly-to-parents-for-cash/; Rick Lyman and Mary Williams Walsh, "Philadelphia Borrows So Its Schools Open on Time," *NYT*, August 15, 2013.
7. Valerie Strauss, "Philadelphia School District Laying Off 3,783 Employees," *WP*, June 8, 2013; "270 More Layoff Notices Go Out this Week," *PPSN*, June 5, 2012; Martha Woodall, "More than 3,700 School Employees Being Laid Off," *PI*, June 9, 2013.
8. Aaron Moselle, "GHS Principal's Passionate Plea Goes Unheeded, District Mulls Possible Roosevelt Expansion," March 11, 2013, WHYY website, https://whyy.org/articles/ghs-principals-passionate-plea-goes-unheeded-district-mulls-possible-roosevelt-expansion/.
9. Brian Hickey, "Germantown High School's Final Graduation was a Celebration, Not a Funeral," June 19, 2013, WHYY, reprinted, https://philadelphia.chalkbeat.org/2013/6/20/22183931/germantown-high-school-s-final-graduation-was-a-celebration-not-a-funeral; Aaron Moselle, "On the Scene for the Last Day of Germantown High School's Life (1914–2013)," June 21, 2013, WHYY website, https://whyy.org/articles/on-the-scene-for-the-last-day-of-germantown-high-schools-life-1914-2013/.

10. For examples of these works, see Sugrue, *Origins of the Urban Crisis*; Hirsch, *Making the Second Ghetto*; Neckerman, *Schools Betrayed*; Katz, *Class, Bureaucracy, and Schools*; Erickson, *Making the Unequal Metropolis*; Mirel, *Rise and Fall of an Urban School System*; Labaree, *Making of an American High School*; Steele, *Making a Mass Institution*.

11. My dissertation advisor, Michael B. Katz, constantly pushed me to look for and recognize these alternatives; my mentor, Michael Silverman, helped me understand why they were not always possible.

12. Most historical scholarship on philanthropy and education focuses on the ways that foundations influenced educational policy and practice. For examples, see Lagemann, *Politics of Knowledge*; Lagemann, *Elusive Science*; Anderson, *Education of Blacks in the South*; Tompkins-Stange, *Policy Patrons*.

13. Clark, *Financing the Public Schools*, 17, 106; Ayers, *Cleveland School Survey*, 56, 328–42; Albert McMichael, "President's Report," *ARBPE-D*, 1914, 9–10; George Auch, "Report of the President," *ARBPE-D*, 1916, 9.

14. Henry Edmunds, "Report of the President," *ARBPE-P*, 1916, 1–13.

15. United States Commission on Civil Rights, *Public Education Funding Inequity*, 49.

16. Emma Brown, "Pa. Schools Are the Nation's Most Inequitable," *WP*, April 22, 2015.

17. Goldin and Katz, *Race Between Education and Technology*; Rizga, "Black Teachers Matter."

18. Sugrue, *Sweet Land of Liberty*; Massey and Denton, *American Apartheid*; Self, *American Babylon*; Ryan, *Five Miles Away*.

19. Countryman, *Up South*; Erickson, *Making the Unequal Metropolis*.

20. Labaree, *Making of an American High School*; Angus and Mirel, *Failed Promise of the American High School*; Mirel, *Rise and Fall of an Urban School System*; Goldin and Katz, *Race Between Education and Technology*.

21. Erickson, *Making the Unequal Metropolis*; Dougherty, *On the Line*; Sugrue, *Sweet Land of Liberty*.

22. Franklin, *Education of Black Philadelphia*.

23. Cucchiara, *Marketing Schools, Marketing Cities*; Bulkey, Mundell, and Riffer, *Contracting Out Schools*.

24. Labaree, *Making of an American High School*; Neckerman, *Schools Betrayed*.

25. Neckerman, *Schools Betrayed*.

26. Mirel, *Rise and Fall of an Urban School System*; Goldin and Katz, *Race Between Education and Technology*. Others have challenged the idea of a golden age of education; see Katz, *Irony of Early School Reform*; Labaree, *Making of an American High School*; Neckerman, *Schools Betrayed*.

27. Clark, *Financing the Public Schools*, 17, 106; Ayers, *Cleveland School Survey*, 56, 328–42; McMichael, "President's Report," 9–10; Auch, "Report of the President," 9.

28. For a history of this in the Progressive period, see Nasaw, *Children of the City*.

29. Cory Turner, "A Looming Financial Meltdown for America's Schools," *NPR.org*, May 26, 2020, https://www.npr.org/2020/05/26/858257200/the-pandemic-is-driving-americas-schools-toward-a-financial-meltdown; Domingo Morel, "Education and Democracy in Covid-19 America," *Items: Insight from Social Science*, June 11, 2020, https://items.ssrc.org/covid-19-and-the-social-sciences/democracy-and-pandemics/education-and-democracy-in-covid-19-america/; Partelow, Yin, and Sargrad, "Why K-12 Education Needs More Federal Stimulus Funding."

30. Baker, *Does Money Matter in Education?*

31. Thanks to Charles Payne who reminded me of the importance of financial resources to augment educational opportunities. As Payne suggests, money allows upper- and middle-income families to finance extracurricular activities that are correlated with academic achievement and raise social outcomes. For research on this point, see Heckman, Humphries, and Kautz, eds., *Myth of Achievement Tests*. For recent studies that show the importance of funding on student achievement, see Baron, "School Spending and Student Outcomes"; Kreisman and Steinberg, "Effect of Increased Funding on Student Achievement"; Rauscher, "Delayed Benefits"; Abbott et al., "School District Operational Spending."

32. Hess and Henig, eds., *New Education Philanthropy*

33. For an exploration of the tensions between public and private in social welfare programs that have influenced my own thinking around this, see Katz, *In the Shadow of the Poorhouse.*

34. Kantor and Tyack, eds., *Work, Youth, and Schooling*; Neckerman, *Schools Betrayed*; Angus and Mirel, *Failed Promise of the American High School*; Lazerson and Grubb, eds., *American Education and Vocationalism.*

35. Sizer, *Horace's Compromise*; Kantor and Lowe, "Class, Race, and the Emergence of Federal Education Policy"; Kantor and Brenzel, "Urban Education and the 'Truly Disadvantaged'"; Tyack and Cuban, *Tinkering Toward Utopia*; Payne, *So Much Reform, So Little Change.*

36. Payne, *So Much Reform, So Little Change.*

37. See Appendix for Methods and Analysis. Labaree, *Making of an American High School*, influenced my thinking about these methods.

38. Hammersley and Atkinson, *Ethnography*; Emerson, Fretz, and Shaw, *Writing Ethnographic Fieldnotes.*

39. Douglas, "Are Private Schools Immoral?"; Darling-Hammond, "Inequality and Access to Knowledge."

Chapter 1

1. M. G. Brumbaugh, Superintendent of Schools Report, *JBPE-P*, October 1907, 202, Free Library of Philadelphia (FLP); Gilbert Fisher, 1910 United States Census, Philadelphia County, ancestry.com.

2. In this work, the term bourgeois refers to the social class and cultural capital that gave Germantown residents their networks of privilege and power, see Bourdieu and Passeron, *Inheritors.*

3. Wood, *Freedom of the Streets.* The long skirts that young women wore at the time frequently caught on fire while on the trolley, so some of these concerns about the commute might have been valid. See "Girl in Flames on Crowded Trolley," *EB*, June 10, 1907; and "One Killed and Several Hurt in Train Crash," *EB*, June 27, 1907, both EBC-FLP.

4. Henry Edmunds, "Report of the President," *ARBPE-P*, 1913, 15–17.

5. For those that support the golden-age argument, see Mirel, *Rise and Fall of an Urban School System*; Goldin and Katz, *Race Between Education and Technology.*

6. These authors discuss the reluctance to fund high schools in the 19th century: Katz, *Irony of Early School Reform*; Reese, *Origins of the American High School.*

7. Hall, *Adolescence.*

8. The following books have influenced my thinking about the connections between space, race, sexuality, and the female body: Wood, *Freedom of the Streets*; Peiss, *Cheap Amusements*; Odem, *Delinquent Daughters*; Ko, *Teachers of the Inner Chambers*; Ryan, *Women in Public*; Stansell, *City of Women*; Brown, *Foul Bodies*; Laqueur, *Making Sex*; Butler, *Undoing Gender*. Typically, the word suburb refers to communities outside the city. This book challenges this view and asserts that Germantown residents in the 20th century and sometimes still today think of themselves and their community as geographically, politically, and racially removed from the city. See Contosta, *Suburb in the City*, and Hepp, *Middle-Class City*.

9. McCaffery, *When Bosses Ruled Philadelphia*; Amsterdam, *Roaring Metropolis*.

10. Labaree, *Making of an American High School*, 45–48.

11. Licht, *Getting Work*, 67–69; Ciampa, "Martin Grove Brumbaugh"; Issel, "Modernization in Philadelphia School Reform"; Steffens, *Philadelphia*; Shaw, "Public Schools of a Boss-Ridden City"; Woodruff, "Corrupt School System."

12. M. G. Brumbaugh, "Report of the Superintendent of Schools," *ARBPE-P*, 1908, 57–59; "Children Huddle in Dingy Schools," *EB*, September 12, 1907, EBC-FLP; "School Board Finances," *PL*, September 25, 1907; "$5,000,000 Will Not Fill School Bill," *PL*, September 26, 1907, PL-FLP.

13. "Educators Will Fight for Loan," *EB*, September 10, 1907; "Teachers to Work for $5,000,000 Loan," *EB*, September 12, 1907; "Fight for Passage of School Loan," *EB*, September 13, 1907, all EBC-FLP; "Insist That Schools Need $5,000,000 Loan," *PL*, September 19, 1907, PL-FLP.

14. "Will Ask Councils to Pass Loan Bill," *EB*, September 14, 1907; "Mayor Talks of Big School Loan," *EB*, September 16, 1907; "$2,500,000 of Loan for Public Schools," *EB*, September 17, 1907, all EBC-FLP.

15. "Mayor Talks of Big School Loan," *EB*, September 16, 1907, all EBC-FLP.

16. "All Downtown Out to Dedicate School," *PL*, September 22, 1907, PL-FLP; "Southern Manual's Great Dedication," *EB*, September 21, 1907, EBC-FLP.

17. GCHIA Meeting Minutes, October 2, 1907, Germantown and Chestnut Hill Improvement Association Collection.

18. "Big Fat Loan Up to Councils," *EB*, October 3, 1907. See also "School Needs Fail to Shake Mayor," *EB*, September 25, 1907; "Board Shows Need of 5 Million," *EB*, September 26, 1907; "Mayor Puts Blame on Education Board," *EB*, September 27, 1907, all EBC-FLP.

19. "School Board Finances," *PL*, September 25, 1907, PL-FLP.

20. "Vote $2,500,000 to the Schools," *PL*, October 4, 1907, PL-FLP.

21. "Board Calls Off Fight on Loan," *EB*, October 9, 1907, EBC-FLP.

22. Minutes, *JSBE-P*, April 14, 1908, 100. See also Neville, "Origin and Development."

23. Clarke, *Sex in Education*, 20–24. See also Barnes, *Woman in Modern Society*.

24. Tyack and Hansot, *Learning Together*, 146–55; Zschoche, "Dr. Clarke Revisited"; Showalter and Showalter, "Victorian Women and Menstruation." For a history of women's education in this and the Progressive period, see Powers, *"Girl Question" in Education*; Graves, *Girls' Schooling During the Progressive Era*; Rury, *Education and Women's Work*; Nash, *Women's Education in the United States*; Solomon, *In the Company of Educated Women*; Newcomer, *Century of Higher Education for American Women*; Perkins, "Impact of the 'Cult of True Womanhood'"; Newman, ed., *Men's Ideas/Women's Realities*; Brown, "Fear of Feminization."

25. Haines, "American Fertility in Transition."

26. Roosevelt, "Prefatory Letter for Theodore Roosevelt," in *Woman Who Toils*. See also Emerick, "College Women and Race Suicide"; G. S., "Race Suicide"; Grant, "Race Suicide"; Smith, "Higher Education of Women and Race Suicide."

27. Hall, *Adolescence*, 2:575.

28. Ibid., 2:575.

29. Ibid., 2:636.

30. Martin, *Unrest of Women*; Hutchinson, "Girl Versus the High School"; Russell, "Co-Education in High Schools"; see also Rury, *Education and Women's Work*; Graves, *Girls' Schooling During the Progressive Era*; Horowitz, "Body in the Library."

31. "Germantown Hits Out from Shoulder," *IG*, May 15, 1908.

32. "They Mean Business," *IG*, May 1, 1908; "Fight for High School," *GN*, April 30, 1908; "Work for High School," May 2, 1908, Jane Campbell Scrapbook Collection; "Business Men Urge High School," Jane Campbell Scrapbook Collection; GCHIA Minutes, May 1908; Business Men's Association of Germantown, Phila. Mass Meeting Letter, May 2, 1908, Business Men's Association of Germantown Collection; "District High School for Germantown," *IG*, May 8, 1908.

33. "A District High School Demanded," GCHIA Minutes, May 14, 1908, Germantown and Chestnut Hill Improvement Association Collection.

34. "No Money for High Schools," *PL*, June 8, 1908; "Will Fight for High Schools," *PR*, June 18, 1908; "Citizens Organize to Get High Schools," *NA*, June 18, 1908, all George Darrow Scrapbook.

35. Minutes, September 14, 1909, *JBPE-P*, 168–73.

36. For a similar class tension in the 19th century, see Katz, *Irony of Early School Reform*.

37. "Advocates of Loan Plead for Schools," *PL*, December 4, 1909, George Darrow Scrapbook.

38. "United Demand for High School," *PR*, December 4, 1909, George Darrow Scrapbook.

39. Ibid.

40. "Schools for Poor Only—M'Allister," *No Name*, December 3, 1909, George Darrow Scrapbook.

41. "United Demand for High School," *PR*, December 4, 1909, George Darrow Scrapbook.

42. Map of Residence of High School and Eighth-Grade Pupils, *ARBPE-P*, 1909.

43. Brumbaugh, "Report of the Superintendent," *ARBPE-P*, 1909, 84.

44. "High School a Certainty," *IG*, June 23, 1910; "Club House Can Be Leased for School," *IG*, June 17, 1910; Minutes, July 12, 1910, *JSBE-P*, 180.

45. Jane Campbell Scrapbook, September 1910; GCHIA Minutes, October 1910, Germantown and Chestnut Hill Improvement Association Collection; "Report of the Principal," *ARBPE-P*, 1910, 241; "Good Results," *IG*, October 21, 1910, Jane Campbell Scrapbook; "More Students," *IG*, February 3, 1911, Jane Campbell Scrapbook.

46. "High School Pupils Sent Down Town," *IG*, February 2, 1912; "Six Mass Meetings for High Schools," *IG*, March 22, 1912, both Jane Campbell Scrapbook; "People Will Rally for High School," *IG*, February 23, 1912; "Enthusiastic in High School Fight," March 8, 1912; "High Schools Coming," *IG*, April 5, 1912; Minutes, April 9, 1912, *JBPE-P*, 62.

47. Edmunds, "Report from the President," *ARBPE-P*, 1912, 1–12.

48. Edmunds, "Report of the President," *ARBPE-P*, 1913, 12.

49. Edmunds, "Report of the President," *ARBPE-P*, 1913, 16.

50. "Germantown High School, The Laying of the Cornerstone," September 26, 1914, box 1, Germantown Public Schools Collection; "School's Cornerstone," September 25, 1914, George Darrow Scrapbook.

Chapter 2

1. "Germantown High School Opens," November 4, 1915, Jane Campbell Scrapbook; "Got High School by 11 Years' Works," *IG*, November 12, 1915, box 1, Germantown Public Schools Collection; "Germantown High Opens," *EB*, November, no date, 1915, EBC-TUUA.

2. Numerous scholars have examined how these factors shape educational inequality, but none have looked at how these four factors worked together to shape educational inequality. For some examples, see Mirel, *Rise and Fall of an Urban School System*; Angus and Mirel, *Failed Promise of the American High School*; Erickson, *Making the Unequal Metropolis*; Neckerman, *Schools Betrayed*; Labaree, *Making of an American High School*; Reese, *Origins of the American High School*; Kantor and Brenzel, "Urban Education and the 'Truly Disadvantaged'"; Kantor and Lowe, "Class, Race, and the Emergence of Federal Education Policy"; Katz, *Class, Bureaucracy, and Schools*; Anderson, *Education of Blacks in the South*.

3. Franklin, *Education of Black Philadelphia*.

4. Scott, "Letters of Negro Migrants," 298–99. See also McMillen, *Dark Journey*; Grossman, *Land of Hope*; Henri, *Black Migration*; Hahn, *Nation Under Our Feet*; Lehmann, *Promised Land*.

5. United States Census, Philadelphia County, 1910 and 1930.

6. Mossell, *Standard of Living*; Pennsylvania Department of Welfare, *Negro Survey of Pennsylvania*.

7. Wolfinger, *Philadelphia Divided*, 25–26; Licht, *Getting Work*, 228–37; Willits, *Steadying Employment*, 5; Amsterdam, *Roaring Metropolis*, 106.

8. Warner, *Private City*, 172.

9. United States Census, Philadelphia County, 1920 and 1930.

10. Brumbaugh, "Report of the Superintendent," *ARBPE-P*, 1907, 42–43.

11. Franklin, *Education of Black Philadelphia*, 193.

12. Franklin, *Education of Black Philadelphia*, 49.

13. John Garber, "Report of the Superintendent," *ARBPE-P*, 1919, 31; Simon Gratz, "Report of the President," *ARBPE-P*, 1920, 12. For a discussion of overcrowded conditions in other districts, see Charles Chadsey, Report of the Superintendent," *ARBPE-D*, 1918, 3; Du Bois, "Segregation"; Franklin, *Education of Black Philadelphia*, 71–86.

14. Franklin, *Education of Black Philadelphia*, 49.

15. "Colored Child Barred from Keyser School," *PT*, October 23, 1926.

16. Pennsylvania Department of Welfare, *Negro Survey of Pennsylvania*, 58; Franklin, *Education of Black Philadelphia*, 83. See also "The Tribune Fund," *PT*, October 9, 1926; "Public Meeting in Interest," *PT*, October 16, 1926; "A Dastardly Outrage," *PT*, October 23, 1926; Orrin Evans, "Segregation in the Public Schools to be Carried to the Highest Courts," *PT*, December 11, 1926; "School Board Prepares," *PT*, December 18, 1926; Orrin Evans, "Meehan School Erected Solely for Colored," *PT*, January 1, 1927; Samuel Comfort, "Fight against Jim Crowism Must Be Taken into Court," *PT*, January 15, 1927.

17. Franklin, *Education of Black Philadelphia*, 60–86.

18. Steffes, *School, Society, and State*, 119–153; Goldin and Katz, *Race Between Education and Technology*; Angus and Mirel, *Failed Promise*.

19. Goldin and Katz, *Race Between Education and Technology*, Table B.4; School Census, *ARBPE-P*, 1890, 37; School Census, *ARBPE-P*, 1918, 54. See also Tyack, *The One Best System*, 182–83; Counts, *The Selective Character of American Secondary Education*, 1; "The Philadelphia Schools," *S&S*, no. 514 (November 1, 1924): 563–64.

20. Edmunds, "Report of the President," *ARBPE-P*, 1916, 1–13; William Dick, "Report of the Secretary," *ARBPE-P*, 1917, 211–13; Garber, "Report of the Superintendent," *ARBPE-P*, 1918, 15–17; Garber, "Report of the Superintendent," *ARBPE-P*, 1919, 37–38; Gratz, "Report of the President," *ARBPE-P*, 1920, 20–21.

21. Gratz, "Report of the President," *ARBPE-P*, 1920, 17–19.

22. William Rowen, "Report of the President," *ARBPE-P*, 1921, 20–21; Edwin Broome, "Report of the Superintendent," *ARBPE-P*, 1925, 175–77.

23. Garber, "Report of the Superintendent," *ARBPE-P*, 1916, 49–51. For a discussion of the Annual Welfare Drive, see "Wm. Penn Arrives in Welfare Flight," *EB*, November 14, 1921; "League of Hearts Is Urged in Drive," *EB*, October 24, 1923; "Welfare Workers Open Annual Drive," *EB*, November 6, 1924, all folders, Welfare Federation of Phila Drives, 1921–25, EBC-TUUA; "Helping the Helpless," *Germantown Beehive*, October 1925.

24. "Report of Compulsory Education," *ARBPE-P*, 1921, 145–46; Garber, "Report of the Superintendent," *ARBPE-P*, 1916, 83–84.

25. Brumbaugh, "Report of the Superintendent," *ARBPE-P*, 1909, 72–73. See also Garber, "Report of the Superintendent," *ARBPE-P*, 1916, 84.

26. Garber, "Report of the Superintendent," *ARBPE-P*, 1916, 52; Garber, "Report of the Superintendent," *ARBPE-P*, 1918, 35–36.

27. Public Education and Child Labor Association of Pennsylvania, *Generation of Progress*, 33; Rowen, "Report of the President," *ARBPE-P*, 1921, 19–20; "Report of Compulsory Education," *ARBPE-P*, 1919, 139–40; "Report of Compulsory Education," *ARBPE-P*, 1921, 145–46.

28. Brumbaugh, "Report of the Superintendent," *ARBPE-P*, 1908, 51. See also Cavallo, *Muscles and Morals*; Nasaw, *Children of the City*, 17–38; Peterson, "Voting for Play."

29. "Educational Department of the Philadelphia Museum of Art," 497; Garber, "Report of the Superintendent," *ARBPE-P*, 1916, 81–82.

30. Garber, "Report of the Superintendent," *ARBPE-P*, 1918, 51. For an earlier discussion, see Brumbaugh, "Report of the Superintendent," *ARBPE-P*, 1909, 75–79.

31. Gratz, "Report of the President," *ARBPE-P*, 1920, 10–11.

32. "Philadelphia Schools," 563–64.

33. While these books do not focus on education, they have influenced my thinking about the tensions between the public and private in welfare provisions in the United States and how these tensions exacerbate racial inequities: Skocpol, *Protecting Soldiers and Mothers*; Gordon, *Pitied but Not Entitled*; Mink, *Wages of Motherhood*; Fox, *Three Worlds of Relief*; Katz, *In the Shadow of the Poorhouse*.

34. "Report of Compulsory Education," *ARBPE-P*, 1915, 154; "Report of Compulsory Education," *ARBPE-P*, 1917, 172–73; "Report of Compulsory Education," *ARBPE-P*, 1918, 164–65; "Report of Compulsory Education," *ARBPE-P*, 1918, 164–65; "Report of Compulsory Education," *ARBPE-P*, 1919, 146–47; "Report of Compulsory Education," *ARBPE-P*, 1920, 177–78; "Report of Compulsory Education," *ARBPE-P*, 1921, 152–53; "Report of Compulsory Education," *ARBPE-P*, 1922, 210–12. Data are not available for the 1916 Annual Report.

35. Emlen, "Movement for the Betterment of the Negro," 84–85.

36. Licht, *Getting Work*.

37. Labaree, *Making of an American High School*.

38. Philadelphia High School for Girls Yearbook, 1919; United States Census, Philadelphia County, 1930.

39. Snyder, ed., *120 Years of American Education*, 27; Franklin, *Education of Black Philadelphia*, 147; Labaree, *Making of an American High School*.

40. Labaree, *Making of an American High School*.

41. Archibald Childs, interview by Louise Strawbridge, October 21, 1991, Germantown Between the Wars Collection.

42. Edmunds, "Report of the President," *ARBPE-P*, 1915, 20. See also Brumbaugh, "Report of the Superintendent," *ARBPE-P*, 1914, 37.

43. Rizga, "Black Teachers Matter."

44. This sample includes Germantown High School graduates of the 1919, 1920, and 1921 classes.

45. "Scholarship," *TC*, December 1921, 8–9; Garber, "Report of the Superintendent," *ARBPE-P*, 1919, 30–31; "Scholarships," *ARBPE-P*, 1920, 31–32; "Germantown High School Stands High in Opinion of Colleges," *Germantown Beehive*, July 1924, 7–14.

46. United States Census, Philadelphia County, Wards 22 and 42, 1920.

47. Data and analysis in author's possession.

48. "Alumni," *TC*, June 1923, 5; Douglas Walter Eiseman, ancestry.com, United States Census, Philadelphia County, 1930.

49. "G.H.S. Alumni," *TC*, April 1922, 28; Barbara Manley, ancestry.com, United States Census, Philadelphia County, 1930.

50. Alice Craigmile, ancestry.com, United States Census, Philadelphia County, 1930.

51. Childs, interview by Strawbridge. See also Marion Campbell, interview by author, April 23, 2011.

52. Florence E. Baugh, ancestry.com, *Philadelphia, Pennsylvania, U.S., Marriage Index, 1885–1951* [database online].

53. For a contemporary analysis of the importance of extracurricular activities for social mobility and academic achievement, see Snellman et al., "Engagement Gap"; Heckman, Humphries, and Kautz, eds., *Myth of Achievement Tests*.

54. "Glee Club," *TC*, November 1917, 38; "Latin Club," *TC*, November 1917, 39; "Activities," GHS Yearbook, February 1926.

55. "School Notes," *TC*, September, 1917, 22–25; "Senate," *TC*, December 1917, 19; "More Preaching," *TC*, February 1919, 7; "Minutes of the Senate," *TC*, February 1919, 22.

56. "Washington Trip Great Success," *CC*, October 20, 1928.

57. "Say Young Fellow," *TC*, October 1918, 24. See also "To All Freshmen," *TC*, February 1917, 28; "Club Notes," *TC*, February 1917, 37–39.

58. "Mothers' Association," *CC*, October 1924; "Mothers' Association," *CC*, March 1925; John B. Shackleton, "Father's Association," *TC*, June 1923, 18–19.

59. "The Light Green Ticket," *TC*, October 1916, 5.

60. "Girls 'B' Class Notes," *TC*, November 1916, 38; "Girls 'A' Class Notes," *TC*, April 1918, 20; "Boys 'C' Class Notes," *TC*, April 1918, 22; "The Senate," *TC*, November 1917, 30; "Senate," *TC*, April 1918, 19–20.

61. "The Frolic of 1921," *TC*, December 1921, 27–28; "The Frolic of 1922," *TC*, January 1923, 8–9.

62. "Girls 'B' Class Notes," *TC*, December 1916, 28; "The Frolic of 1921," *TC*, December 1921, 27–28.

63. "Editorial," *TC*, June 1919; GCHIA Meeting Minutes, May 15, 1923; GCHIA Meeting Minutes, October 16, 1923, both Germantown and Chestnut Hill Improvement Association Collection; "$400,000 Campaign," *Germantown Beehive*, February 1927; "$400,000 Campaign," *Germantown Beehive*, March 1927; "Mayor Here to See Field Site," *GB*, December 20, 1928.

64. "Assembly Notes," *TC*, November 1917, 25–27; "Fund for Civic Prizes," March 1922, Public Schools Papers; "New Prizes Offered," 1926, Germantown Public Schools Collection.

65. GCHIA Meeting Minutes, May 15, 1923, Germantown and Chestnut Hill Improvement Association Collection.

66. Engineering Club, GHS Yearbook, February 1922; "Clubs," *TC*, October 1925, 29–31.

67. GHS Yearbook, June 1919, 121; GHS Yearbook, June 1920, 52. See also Cahn, *Coming on Strong*.

68. "Geneva E. Edney," *Germantown Crier* 56, no. 2 (Fall 2006): 56. See also Louise Strawbridge, "John 'Archie' Child," *Germantown Crier* 56, no. 2 (Fall 2006): 53.

69. "When There's a Will, There's a Way," *TC*, May 1923, 6–7.

70. "Seven O'Clock," 26, Germantown YMCA Collection; "A Seashore Outing for 1000 Children," *IG*, July 20, 1922.

71. Wissahickon School Club, Ninth Annual Report, 1912, Wissahickon Boys Club Collection; "1870–1960, YWCA, Germantown Annual Meeting, 1960," Germantown YMCA Collection.

72. M. Frances Hunter, interview by author, August 6, 2010.

73. Savage, "'In the Interest of the Colored Boys.'"

74. Wissahickon School Club, Eighth Annual Report, 1911, Wissahickon Boys Club Collection.

75. Charles Shirley, interview by author, July 26, 2010; Coleman, *Counsel for the Situation*, 15.

76. William T. Coleman Jr., interview by author, August 10, 2010.

77. Beaupre, "Negro Boys' Activities at Wissahickon," 14.

Chapter 3

1. Marion Garrison, interview by author, April 23, 2011.

2. de Schweinitz, "Philadelphia Takes Heart"; "Philadelphia's Survey Shows Peak of Unemployment Passed," 10; Fox, "Unemployment Relief in Philadelphia," 90; Dewhurst and Nathan, *Social and Economic Character of Unemployment in Philadelphia*, 22–23.

3. Willits, "Some Impacts of the Depression upon the Negro in Philadelphia," 202.

4. Palmer, *Recent Trends in Employment and Unemployment in Philadelphia*, 36; Willits, "Some Impacts of the Depression upon the Negro in Philadelphia," 202.

5. Tyack, Lowe, and Hansot, *Public Schools in Hard Times*, 103–32.

6. Tyack, Lowe, and Hansot, *Public Schools in Hard Times*, 144–50.

7. *ARBPE-P*, 1929, and *ARBPE-P*, 1939.

8. United States Census, Characteristics of the Population, Pennsylvania, 1940.

9. Welch, "Duration of Unemployment in Philadelphia."

10. United States Census, Philadelphia County, 1930.

11. Rosalie August, interview by author, May 10, 2009.

12. Alyce Jackson Alexander, interview by George Woods, August 6, 1992, GBWC; Vincenza Iannuzzi Cerrato, interview by author, June 29, 2011.

13. August, interview by author; Alexander, interview by Woods; Cerrato, interview by author.

14. Erickson, *Making the Unequal Metropolis*; Clapper, "Constructed World of Postwar Philadelphia Area Schools."

15. Central, Girls, Gratz, and GHS 1930 Yearbooks; United States Census, Philadelphia County, 1930, ancestry.com.

16. Charles Cauthorn, interview by Gregory Woods, June 22, 1992, GBWC. For a similar story, see Helen Faust, interview by author, July 26, 2010.

17. Cauthorn, interview by Woods. See also Neckerman, *Schools Betrayed*, 32–126.

18. Cauthorn, interview by Woods.

19. Alexander, interview by Woods.

20. William Rowen et al., "Report of the President," *ARBPE-P*, 1931, 11–14.

21. Edwin Broome, "Report of the Superintendent," *ARBPE-P*, 1933, 32; Broome, "Report of the Superintendent," *ARBPE-P*, 1934, 100–17; Broome, "Report of the Superintendent," *ARBPE-P*, 1936, 9.

22. Broome, "Report of the Superintendent," *ARBPE-P*, 1936, 9.

23. Broome, "Report of the Superintendent," *ARBPE-P*, 1933, 32.

24. Broome, "Report of the Superintendent," *ARBPE-P*, 1934, 100.

25. Broome, "Report of the Superintendent," *ARBPE-P*, 1933, 161–62.

26. "Unemployment Relief in Philadelphia, 1930–1931–1932," Bureau of Unemployment Relief Papers.

27. "Report of Compulsory Attendance," *ARBPE-P*, 1933, 12–15; "Report of Compulsory Attendance," *ARBPE-P*, 1934, 229–30.

28. Hallgren, "Mass Misery in Philadelphia," 275.

29. Works, *Philadelphia Public School Survey*, 1:12–25.

30. It should be noted that federal dollars represented a small percentage of any school district budget at the time.

31. Works, *Philadelphia Public School Survey*, 2:61.

32. Works, *Philadelphia Public School Survey*, 2:26–74.

33. Works, *Philadelphia Public School Survey*, 2:64.

34. Works, *Philadelphia Public School Survey*, 2:64–68.

35. Annual Report of the Superintendent, *CPS-AR*, 1933–1934, 77–85; *ARBPE-D*, 1930, 46–47. See also Au, *Unequal By Design*; Gould, *The Mismeasure of Man*.

36. School District of Philadelphia, The Board of Public Education, *Program of Studies of Senior High & Vocational Schools* (Philadelphia, 1942), 34.

37. Broome, "Report of the Superintendent of Schools," *ARBPE-P*, 1937, 102–5; "Board to Appeal 85c School Tax Limit Order," *EB*, October 23, 1937, EBC-FLP.

38. "Board to Appeal 85c School Tax Limit Order"; "Board Will Appeal Limit on School Tax," *PL*, October 23, 1937, PL-FLP; "Court Curbs School Board Tax Power," *PR*, October 23, 1937; "School Board Speeds Appeal on Tax Slash," *PI*, October 24, 1937; "School Board to Appeal Tax Ruling," *PR*, October 24, 1937.

39. "Payless Pay Days Facing Teachers," *EB*, October 25, 1937, EBC-FLP.

40. "School Tax Stays at 92½ Cents Two Years," *EB*, November 16, 1937, EBC-FLP; "Supreme Court Bars Rise in School Taxes," *PL*, November 16, 1937, PL-FLP.

41. Birger, "Race, Reaction, and Reform," 184–85; Spencer, *In the Crossfire*, 143.

42. Krug, *Shaping of the American High School*, 2:307–14.

43. Davis, *Lost Generation*.

44. Krug, *Shaping of the American High School*, 2:307–14. See also Melvin, *Youth—Millions Too Many?*; Rainey, *How Fare American Youth?*; Davis, *Youth in the Depression*.

45. "Failure of Home Retarding Youth," *GC*, March 10, 1937.

46. High School Enrollment, *ARBPE-P*, 1929 and 1938.

47. Garrison, interview by author.

48. "Counselors Corner," *CC*, October 22, 1929; "College Stuff," *CC*, November 5, 1929; "High Scholarship Wins Haverford," *CC*, December 17, 1929; "Junior College Offers Tuition," *CC*, January 14, 1930; "Beaver College Oldest Woman's School," *CC*, February 11, 1930; "Oberlin College," *CC*, February 25, 1930; "Franklin and Marshall College," *CC*, March 11, 1930. Similar programs existed in other school districts; see *ARBPE-D*, 1928, 26; "Union Trust Scholarship Awards," *DEB*, September 1928, 7; "Mercy J. Hayes Student Loan Fund," *DEB*, September 1928, 9.

49. August, interview by author.

50. Marion Campbell, interview by author.

51. Marion Campbell, interview by author. I asked Marion if Black and white students protested together, but she did not remember.

52. Berthold Levy, interview by author, March 10, 2010.

53. Garrison, interview by author.

54. Savannah Holman, interview by author, August 6, 2010.

55. Broome, "Report of the Superintendent," *ARBPE-P*, 1936, 9.

56. Doris Galbraith, "Girls to Promote Theatre Benefit," *CC*, January 14, 1930.

57. "Mothers' Association," *TC*, October 1924, 24; "Mothers' Association," *TC*, March 1925, 33; "Boosters Turn into Salesmen," *CC*, October 22, 1929; "The Student Aid Fund," *CC*, October 27, 1931; "Footlight Club to Aid Students' Fund," *CC*, May 9, 1933; "Baskets Collected and Distributed," *CC*, December 17, 1929; "Pupils Respond Nobly," *CC*, December 22, 1931; "Record Classes Will Provide for Poor Families," *CC*, December 20, 1932.

58. "Report of Compulsory Attendance," *ARBPE-P*, 1933, 12. See also "Report of Compulsory Education," *ARBPE-P*, 1934, 229–30.

59. "Teachers Aid Mothers' Ass'n," *CC*, November 19, 1929; "Faculty-Parents Party a Success," *CC*, November 18, 1930; "School Teachers to Contribute," *CC*, March 10, 1931; "Quilt Offered in Lottery," *CC*, October 27, 1931; "Faculty Members Buy Cakes," *CC*, May 15, 1934; "Funds for Students Raised by Mothers," *GB*, January 30, 1930.

60. "Summer Camps Open," *GB*, June 6, 1929; "Social Events Surround Tournament," *PT*, August 8, 1929; "Boys' Club to Open Vacation House," *GB*, June 22, 1933; "Germantown," *PT*, June 7, 1934; "65 Youths to Get Shore Vacations," *GC*, June 9, 1937: "Ending Local Unemployment," *GC*, January 12, 1938.

61. Coleman Jr., interview by author.

62. "Citizens Do Not Forget Poor," *PT*, January 2, 1930.

63. "Unemployment and Relief Statistics," *GB*, February 20, 1930; "Germantown Charities Do Their Part," *GB*, September 7, 1933; "Ending Local Unemployment," *GC*, January 12, 1938.

64. "Strauss Requests Prompt Payments," *CC*, November 24, 1931; "Senate Election Tax," *CC*, December 8, 1931.

65. "Senate Passes New Laws," *CC*, March 10, 1931; "Annual Senate Dance," *CC*, December 11, 1934.

66. GHS Yearbooks, 1930 and 1940.

67. "Senate Assessment Due in Near Future, 5 Cents," *CC*, April 25, 1932; "Senate Assessment Tax Collected," *CC*, December 19, 1933; "Senate Settles Two Important Questions," *CC*, May 15, 1934; "Annual Senate Dance Scheduled for Friday, Jan. 4 in Girls' Gym," *CC*, December 11, 1934; "Assessment Tax," *CC*, January 14, 1936.

68. GHS Yearbooks, 1929 and 1939.

69. "Faculty Faces: Dr. Anna Mullikin," *CC*, March 24, 1953; "Dr. Mullikin," *CC*, March 18, 1958; Bartlow and Zitarelli, "Who Was Miss Mullikin?" 2, 99.

70. David Alcorn, interview by author, November 16, 2010.

71. Margaret (Engle) Bjorseth, interview by author, June 29, 2011.

72. For ease of reading, I will refer to Coleman Jr. as William and will retain Coleman Sr. when referring to his father.

73. Coleman Jr., interview by author.

74. Coleman Jr., interview by author.

Chapter 4

1. Coleman Jr., interview by author; "Cong. Mitchell Appoints Boy to West Point," *CD*, April 1, 1939; "Party Time in Harlem," *NYAN*, November 11, 1939.

2. "Tresville Appointed to Military Academy," *CC*, April 20, 1939.

3. Patricia Sullivan, "West Point Graduate Clarence M. Davenport, Jr.," *WP*, August 9, 2007.

4. "Smiles of Pride and Joy," *PC*, January 20, 1943; "Local 99th Officer Missing in Action," *PT*, July 15, 1944; "Billie Rowe's Notebook," *PC*, July 22, 1944; "I Saw Capt. Tresville Die," *PC*, December 9, 1944.

5. T. Rees Shapiro, "Vivien Rowan, 89; Fierce Foe of Racial Discrimination," *WP*, April 16, 2011.

6. McKee, *Problem of Jobs*, 18–40; Adams et al., *Philadelphia*, 30–65.

7. United States Census, Housing and Population, 1940 and 1950.

8. Wolfinger, *Philadelphia Divided*, 98; Sobek, "New Statistics on the U.S. Labor Force," table 9; Franklin, *Education of Black Philadelphia*, 151–56.

9. Sugrue, *Origins of the Urban Crisis*, 27; Countryman, *Up South*, 29; Palmer, *Philadelphia Labor Market in 1944*, 6–9.

10. Bauman, *Public Housing, Race, and Renewal*, 87.

11. Charles Cauthorn, interview by Gregory Woods, June 22, 1992, GBWC.

12. Wolfinger, *Philadelphia Divided*, 87.

13. Spencer, *In the Crossfire*, 41–52; Countryman, *Up South*, 28–33; Adams et al., *Philadelphia*, 30–99; McKee, *Problem of Jobs*, 1–41.

14. Kitzmiller, "Nellie Rathbone Bright"; Ernest Cuff, interview by author, August 6, 2010.

15. "Slum Clearance Prospects Here Aired," *GC*, February 24, 1938; Hillier, "Redlining and the Home Owners' Loan Corporation."

16. B.W. Frazier to Frank Smith, April 17, 1939, and James Kelly to B.W. Frazier, April 26, 1939, box 57, folder 32, Germantown Community Council Papers.

17. "Germantown Gets 6 Million Slum Project," *PI*, August 10, 1939, box 57, folder 32, Germantown Community Council Papers.

18. "Rehousing Project Favored by Local Civic Groups," *GC*, August 24, 1939, box 57, folder 32, Germantown Community Council Papers.

19. Weir, "Urban Poverty and Defensive Localism."

20. "Second Battle of Germantown Rages," *GC*, February 8, 1940; "Haines-Baynton Re-Housing Project Reaches Stalemate," *GC*, February 22, 1940; "Housing Opposition Opens Office and Pickets Streets; Hearings Again Delayed," *GC*, April 11, 1940.

21. "Opens Gtn. Project Information Office," *PT*, April 4, 1940.

22. "Housing: Local Projects Disapprove by Lamberton," *PT*, May 16, 1940.

23. Hunter, *Black Citymakers*, 108–9; Bauman, *Public Housing, Race, and Renewal*, 54–56; Wolfinger, *Philadelphia Divided*, 69–70.

24. Cerrato, interview by author.

25. City Summary, *ARBPE-P*, 1925, 475; Annual School Census, *ARBPE-P*, 1945, 126.

26. Phillips, "Struggle for School Desegregation in Philadelphia," 67.

27. *Wartime Handbook for Education*, 17; Morgan, "NCPT Mobilizes for War," 99; Howell, "Schools and Wartime Delinquency," 151–52.

28. "School-Work Plan Now Under Way," *CC*, October 12, 1943; "Labor Shortage Affects Schools," *CC*, December 14, 1943.

29. School District of Philadelphia, *Statistical Reports of the Department of Instruction for the School Year 1945–1946*, Table no. 45, Employment Certificates, Exemption Permits, and Age Certificates, Comparative Statements, 1937–1946, 57.

30. Melvin, *Youth—Millions Too Many?*

31. Palmer, *Philadelphia Labor Market in 1944.*

32. McKee, *Problem of Jobs*, 22–25; Merritt and Rifkind, "Unemployment Among the Teen-Aged in 1947–49"; Katz, "Employment of Students, October 1959"; Johnson, "Employment Problems of Out-of-School Youth"; Gilbert Fuller Sr., interview by author, August 8, 2010.

33. Committee on Human Relations, "Philadelphia's Negro Population: Facts on Housing," cited in Delmont, *Nicest Kids in Town*, 15.

34. Abraham Tucker, "Germantown Human Relations Committee: A Study in Community Organization," 1952?, box 50, folder 23, Germantown Community Council Papers.

35. Donald Hamilton, "An Appraisal of Our Community Problems," 1958, box 3, folder 6, Germantown Community Council Papers.

36. Hamilton, "Appraisal of Our Community Problems"; Kitzmiller, "Nellie Rathbone Bright."

37. Seligman, *Block by Block*; Todd-Breland, *Political Education.*

38. Monthly Report, June 1951, box 50, folder 14, Germantown Community Council Papers.

39. Germantown Settlement, "Second Reports on Development of Neighborhood Block Project," May to August 1954, box 54, folder 49, Germantown Community Council Papers.

40. PHA, Public Hearings, Rittenhouse Site, July 19, 1950, box 430, Housing Association of Delaware Valley, Pamphlets; "H-Authority Hears Argument," *GC*, July 27, 1950, box 50, folder 12, Germantown Community Council Papers; Minutes of the 22nd Ward Planning Committee Meeting, June 15, 1950, box 11, folder 25, Germantown Community Council Papers; "Germantown Housing Plan Held Up," *EB*, September 21, 1950, box 50, folder 12, Germantown Community Council Papers; Levenstein, *Movement Without Marches*, 89–93; Bauman, *Public Housing, Race, and Renewal*, 172–73; Countryman, *Up South*, 75–79.

41. Philadelphia Housing Authority, Public Hearings, Rittenhouse Site, July 19, 1950, box 430, Housing Association of Delaware Valley, Pamphlets; "Germantown Housing Plan Held Up After Long Debate," *EB*, September 21, 1950, box 50, folder 12, Germantown Community Council Papers; Levenstein, *Movement Without Marches*, 89–93; Bauman, *Public Housing, Race, and Renewal*, 172–73; Countryman, *Up South*, 75–79.

42. Perkiss, *Making Good Neighbors*.

43. US Commission on Civil Rights, *Racial Isolation in the Public Schools*, vol. 1 (Washington, DC, 1967), 9, cited in Franklin, *Education of Black Philadelphia*, 168; "Germantown Community Council: Committee on Schools," January 23, 1957, box 13, folder 36, Germantown Community Council Papers.

44. Delmont, *Nicest Kids in Town*, 72; Countryman, *Up South*, 238.

45. Levenstein, *Movement Without Marches*, 126; Binzen, *Whitetown, U.S.A.*, 275; Birger, "Race, Reaction, and Reform," 27.

46. Martin, "Role of the School-Community Organization," 6–7.

47. Levenstein, *Movement Without Marches*, 126.

48. For the history of this process in Nashville, see Erickson, *Making the Unequal Metropolis*.

49. Clapper, "Constructed World of Postwar Philadelphia Area Schools," 32.

50. Clapper, "Constructed World of Postwar Philadelphia Area Schools"; Levenstein, *Movement Without Marches*, 130–31.

51. Delmont, *Nicest Kids in Town*, 68–100; Spencer, *In the Crossfire*, 41–52; Daniel A. Brooks, "Thirty Years in Philadelphia Schools," *PT*, April 27, 1946; "Segregation in Schools Condemned," *Hartford Courant*, March 21, 1946. For a similar story about Chicago, see Todd-Breland, *Political Education*.

52. Delmont, *Nicest Kids in Town*, 73–77; Powdermaker and Storen, *Probing Our Prejudice*; Burkholder, *Color in the Classroom*; Perrillo, "White Teachers and the 'Black Psyche.'"

53. Floyd Logan to Louis Hoyer, December 2, 1948, box 2, folder 9, Floyd Logan Collection. See also "Organize State Fight Against Bias," *PT*, November 25, 1947; Floyd Logan to Walter Biddle Saul, March 3, 1949, box 2, folder 9, Floyd Logan Collection; "'Alarming Growth' of 'Negro' Schools," *PT*, July 19, 1949.

54. "Urge State to Pass Anti-Bias School Bill," *PT*, April 5, 1949.

55. "Local NAACP Chapter Joins School Protest," *PT*, March 22, 1949.

56. Todd-Breland, *Political Education*, 26.

57. Nathaniel Morgan, Minutes of the Education Sub-committee, January 12, 1956, box 54, folder 45, Germantown Community Council Papers.

58. Middle States, "Report of the Visiting Committee on the Evaluation of the Benjamin Franklin High School," May 25, 1951, box 20, folder 26, Floyd Logan Collection; "Report on Franklin High," *PT*, October 9, 1951.

59. "Ben Franklin Probe," *PT*, October 13, 1951.

60. "Tribune Articles Inspire Meeting," *PT*, October 13, 1951; Report of the Committee on Schools to Germantown Community Council, June 5, 1957, box 13, folder 36, Germantown Community Council Papers.

61. Blaustein, "Philadelphia, PA," 131–33; Kim Hirschman, interview by author, February 16, 2010; "Residents Press for New Grade School in Area," *GC*, June 14, 1951, box 62, folder

71, Germantown Community Council Papers; "School Sites Submitted by Wister Group," *GC*, October 4, 1951, box 54, folder 52, Germantown Community Council Papers.

62. Bonnie Marglous, Germantown Human Relations Committee Meeting Notes, December 6, 1954, box 54, folder 44, Germantown Community Council Papers; "Germantown Community Council: Committee on Schools," January 23, 1957, box 13, folder 36, Germantown Community Council Papers; "Segregation Up in Germantown, Says GCC Aide," *GC*, June 16, 1955.

63. Roger Scattergood, December 31, 1955, box 54, folder 45, Germantown Community Council Papers.

64. Morgan, Minutes of the Education Sub-Committee, January 12, 1956, box 54, folder 45, Germantown Community Council Papers.

65. Minutes of the Human Relations Committee, February 26, 1956, box 54, folder 45, Germantown Community Council Papers.

66. Letter from Myers to Giles, March 13, 1956, box 22, folder 45, Germantown Community Council Papers.

67. "A Conference of Community Organizations in Germantown and Mt. Airy," April 19, 1956, box 4, folder 17, Germantown Community Council Papers.

68. Religious Community Council of Stenton and the Emlen Federation of Civic Organizations, June 5, 1956, box 13, folder 36, Germantown Community Council Papers; Church Community Relations Council of Pelham et al., June 5, 1956, box 13, folder 36, Germantown Community Council Papers; "Groups Ask Integrated Schools, Staff," *GC*, June 14, 1956, box 13, folder 36, Germantown Community Council Papers; "School Bias Upsets Germantown," *PT*, June 16, 1956.

69. "Groups Ask Integrated Schools, Staff," *GC*, June 14, 1956.

70. "Groups Ask Integrated Schools, Staff," *GC*, June 14, 1956; Mercedes Dodds, "Letter to the Editor," *GC*, June 22, 1956, box 13, folder 36, Germantown Community Council Papers; Meeting Minutes of the Executive Committee of the Human Relations Committee of Germantown, September 18, 1956, box 54, folder 44, Germantown Community Council Papers; Ruth Miller to a friend, September 24, 1956, Enclosed, "A Statement for Better Integrated Schools in Philadelphia," box 13, folder 36, Germantown Community Council Papers.

71. GHS Yearbooks, January and June 1950

72. "Students Hear President," *CC*, December 16, 1941.

73. "Men Learn Skills in Gtn. Shop," *CC*, November 21, 1940; *Wartime Handbook for Education*, 11; Adult Education Department of the Long Beach Public Schools, "America's Answer: Education for Victory," 1942; "Adults to Learn Sales," *CC*, November 3, 1942; "Sales Course Ends Tomorrow," *CC*, November 18, 1942; "Faculty and Students Start Defense Work," *CC*, January 20, 1942; "Students, Faculty in Defense Work," *CC*, May 14, 1942.

74. "12B's Given Extra Period of Gym," *CC*, November 17, 1942; "Doubling the Gym Period."

75. "A Necessary Sacrifice," *CC*, January 20, 1942. See also "School Show Dropped at G.H.S. This Term," *CC*, October 13, 1942; *Wartime Handbook for Education*, 34–35. "Students Launch Victory Corps," *CC*, November 3, 1942; "Why Join the Victory Corp?" *CC*, December 16, 1942; "New Victory Corps Activities Began," *CC*, January 19, 1943; "Victory Corps Aids Varied Programs," *CC*, February 24, 1944; Ugland, "Education for Victory."

76. "Faculty and Students Start Defense Work," *CC*, January 20, 1942; "Sewing Classes Work for Red Cross," *CC*, January 20, 1942; "G.H.S. Prepares Gift Packages," *CC*, December 12, 1944.

77. "Senate Sponsors Buy-a-Bond Week," *CC*, May 14, 1942; "Students, Faculty in Defense Work," *CC*, May 14, 1942.

78. "Bond Sales Top $15,000," *CC*, November 3, 1942.

79. "Bond Sales Now Top $63,000," *CC*, December 16, 1942; "Bond, Stamp Sales Reach $102,000," *CC*, April 6, 1943; "Honor Society Boosts Stamp Sales," *CC*, June 10, 1943; "GHS Buys Bomber; Sales Increasing," *CC*, November 4, 1943; "Did Your Bonds Buy This Bomber," *CC*, April 25, 1944.

80. "Hospital Plan Is Xmas Goal," *CC*, October 31, 1944; "G.H.S. Goal for Sixth War Loan," *CC*, November 21, 1944; "Sixth War Loan," *CC*, November 21, 1944.

81. "Bye-Bye Dumb-Belles," *CC*, January 20, 1948.

82. Frank Selemno, interview by author, July 18, 2010.

83. "Senate Plans for New Term; Student Participation Stressed," *CC*, October 15, 1946; Angie Luongo, "Payment for Uniforms," *CC*, October 28, 1947; "Busy Term Ahead Projects Listed," *CC*, November 25, 1947; "It's Cheaper to Flunk," *CC*, January 20, 1948; "Senate Discusses New A.A. Tickets," *CC*, June 15, 1950.

84. Charles Shirley Jr., interview by author, July 27, 2010. See also M. Frances Hunter, interview by author, August 6, 2010.

85. Donald Hamilton, "An Appraisal of Our Community Relations," 1958, box 3, folder 6, Germantown Community Council Papers.

86. "Recreational Facilities are Urged for Negroes," *PI*, March 10, 1948, box 11, folder 17, Germantown Community Council Papers; "Adequate Facilities Must Be Provided for Gtn. Recreation," *GC*, May 5, 1949, box 63, Germantown Community Council Papers.

87. McKee, *Problem of Jobs*, 22–25.

88. *Wartime Handbook for Education*, 34–35; Dorn, *Creating the Dropout*.

89. Jones and Gregory, *Life Adjustment Education for Every Youth*, iii.

90. Jones and Gregory, *Life Adjustment Education for Every Youth*; Dorn, *Creating the Dropout*; Dillon, *Early School Leavers*; Educational Policies Commission, *Education for All American Youth*.

91. Jones and Gregory, *Life Adjustment Education for Every Youth*, 15.

92. Jones and Gregory, *Life Adjustment Education for Every Youth*; Ravitch, *Left Back*, 327–35; Kliebard, *Struggle for the American Curriculum*, 241–59; Zeran, *Life Adjustment Education in Action*.

93. The distributive education program prepared students for clerical jobs, while the vocational arts program was a college preparatory program; there were only three students in the agricultural track.

94. "G.H.S. Activities, Integrated Arts Class," *CC*, May 18, 1948. See also "Arts Dep't Offers Craft Courses," *CC*, October 12, 1950; "D.E. Class Working on Full Time Schedule," *CC*, December 14, 1950; "Clerical Practice New Major Course," *CC*, January 24, 1950; "G.H.S. Girls to Enter first X-Ray Course," *CC*, January 25, 1951; "G.H.S. Offers First Course in Home Nursing," *CC*, April 24, 1952; "Students Practice Home Nursing," *CC*, October 28, 1952; "Home Nursing Boys Make Better Beds," *CC*, October 27, 1953; "117 Receive Home Nursing Certificate," *CC*, March 22, 1955.

95. "Germantown Offers New Students Extensive Guidance Program," *CC*, September 12, 1951.

96. "College Guidance Offered Students," *CC*, February 3, 1948; "College Bound," *CC*, September 12, 1949; "Get Requirements for College in 103," *CC*, February 24, 1955; "Tenth Grade Not Too Soon," *CC*, November 20, 1956.

97. See appendix for data and analysis.

98. Snyder, ed., *120 Years of American Education*, 75; Komarovsky, "Cultural Contradictions and Sex Roles," 184–89; Peirs and Neisser, "Is She Ready for College?" 32–33; Kessler-Harris, *Out to Work*.

99. August, interview by author.

100. Cerrato, interview by author; United States Census, Philadelphia County, 1940. See also Helene C. Kaelin, interview by author, July 29, 2009.

101. Gabler, "They Learn to Be Good Neighbors," *EB*, January 25, 1956; Fowler, "Citizens, Junior Grade."

102. Adrianne Valentine Morrison, interview by author, November 8, 2011; United States Census, Philadelphia County, 1940.

103. "Fellowship Club Plans Barn Dance," *CC*, April 24, 1952; "Germantown Week Theme Is 'Unity,'" *CC*, May 13, 1952; "Fellowship Group Will Present 'The Legend,'" *CC*, May 11, 1954.

104. "The Germantown Way," *CC*, October 8, 1957.

105. August, interview by author; Kaelin, interview by author.

106. Meeting Notes, Committee on Human Relations, March 8, 1949, box 50, folder 23, Germantown Community Council Papers.

107. August, interview by author; Meeting Notes, November 1949, box 50, folder 23, Germantown Community Council Papers.

108. Cuff, interview by author, August 6, 2010. See also Neckerman, *Schools Betrayed*.

Chapter 5

1. Fuller, interview by author, August 8, 2010. See also Countryman, *Up South*, 58–62; Herbert Rodville, Herbert S. Interview by Gregory Woods, July 7, 1992, GBWC.

2. For the long arc of this story in Chicago, see Todd-Breland, *Political Education*.

3. Delmont, *Nicest Kids in Town*, 93–94.

4. Bacon, *Design of Cities*, 13.

5. Heller, *Ed Bacon*, 50–53.

6. Heller, *Ed Bacon*, 58–59.

7. United States Census, 1950 and 1970, Philadelphia County, Social Explorer, www.socialexplorer.com.

8. Churchill and Kendree, *Preliminary Study of Germantown*; Magaziner, *Proposal for the Revitalization of the Heart of Germantown*.

9. "A Fact Sheet on the Local Town Meetings," January 15, 1961, box 10, folder 7, Germantown Community Council Papers.

10. "Section I: Upper Germantown and Mt. Airy"; "Germantown Settlement Statement to Town Meeting," March 3, 1961; Morton Neighborhood Council, "Report to Physical Planning Committee of Germantown Community Council," March 9, 1961; Penn Knox Neighborhood Association, "Community Planning Problems, 1961," March 23, 1961; and Wister Neighborhood Council, "Statement to the Town Meeting" March 23, 1961, all box 10, folder 7, Germantown Community Council Papers.

11. United States Census 1940 and 1960, Philadelphia County, socialexplorer.com.

12. Levenstein, *A Movement Without Marches*, 127; Phillips, "A History of the Struggle for School Desegregation in Philadelphia," 52–53.

13. Lavell, "Philadelphia's Non-white Population," 2, Philadelphia City Archives; Franklin, *The Education of Black Philadelphia*, 188; Binzen, "Transfers Help Integration" *PI*, December 13, 1962, TUUA Box 207.

14. Bruce McDowell, interview by author, August 31, 2010.

15. Linda Singleton, interview by author, February 2, 2012.

16. Lewis, *Report of the Special Committee on Nondiscrimination*, 12.

17. Philadelphia Board of Education, Division of Research, "A Ten-Year Summary of the Distribution of Negro Pupils in the Philadelphia Public Schools, 1957–1966," December 23, 1966, box 23, folder 6, Floyd Logan Collection; "Number of Negro Teachers and Percentage of Negro Students in Philadelphia Senior High Schools, 1956–1957 [n.d.]," box 14, folder 10, Floyd Logan Collection, cited in Delmont, *Nicest Kids in Town*, 93–94.

18. Bob Queen, "NAACP Suit Testing North's School Bias," *PC*, June 17, 1961.

19. Phillips, "History of the Struggle for School Desegregation in Philadelphia," 54–55; Levenstein, *Movement Without Marches*, 128.

20. Phillips, "History of the Struggle for School Desegregation in Philadelphia," 55. See also Douglas, *Jim Crow Moves North*; Ryan, *Five Miles Away*.

21. Phillips, "Struggle for School Desegregation in Philadelphia," 118.

22. John Gillespie, "True Integration Unlikely, School Aides Fear," *EB*, November 17, 1963, Philadelphia Public Schools Desegregation, 1960s.

23. Phillips, "Struggle for School Desegregation in Philadelphia," 127.

24. Phillips, "Struggle for School Desegregation in Philadelphia," 129–33; Thomas Dau and Peter Janssen, "School Board Files Integration Report," *PI*, March 16, 1965, Philadelphia Public Schools Desegregation, 1960s.

25. Art Peters, "Board of Education Committee to Study Lack of Negro Principals," *PT*, February 9, 1963. See also Lewis, *Report of the Special Committee on Nondiscrimination*, 5.

26. Lewis, *Report of the Special Committee on Nondiscrimination*, 16; "Summary of Reports," *PI*, July 24, 1964.

27. William Collins, "Study of City Schools Hits Race Inequality," *PI*, July 26, 1964, Philadelphia Public Schools Desegregation, 1960s.

28. Lewis, *Report of the Special Committee on Nondiscrimination*, 36. See also Riessman, *Culturally Deprived Child*; Phillips, "Struggle for School Desegregation in Philadelphia," 139.

29. Lewis, *Report of the Special Committee on Nondiscrimination*, 208–10.

30. Lewis, *Report of the Special Committee on Nondiscrimination*, 158.

31. Odell, *Educational Survey Report*, 44–52, 196–98.

32. Odell, *Educational Survey Report*, 340–49.

33. Odell, *Educational Survey Report*, 197.

34. J. Brantley Wilder and Mark Bricklin, "Odell Survey of Schools is $125,000 Flop," *PT*, March 9, 1965.

35. Odell, *Educational Survey Report*, 385

36. J. Brantley Wilder and Mark Bricklin, "Odell Survey of Schools is $125,000 Flop," *PT*, March 9, 1965; "Odell Report 47 Years Late," *PT*, April 6, 1965.

37. J. Williams Jones, "Board Plans to Bus Pupils to Schools in Northeast," *EB*, March 26, 1965, box 62, Germantown Community Council Papers.

38. Jim Magee, "School Board Names Comm. for Integration: 18 Negroes on 52-Citizen Unit; Set April Meet," *PT*, March 27, 1965.

39. "NAACP Calls Report," *EB*, March 30, 1965.

40. Mark Bricklin, "Becomes Highest Ranking Negro Educator in U.S.: Vows to Speed Integration and Tan Principals," *PT*, June 26, 1965.

41. "Teacher Integration Plan Shelved After Clash at Stormy Meeting," *PT*, October 16, 1965.

42. "Englewood Educator Named Head of Philadelphia Schools," *NYT*, December 1, 1966; J. Porter, "Dr. Whittier, Departing School Head, Didn't Get Fair Chance, Says Nichols," *PT*, December 3, 1966.

43. Birger, "Race, Reaction, and Reform," 170.

44. Mark Shedd, "Address to the Staff," Philadelphia, May 18, 1967, cited in Birger, "Race, Reaction, and Reform," 170–71.

45. "A Fair Chance for Dr. Shedd's Ideas," *PT*, June 3, 1967; John Wilder, "New School Superintendent Sending His Children to 90% Negro School," *PT*, September 12, 1967.

46. August, interview by author; Pearl Aldrich, "Sharing, Shifting, Extra Free Time Ill of Germantown HS Overcrowding," *PI*, box 13, folder 36, Germantown Community Council Papers.

47. School District of Philadelphia, *Statistical Reports of the Department of Instruction*, 1941–1957, School District of Philadelphia Archives.

48. Meeting of the Schools Committee of the Germantown Community Council, January 6, 1957, box 13, folder 36, Germantown Community Council Papers.

49. Meeting of the Schools Committee of the Germantown Community Council, January 6, 1957. See also Earle N. Barber Jr. to GCC, December 3, 1957, box 13, folder 36; John Gummere to GCC, December 9, 1957, box 13, folder 36; Gummere to GCC, January 17, 1958, box 3, folder 33; Leon Obermayer to Gummere, January 20, 1958, box 13, folder 36, all Germantown Community Council Papers.

50. "GHS Expansion Costs $1¼ Million," May 1958, box 13, folder 36, Germantown Community Council Papers.

51. Conant, *American High School Today*.

52. Cathy Spears Schuler, interview by author, April 30, 2015.

53. Michelle Deal Winfield, interview by author, March 16, 2015.

54. Singleton, interview by author.

55. Walter Ballard, interview by author, April 11, 2016.

56. Marianna Eckhardt, interview by author, October 18, 2011.

57. Mary Ellen Brown to Joseph, April 4, 1964, box 15, folder 64, Germantown Community Council Papers.

58. Brown to Joseph, April 4, 1964. See also Stanwood Kenyon, Memo, January 11, 1965, box 19, folder 193, Germantown Community Council Papers; "Germantown High Visit Impresses 34 Pupils," *PI*, December 20, 1964, box 64, Germantown Community Council Papers.

59. "Youth Aide Predicts," *PI*, October 29, 1964, box 64; Martin Herman, "Germantown Gangs Called Worst," *EB*, March 17, 1965, box 64; "Boy Fined $25," *EB*, October 29, 1963, box 92; "Man, 2 Youths Shot," *PI*, October 22, 1964, box 64, all Germantown Community Council Papers.

60. Kean, "Student Unrest and Crisis," 103–7.

61. Junius Bond, "3 Youths Held in Attack On Gtn. High 'A' Student," *PT*, October 27, 1962.

62. Chet Coleman, "Boy, 15, Arrested in Germantown High School Stabbing Incident," *PT*, December 8, 1964.

63. "15 Invade High School; 2 Shot in Gang Fracas," *EB*, October 17, 1967, box 92, folder, GHS-Student Activities Prior to 1968, EBC-TUUA.

64. "15 Invade High School," *EB*, October 17, 1967; "8 Germantown Boys Seized," *EB*, October 18, 1967. For earlier incidents, see "Pupil Accused of Taking Razor," *EB*, May 12, 1963, box 92, folder, GHS-Student Activities Prior to 1968, EBC-TUUA.

65. George Riley, "Schools Adopt Tough Policies with Rowdies," *EB*, February 14, 1957, box 92, folder, Schools-Phila. Miscel. 1964 and Prior, EBC-TUUA.

66. "'Behavior Code' Guiding Germantown," *EB*, November 5, 1963, box 92, folder, Germantown High School, EBC-TUUA; "15 Invade High School," *EB*, October 17, 1967, EBC-TUUA.

67. Margaret Halsey, "Police Team of Reihley and Riley Keeps Germantown Pupils in Line," *EB*, October 10, 1968, Germantown High School, EBC-TUUA.

68. Noguera, "Schools, Prisons, and Social Implications of Punishment"; Hinton, *From the War on Poverty to the War on Crime.*

69. Earle N. Barber Jr. to Members of the Germantown Community Council, March 24, 1965, box 3, folder 37, Germantown Community Council Papers.

70. This figure is not the official poverty rate. In 1960, the weighted average poverty threshold according to the United States Census was $3,022 for a family of four. These figures were calculated by the author using that rate. United States Census, Historical Poverty Tables: People and Families, 1959 to 2019, https://www.census.gov/data/tables/time-series/demo/income-poverty/historical-poverty-people.html.

71. Wert Hooper, "Germantown Folk Hit Plan to Close Camp Emlen This Summer," *PT*, April 20, 1957; Germantown Settlement, Annual Board Meeting, June 1958–June 1959, folder, GS-AD, Germantown Settlement Records; YMCA of Germantown, Proposed Budget, 1960–61, folder, Budget, 1959–1962, Young Men's Christian Association (Philadelphia, Pa.), Germantown Branch Records.

72. Clarice Herbert, interview by Stephanie Y. Felix, September 9, 1996, cited in Felix, "Committed to Their Own," 222.

73. Felix, "Committed to Their Own," 220–23.

74. S. Kenyon, "Evaluation of 'GIPSY '64,'" August 17, 1964, box 35, folder 59; W.T. Vandever Jr., "Evaluation and Suggestions for 'GIPSY '64,'" August 16, 1964, box 35, folder 59; Germantown Community Council, "Rough Draft: Report of the 1964–65 Recreation Committee," May 17, 1965, box 11, folder 22; "Youth to Toil, Absorb Values," *PI*, April 12, 1964, box 35, folder 54; M. Bailey, Wister Neighborhood Council, to Members and Friends, August 4, 1966, box 35, folder 52, all Germantown Community Council Papers.

75. "$1¼ Million Improvement Planned," *GC*, October 29, 1964, box 64, Germantown Community Council Papers.

76. David Umansky, "Overcrowding Taxes School," *PI*, January 21, 1965, folder, Germantown High School, Buildings, EBC-TUUA; McDowell, interview by author.

77. J. William Jones, "Campus School Complex Planned in Germantown," *EB*, March 6, 1964, box 64, Acc 39; Peter Janssen, "Campus Urged for All Schools in Germantown," *PI*, March 7, 1964, box 92, folder, Germantown (Section) Schools, EBC-TUUA; "Education Park

Urged," *PI*, January 14, 1965, box 64, Germantown Community Council Papers; "Education Park Plan Is Defended," *PI*, January 21, 1965, box 64, Germantown Community Council Papers.

78. J. William Jones, "Calif. Firm Hired to Study Germantown 'Campus' Plan," *EB*, December 1, 1964; J. William Jones, "School Project to Preserve 'Character,'" *EB*, December 3, 1964; Lois Morasco, "Civic Units Back Education Study," *EB*, April 26, 1964, all box 64, Germantown Community Council Papers.

79. Maurice Lewis Jr., "Renewal Role Urged for Schools," *EB*, January 17, 1965, box 92, folder, Gtw. (Section) Schools, EBC-TUUA.

80. Peter Binzen, "$36.7 Million School Reorganization," *EB*, August 19, 1965, box 92, folder, Gtw. (Section) Schools, EBC-TUUA.

81. Todd-Breland, *Political Education*, 54.

82. "Youth Group Plans Negro History Fete," *EB*, February 17, 1966, box 64; "Germantown Pupils Slate 'Freedom Day,'" *PI*, February 13, 1966, box 63, both Germantown Community Council Papers.

83. Countryman, *Up South*, 239.

84. Countryman, *Up South*, 229.

85. Germantown Community Council, Schools Progress Report, November 1965, box 14, folder 43, Germantown Community Council Papers.

86. "Statement by the Schools Committee," October 1965, box 14, folder 42; J. Harry LaBrum to Mrs. Thornhill Cosby, September 22, 1965, box 14, folder 42; Cosby to Neighbor, October 15, 1965, box 14, folder 43; Germantown Community Council Schools Committee, November 1965, box 14, folder 43; Schools Proposals for Board of Directors, November 18, 1965, box 2, folder 24, all Germantown Community Council Papers.

87. Central Germantown Residential Survey, February 4, 1966, box 10, folder 9, Germantown Community Council Papers.

88. Todd-Breland, *Political Education*, 54.

89. "Black Power Pickets Battle Police," and "Dilworth Blames Police," *EB*, November 17, 1967; "Mathis Says He Was a Peacemaker," *EB*, November 21, 1967, cited in Countryman, *Up South*, 223–24.

90. Countryman, *Up South*, 223–25.

91. Countryman, *Up South*, 226; Ron Whitehorn, "1967: Black Students Strike," *PPSN*, September 25, 2002.

92. Countryman, *Up South*, 228.

Chapter 6

1. John Gillespie, "Board Orders Schools Closed as Pact Ends" *EB*, September 8, 1970, EBC-FLP.

2. William Mandel, "Parents Work to Keep Open 'Get Set' Units," *EB*, September 9, 1970; William Kennedy and Adolph Katz, "Volunteers Step in as Teachers," *EB*, September 10, 1970; William Mandel, "Ready to Work Even as Volunteers," *EB*, September 10, 1970; Kennedy, "Volunteers Teach Pupils at over 100 Sites," *EB*, September 10, 1970, all EBC-FLP; John Wilder, "Do Not Interfere, Judge Warns Board and Union," *PT*, September 12, 1970; Fred Hechinger, "Education: A Money Squeeze Marks the Opening of Schools," *NYT*, September 13, 1970; "Annual Report, 1970–1971," box 35, folder 1, Fellowship Commission Records.

3. John Gillespie, "City Pupils Return Tomorrow under 30-Day Agreement," *EB*, September 14, 1970; John Gillespie, "290,000 Begin First Day of Classes Here," *EB*, September 15, 1970, both EBC-FLP; "Schools to Reopen in Philadelphia," *NYT*, September 15, 1970.

4. Katrina Dyke and John Gillespie, "Teachers Strike City Public School System," *EB*, October 16, 1970; William Kennedy, "Teacher Union Leaders Cited for Contempt," *EB*, October 16, 1970; William Kennedy, "Union Won't Capitulate," *EB*, October 17, 1970, all EBC-FLP; "Philadelphia Schools Hit by Teachers Strike," *WP*, October 17, 1970; "Philadelphia Teachers Strike on Pay," *NYT*, October 17, 1970; "Philadelphia Teachers Strike," *LAT*, October 17, 1970; Pamela Haynes, "Many Black Principals Operating Schools," *PT*, October 20, 1970.

5. John Gillespie and William Kennedy, "Union Agrees to End Teachers Strike," *EB*, October 20, 1970; John Gillespie, "$57.3 Million Pact Sends Teachers Back to Work," *EB*, October 21, 1970, both EBC-FLP; John Gaudiosi, "Philly Strike Is Over," *CDD*, October 22, 1970.

6. James Lytle, interview by author, March 23, 2015.

7. United States Census, Philadelphia County, 1940 and 1980, socialexplorer.com.

8. "Philadelphia Is Scene of Black Student Walkout," *CDD*, October 9, 1968; John Wilder, "200 Students Walk Out of Bok," *PT*, October 8, 1968; "Police Guarding Tense Philly High School," *CDD*, October 10, 1968; "Ten Days of Disorders," *EB*, October 20, 1968, folder, Racial Tensions, EBC-FLP.

9. Lombardo, *Blue-Collar Conservatism*.

10. Linda Hefner, "Government and People Demand Better Results for School Dollar," *EB*, September 8, 1970; Perrillo, *Uncivil Rights*.

11. Watson, "What Do You Mean When You Say Urban."

12. "Senate Witness Bids U.S. Fund 25 Big Urban School Systems," *NYT*, September 22, 1971. See also "U.S. Asked to Run Big City Schools," *WP*, September 22, 1971.

13. Stephen Isaacs, "Philadelphia: A Referendum on Rizzo," *WP*, October 31, 1971; "Ex-Police Official Wins Philadelphia Mayorality," *LAT*, November 3, 1971; "Lack of Response Kills Voter Guide," *PT*, October 5, 1971.

14. "Board Moves to Dismiss School Chief," *WP*, December 1, 1971.

15. Peter Milius, "First Casualty," *WP*, December 12, 1971; "School Head Out in Philadelphia," *NYT*, December 12, 1971.

16. "Board in Philadelphia Names School Chief," *NYT*, December 17, 1971; John Wilder, "New School Head," *PT*, January 8, 1972.

17. "Costanzo in DC Seeking School Aid," *EB*, February 25, 1972; Linda Heffner, "Costanzo Gets Sympathy, No Aid in Washington," *EB*, February 26, 1972, both in folder, Costanzo, Matthew W., Finances School, 1971–72, EBC-TUUA.

18. Charles Thomson, "State Rejects Phila. Plea for School Funds," *EB*, June 21, 1972, folder, Costanzo, Matthew W., Finances School, 1971–72, EBC-TUUA.

19. Charles Thomson, "Costanzo Seeks Revised School Aid," *EB*, October 17, 1972, folder, Costanzo, Matthew W., Finances School, 1971–72, EBC-TUUA.

20. United States Census, 1970.

21. Charles Thomson and Paula Herbert, "2 Councilwomen Ask School Pact Extension," *EB*, September 1, 1972, FLP Newspaper Collection; Charles Thomson, "City School Strike," *EB*, September 4, 1972, FLP Newspaper Collection; Louise Cook, "Strikes Could Delay Many School Starts," *WP*, September 1, 1972; "Philadelphia Teachers Strike, Suburbs also Face

Walkouts," *NYT*, September 5, 1972; "From New York to Missouri: Strikes Delay Start of School," *LAT*, September 7, 1972.

22. J. Brantley Wilder, "Open Centers to Teach High School Youth During Strike," *PT*, September 9, 1972; J. Brantley Wilder, "Education Confrontation," *PT*, September 23, 1972; Lytle, interview by author.

23. Ronald Booner, "Photo Standalone 15," *PT*, September 19, 1972; Gene Harris, "Mothers and Children Confront Rizzo on Schools," *EB*, September 8, 1972, EBC-FLP; "Students Picket in Philadelphia," *HC*, September 10, 1972; "Strike Protesters Confront Councilmen," *HC*, September 23, 1972; Len Lear, "Students, Teachers Unite Politically," *PT*, September 23, 1972.

24. "Teachers Strike Postpones School," *HC*, September 14, 1972; Robert Donin, "Philadelphia Teacher Strike Settlement Is Weeks Away," *WP*, September 21, 1972; Pamela Haynes, "Right On!" *PT*, September 26, 1972.

25. Len Lear, "School Strike Lawsuit Lists Permanent Damage," *PT*, September 26, 1972. See also "Need to Better Represent Children," *PT*, February 10, 1968.

26. Lear, "School Strike Lawsuit Lists Permanent Damage," *PT*, September 26, 1972.

27. "Philadelphia Teachers Vote to Return to Classrooms," *WP*, September 28, 1972; J. Brantley Wilder, "Schools Opened as Court Intervenes," *PT*, September 30, 1972.

28. Charles Thomson, "Board Files for Injunction to Bar Teachers' Strike," *EB*, January 4, 1973; Charles Thomson, "School Board Ask Court to Block Teachers Strike," *EB*, January 5, 1973; "Pay, Length of Faculty Day Are Keys to School Impasse," *EB*, January 7, 1973; "School Impasse," *EB*, January 8, 1973, all EBC-FLP.

29. Charles Thomson and S. Robert Jacobs, "Rizzo Exhorts Teachers to Work Despite Strike," *EB*, January 6, 1973, EBC-FLP.

30. Charles Thomson, "Strike by Teachers 'Certain as Can Be,'" *EB*, January 7, 1973; "130 School Close as Teachers Strike," *EB*, January 8, 1973, EBC-FLP.

31. Harmon Gordon and Martin Herman, "Court Issues Injunction, Teachers Voice Defiance," *EB*, January 11, 1973, EBC-FLP.

32. "Women and Children Picket Against Teachers," *EB*, January 17, 1973, EBC-FLP.

33. "Pa. Board Defies Rizzo, Hires Teachers," *WP*, February 8, 1973; "TV-3 Airs Math Course," *PT*, February 6, 1973.

34. "Prison for Two in School Strike in Philadelphia," *CT*, February 10, 1973; Wayne King, "Rizzo Lifts Offer in School Strike," *NYT*, February 10, 1973; David Freudberg, "Two Jailed in Pa. Teacher's Strike," *WP*, February 10, 1973.

35. Wayne King, "Teachers Seized in Philadelphia," *NYT*, February 16, 1973; "Pickets Seized in Pa. Strike," *WP*, February 17, 1973; "319 Jailed in Teacher Strike in Philadelphia," *LAT*, February 17, 1973; "383 in Philadelphia Charged on Strike," *NYT*, February 20, 1973; "Police Arrest 417 Striking Teachers in Philadelphia," *ADW*, February 20, 1973.

36. "Philadelphia School Head Quits," *NYT*, February 21, 1973; "School Chief Bows Out in Phila.," *WP*, February 21, 1973.

37. "Federal Aide Seeks to End Philadelphia School Strike," *NYT*, February 23, 1973; "Quick End Seen in Strike of Philadelphia Teachers," *NYT*, February 24, 1973; "Philadelphia School Strike Settled," *HC*, February 28, 1973; Jon Katz, "Rizzo Concedes Higher Cost of Teachers Pact," *WP*, March 1, 1973.

38. "Philly School Problems Seen as Both Racial, Financial," *ADW*, March 1, 1973.

39. Lytle, interview by author; J. Brantley Wilder, "J. Kelly School Losing Students," *PT*, February 27, 1973.

40. Paul Bennett, "Costanzo Resigns, Poindexter Will Serve in Interim," *PT*, July 8, 1975; Steve Twomey, "The Enigma of Costanzo, a Fighter Who Ran Away," *PI*, August 31, 1975, folder, Costanzo, Matthew, Inquirer Interview, 8-31-75, EBC-TUUA.

41. Steve Twomey, "Public Sick of Higher Cost, Taxes," *PI*, May 5, 1976; Steve Twomey, "Marcase Says Schools Need Funds for Survival," *PI*, May 14, 1976, folder, Marcase, Michael, Superintendent of Schools, Philadelphia, 1976, EBC-TUUA.

42. Carole Rich, "Phila. Unveils Integration Plan," *EB*, May 11, 1976; Carole Rich, "2 Black Leaders Rip Pupil Integration Plan," *EB*, May 11, 1976; Carole Rich, "Unit Seeks to Skirt Busing," *EB*, April 27, 1976, folder, Marcase, Michael, Superintendent of Schools Philadelphia, 1976, EBC-TUUA.

43. "Public School Teachers Ready to Go on Strike," *PT*, August 3, 1976; "Teachers' Strike Can Be Averted," *PT*, August 17, 1976.

44. Lorraine Branham, "Parents' Group Slates Workshop in Readiness for Teachers' Strike," *PT*, August 24, 1976; Lorraine Branham, "350 Volunteers to Teach If Strike Shuts Public Schools," *PT*, August 31, 1976.

45. Lorraine Branham, "City Hall to Play Big Role in PFT, School Board Talks," *PT*, September 4, 1976. See also Lorraine Branham, "Students Want Role in School Contract Talks with the PFT," *PT*, September 7, 1976.

46. Carole Rich and W. Robert Bridgeo, "Contract Approved by Phila. Teachers," *EB*, September 7, 1976, folder, Marcase, Michael, Superintendent of Schools Philadelphia, 1976, EBC-TUUA.

47. Carole Rich, "Budget Cuts Rouse Phila. Teachers Union," *EB*, March 19, 1977; Rich, "'No Fat' School Budget?" *EB*, April 24, 1977; Carole Rich, "Schools Slash Shocks Officials, Staff," *EB*, May 1, 1977; Carole Rich, "Marcase Expects 5,000 to Lose Jobs," *EB*, May 8, 1977; Carole Rich, "9,731 Jobs Face Ax in Budget," *EB*, May 14, 1977, all folder, Marcase, Michael, School Supt, Budget 77–78, EBC-TUUA.

48. Michael Coakley, "Council Plans $10 Million for Schools," *EB*, June 18, 1977; Carole Rich, "Schools Still Need $84 Million," *EB*, August 21, 1977, all folder, Marcase, Michael, School Supt, Budget 77–78, EBC-TUUA.

49. Michael Coakley, "Council Plans $10 Million for Schools," *EB*, June 18, 1977; Carole Rich, "Schools Still Need $84 Million," *EB*, August 21, 1977, both, folder, Marcase, Michael, School Supt, Budget 77–78, EBC-TUUA; Oakes, "A Demoralizing Summer and Still No Solution," *Oakes Newsletter*, September 20, 1977, box 1, folder 4, Helen Oakes Papers, Acc 995, TUUA.

50. "Phil. Schools Abandon Hope of Integration," *AA*, March 28, 1970; Oakes, "Integration," *Oakes Newsletter*, April 15, 1971, box 32, Helen Oakes Papers; Donald Janson, "Pupil Balance Set by Pennsylvania," *NYT*, June 19, 1971.

51. Richardson Dilworth, "Let's Regionalize the Schools," *EB*, January 22, 1971; "Can Suburban and Phila. Schools Work Together," *EB*, February 21, 1971; William Kennedy, "Merger of Phila.-Suburban Schools Proposed," August 29, 1971, box 209, folder Schools-Phila-Suburban 1968–1971, EBC-TUUA.

52. Robert Hightower, "Building Black, Learning Power," *PT*, September 19, 1971; "Educator Rejects Token Integration," *AA*, August 21, 1971.

53. J. Brantley Wilder, "Bowser Claims School Board's Worse than KKK," *PT*, November 24, 1973. See also "Task Force to Oversee City School Integration," *PI*, September 9, 1973;

Elizabeth Williams, "Schools Calmly Greet Desegregation Deadline," *EB*, November 11, 1973, folder, Segregation, 1970–1974, FLP Newspaper Clippings Collection, Education.

54. J. Brantley Wilder, "'We Won't Bus;' Is Scream of Desegregation Foes," *PT*, January 19, 1974.

55. Wilder, "'We Won't Bus,'" *PT*, January 19, 1974.

56. Paul Taylor, "Expert Gives Plan for Phila. Desegregation," *PI*, August 30, 1974, folder, Segregation, 1970–1974, FLP Newspaper Clippings Collection, Education.

57. Peter Milius, "High Court Draws Final Line," *WP*, July 26, 1974; Meinke, "Milliken v. Bradley," 20–22.

58. Ryan, *Five Miles Away*; Bell, *Silent Covenants*; Kluger, *Simple Justice*; Clotfelter, *After "Brown"*; Orfield, *Dismantling Desegregation*.

59. Gerald McCullough and Thomas Breen, 3rd, "New Phila. School Racial Plan Avoids 'Massive' Pupil Busing," *EB*, August 30, 1974, folder, Desegregation, 1975, FLP Newspaper Clippings Collection, Education; J. Brantley Wilder, "School Plan Is a Delaying Tactic," *PT*, September 3, 1974; James Wooten, "Busing May Change the Philadelphia Story," *NYT*, August 3, 1975.

60. Steve Twomey, "School Board Ready to Reject Bias Plan," *PI*, June 4, 1975, folder, Desegregation, 1975, FLP Newspaper Clippings Collection, Education.

61. Carole Rich, "Integration Plan Ripped at Hearing," *EB*, June 6, 1975; Steve Twomey, "Angry Parents Jam Hearings to Protest Desegregation Plans," *PI*, June 3, 1975, folder, Desegregation, 1975, FLP Newspaper Clippings Collection, Education.

62. Elizabeth Williams, "Schools Calmly Greet," *EB*, November 11, 1973, folder, Segregation, 1970 -74, FLP Newspaper Clippings Collection, Education.

63. "'Liberation' Seen Behind Gang Problem in Germantown," *PT*, May 23, 1970.

64. "350 Youth Off to Camp Wm. Penn," *PT*, July 28, 1970; "Autumn Time Fun-Learning at Germantown 'Y,'" *PT*, September 1, 1970.

65. Len Lear, "G'twn Civic Group Provides Housing for 43 Families," *PT*, October 3, 1970.

66. "Belfield Court Apt. Residents Must Carry Knives for Protection," *PT*, April 21, 1970; Len Lear, "G'twn Apartment House Declared Unfit," *PT*, September 11, 1970; "Gang War Claims Its 39th Victim," *AA*, October 27, 1973.

67. McKee, *Problem of Jobs*, 251.

68. "Greater G'twn Appeal to Solicit Area Businesses," *PT*, August 18, 1973; "Is It Easy or Hard to Find a Job These Days," *PT*, September 11, 1973.

69. Pamela Haynes, "Gtn. Students Kept in Freezing 'Squirrel Cages,'" *PT*, December 17, 1968.

70. Margaret Halsey, "Wire Ceilings Used to Block Missiles at Germantown High," *EB*, date not legible; Margaret Halsey, "New 'Classrooms' at Germantown Have No Ceilings; Result: 'Bedlam,'" *EB*, October 19, 1968, both folder Germantown High School, Misc, EBC-TUUA.

71. John Wilder, "Jeremiah X Tricked School," *PT*, February 24, 1968.

72. "Bellis, Dilworth to Confer on School Issues," *EB*, March 14, 1968, folder, Germantown High School, EBC-TUUA.

73. "Boy Wounded Near School," *EB*, March 27, 1968, folder GHS-Student Activities Prior to 1968, EBCF; "200 Germantown Teen-Agers Fight, One Boy Is Shot, Another Stabbed," *EB*, March 28, 1968, folder, Germantown High School, EBC-TUUA.

74. Spencer, *In the Crossfire*, 172–73.

75. Len Lear, "Parents of G'tn High 'Exiles' Called Bigots," *PT*, January 13, 1968.

76. Julie Moshinsky, "Germantown High School Coordinator Wants Better for Her School," *EB*, March 7, 1968, folder, Germantown High School, EBC-TUUA.

77. Margaret Halsey, "Germantown High Is Given Extra Guards," *EB*, February 6, 1969. See also Margaret Halsey, "Police Team of Reihley and Riley Keep Germantown Pupils in Line," *EB*, October 10, 1968, both folder, Germantown High School, EBC-TUUA; "Greater Security Sought in Schools," *AA*, February 15, 1969.

78. Alexander, *New Jim Crow*; Goffman, *On the Run*.

79. Noguera, "Schools, Prisons, and Social Implications of Punishment"; Shedd, *Unequal City*; Hinton, *From the War on Poverty to the War on Crime*; Thompson, "Criminalizing Kids," in Rose and Katz, *Public Education Under Siege*.

80. "Germantown High's New Principal Was Athletic Champion at Temple U.," *PT*, January 6, 1970; "Germantown High School Gets 'Tough' Principal," *AA*, January 17, 1970.

81. William Kennedy, "Germantown High to Close Lunchroom Indefinitely," *EB*, November 25, 1970, box 92, folder, Germantown High School, Misc., EBC-TUUA; Janet Malloy, interview by author, February 10, 2015.

82. D. D. Eisenberg, "School—This Time for Seniors Only," *EB*, January 17, 1973, EBC-FLP.

83. Eisenberg, "School—This Time for Seniors Only," *EB*, January 17, 1973, EBC-FLP.

84. Len Lear, "What's the Most Serious Problem in Philadelphia?" *PT*, October 17, 1972.

85. Lytle, interview by author.

86. United States Census, Philadelphia County, 1960 and 1980, socialexplorer.com.

87. Lombardo, *Blue-Collar Conservatism*.

88. Joyce Gemperlein, Lucinda Fleeson, and Mary Bishop, "Court Orders Teachers Back," *PI*, October 8, 1981.

89. John Gillespie, "Negro School Enrollment Now Close to 60 Pct. Here," *EB*, June 12, 1970, EBC-TUUA.

90. "Martin Luther King High," *PT*, February 5, 1972.

91. Arthur Ridgeway, "3 Youths Are Stabbed," *EB*, December 5, 1972; Charles F. Thomson, "Gang Fights, Pupil Assaults," *EB*, June 6, 1972, both EBC-TUUA.

92. "G'town 'Y' Membership Drive Needs Support," *PT*, April 7, 1973; "Greater G'twn Appeal Still Seeking Funds," *PT*, August 18, 1973; "G'twn Boys' Club Starts 87th Year," *PT*, September 25, 1973; "Germantown 'YW' Notes 104 Years," *PT*, March 9, 1974.

93. Timothy Dougherty, "Residents of Germantown 'Y' Hoping for a HUD Loan," *PT*, August 18, 1978; Timothy Dougherty, "Germantown YMCA's Money Loss Is OIC's Gain," *PT*, October 6, 1978; "Community Agency Gets City Grant," *PT*, September 12, 1980; Gwen McKinney, "U.S. Grant Hopes to Boost Germantown Youth Program," *PT*, December 23, 1980.

94. Lou Antosh, "King School Construction 'a Travesty,' Teacher Says," *EB*, August 28, 1977, folder Martin Luther King, 1977, EBC-TUUA; Timothy Dougherty, "Student's Gripe Brings Results at King High," *PT*, April 29, 1978.

95. Clark Deleon, "The Scene-in Philadelphia and Its Suburbs," *PI*, April 10, 1981; Rick Nichols, "Not Marcase, but the Teacher's Union Incurs Council's Wrath," *PI*, April 12, 1981.

96. Mike Leary and Steve Twomey, "City Judge Intervenes on Schools," *PI*, July 16, 1981; Carol Honer, "Man in the News," *PI*, August 10, 1981; Thomas Ferrick Jr. and Steve Twomey, "Can the School District Be Put Back Together?" *PI*, July 23, 1981.

97. Thomas Ferrick Jr., "City Schools Run Poorly Audit Says," *PI*, July 29, 1981.

98. Thomas Ferrick Jr. and Mary Bishop, "Strike Fears Mount," *PI*, August 16, 1981; Rick Nichols, "Teachers Take the Offensive," *PI*, August 18, 1981; Maida Odom, "PFT Head Calls Strike Inevitable," *PI*, August 31, 1981; Mary Bishop and Rick Nichols, "Union Rejects Green's Plan," *PI*, September 1, 1981; Rick Nichols, "PFT Votes for a Strike Scorns Green," *PI*, September 2, 1981; Joyce Gemperlein, "Teachers Are Rebuffed in Court," *PI*, September 5, 1981.

99. Joyce Gemperlein, Lucinda Fleeson, and Mary Bishop, "Court Orders Teachers Back," *PI*, October 8, 1981; Thomas Ferrick Jr., Mary Bishop, and Lucinda Fleeson, "The Strike: Meetings Bring Hope," *PI*, October 4, 1981; Lucinda Fleeson, "Schools Talks on in Secret," *PI*, October 5, 1981; Steve Twomey, Mary Bishop, and Lucinda Fleeson, "'Amicable' School Talks Press Ahead," *PI*, October 6, 1981; Steve Twomey, Lucinda Fleeson, and Mary Bishop, "Teacher Talks Break Off," *PI*, October 7, 1981.

100. Mary Bishop and Thomas Ferrick Jr., "Teachers Mass at N. Phila. School," *PI*, October 10, 1981.

101. Robert Kilborn Jr., "Philadelphia: No General Strike, But Teacher Dispute Not Fully Settled," *CSM*, October 29, 1981.

102. Mary Bishop, "A Quiet Storm in Schools—After the Strike, Muffled Discord," *PI*, November 8, 1981.

103. Mary Bishop, Thomas Ferrick Jr., and Donald Kimelman, "The Shame of the Schools—How the City's Children Are Neglected by the System," *PI*, August 30, 1981.

104. Bishop, Ferrick Jr., and Kimelman, "The Shame of the Schools," *PI*, August 30, 1981.

Chapter 7

1. Vernon Loeb, "It's Formal: Clayton Heads Schools," *PI*, October 5, 1982; "First Black Woman Chosen," *LAT*, October 5, 1982; "Black Woman Elected Philadelphia School Chief," *NYT*, October 10, 1982; Pamela Smith, "Dr. Constance Clayton: Education, Children, Women are Personal Issues for the New Supt," *PT*, October 12, 1982.

2. "Educators Set Rescue Plan for Urban Schools," *BG*, January 15, 1991.

3. Loeb, "It's Formal: Clayton Heads Schools," *PI*, October 5, 1982; Oscar Berryman, "'Children Come First for the New Superintendent,'" *PT*, October 8, 1982.

4. Schuler, interview by author.

5. Vernon Loeb, "Some Fear More Courses," *PI*, May 9, 1984. See also Adams et al., *Philadelphia*.

6. Bob Warner, "Phila. Poor Rose in '70s to One in 5," *PI*, December 17, 1982.

7. Vernon Loeb, "Clayton: Schools to Be Visited—Aides to Drop in Unannounced," *PI*, October 27, 1982. See also Gar Joseph, "District Execs Ordered to Visit Schools," *PDN*, October 27, 1982; Vernon Loeb, "Visitations Produce Candid School Critiques," *PI*, December 12, 1982.

8. Joyce Gemperlein, "Clayton, Liacouras Blast Reagan's Budget," *PI*, March 13, 1985; Vernon Loeb, "School District to Lose 14.4% of Federal Aid, Board Told," *PI*, April 6, 1982; Vernon Loeb, "School Board Given Budget Changes," *PI*, April 29, 1983; Jane Eisner, "School District Proposes Tax Hike for the $20.1 Million Deficit," *PI*, May 3, 1983; Jane Eisner and Linda Lloyd, "Cuts to Hit Schools and City Hard—Total Shortfall is $141 Million," *PI*, July 13, 1983.

9. Yvonne Reynolds, "Six Exemplary High Schools Receive Grants," *PT*, June 14, 1983; United States Department of Education, *Nation Responds*, 228; Editorial, "Clayton's Educational Partners," *PI*, January 28, 1984; Vernon Loeb, "The Director—Her Private Program

Brings Humanities to City Schools," *PI*, June 1, 1984; James Asher, "Phila. Foundation Awards $716,800," *PI*, January 29, 1985; Dale Mezzacappa, "City Schools Map New Course in World History," *PI*, March 22, 1987.

10. Hart, "Adopt-a-School Program Adds Depth to City's Schools," 58.

11. Lini Kadaba, "Raising Funds for Luxuries—And Books," *PI*, June 18, 1987; Valeria Russ, "Beating the Drum for Public School Alumni Associations," *PDN*, October 19, 1987.

12. Dan Rottenberg, "Untapped Assets for Public Schools," *PI*, September 24, 1984. See also Kadaba, "Raising Funds for Luxuries—And Books," *PI*, June 18, 1987; Russ, "Beating the Drum for Public School Alumni Associations," *PDN*, October 19, 1987.

13. United States Census, 1960 and 1980, Social Explorer, socialexplorer.com.

14. Vernon Loeb, "School Board and State Panel Reach Agreement on Desegregation Plan," *PI*, October 25, 1983.

15. School District of Philadelphia School Board Meeting Notes, October 3, 1983, *Journal of the Board of Public Education*, 687, School District of Philadelphia Archives.

16. Marcia Slacum, "Clayton Preparing Plan to Improve Desegregation," *PI*, March 8, 1983.

17. I have chosen to use the terms that Clayton used to describe her plan.

18. Vernon Loeb, "What's New in Clayton's Desegregation Plan," *PI*, October 6, 1983.

19. Vernon Loeb, "School Board and State Panel Reach Agreement on Desegregation Plan," *PI*, October 25, 1983.

20. "Dr. Clayton's Desegregation Plan," *PT*, August 12, 1983.

21. Steven Marquez, "Elementary: First Day, First Grade," *PDN*, September 6, 1985.

22. Dale Mezzacappa, "School Desegregation: Many Apply—and Lose Out," *PI*, October 10, 1988

23. Lori Cornish, "Parents Claim Discrimination in Phila's School Desegregation Program," *PT*, April 22, 1986. See also Debbie Stone, "Report Says City Schools Treat Black Students Unfairly," *PDN*, October 31, 1990.

24. Cornish, "Parents Claim Discrimination," *PT*, April 22, 1986.

25. Vernon Loeb, "School Board and State Panel Reach Agreement on Desegregation Plan," *PT*, October 25, 1983; School Enrollment Data, 1990, School District of Philadelphia Archives.

26. Dale Mezzacappa, "Pew Grant Lets Schools Think Big About Change," *PI*, April 24, 1989. Based on the success of the reform, Pew allocated more funding to the initiative; see Dale Mezzacappa, "Pew Gives Funds for Schools," *PI*, June 19, 1992; Leigh Jackson, "Schools Hail Results of $20M in Grants," *PDN*, June 19, 1992.

27. Christman and Macpherson, *Five School Study*, 5; Dina Portnoy, interview by author, May 7, 2015.

28. Sizer, *New American High School*; Meier, *Power of Their Ideas*.

29. Christman and Macpherson, *Five Schools Study*, 22–24. See also McMullan, Sipe, and Wolf, *Charters and Student Achievement*.

30. Portnoy, interview by author.

31. Portnoy, interview by author. The seniority provisions in the PFT contract offered veteran teachers certain benefits such as the right to transfer to a new school and added protections during district wide layoffs. For a discussion of how these provisions and the PFT contract negotiations blocked the collaborative, see Leigh Jackson, "Both Sides Claiming Vic-

tory and Students will Return as Scheduled," *PDN,* September 9, 1992; Dale Mezzacappa, "Plan to Decentralize High Schools Spurs Brisk Debate," *PI,* March 27, 1993.

32. 1990 SDP Data, Author has copy.

33. Portnoy, interview by author.

34. Gloria Williams, "Secondary Education: Lankenau School: It Has Everything Going for It," *PT,* March 2, 1982.

35. Gloria Williams, "Secondary Education: Lankenau School: It Has Everything Going for It," *PT,* March 2, 1982.

36. Kathy Bagley, interview by author, July 6, 2015.

37. School Enrollment Data, 1990, author has copy.

38. Bagley, interview by author.

39. Deborah Grill, interview by author, March 15, 2015.

40. "In Your Community," *PT,* May 27, 1983; "The Germantown 'Y' Springs to a New Beginning," *PT,* May 27, 1983; "In Your Community-Teen Parent Support," *PT,* January 12, 1988; "Germantown YWCA Has Basketball League," *PT,* July 25, 1989; "Job Training Offered by Germantown Agency," *PT,* October 13, 1992.

41. Caroline Maxwell, interview by author, December 13, 2015.

42. Christman and Macpherson, *Five School Study.*

43. Dennis Barnaby, interview by author, March 15, 2015.

44. Dale Mezzacappa, "A Struggle with Crowded Schools: High Schools, Especially, Are Brimming," *PI,* November 11, 1992.

45. Barnaby, interview by author.

46. Mezzacappa, "A Struggle with Crowded Schools: High Schools, Especially, Are Brimming," *PI,* November 11, 1992.

47. Schwartz, "Restructuring Philadelphia's Neighborhood High Schools."

48. Levin and Baker, *Educational Equity, Adequacy, and Equal Opportunity in the Commonwealth*; United States Commission on Civil Rights, *Public Education Funding Inequity*; Travers, "Philadelphia School Reform."

49. Schwartz, "Restructuring Philadelphia's Neighborhood Schools," 122.

50. Dale Mezzacappa, "School Reform Tab: $300 Million," *PI,* September 16, 1994.

51. Pennsylvania Human Relations Commission v. School District of Pennsylvania, 651 A.2d. 186 (Pa. Cmwlth. 1994). For details on this, see Malik Morrison, "An Examination of Philadelphia's School Desegregation Litigation."

52. Dale Mezzacappa, "In 4 Years under Clayton's Plan, Desegregation Has Progressed," *PI,* June 14, 1987.

53. Dale Mezzacappa, "New Review Set on School Integration," *PI,* June 28, 1988; Michael Days, "State, City Stalemated on School Desegregation Plan," *PDN,* June 28, 1988.

54. Dale Mezzacappa, "Clayton Announces Retirement," *PI,* July 17, 1993.

55. M. McCollum, "Hornbeck Is Elected as School Board's Superintendent," *PT,* July 26, 1994.

56. Dale Mezzacappa, "Not Much Will—And Too Many Won'ts," *PI,* September 18, 1994.

57. Dale Mezzacappa, "School Reform Tab: $300 Million," *PI,* September 16, 1994.

58. Mezzacappa, "School Reform Tab," *PI,* September 16, 1994.

59. Corcoran and Christman, *Limits and Contradictions of System Reform,* 7.

60. Christman and Rhodes, *Civic Engagement and Urban School Improvement,* 17.

61. Dale Mezzacappa, "Judge Hears Schools Plan: David Hornbeck Tried to Convince Her of Wisdom of His Reform Program," *PI*, October 15, 1994.

62. Dale Mezzacappa, "Judge: Overhaul Phila. Schools," *PI*, November 29, 1994; Yvette Ousley, "A 'Blueprint' for Schools," *PDN*, November 29, 1994; Editorial, "The Judge's Assessment," *PI*, November 30, 1994.

63. Ousley, "A 'Blueprint' for Schools," *PDN*, November 29, 1994; Dale Mezzacappa, "Phila. Schools are Handed Their Toughest Assignment," *PI*, December 4, 1994; Editorial, "Facing 'Challenge' of School Reform," *PDN*, December 2, 1994.

64. Dale Mezzacappa, "Hornbeck Is the Best, Board Told a Rendell-Led Coalition," *PI*, May 24, 1994; Dale Mezzacappa, "Hornbeck Mingles, Pressing the Flesh and His Message," *PI*, September 9, 1994.

65. Dale Mezzacappa, "Phila. Schools Given a Pledge of $50 Million," *PI*, January 27, 1995.

66. Michael Dabney, "Court Orders State to Fund City School Desegregation Costs," *PT*, August 23, 1996.

67. Dale Mezzacappa, "School District Takes Drubbing on 3 Fronts," *PI*, March 8, 1995.

68. Dale Mezzacappa, "Judge Hears Schools Plan," *PI*, October 15, 1994.

69. Marisol Bello, "State Wants Judge in Desegregation Case Out," *PDN*, September 26, 1995.

70. Dabney, "Court Orders State to Fund City School Desegregation Costs," *PT*, August 23, 1996.

71. Richard Jones, Dale Mezzacappa, and Robert Zausner, "Order to Aid City Schools Is Thrown Out," *PI*, September 11, 1996.

72. Gallo Jr., "Reforming the 'Business' of Charter Schools in Pennsylvania."

73. Michelle Welk, "A Brief History of Charters," *PPSN*, Summer 2010, 16.

74. Howard Goodman and Dale Mezzacappa, "Phila. to Sue State Over School Funds, Alleging Racial Bias," *PI*, January 28, 1998.

75. Dale Mezzacappa, "School Suit Goes to Top Pa. Court," *PI*, February 4, 1998.

76. Editorial, "Ridge Budget Shortchanges Future," *PDN*, February 5, 1998; Dale Mezzacappa, "With Budget, Hornbeck Gets Tough," *PI*, February 22, 1998.

77. Dale Mezzacappa, "Panel Deals Blow to City Schools," *PI*, March 3, 1998.

78. Dale Mezzacappa, "Bias Alleged in Pa. School Aid Formula," *PI*, March 10, 1998; Kevin Haney, "City, Schools Based Funds Suit on Race," *PDN*, March 10, 1998.

79. James O'Neill, "Federal Judge Dismisses City's School-Funding Suit," *PI*, November 24, 1998; Ryan, *Five Miles Away*.

80. Dale Mezzacappa, "Hornbeck Renews Criticism of Pa. Funding of Schools State Policies Discriminate Against Poor, Minority Disabled Children, He Said," *PI*, November 10, 1999.

81. John Baer, "Hornbeck Ripped for Remarks Lawmaker Wants Apology for Speech Linking Race, School $," *PDN*, November 17, 1999; See also Editorial, "Being School Superintendent Means Never Having to Say 'I'm Sorry,'" *PDN*, November 18, 1999.

82. John Baer, "Ridge Signs Takeover Law," *PDN*, April 28, 1998.

83. Mensah Dean, "Kids at the Capitol," *PDN*, April 29, 1998; Kevin Haney, "4 Groups Oppose Pa. Takeover," *PDN*, May 6, 1998; Richard Jones, "4 Parent Groups Vow to Fight Pa. If It Moves to Take Over City Schools," *PI*, May 7, 1998.

84. Kevin Haney, "Guv Asks $$ to Run Schools," *PDN*, April 21, 2000.

85. Susan Snyder, "Phila. Schools to Detail Big Cuts," *PI*, May 31, 2000.

86. Susan Snyder, Dale Mezzacappa, and Robert Sanchez, "City, Pa. Reach School Accord the One-Year Deal Will Avert a State Takeover," *PI*, June 1, 2000

87. Board, "David Hornbeck Without Tears: Some Progress, Some Pain from the Departing Superintendent," *PDN*, June 6, 2000. See also John Baer, "Funding Still the Hot Issue: Most Feel Departure Won't Impact on $$," *PDN*, June 6, 2000; Kevin Haney and Mark McDonald, "'F' for Funding: Hornbeck Grades His Stewardship," *PDN*, June 6, 2000; Dale Mezzacappa, "Staunch Backers and Strong Critics Love or Hate Hornbeck," *PI*, June 6, 2000; Kevin Haney, "Supe Gone, Plan Stays: Street Wants Hornbeck's Replacement to Stick with Children Achieving Policy," *PDN*, June 7, 2000.

88. Mindy Noble, interview by author, March 10, 2015.

89. Barnaby, interview by author.

90. George Schuler, interview by author, April 30, 2015.

91. Bornstein, "Search for Sanity," 10. Author has copy, courtesy of Dennis Barnaby.

92. Renee Connor, interview by author, June 10, 2015.

Chapter 8

1. Mensah Dean and Yvette Ousley, "Schools' on for Tomorrow as Talks Continue, Teachers Give OK to Call Strike," *PDN*, September 6, 2000.

2. Susan Snyder, "Phila. High School Students Stage Protest," *PI*, June 10, 2000.

3. Susan Snyder, "Phila. School Board Considers Hiring CEO to Run District," *PI*, August 11, 2000; Martha Woodall, "Of Phila. Schools or Edison, Who's Really Rescuing Whom?," *PI*, August 19, 2001; Ros Purnell, "From Coast to Coast, Edison Under Fire," *Philadelphia Public School Notebook* 9, no. 2 (Winter 2001–2002): 6.

4. Jacques Steinberg, "In Largest School Takeover, State Will Run Philadelphia's," *NYT*, December 22, 2001; Daniel Denvir, "How to Destroy," *The Nation*, September 24, 2014; Elizabth Useem, Jolley Bruce Christman, and William Lowe Boyd, "The Role of District Leadership in Radical Reform," July 2006.

5. Barbara Laker, "Schools Start Year Under State Control," *PDN*, January 2, 2002.

6. Travers, "Philadelphia School Reform."

7. Paul Socolar, "Deadlines Loom: No Sign of A Solution," *PPSN*, Fall 2001; Benjamin Herold, "Where Charters Run the Neighborhood Schools," *PPSN*, October 17, 2012.

8. Useem, "Big City Superintendent as Powerful CEO," 305; Useem, "Impact of NCLB and Related State Legislation."

9. Christman, Gold, and Herold, *Privatization "Philly Style,"* 4.

10. Useem, "Big City Superintendent as Powerful CEO."

11. Christman, Gold, and Herold, *Privatization "Philly Style,"* 7; Gill et al., *State Takeover, School Restructuring, Private Management, and Student Achievement in Philadelphia*; Useem, "Impact of NCLB and Related State Legislation"; Bulkey, Mundell, and Riffer, *Contracting Out Schools*.

12. Dale Mezzacappa, "Vallas Stresses 'Human Capital'—As the Keystone of His Effort to Recruit Good Teachers, the City Schools Chief Wants to Bring Together Experts to Brainstorm," *PI*, November 21, 2002; Mensah M. Dean, "Money, Mentors Part of the Plan to Lure Teachers," *PDN*, December 19, 2002.

13. Martha Woodall, "Phila. Testing Program Gets Positive Marks," *PI*, February 8, 2004; Dale Mezzacappa and Connie Langland, "Teachers Feel Heat of Accountability," *PI*, March 6, 2005.

14. Mensah Dean, "State: Philly 'Not Dealing,'" *PDN*, August 17, 2002; Susan Snyder, "Vallas: No Shuffling of Violent Students," *PI*, August 22, 2002.

15. Caroline Maxwell, interview by author, December 13, 2015.

16. "Core Curriculum Brings Unity, Challenges," *PPSN*, September 22, 2004; See also Cochran-Smith and Lytle, "Troubling Images of Teaching in No Child Left Behind."

17. "Groups Charge Curriculum Falls Short in Addressing Diversity," *PPSN*, September 22, 2004. For the importance of culturally relevant curriculum, see Ladson-Billings, "But That's Just Good Teaching!"

18. Daniel Denvir, "Discipline Schools Charged," *PPSN*, April 1, 2010; Kristen Graham, "At Philly Disciplinary School," *PI*, March 30, 2011.

19. Mensah Dean, "Idea of Arming School Cops," *PDN*, March 18, 2004.

20. Paul Socolar, "Criticisms Fly About Selection of 70 Schools for Overhaul," *PPSN*, Summer 2002.

21. Susan Snyder, "27 Phila. Schools Labeled Dangerous," *PI*, August 23, 2003.

22. Dale Mezzacappa, "Phila.'s Stricter School Discipline Comes Under Fire," *PI*, December 19, 2002.

23. "About Center City District," Center City District website, https://www.centercityphila.org/ccd-services.

24. *Center City Reports*; Cucchiara, *Marketing Schools, Marketing Cities*.

25. Hartmann et al., *Going Small*; School Enrollment Data, 2010, copy in author's possession.

26. "New Fund Brings Art," *PPSN*, November 28, 2002; "Efforts Seeks to Position Center City," *PPSN*, December 2, 2004; "Center City Residents," *PPSN*, May 25, 2005; "Principals Who Strive," *PPSN*, May 24, 2006.

27. *Center City Reports*. See also Nina Feldman, "Why Your Neighborhood School Probably Doesn't Have a Playground," February 6, 2019, WHYY website, https://whyy.org/articles/uneven-play-most-philadelphia-public-schools-dont-have-playgrounds-thats-slowly-changing/.

28. Cucchiara, *Marketing Schools, Marketing Cities*.

29. Lipman, *New Political Economy of Urban Education*; Anyon, *Radical Possibilities*; Payne, *So Much Reform, So Little Change*.

30. Dave Davies, "Vallas Orders Principals to Trim Costs," *PDN*, February 2, 2005.

31. Susan Snyder, "District Cuts Discretionary Spending by 30%," *PI*, February 2, 2006.

32. Susan Snyder, "Balanced Budget Draws Fire," *PI*, April 4, 2006. See also Mensah Dean, "Look for Some Cuts in $2B School Budget," *PDN*, April 4, 2006; Susan Snyder, "An A-Plus Paper Struggles to Press On," *PI*, April 4, 2006.

33. Levin and Baker, *Educational Equity, Adequacy, and Equal Opportunity in the Commonwealth*; United States Commission on Civil Rights, *Public Education Funding Inequity*.

34. Michael Masch, Report on the Financial Situation, cited in Zimmer et al., *Evaluating the Performance of Philadelphia's Charter Schools*, 5.

35. Mensah Dean, "School Admission, Transfer Policy Approved," *PDN*, February 16, 2006; Ronnie Polaneczky, "Find the Right Mix," *PDN*, February 16, 2006; Susan Snyder, "Neighbors Get an Edge in Getting into Center City Schools," *PI*, February 16, 2006; Valeria Russ, "Parents Feel Cheated by New District Policy," *PDN*, March 15, 2006; Valeria Russ, "Activist: Schooling by Zip Code Creates a 'Separate, Unequal District,'" *PDN*, March 15, 2006.

36. Zimmer et al., *Evaluating the Performance of Philadelphia's Charter Schools*, iii.

37. Mensah Dean and Valeria Russ, "$21M Schools Deficit to Force Layoffs, Cuts," *PDN*, October 11, 2006.

38. Mensah Dean, "Schools Will Have to Make $70M in Cuts," *PDN*, October 19, 2006.

39. Mensah Dean, "$90 in Cuts Eyed to Rid District's Deficit," *PDN*, October 24, 2006.

40. Susan Snyder and Kristen Graham, "Vallas Gets Heat on School Cuts," *PI*, November 9, 2006.

41. Kristen Graham, "Deficit Is Closed in School Budget," *PI*, December 9, 2006.

42. Gill et al., *State Takeover, School Restructuring, Private Management, and Student Achievement in Philadelphia.*

43. Susan Snyder, "Report: Managers Fall Short in Phila. Schools," *PI*, February 1, 2007.

44. Susan Snyder and Martha Woodall, "District Deficit May be Massive," *PI*, February 13, 2007.

45. Mensah Dean, "Vallas Goin' South?" *PDN*, April 12, 2007; Susan Snyder, "Vallas to Leave City Schools Post," *PI*, April 12, 2007.

46. Mensah Dean, "Schools Post for Ackerman?" *PDN*, February 19, 2008; Susan Snyder, "A New Schools Chief for Phila.," *PI*, February 19, 2008; Mensah Dean, "Mayor, Guv Rally 'Round Schools CEO Choice," *PDN*, February 20, 2008.

47. Susan Snyder, "Phila Schools Facing Shake-up, With Input," *PI*, February 24, 2008; Chris Satullo, "Citizens' Voices Finding an Ear," *PI*, February 26, 2008; Dale Mezzacappa, "Talking Equality," *PPSN*, Winter 2008; Editorial, "Changing the Odds," *PPSN*, Winter 2008; Mensah Dean, "SRC to Formally Extend CEO Job Offer," *PDN*, March 19, 2008; Editorial Board, "Leaving School-Dropping Out of Sight," *PI*, April 23, 2008; Rita Giordano, "A Doorway Back: With the Dropout Problem in Philadelphia at Crisis Proportions," *PI*, May 4, 2008; Mensah Dean, "Ackerman Challenges District's Principals," *PDN*, August 12, 2008; Kristen Graham, "Phila. School Test Scores Up for Sixth Straight Year," *PI*, July 1, 2008.

48. Dale Mezzacappa, "Talking Equality," *PPSN*, Winter 2008; Editorial, "Changing the Odds," *PPSN*, Winter 2008.

49. Nelson, "Key Dates (2010)," *PPSN*, February 2, 2010; "Facts About School Advisory Councils," *PPSN*, February 4, 2010.

50. Kristen Graham, "Phila. Students Challenge 'Imagine 2014' Plan," *PI*, February 26, 2009; Mensah Dean, "Ackerman and Students to Meet on Reform Plans," *PDN*, February 26, 2009.

51. Fernando Gallard, "Imagine 2014," February 25, 2009, cited in "Below Is District Fact Sheet on Turnaround School Plan," *PPSN*, February 25, 2009.

52. Mensah Dean, "New School Plan Ready," *PDN*, April 16, 2009; Mensah Dean, "School Reform Plan Costs to Be Aired Tonight," *PDN*, April 22, 2009; Kristen Graham, "Board to Vote on Five-Year Schools Plan," *PI*, April 22, 2009; Paul Socolar, "Stimulus Funding Boost Is Not a Sure Thing," *PPSN*, May 27, 2009.

53. Kristen Graham, "School District Pitches Funding Requests," *PI*, May 13, 2009.

54. Dale Mezzacappa, "Strategic Plan: A Vast List but a Modest Price Tag," *PPSN*, March 5, 2009.

55. Kristen Graham, "School Panel to Vote on $3.2 Billion Budget Today," *PI*, May 27, 2009; Kristen Graham, "SRC Adopts $3.2 Billion Schools Budget," *PI*, May 28, 2009.

56. Remarks by President in Back-to-School Speech in Philadelphia, Pennsylvania, September 14, 2010, https://obamawhitehouse.archives.gov/the-press-office/2010/09/14/remarks-president-back-school-speech-philadelphia-pennsylvania.

57. Kate Nelson, "The Renaissance Schools Plans: What It All Means," *PPSN*, February 2, 2010.

58. "Charter School Conversion Plan Rankles S. Philly Parents," WHYY website, February 11, 2011, https://whyy.org/articles/11bhparent/. See also Ben Herold, "Fireworks at Audenreid," *PPSN*, February 9, 2011; Ben Herold, "No Exceptions for West on Ousting of Staff," *PPSN*, February 8, 2011.

59. Gallard, "Imagine 2014."

60. Kristen Graham, "Phila. Students Challenge 'Imagine 2014' Plan," *PI*, February 26, 2009; Mensah Dean, "Ackerman and Students to Meet on Reform Plans," *PDN*, February 26, 2009; Herold, "Charter School Conversion Plan Rankles S. Philly Parents."

61. Michael Silverman, interview by author, July 8, 2008.

62. Ben Herold, "'Not a Minute to Waste,'" *PPSN*, November 2, 2010; Ben Herold, "Teaching at Mastery," *PPSN*, December 1, 2010; Ben Herold, "Considering 'Cultural Competencies,'" *PPSN*, December 1, 2010.

63. Ben Herold, "Ackerman Hears from Parents," *PPSN*, December 17, 2010.

64. SDP Data, author copy, received from Audrey L. Buglione, SDP, Assistant General Counsel, October 16, 2016.

65. School District of Philadelphia, Germantown/Lankenau High School, NCLB Report Card, 2002–2003.

66. Carter and Welner, eds., *Closing the Opportunity Gap*; Duncan and Murnane, eds., *Whither Opportunity?*.

67. Barnaby, interview by author; Grill, interview by author; Lisa Haver, interview by author, May 27, 2015; Ilene Poses, interview by author, May 27, 2015; Karel Kilinik, interview by author, May 27, 2015; Ken Derstine, interview by author, May 27, 2015.

68. Morel, *Takeover*.

69. Morel, *Takeover*; Welsh and Williams, "Incentivizing Improvement or Imposition?" 124.

70. Daniel Campbell, interview by author, February 11, 2008.

71. Daniel Campbell, interview by author; Maxwell, interview by author, December 13, 2015; Barnaby, interview by author.

72. Morel, *Takeover*.

73. Welsh, Graham, and Williams, "Acing the Test"; Hargrove et al., "Unintended Consequences of High-Stakes Testing in North Carolina," 21; Rentner et al., *From the Capital to the Classroom*.

74. Bryk et al., *Organizing Schools for Improvement*.

75. Daniel Campbell, interview by author; Maxwell, interview by author; Barnaby, interview by author.

76. Maxwell, interview by author.

77. Grill, interview by author.

78. Cochran-Smith and Lytle, "Troubling Images of Teaching in No Child Left Behind"; Freire, *Pedagogy of the Oppressed*; Ladson-Billings, "But That's Just Good Teaching!"; hooks, *Teaching to Transgress*; Rose, *Possible Lives*; Nieto, *The Light in Their Eyes*.

79. Payne, *So Much Reform, So Little Change*.

80. Grill, interview by author.

81. Daniel Campbell, interview by author; Matthew Rodgers, interview by author, April 4, 2008; Maxwell, interview by author.

82. Daniel Campbell, interview by author.

83. Grill, interview by author.

84. Annie Phillips, interview by author, June 2, 2008.

85. Frank Burd and Ed Klein, interview by Terry Gross, *Fresh Air*, NPR, June 26, 2008.

86. Joseph Gambardello and Robert Moran, "Teacher Assaulted in School Hallway," *PI*, February 24, 2007.

87. Martha Woodall, "Burd Attackers Offer Apologies Before Sentencing," *PI*, April 26, 2007.

88. Shedd, *Unequal City*; Hinton, *From the War on Poverty to the War on Crime*.

89. Lesli Maxwell, "Phila. Cracks Down on Assaults by Students," *EW*, March 21, 2007.

90. "Study: Many Schools See Breakdown in Discipline," *PPSN*, March 8, 2007.

91. Martha Woodall and Susan Snyder, "City Special-ed Lapses," *PI*, May 20, 2007.

92. Emily Sanders, interview by author, December 17, 2015.

93. Silverman, interview by author.

94. Silverman, interview by author.

95. Michael Silverman, Personal Notes, September 4, 2007.

96. Bonnie Uditsky, interview by author, September 1, 2015.

97. Daniel Campell, interview by author; Grill, interview by author.

98. Daniel Campell, interview by author.

99. John Grayford, interview by author, May 14, 2008.

100. Tim Hopkins, interview by author, May 25, 2008.

101. Silverman, interview by author.

102. Sanders, interview by author.

103. Phillips, interview by author.

104. James Downing, interview by author, April 10, 2008.

105. Bryk et al., *Organizing Schools for Improvement*.

106. Louisa Williams, interview by author, February 25, 2008.

107. Payne, *So Much Reform, So Little Change*, 17–47.

108. Grill, interview by author.

109. Angela Foster, interview by author, April 5, 2008.

110. Maggie Johnson, interview by author, April 28, 2008.

111. Marcia Gelbert, "City Ends Longtime Agency's Contracts," *PI*, September 24, 2009.

112. Sanders, interview by author.

113. Bill Hangley Jr., "3 Schools in Northwest on Renaissance List," *PSN*, January 27, 2011.

114. "Seeking Stability at Germantown High," February 25, 2011, WHYY website, https://whyy.org/articles/scenes-from-the-renaissance-seeking-stability-in-germantown/.

115. Dale Mezzacappa, "Finally, It's Closing Time," *PPSN*, February 2, 2011.

116. Sanders, interview by author.

117. Maxwell, interview by author.

118. "Seeking Stability at Germantown High," February 25, 2011, WHYY website; Payne, *So Much Reform, So Little Change*, 31.

119. Celeste Levin, "1,000 Rally Outside District Headquarters," *PPSN*, March 14, 2011; Martha Woodall, "Philadelphia Schools Raise Shortfall Estimate to $629 Million, Warn of Major Cuts," *PI*, March 31, 2011.

120. For this history in Philadelphia and similar reforms in Newark and Chicago, see Morel, *Takeover*; McWilliams, *Compete or Close*; Ewing, *Ghosts in the Schoolyard*; McWilliams and Kitzmiller, "Mass School Closures and the Politics of Race, Value, and Disposability in Philadelphia."

121. Kristen Graham, "Parents Blast District Budget," *PI*, May 4, 2011.

122. Jenny Swigoda, "Mt. Airy Residents Speak Out Against Gov. Corbett's Plan to Lower School Spending," May 16, 2011, WHYY website, https://whyy.org/articles/residents-in-mt-airy-fear-state-education-cuts-are-too-deep/; George Anastasia, "Nearly 200 Rally Against Phila. School Budget Cuts," *PI*, May 16, 2011.

123. Mayor Michael Nutter to the Members of the SRC, June 5, 2011, http://media.philly.com/documents/Letter+to+School+Reform+Commission.pdf.

124. Ben Herold and Dale Mezzacappa, "Confidential Document Lists Dozens of Possible Closings, Consolidations," *PPSN*, June 25, 2011. For document, see "Imagine 2014: Preliminary FMP Options Report," URS Corporation, March 18, 2011, http://thenotebook.org/sites/default/files/school-closings-report-full.pdf; Paul Socolar, "More Leaked Details on Facilities Plan," *PPSN*, June 27, 2011.

125. Dale Mezzacappa, "A Long, Tumultuous Final Act," *PPSN*, August 22, 2011. See also Ben Herold, "Amid Outrage, SRC Approves Buyout," *PPSN*, August 24, 2011.

Chapter 9

1. Fernando A. Gallard, "School District of Philadelphia Releases Reorganization Plan for Schools," The School District of Philadelphia, Press Release, December 13, 2012, https://web.archive.org/web/20170710155800/https://webapps.philasd.org/news/display/articles/1267.

2. Michael Masch, "Philadelphia's Schools Have Been Singled Out by Pa. for Unfair Treatment," *PPSN*, October 14, 2014.

3. Martha Graham, "Phila. SD wants to close 9 schools," *PI*, November 2, 2011.

4. Caskey and Kuperberg, "Philadelphia School District's Ongoing."

5. Transcript School District of Philadelphia Community Meeting, Martin Luther King Jr. High School, December 19, 2012, accessed February 6, 2016, http://webgui.phila.k12.pa.us/offices/f/facilities-master-plan/community-forums.

6. McWilliams and Kitzmiller, "Mass School Closures and the Politics of Race, Value, and Disposability in Philadelphia."

7. McWilliams and Kitzmiller, "Mass School Closures and the Politics of Race, Value, and Disposability in Philadelphia," 11.

8. SRC Meeting Transcript, March 7, 2013. See also Moselle, "GHS Principal's Passionate Plea Goes Unheeded, District Mulls Possible Roosevelt Expansion," March 11, 2013, PPSN Website, https://philadelphia.chalkbeat.org/2013/3/11/22183201/ghs-principal-s-plea-to-src-goes-unheeded-district-mulls-possible-roosevelt-expansion; Bach, McWilliams, and Simon, "This Is about Racism and Greed."

9. "Philly School-Closings Vote Marked by Protests, Arrests, and Raw Emotion," March 8, 2013, WHYY website; Moselle, "GHS Principal's Passionate Plea Goes Unheeded, District Mulls Possible Roosevelt Expansion," March 11, 2013, WHYY website.

10. Anonymous GHS Teacher, interview by Deborah Grill, April 24, 2014.

11. Neema Roshania Patel, "A Disappointing Morning After at Germantown High and Fulton Elementary," March 8, 2013, WHYY website, https://whyy.org/articles/a-disappointing-morning-after-at-germantown-high-and-fulton-elementary/; Herold, "School Reform Commission Votes to Close 23 Philadelphia Public Schools, Sparking Anger and Despair for Students, Parents, Teachers," March 8, 2013, WHYY website, https://whyy.org/articles/school

-reform-commission-votes-to-close-23-philadelphia-schools/; Anonymous GHS Teacher, interview by Deborah Grill, May 4, 2014.

12. Maxwell, interview by author.

13. Anonymous GHS Teacher, interview by Deborah Grill, May 4, 2014.

14. Author's fieldnotes and transcript of the Lest We Forget Ceremony, June 19, 2013, Germantown High School.

15. Hickey, "Germantown High School's Final Graduation was a Celebration, Not a Funeral," June 19, 2013, WHYY; Moselle, "On the Scene for the Last Day of Germantown High School's Life (1914–2013)," June 21, 2013, WHYY website.

16. "Hatching a Plan to Prevent Shuttered Philly Schools from Turning to Blight," June 14, 2013, WHYY website, https://whyy.org/articles/hatching-a-plan-to-prevent-shuttered-philly -schools-from-turning-to-blight/.

17. Brian Hickey, "The Final Month: From Seattle, She Mourns the Loss of Germantown High School," June 7, 2013, WHYY website, https://whyy.org/articles/the-final-month-from -seattle-she-mourns-the-loss-of-germantown-high-school/; Aaron Moselle, "The Final Month: Kevin Eubanks Recalls Voyage from GHS to 'The Tonight Show,'" June 11, 2013, WHYY website, https://whyy.org/articles/the-final-month-kevin-eubanks-recalls-voyage-from-ghs-to-the -tonight-show/; Brian Hickey, "The Final Month: Comcast Founder Ralph J. Roberts, 'Proud to be Associated' with Germantown High," May 23, 2013, WHYY website, https://whyy.org /articles/the-final-month-comcast-founder-ralph-j-robertsproud-to-be-associated-with -germantown-high/.

18. Benjamin Herold, "In Philly, the Struggle to Make High School Work Pits Sentiment vs. Data," March 5, 2013, WHYY website, https://whyy.org/articles/in-philly-the-struggle-to -make-high-schools-work-pits-nostalgia-vs-data/. See also Aaron Moselle, "On the Scene for the Last Day of Germantown High School's Life (1914–2013), June 21, 2013.

19. Marty Moss-Coane, "A Conversation with Philadelphia School Chief William Hite," *Radio Times*, January 8, 2013, WHYY website, https://whyy.org/episodes/a-conversation -with-philadelphia-schools-chief-william-hite-2/.

20. Brian Hickey, "'Welcoming Committee' Cheers for MLK High Students on the First Day of School," September 9, 2013, WHYY website, https://whyy.org/articles/welcoming -committee-greets-mlk-high-students-on-first-day-of-school/.

21. Damon Williams, "Mayor Asks City to Donate for School Supplies," *PT*, September 12, 2013.

22. Valeria Strauss, "Philadelphia School District Laying Off 3,783 Employees," *WP*, June 8, 2013; "270 More Layoff Notices Go Out This Week," *PPSN*, June 5, 2012; Martha Woodall, "More Than 3,700 School Employees Being Laid Off," *PI*, June 9, 2013.

23. Jennifer Berkshire, "Why Do We Keep Insisting That Education Can Solve Poverty?" *Salon*, September 23, 2017.

24. Rizga, "Black Teachers Matter"; Goldin and Katz, *Race Between Education and Technology*.

25. Katz, *Irony of Early School Reform*; Bowles and Gintis, *Schooling in Capitalist America*; Labaree, *Making of an American High School*.

26. Douglas, "Are Private Schools Immoral?"

27. Pew Charitable Trusts, *Philadelphia 2020: State of the City*, 13.

28. Philadelphia Research Initiative, *Philadelphia's Poor*.

29. United States Commission on Civil Rights, *Public Funding Educational Inequity*, 49.

30. Tajma Cameron, "Philly Should Use the Schools Reopening Debate to Fix Longer-Term Problems," *PI*, February 15, 2021; Darling-Hammond, Schachner, and Edgerton, "Restarting and Reinventing School."

31. United States Commission on Civil Rights, *Public Funding Educational Inequity*, 49–50.

32. Contosta, *Suburb in the City*.

33. Heckman, Humphries, and Kautz, *Myth of Achievement Tests*.

34. Payne, *So Much Reform, So Little Change*.

35. Heckman, Humphries, and Kautz, *The Myth of Achievement Tests*.

36. Snyder, de Brey, and Dillow, *Digest of Education Statistics 2015*.

37. Cucchiara, *Marketing Schools, Marketing Cities*.

38. See Hess and Henig, eds., *New Education Philanthropy*; Brown, *Good Investment?*; McGoey, *No Such Thing as a Free Gift*; Cassidy, "Mark Zuckerberg and the Rise of Philanthrocapitalism": Tompkins-Stange, Megan E. *Policy Patrons*.

39. Ferman, *Fight for America's Schools*; Rose and Katz, *Public Education Under Siege*.

40. Maxwell, interview by author.

41. William M. Meredith School, Demographics, School District of Philadelphia Website, Accessed October 2, 2014; Economic Disadvantage data, Education Law Center website, http://www.elc-pa.org/wp-content/uploads/2015/04/District-Charter-Economic-Disadvantage-2013-2014.pdf.

42. Sample kindergarten supply list, https://meredithhomeandschool.files.wordpress.com/2012/10/kindergarten-supply-list-room-105.pdf.

43. Rick Lyman and Mary Williams Walsh, "Philadelphia Borrows So Its Schools Open on Time," *NYT*, August 15, 2013.

44. Kristen Graham, "Philly's Central High Gets $10M Gift," *PI*, November 29, 2017.

45. "Philly School Principals Are Appealing Directly to Parents for Cash," *PPSN*, August 9, 2013; Lyman and Walsh, "Philadelphia Borrows So Its Schools Open on Time," *NYT*, August 15, 2013; Kevin McCorry, "Philly School Principals Appeal Directly to Parents for Cash," August 9, 2013, WHYY website; Anne Pomerantz, "Why the 'Good School' vs 'Bad School' Debate Is All Wrong," *WP*, December 9, 2013.

46. Alane Mason, "Fed Up with Fund-Raising for My Kids' School," *NYT*, October 10, 2012.

47. Marilyn Gelber, "Next Mayor Must Embrace Philanthropy," *City Limits*, November 1, 2013; Kate Taylor, "Public Schools Fund, Under de Blasio, Is Struggling to Lure Wealthy Donors," *NYT*, May 12, 2015.

48. donorschoose.org, accessed February 3, 2021.

49. Rob Reich, "Not Very Giving," *NYT*, September 4, 2013.

50. Wayland Public Schools Foundation, http://www.waylandpublicschoolsfoundation.org; Reich, "Not Very Giving," *NYT*, September 4, 2013.

51. Reich, "Not Very Giving," *NYT*, September 4, 2013. See also Rob Reich, "A Failure of Philanthropy," *Stanford Social Innovation Review*, Winter 2005.

52. Dylan Peers McCoy, "IPS Seeks Donations to Address the 'Fundamentally Inequitable' Coronavirus Impact," *Chalkbeat*, April 10, 2020, https://in.chalkbeat.org/2020/4/10/21225460/ips-seeks-donations-to-address-the-fundamentally-inequitable-coronavirus-impact; Matt Bar-

num, "How Education Philanthropy Is Beginning to Respond to the Coronavirus," *Chalk-beat*, April 15, 2020, https://www.chalkbeat.org/2020/4/15/21225506/how-education-philanthropy -is-beginning-to-respond-to-the-coronavirus; Alex Zimmerman, "NYC School Can Hold Classes Outside This Fall," *Chalkbeat*, August 24, 2020, https://ny.chalkbeat.org/2020/8/24 /21400017/outdoor-learning-nyc-schools.

53. Jessica Calarco, "What Is Betsey DeVos Thinking?" *NYT*, July 15, 2020; Erica Green, "The Latest in School Segregation," *NYT*, July 22, 2020; Christina Cauterucci, "I Have a 'Quarantine Bubble' with People Outside My House. You Should Too," *Slate*, May 19, 2020, https://slate.com/human-interest/2020/05/why-i-decided-to-join-a-quarantine-bubble-and -you-should-too.html; Dan Kois, "When Learning Pods Came to Greenbrier Elementary," *Slate*, October 22, 2020, https://slate.com/human-interest/2020/10/learning-pods-greenbrier -elementary-charlottesville-divided-racial-lines.html.

54. Erika M. Kitzmiller and Deborah Grill, "Mourning the Loss of Germantown High School," *Germantown Crier*, Summer 2014.

55. Maxwell, interview by author.

Appendix

1. For the codes, see IPUMS USA, Occ1950, https://usa.ipums.org/usa-action/variables /OCC1950#description_section.

2. For similar methods and analysis, see Labaree, *Making of an American High School*.

BIBLIOGRAPHY

Archival Collections

CENTRAL HIGH SCHOOL ARCHIVES

Central High School Yearbooks

FREE LIBRARY OF PHILADELPHIA

Annual Reports of the Board of Public Education, Philadelphia (ARBPE-P)
Evening Bulletin Collection, FLP (EBC-FLP)
Journal of the Board of Public Education, Philadelphia (JBPE-P)
Newspaper Clippings Collection, Education (FLP Newspaper Clippings)
Public Ledger Collection (PL-FLP)

GERMANTOWN HIGH SCHOOL

The Cliveden Clipper (GHS student newspaper, October 1924–June 1961, CC)
The Cliveden Collection (GHS student journal, 1916–1929, TC)
Germantown High School Yearbooks

GERMANTOWN HISTORICAL SOCIETY

Business Men's Association of Germantown Collection
Germantown Beehive Collection
Germantown Between the Wars Collection (GBWC)
Germantown and Chestnut Hill Improvement Association Collection
Germantown Crier Collection
Germantown Public Schools Collection
Germantown YMCA
Jane Campbell Scrapbook Collection
Public School Papers
Wissahickon Boys Club Collection

HARVARD GUTMAN LIBRARY, SPECIAL COLLECTIONS

Cleveland Public School, Annual Reports
Detroit Annual Reports
Detroit Educational Bulletin (DEB)
Education for Victory Collection

HISTORICAL SOCIETY OF PENNSYLVANIA

Bureau of Unemployment Relief Collection (BUR)

OLNEY HIGH SCHOOL

Olney High School Yearbooks

SIMON GRATZ HIGH SCHOOL

Simon Gratz Yearbooks

TEMPLE UNIVERSITY URBAN ARCHIVES

Fellowship Commission Records, SCRC 259
Floyd Logan Collection, Acc 469
George D. McDowell Philadelphia Evening Bulletin Mounted Clippings Collection (EBC-TUUA)
Germantown Community Council (Philadelphia, Pa.) Records, Urb 39
Germantown Settlement Records, Acc 220
Helen Oakes Paper Collection, Acc 995
Housing Association of Delaware Valley, Pamphlets, box 430
Young Men's Christian Association (Philadelphia, Pa.), Germantown Branch Records

THE PHILADELPHIA HIGH SCHOOL FOR GIRLS

The Philadelphia High School for Girls Yearbooks

SCHOOL DISTRICT OF PHILADELPHIA ARCHIVES

Journal of the Board of Education, Philadelphia, 1983
School District of Philadelphia, *Statistical Reports of the Department of Instruction*, 1941–1957
School Enrollment Data, 1990, 2000, 2010

Abbreviated Newspapers

Afro-American (AA)
Atlanta Daily World (ADW)
Boston Globe (BG)
Chicago Defender (CD)
Christian Science Monitor (CSM)
Education Week (EW)
Evening Public Record (EPR)
Germantown Bulletin (GB)
Germantown Courier (GC)
Germantown News (GN)
Hartford Courant (HC)
Independent Gazette, Germantown *(IG)*
Los Angeles Times (LAT)
New York Amsterdam News (NYAN)
New York Times (NYT)
North American (NA)
Pennsylvania History (PH)

Philadelphia Daily News (PDN)
Philadelphia Evening Bulletin (EB)
Philadelphia Inquirer (PI)
Philadelphia Public School Notebook (PPSN)
Pittsburgh Courier (PC)
Public Ledger (PL)
Public Record (PR)
Philadelphia Tribune (PT)
Washington Post (WP)

Oral History Interviews by Author

Alcorn, David, GHS Alumnus, November 16, 2010.
August, Rosalie, GHS Alumna and Teacher, May 10, 2009.
Bagley, Kathy, GHS Teacher, July 6, 2015.
Ballard, Walter, GHS Alumnus, April 11, 2016.
Barnaby, Dennis, GHS Teacher, March 15, 2015.
Bjorseth, Margaret (Engle), GHS Alumna, June 29, 2011.
Campbell, Daniel, GHS Teacher, February 11, 2008.*
Campbell, Marion, GHS Alumna, August 6, 2010.
Cerrato, Vincenza Iannuzzi, GHS Alumna, June 29, 2011.
Coleman, William T., Jr., GHS Alumnus, August 10, 2010.
Connor, Renee, GHS Alumna, June 10, 2015.
Cuff, Ernest, GHS Student, August 6, 2010.
Derstine, Ken, SDP Teacher, May 27, 2015.
Downing, James, GHS Student April 10, 2008.*
Eckhardt, Marianna, GHS Alumna, October 18, 2011.
Faust, Helen, SDP Educator, July 26, 2010.
Foster, Angela, GHS Student April 5, 2008.*
Fuller, Gilbert, Sr., GHS Parent, August 8, 2010.
Garrison, Marion, GHS Alumna, April 23, 2011.
Grayford, John, GHS Teacher, May 14, 2008.*
Grill, Deborah, GHS Teacher, March 15, 2015.
Haver, Lisa, SDP Teacher, May 27, 2015.
Hirschman, Kim, GHS Alumna, February 16, 2010.
Holman, Savannah, GHS Alumna, August 6, 2010.
Hopkins, Tim, GHS Teacher, May 25, 2008.*
Hunter, M. Frances, Germantown Resident, August 6, 2010.
Johnson, Maggie, GHS Student, April 28, 2008.*
Kaelin, Helene C., GHS Alumna, July 29, 2009.
Kilimnik, Karel, SDP Teacher, May 27, 2015.
Levy, Berthold, GHS Alumnus, March 10, 2010.
Lytle, James, SDP Administrator and Chestnut Hill Resident, March 23, 2015.
Malloy, Janet, GHS Alumna, February 10, 2015.
Maxwell, Caroline, GHS Teacher and Resident, December 13, 2015.*
McDowell, Bruce, GHS Alumnus, August 31, 2010.
Morrison, Adrianne Valentine, GHS Alumna, November 8, 2011.

Noble, Mindy, GHS Teacher, March 10, 2015.

Phillips, Annie, GHS Student, June 2, 2008.*

Portnoy, Dina, SDP Teacher and Germantown Resident, May 7, 2015.

Poses, Ilene, SDP Teacher, May 27, 2015.

Rodgers, Matthew, GHS Teacher, April 4, 2008.*

Sanders, Emily, GHS Teacher, December 17, 2015.*

Selemno, Frank, GHS Alumnus, July 18, 2010.

Schuler, Cathy Spears, GHS Alumna, April 30, 2015.

Schuler, George, GHS Alumnus and Principal, April 30, 2105.

Shirley, Charles, Jr., Germantown Resident, Gratz Alumnus, and SDP Teacher, July 27, 2010.

Silverman, Michael, GHS Principal and Resident, July 8, 2008.

Singleton, Linda, GHS Alumna/GHS School Counselor, February 2, 2012.

Uditsky, Bonnie, GHS Assistant Principal, September 1, 2015.

Williams, Louisa, GHS Student, February 25, 2008.*

Winfield, Michelle Deal, GHS Alumna, March 16, 2015.

*Indicates pseudonym

Other Oral History Interviews

Alexander, Alyce Jackson. Interview by George Woods, August 6, 1992. GBWC, Germantown Historical Society.

Anonymous GHS Teacher, interview by Deborah Grill, April 24, 2014.

Anonymous GHS Teacher, interview by Deborah Grill, May 4, 2014.

Cauthorn, Charles. Interview by Gregory Woods, June 22, 1992. GBWC, Germantown Historical Society.

Childs, Archibald. Interview by Louise Strawbridge, October 21, 1991. GBWC, Germantown Historical Society.

Rodville, Herbert S. Interview by Gregory Woods, July 7, 1992. GBWC, Germantown Historical Society.

Film/Radio

Berkshire, Jennifer. "Why Do We Keep Insisting That Education Can Solve Poverty? An Interview with Harvey Kantor." *Salon*, September 23, 2017. https://www.salon.com/2017/09/23/why-do-we-keep-insisting-that-education-can-solve-poverty_partner/.

Burd, Frank. "Philadelphia Teacher Frank Burd." Interview by Marty Moss-Coane. *Radio Times*, July 16, 2008. https://whyy.org/episodes/philadelphia-teacher-frank-burd-2/.

Government Documents

Blaustein, Albert P. "Philadelphia, PA." In *Civil Rights U.S.A.: Public Schools; Cities in the North and West*. Washington, DC: United States Commission on Civil Rights, 1962, 105–74.

Churchill, Henry S., and Jack M. Kendree. *A Preliminary Study of Germantown Prepared for Concern for Germantown*. Philadelphia: February 1960.

Gallard, Fernando A. "School District of Philadelphia Releases Reorganization Plan for Schools." School District of Philadelphia, press release, December 13, 2012.

Jones, Galen, and Raymond W. Gregory. *Life Adjustment Education for Every Youth*. Washington, DC: Federal Security Agency/Office of Education, 1948.

Lewis, Ada H. *Report of the Special Committee on Nondiscrimination*. Philadelphia: Philadelphia Board of Education, 1964.

Magaziner, Henry J. *A Proposal for the Revitalization of the Heart of Germantown*. Philadelphia: A.I.A. and Wright, Andrade & Amenta, A.I.A., Architects, May 1963.

Odell, William R., and the Survey Staff. *Educational Survey Report for the Philadelphia Board of Public Education*. Philadelphia: Board of Public Education, 1965.

Palmer, Gladys L. *Recent Trends in Employment and Unemployment in Philadelphia*. Philadelphia: Works Progress Administration National Research Project and Industrial Research Department, University of Pennsylvania, December 1937.

Pennsylvania Department of Welfare. *Negro Survey of Pennsylvania*. 1928.

School District of Philadelphia. *Program of Studies of Senior High & Vocational Schools*.

———. *Statistical Reports of the Department of Instruction*. 1941–1957.

Snyder, Thomas D., ed. *120 Years of American Education: A Statistical Portrait*. Washington, DC: National Institute for Educational Sciences, 1993. https://nces.ed.gov/pubsearch/pubsinfo.asp?pubid=93442.

Snyder, Thomas, Cristobal de Brey, and Sally A. Dillow. "Digest of Education Statistics, 2015." Washington, DC: National Center for Educational Statistics, December 2016. https://nces.ed.gov/pubs2016/2016014.pdf.

United States Commission on Civil Rights. *Civil Rights U.S.A.: Public Schools Cities in the North and West*. Washington, DC, 1962.

———. *Public Education Funding Inequity in an Era of Increasing Concentration of Poverty and Resegregation*. Washington, DC, January 2018. https://www.usccr.gov/pubs/2018/2018-01-10-Education-Inequity.pdf.

———. *Racial Isolation in the Public Schools*, vol. 1. Washington, DC, 1967.

United States Department of Education. *The Nation Responds: Recent Efforts to Improve Education*. Washington, DC: United States Department of Education, May 1984.

Wartime Handbook for Education. Washington, DC: National Education Association of the United States, January 1943.

Published Works

Abott, Carolyn, Vladimir Kogan, Stéphane Lavertu, and Zachary Peskowitz. "School District Operational Spending and Student Outcomes: Evidence from Tax Elections in Seven States." EdWorkingPaper: 20–25, Brown University, Annenberg Institute, May 2019. https://www.edworkingpapers.com/ai19-25.

Adams, Carolyn, David Bartelt, David Elesh, Ira Goldstein, Nancy Kleniewski, and William Yancy. *Philadelphia: Neighborhoods, Division, and Conflict in a Postindustrial City*. Philadelphia: Temple University Press, 1991.

Alexander, Michelle. *The New Jim Crow: Mass Incarceration in the Age of Colorblindness*. New York: New Press, 2010.

Amsterdam, Daniel. *Roaring Metropolis: Businessmen's Campaign for a Civic Welfare State*. Philadelphia: University of Pennsylvania Press, 2016.

Anderson, James D. *The Education of Blacks in the South, 1860–1935*. Chapel Hill: University of North Carolina Press, 1988.

Angus, David L., and Jeffrey Mirel. *The Failed Promise of the American High School, 1890–1995*. New York: Teachers College Press, 1999.

Anyon, Jean. *Radical Possibilities: Public Policy, Urban Education, and a New Social Move-ment.* New York: Routledge, 2005.

Ayers, Leonard P. *The Cleveland School Survey.* Cleveland: The Survey Committee of the Cleveland Foundation, 1917.

Bach, Amy J., Julia A. McWilliams, and Elaine Simon. "'This Is about Racism and Greed': Photographs of Philadelphia's Mass School Closures." *Society for Cultural Anthropology,* October 29, 2019. https://culanth.org/fieldsights/this-is-about-racism-and-greed.

Bacon, Edmund. *Design of Cities.* New York: Viking, 1967.

Baker, Bruce D. *Does Money Matter in Education?* Washington, DC: Albert Shanker Institute, 2016. https://www.shankerinstitute.org/resource/does-money-matter-second-edition.

Barnes, Earl. *Woman in Modern Society.* New York: B. W. Huebsch, 1912.

Baron, E. Jason. "School Spending and Student Outcomes: Evidence from Revenue Limit Elec-tions in Wisconsin." *SSRN,* November 5, 2019. https://papers.ssrn.com/abstract=3430766.

Bartlow, Thomas L., and David E. Zitarelli. "Who Was Miss Mullikin?" *American Mathemat-ical Monthly* 116, no. 2 (February 2009): 99–114.

Bauman, John F. *Public Housing, Race, and Renewal: Urban Planning in Philadelphia, 1920–1974.* Philadelphia: Temple University Press, 1987.

Bell, Derrick A. *Silent Covenants: Brown v. Board of Education and the Unfulfilled Hopes for Racial Reform.* Oxford: Oxford University Press, 2004.

Beaupre, Eugene. "Negro Boys' Activities at Wissahickon: The Leading Boys' Club of the B.C.F." *Boys' Workers Round Table,* Autumn 1928.

Binzen, Peter. *Whitetown, U.S.A.* New York: Vintage Books, 1971.

Birger, Jon S. "Race, Reaction, and Reform: The Three Rs of Philadelphia School Politics, 1965–1971." *Pennsylvania Magazine of History and Biography* 120, no. 3 (July 1996): 163–216.

Bourdieu, Pierre, and Jean-Claude Passeron, *The Inheritors: French Students and Their Rela-tions to Culture.* Chicago: University of Chicago Press, 1979.

Bowles, Samuel, and Herbert Gintis. *Schooling in Capitalist America: Educational Reform and the Contradictions of Economic Life.* New York: Basic Books, 1976.

Brown, Amy. *A Good Investment? Philanthropy and the Marketing of Race in an Urban Public School.* Minneapolis: University of Minnesota Press, 2015.

Brown, Kathleen M. *Foul Bodies: Cleanliness in Early America.* New Haven: Yale University Press, 2009.

Brown, Victoria Bissell. "The Fear of Feminization: Los Angeles High Schools in the Progres-sive Era." *Feminist Studies* 16, no. 3 (1990): 493–518.

Bryk, Anthony S., Penny Bender Sebring, Elaine Allensworth, Stuart Luppescu, and John Q. Easton. *Organizing Schools for Improvement: Lessons from Chicago.* Chicago: University of Chicago Press, 2010.

Bulkey, Katrina, Leah Mundell, and Morgan Riffer. *Contracting Out Schools: The First Year of the Philadelphia Diverse Provider Model.* Philadelphia: Research for Action, 2004. https://www.researchforaction.org/publications/contracting-out-schools-the-first-year-of-the-philadelphia-diverse-provider-model/.

Burkholder, Zoe. *Color in the Classroom: How American Schools Taught Race, 1900–1954.* Oxford: Oxford University Press, 2014.

Butler, Judith. *Undoing Gender.* New York: Routledge, 2004.

Cahn, Susan K. *Coming on Strong: Gender and Sexuality in Women's Sports.* Cambridge, MA: Harvard University Press, 1994.

Carter, Prudence L., and Kevin G. Welner, eds. *Closing the Opportunity Gap: What America Must Do to Give Every Child an Even Chance*. New York: Oxford University Press, 2013.

Caskey, John, and Mark Kuperberg. "The Philadelphia School District's Ongoing Financial Crisis." *Education Next* 14, no. 4 (Fall 2014).

Cassidy, John. "Mark Zuckerberg and the Rise of Philanthrocapitalism." *New Yorker*, December 2, 2015. http://www.newyorker.com/news/john-cassidy/mark-zuckerberg-and-the-rise-of-philanthrocapitalism.

Cavallo, Dominick, *Muscles and Morals: Organized Playgrounds and Urban Reform, 1880–1920*. Philadelphia: University of Pennsylvania Press, 1981.

Center City Reports. *Growing Smarter: The Role of Center City's Public Schools in Enhancing the Competitiveness of Philadelphia*. Philadelphia: Center City District, November 2004. https://centercityphila.org/uploads/attachments/citfvwvd100j40wqdkmso00ne-growingsmarterreport2004.pdf.

Christman, Jolley Bruce, Eva Gold, and Benjamin Herold. *Privatization "Philly Style": What Can Be Learned from Philadelphia's Diverse Provider Model of School Management (Updated Edition with Important New Information and Findings)*. Philadelphia: Research for Action, 2005. https://www.researchforaction.org/publications/privatization-philly-style-what-can-be-learned-from-philadelphias-diverse-provider-model-of-school-management-updated-edition-with-important-new-information-and-findings/.

Christman, Jolley, and Pat Macpherson. *The Five School Study: Restructuring Philadelphia's Comprehensive High Schools*. Philadelphia: Research for Action, 1996.

Christman, Jolley, and Amy Rhodes. *Civic Engagement and Urban School Improvement: Hard-to-Learn Lessons from Philadelphia*. Philadelphia: Consortium for Policy Research in Education, June 2002, https://repository.upenn.edu/cpre_researchreports/27/.

Churchill, Henry S., and Jack M. Kendree. *A Preliminary Study of Germantown Prepared for Concern for Germantown*. Philadelphia: Concern for Germantown, 1959.

Ciampa, V. A. "Martin Grove Brumbaugh, Pioneering Superintendent of the Philadelphia Public Schools." *Pennsylvania History* 7, no. 1 (January 1940): 31–41.

Clark, Earle. *Financing the Public Schools*. Cleveland: The Survey Committee of the Cleveland Foundation, 1915.

Clarke, Edward H. *Sex in Education; or, A Fair Chance for Girls*. Boston: James R. Osgood and Company, 1875.

Clotfelter, Charles T. *After "Brown": The Rise and Retreat of School Desegregation*. Princeton: Princeton University Press, 2006.

Cochran-Smith, Marilyn, and Susan L. Lytle. "Troubling Images of Teaching in No Child Left Behind." *Harvard Educational Review* 76, no. 4 (Winter 2006): 668–97.

Coleman, William T. *Counsel for the Situation: Shaping the Law to Realize America's Promise*. Washington, DC: Brookings Institution Press, 2010.

Conant, James Bryant. *The American High School Today: A First Report to Interested Citizens*. New York: McGraw-Hill Book Company, Inc., 1959.

Contosta, David R. *Suburb in the City: Chestnut Hill, Philadelphia, 1850–1990*. Columbus: Ohio State University Press, 1992.

Corcoran, Tom, and Jolley Bruce Christman. *The Limits and Contradictions of System Reform: The Philadelphia Story*. Philadelphia: Consortium for Policy Research in Education, November 2002.

Countryman, Matthew. *Up South: Civil Rights and Black Power in Philadelphia*. Philadelphia: University of Pennsylvania Press, 2006.

Counts, George Sylvester. *The Selective Character of American Secondary Education*. Chicago: University of Chicago Press, 1922.

Cucchiara, Maia Bloomfield. *Marketing Schools, Marketing Cities: Who Wins and Who Loses When Schools Become Urban Amenities*. Chicago: University of Chicago Press, 2013.

Darling-Hammond, Linda. "Inequality and Access to Knowledge." In *Handbook of Research on Multicultural Education*, edited by James A. Banks and C. Banks. New York: MacMillan, 1995.

Darling-Hammond, Linda, Abby Schachner, and Adam K. Edgerton. "Restarting and Reinventing School: Learning in the Time of COVID and Beyond." Washington, DC: Learning Policy Institute, August 2020. https://restart-reinvent.learningpolicyinstitute.org/sites/default/files/product-files/Restart_Reinvent_Schools_COVID_REPORT.pdf.

Davis, Kingsley. *Youth in the Depression*. Chicago: University of Chicago Press, 1935.

Davis, Maxine. *The Lost Generation: A Portrait of American Youth Today*. New York: MacMillan, 1936.

Delmont, Matthew. *The Nicest Kids in Town: American Bandstand, Rock 'n' Roll, and the Struggle for Civil Rights in 1950s Philadelphia*. Berkeley: University of California Press, 2012.

de Schweinitz, Karl. "Philadelphia Takes Heart." *Survey* 66 (May 15, 1931): 217–19.

Dewhurst, J. Frederic, and Robert R. Nathan. *Social and Economic Character of Unemployment in Philadelphia, April, 1930*. Bulletin of the United States Bureau of Labor Statistics. Philadelphia: Industrial Research Department, Wharton School of Finance and Commerce, University of Pennsylvania, March 1932.

Dillon, Harold J. *Early School Leavers: A Major Educational Problem*. New York: National Child Labor Committee, 1949.

Dorn, Sherman. *Creating the Dropout: An Institutional and Social History of School Failure*. Westport: Praeger, 1996.

"Doubling the Gym Period." *The School Review* 51, no. 7 (September 1943): 390–91.

Dougherty, Jack. *On the Line: How Schooling, Housing, and Civil Rights Shaped Hartford and Its Suburbs*. Hartford: Amherst College Press, 2016. https://ontheline.trincoll.edu/.

Douglas, Davison M. *Jim Crow Moves North: The Battle over Northern School Segregation, 1865–1954*. Cambridge: Cambridge University Press, 2005.

Douglas, Dianna. "Are Private Schools Immoral?" *Atlantic*, December 14, 2017. https://www.theatlantic.com/education/archive/2017/12/progressives-are-undermining-public-schools/548084/.

Du Bois, W. E. B. "Segregation." *Crisis*, November 1910.

Duncan, Greg J., and Richard J. Murnane, eds. *Whither Opportunity? Rising Inequality, Schools, and Children's Life Chances*. New York: Russell Sage Foundation, 2011.

"The Educational Department of the Philadelphia Museum of Art." *School and Society* 27, no. 696 (1928): 497.

Educational Policies Commission. *Education for All American Youth*. Washington, DC: National Educational Association of the United States and the American Association of School Administrators, 1944.

Emerick, Charles Franklin. "College Women and Race Suicide." *Political Science Quarterly* 24 (June 1909): 269–83.

Emerson, Robert M., Rachel I. Fretz, and Linda L. Shaw. *Writing Ethnographic Fieldnotes.* Chicago: University of Chicago Press, 1995.

Emlen, John. "The Movement for the Betterment of the Negro in Philadelphia." *Annals of the American Academy of Political and Social Science* 49 (September 1913): 81–92.

Erickson, Ansley T. *Making the Unequal Metropolis: School Desegregation and Its Limits.* Chicago: University of Chicago Press, 2016.

Ewing, Eve. *Ghosts in the Schoolyard: Racism and School Closings on Chicago's South Side.* Chicago: University of Chicago Press, 2018.

Ferman, Barbara. *The Fight for America's Schools: Grassroots Organizing in Education.* Cambridge: Harvard Education Press, 2017.

Franklin, Vincent P. *The Education of Black Philadelphia: The Social and Educational History of a Minority Community, 1900–1950.* Philadelphia: University of Pennsylvania Press, 1979.

Fowler, Burton P. "Citizens, Junior Grade." *Community* 24, no. 8 (April 1949): 144–45.

Fox, Bonnie R. "Unemployment Relief in Philadelphia, 1930–1932: A Study of the Depression's Impact on Voluntarism." *Pennsylvania Magazine of History and Biography* 93, no. 1 (January 1969): 86–108.

Fox, Cybelle. *Three Worlds of Relief: Race, Immigration, and the American Welfare State from the Progressive Era to the New Deal.* Princeton: Princeton University Press, 2012.

Freire, Paulo. *Pedagogy of the Oppressed.* Translated by Myra Bergman Ramos. New York: Continuum, 1970.

Gallo, Patrick J., Jr. "Reforming the 'Business' of Charter Schools in Pennsylvania." *Brigham Young University Education and Law Journal* 2014, no. 2 (Summer 2014): 207–32.

Gill, Brian, Ron Zimmer, Jolley Christman, and Suzanne Blanc. *State Takeover, School Restructuring, Private Management, and Student Achievement in Philadelphia.* Santa Monica: Rand Corporation, 2007. http://www.rand.org/content/dam/rand/pubs/monographs/2007/RAND_MG533.pdf.

Goffman, Alice. *On the Run: Fugitive Life in an American City.* New York: Picador/Farrar, Straus and Giroux, 2014.

Goldin, Claudia, and Lawrence F. Katz, *The Race Between Education and Technology.* Cambridge, MA: Harvard University Press, 2010.

Gordon, Linda. *Pitied but Not Entitled: Single Mothers and the History of Welfare, 1890–1935.* Cambridge, MA: Harvard University Press, 1998.

Grant, Margaret. "Race Suicide." *Beauty and Health,* August 1, 1903, 227.

Graves, Karen. *Girls' Schooling During the Progressive Era: From Female Scholar to Domesticated Citizen.* New York: Routledge, 1998.

Grossman, James R. *Land of Hope: Chicago, Black Southerners, and the Great Migration.* Chicago: University of Chicago Press, 1991.

G. S. "Race Suicide." *Lancet,* June 27, 1908, 786–87.

Hahn, Steven. *A Nation Under Our Feet: Black Political Struggles in the Rural South from Slavery to the Great Migration.* Cambridge, MA: Harvard University Press, 2003.

Haines, Michael R. "American Fertility in Transition: New Estimates of Birth Rates in the United States, 1900–1910." *Demography* 26, no. 1 (1989): 137–48.

Hall, G. Stanley. *Adolescence: Its Psychology and Its Relations to Physiology, Anthropology, Sociology, Sex, Crime, Religion and Education.* Volumes 1 and 2. New York: D. Appleton, 1916.

Hallgren, Mauritz A. "Mass Misery in Philadelphia." *Nation,* March 9, 1932, 275–76.

Hammersley, Martyn, and Paul Atkinson. *Ethnography: Principles in Practice*. London: Routledge, 1995.

Hargrove, Tracy Y., M. Gail Jones, Brett D. Jones, Lisa Chapman, and Belinda Hardin. "Unintended Consequences of High-Stakes Testing in North Carolina: Teacher Perceptions." *ERS Spectrum* 18, no. 4 (2000): 21.

Hart, Charles. "Adopt-a-School Program Adds Depth to City's Schools." *Focus*, August 13, 1986.

Hartmann, Tracey A., Rebecca Reumann-Moore, Shani Aida Evans, Clarisse Haxton, Holly Plastaras Maluk, and Ruth Curran Neild. *Going Small: Progress and Challenges of Philadelphia's Small High Schools*. Philadelphia: Research for Action, July 2009. https://www.researchforaction.org/publications/going-small-progress-and-challenges-of-philadelphias-small-high-schools/.

Heckman, James J., Eric Humphries, and Tim Kautz, eds. *The Myth of Achievement Tests: The GED and the Role of Character in American Life*. Chicago: University of Chicago Press, 2014.

Heller, Gregory L. *Ed Bacon: Planning, Politics, and the Building of Modern Philadelphia*. Philadelphia: University of Pennsylvania Press, 2013.

Henri, Florette. *Black Migration: Movement North, 1900–1920*. Garden City: Doubleday, 1975.

Hepp, John Henry. *The Middle-Class City: Transforming Space and Time in Philadelphia, 1876–1926*. Philadelphia: University of Pennsylvania Press, 2003.

Hess, Frederick M., and Jeffrey Henig, eds. *The New Education Philanthropy: Politics, Policy, and Reform*. Cambridge: Harvard Education Press, 2015.

Hillier, Amy E. "Redlining and the Home Owners' Loan Corporation." *Journal of Urban History* 29, no. 4 (2003): 394–420.

Hinton, Elizabeth. *From the War on Poverty to the War on Crime: The Making of Mass Incarceration in America*. Cambridge, MA: Harvard University Press, 2015.

Hirsch, Arnold R. *Making the Second Ghetto: Race and Housing in Chicago, 1940–1960*. Chicago: University of Chicago Press, 1998.

hooks, bell. *Teaching to Transgress: Education as the Practice of Freedom*. New York: Routledge, 1994.

Horowitz, Helen Lefkowitz. "The Body in the Library." In *The "Woman Question" and Higher Education: Perspectives on Gender and Knowledge Production in America*, edited by Ann Mari May, 11–31. Cheltenham, UK: Edward Elgar, 2008.

Howell, C. E. "Schools and Wartime Delinquency." *Journal National Education Association* 31 (May 1942): 151–52.

Hunter, Marcus Anthony. *Black Citymakers: How "The Philadelphia Negro" Changed Urban America*. Oxford: Oxford University Press, 2013.

Hutchinson, Woods. "The Girl Versus the High School." *Good Housekeeping*, October 1912, 533–38.

Issel, William H. "Modernization in Philadelphia School Reform, 1882–1905." *Pennsylvania Magazine of History and Biography* 94, no. 3 (July 1970): 358–83.

Johnson, Elizabeth S. "Employment Problems of Out-of-School Youth." *Monthly Labor Review* 65, no. 6 (December 1947): 671–74.

Kantor, Harvey, and Barbara Brenzel. "Urban Education and the 'Truly Disadvantaged': The Historical Roots of the Contemporary Crisis, 1945–1990." *Teachers College Record* 94, no. 2 (1992): 278–314.

Kantor, Harvey, and Robert Lowe. "Class, Race, and the Emergence of Federal Education Policy: From the New Deal to the Great Society." *ER* 24, no. 3 (April 1995): 4–21.

Kantor, Harvey, and David B. Tyack, eds. *Work, Youth, and Schooling: Historical Perspectives on Vocationalism in American Education.* Palo Alto: Stanford University Press, 1982.

Katz, Arnold. "The Employment of Students, October 1959." *Monthly Labor Review* 83, no. 7 (July 1960): 705–9.

Katz, Michael B. *Class, Bureaucracy, and Schools: The Illusion of Educational Change in America.* New York: Praeger, 1971.

———. *In the Shadow of the Poorhouse: A Social History of Welfare in America.* New York: Basic Books, 1996.

———. *The Irony of Early School Reform: Educational Innovation in Mid-Nineteenth Century Massachusetts.* Cambridge, MA: Harvard University Press, 1968.

Katz, Michael B., and Mike Rose. *Public Education Under Siege.* Philadelphia: University of Pennsylvania Press, 2013.

Kessler-Harris, Alice. *Out to Work: A History of Wage-Earning Women in the United States.* Oxford: Oxford University Press, 2003.

Kitzmiller, Erika M. "Nellie Rathbone Bright: Acclaimed Author, Educator Activist, Un-American Woman?" *Pennsylvania Magazine of History and Biography* 114, no. 3 (October 2017): 297–328.

Kliebard, Herbert M. *The Struggle for the American Curriculum, 1893–1958.* New York: Routledge, 2004.

Kluger, Richard. *Simple Justice: The History of Brown v. Board of Education and Black America's Struggle for Equality.* New York: Knopf, 1976.

Ko, Dorothy. *Teachers of the Inner Chambers: Women and Culture in Seventeenth-Century China.* Palo Alto: Stanford University Press, 1994.

Komarovsky, Mirra. "Cultural Contradictions and Sex Roles." *American Journal of Sociology* 52, no. 3 (November 1946): 184–89.

Kreisman, Daniel, and Matthew P. Steinberg. "The Effect of Increased Funding on Student Achievement: Evidence from Texas's Small District Adjustment." *Journal of Public Economics* 176 (August 2019): 118–41.

Krug, Edward A. *The Shaping of the American High School.* Vol. 2. New York: Harper & Row, 1964.

Labaree, David F. *The Making of an American High School: The Credentials Market and Central High of Philadelphia, 1838–1939.* New Haven: Yale University Press, 1988.

Ladson-Billings, Gloria. "But That's Just Good Teaching! The Case for Culturally Relevant Pedagogy." *Theory into Practice* 34, no. 3 (Summer 1995): 159–65.

Lagemann, Ellen Condliffe. *An Elusive Science: The Troubling History of Education Research.* Chicago: University of Chicago Press, 2002.

———. *The Politics of Knowledge: The Carnegie Corporation, Philanthropy, and Public Policy.* Chicago: University of Chicago Press, 1992.

Laqueur, Thomas. *Making Sex: Body and Gender from the Greeks to Freud.* Cambridge, MA: Harvard University Press, 1992.

Lazerson, Marvin, and W. Norton Grubb, eds. *American Education and Vocationalism: A Documentary History, 1870–1970.* New York: Teachers College Press, Columbia University, 1974.

Lehmann, Nicholas. *The Promised Land: The Great Black Migration and How It Changed America.* New York: Vintage, 1991.

Levenstein, Lisa. *A Movement Without Marches: African American Women and the Politics of Poverty in Postwar Philadelphia*. Chapel Hill: University of North Carolina Press, 2009.

Levin, Jesse, and Bruce Baker. *Educational Equity, Adequacy, and Equal Opportunity in the Commonwealth: An Evaluation of Pennsylvania's School Finance System*. Washington, DC: American Institutes for Research, October 2014.

Licht, Walter. *Getting Work: Philadelphia, 1840–1950*. Cambridge, MA: Harvard University Press, 1992.

Lipman, Pauline. *The New Political Economy of Urban Education: Neoliberalism, Race, and the Right to the City*. New York: Taylor & Francis, 2013.

Lombardo, Timothy. *Blue-Collar Conservatism: Frank Rizzo's Philadelphia and Populist Politics*. Philadelphia: University of Pennsylvania Press, 2018.

Magaziner, Henry J. *A Proposal for the Revitalization of the Heart of Germantown*. Philadelphia: A.I.A. and Wright, Andrade & Amenta, A.I.A., Architects, 1963.

Martin, Edward S. *The Unrest of Women*. New York: D. Appleton and Company, 1913.

Massey, Douglas S., and Nancy A. Denton, *American Apartheid: Segregation and the Making of the Underclass*. Cambridge, MA: Harvard University Press, 1993.

McCaffery, Peter. *When Bosses Ruled Philadelphia: The Emergence of the Republican Machine, 1867–1933*. University Park: Pennsylvania State University, 1993.

McGoey, Linsey. *No Such Thing as a Free Gift: The Gates Foundation and the Price of Philanthropy*. London: Verso Books, 2015.

McKee, Guian A. *The Problem of Jobs: Liberalism, Race, and Deindustrialization in Philadelphia*. Chicago: University of Chicago Press, 2008.

McMillen, Neil R. *Dark Journey: Black Mississippians in the Age of Jim Crow*. Urbana and Chicago: University of Illinois Press, 1990.

McMullan, Bernard J., Cynthia L. Sipe, and Wendy C. Wolf. *Charters and Student Achievement Early Evidence from School Restructuring in Philadelphia*. Bala Cynwyd: Center for Assessment and Policy Development, 1994.

McWilliams, Julia A. *Compete or Close: Traditional Neighborhood Schools Under Pressure*. Cambridge, MA: Harvard Education Press, 2019.

McWilliams, Julia A., and Erika M. Kitzmiller. "Mass School Closures and the Politics of Race, Value, and Disposability in Philadelphia." *Teachers College Record* 121, no. 2 (2019).

Meier, Deborah. *The Power of Their Ideas: Lessons for America from a Small School in Harlem*. Boston: Beacon Press, 1995.

Meinke, Samantha. "Milliken v. Bradley: The Northern Battle for Desegregation." *Michigan Bar Journal*, September 2011, 20–22.

Melvin, Bruce. *Youth—Millions Too Many? A Search for Youth's Place in America*. New York: Association Press, 1940.

Merritt, Ella A., and Hannah S. Rifkind. "Unemployment Among the Teen-Aged in 1947–49." *Monthly Labor Review* 69, no. 6 (December 1949): 646–48.

Mink, Gwendolyn. *The Wages of Motherhood: Inequality in the Welfare State, 1917–1942*. Ithaca: Cornell University Press, 1996.

Mirel, Jeffrey. *The Rise and Fall of an Urban School System: Detroit, 1907–81*. Ann Arbor: University of Michigan Press, 1999.

Morel, Domingo. *Takeover: Race, Education, and American Democracy*. New York: Oxford University Press, 2018.

Morgan, Joy Elmer. "NCPT Mobilizes for War." *Journal National Education Association* 31 (April 1942): 99.

Morrison, Malik. "An Examination of Philadelphia's School Desegregation Litigation." *Penn GSE Perspectives on Urban Education* 3, no. 1, Fall 2004, https://urbanedjournal.gse.upenn .edu/archive/volume-3-issue-1-fall-2004/examination-philadelphia-s-school-desegrega tion-litigation.

Mossell, Sadie Tanner. *The Standard of Living Among One Hundred Negro Migrant Families in Philadelphia*. Philadelphia: University of Philadelphia, 1921.

Nasaw, David. *Children of the City: At Work and At Play*. Oxford: Oxford University Press, 1986.

Nash, Margaret A. *Women's Education in the United States, 1780–1840*. 1st ed. New York: Palgrave Macmillan, 2005.

National Education Association. *Reforming High Schools for the 21st Century—An Imperative*. Washington, DC: National Education Association, 2008. http://ftp.arizonaea.org/assets /docs/HE/mf_PB06_ReformingHS.pdf.

Neckerman, Kathryn M. *Schools Betrayed: Roots of Failure in Inner-City Education*. Chicago: University of Chicago Press, 2007.

Neville, C. E. "Origin and Development of the Public High School in Philadelphia." *The School Review* 35, no. 5 (1927): 363.

Newcomer, Mabel. *A Century of Higher Education for American Women*. New York: Harper & Brothers Publishers, 1959.

Newman, Louise Michele, ed. *Men's Ideas/Women's Realities*. New York: Pergamon Press, 1985.

Nieto, Sonia. *The Light in Their Eyes*. 10th Anniversary Edition. New York: Teachers College Press, 2010.

Noguera, Pedro. "Schools, Prisons, and Social Implications of Punishment." *Theory into Practice* 42, no. 4 (Autumn 2003): 341–50.

Odem, Mary E. *Delinquent Daughters: Protecting and Policing Adolescent Female Sexuality in the United States, 1885–1920*. Chapel Hill: University of North Carolina Press, 1995.

Orfield, Gary. *Dismantling Desegregation: The Quiet Reversal of "Brown v. Board of Education."* New York: New Press, 1996.

Palmer, Gladys L. *The Philadelphia Labor Market in 1944*. Philadelphia: Industrial Research Department, Wharton School of Finance and Commerce, November 1944.

Partelow, Lisette, Jessica Yin, and Scott Sargrad. "Why K-12 Education Needs More Federal Stimulus Funding." *Center for American Progress*, July 21, 2020. https://www.american progress.org/issues/education-k-12/reports/2020/07/21/487865/k-12-education-needs -federal-stimulus-funding/.

Payne, Charles M. *So Much Reform, So Little Change: The Persistence of Failure in Urban Schools*. Cambridge, MA: Harvard Education Press, 2008.

Peirs, Maria W., and Edith G. Neisser. "Is She Ready for College?" *Today's Health*, June 1950, 32–33, 55–54.

Peiss, Kathy. *Cheap Amusements: Working Women and Leisure in Turn-of-the-Century New York*. Philadelphia: Temple University Press, 1986.

Perkins, L. M. "The Impact of the 'Cult of True Womanhood' on the Education of Black Women." *Journal of Social Issues* 39, no. 3 (1983): 17–28.

Perkiss, Abigail. *Making Good Neighbors: Civil Rights, Liberalism, and Integration in Postwar Philadelphia*. Ithaca: Cornell University Press, 2014.

Perrillo, Jonna. *Uncivil Rights: Teachers, Unions, and Race in the Battle for School Equity.* Chicago: University of Chicago Press, 2012.

———. "White Teachers and the 'Black Psyche': Interculturalism and the Psychology of Race in the New York City High Schools, 1940–1950." In *When Science Encounters the Child: Education, Parenting, and Child Welfare in 20th-Century America*, edited by Barbara Beatty, Emily D. Cahan, and Julia Grant, 157–74. Reflective History Series. New York: Teachers College Press, 2006.

Peterson, Sarah Jo. "Voting for Play: The Democratic Potential of Progressive Era Playgrounds." *Journal of the Gilded Age and Progressive Era* 3, no. 2 (2004): 145–75.

Philadelphia 2020: State of the City. Philadelphia: Pew Charitable Trusts, 2020. https://www.pewtrusts.org/-/media/assets/2020/04/state_of_the_city_2020.pdf.

Philadelphia Research Initiative. *Philadelphia's Poor: Who They Are, Where They Live, and How That Has Changed.* Philadelphia: Pew Charitable Trusts, 2017. https://www.pewtrusts.org/-/media/assets/2017/11/pri_philadelphias_poor.pdf.

"The Philadelphia Schools." *School and Society* 20, no. 514 (1924): 563–64.

"Philadelphia's Survey Shows Peak of Unemployment Passed." *Business Week*, June 11, 1930, 10.

Phillips, Anne E. "A History of the Struggle for School Desegregation in Philadelphia." *PH* 72, no. 1 (Winter 2005): 49–76.

Powdermaker, Hortense, and Helen Frances Storen. *Probing Our Prejudice: A Unit for High School Students.* New York: Harper & Brothers Publishers, 1944.

Powers, Jane Bernard. *The "Girl Question" in Education: Vocational Education for Young Women in the Progressive Era.* London: The Falmer Press, 1992.

Public Education and Child Labor Association of Pennsylvania. *A Generation of Progress in Our Public Schools, 1881–1912.* Philadelphia: Public Education and Child Labor Association of Pennsylvania, 1914.

Rainey, Homer. *How Fare American Youth?* New York: Appleton-Century, 1937.

Rauscher, Emily. "Delayed Benefits: Effects of California School District Bond Elections on Achievement by Socioeconomic Status." *Sociology of Education* 93, no. 2 (April 2020): 110–31.

Ravitch, Diane. *Left Back: A Century of Failed School Reforms.* New York: Simon & Schuster, 2000.

Reese, William J. *The Origins of the American High School.* New Haven: Yale University Press, 1995.

Rentner, Diane Stark, Caitlin Scott, Naomi Chudowsky, Victor Chudowsky, Scott Joftus, and Dalia Zabala. *From the Capital to the Classroom: Year 4 of the No Child Left Behind Act.* Washington, DC: Center on Education Policy, March 2006. https://www.cep-dc.org/displayDocument.cfm?DocumentID=301.

Riessman, Frank. *The Culturally Deprived Child.* New York: Harper & Row, 1962.

Rizga, Kristina. "Black Teachers Matter." *Mother Jones*, October 2016. http://www.motherjones.com/politics/2016/09/black-teachers-public-schools-education-system-philadelphia.

Roosevelt, Theodore. "Prefatory Letter for Theodore Roosevelt." In *The Woman Who Toils: Being the Experience of Two Ladies as Factory Girls*, by Bessie Van Vorst and Marie Van Vorst. New York: Doubleday, 1903. https://www.gutenberg.org/files/15218/15218-h/15218-h.htm.

Rose, Mike. *Possible Lives: The Promise of Public Education in America.* Boston: Houghton Mifflin Co., 1995.

Rury, John L. *Education and Women's Work: Female Schooling and the Division of Labor in Urban America, 1870–1930*. Albany: SUNY Press, 1991.

Russell, James E. "Co-Education in High Schools: Is It a Failure?" *Good Housekeeping*, October 1913, 491–95.

Ryan, James E. *Five Miles Away, A World Apart: One City, Two Schools, and the Story of Educational Opportunity in Modern America*. Oxford: Oxford University Press, 2011.

Ryan, Mary P. *Women in Public: Between Banners and Ballots, 1825–1880*. Baltimore: Johns Hopkins University Press, 1990.

Savage, Carter Julian. "'In the Interest of the Colored Boys': Christopher J. Atkinson, William T. Coleman, and the Extension of Boys' Clubs Services to African-American Communities, 1906–1931." *History of Education Quarterly* 51, no. 4 (November 2011): 486–518.

Schwartz, Robert. "Restructuring Philadelphia's Neighborhood High Schools: A Conversation with Constance Clayton and Michelle Fine." *Journal of Negro Education* 63, no. 1 (1994): 111–25.

Scott, Emmett J. "Letters of Negro Migrants of 1916–1918." *Journal of Negro History* 4, no. 3 (July 1919): 290–340.

Self, Robert O. *American Babylon: Race and the Struggle for Postwar Oakland*. Princeton: Princeton University Press, 2003.

Seligman, Amanda I. *Block by Block: Neighborhoods and Public Policy on Chicago's West Side*. Chicago: University of Chicago Press, 2005.

Shaw, Adele Marie. "The Public Schools of a Boss-Ridden City." *World's Work*, no. 8 (June 1904): 4460–66.

Shedd, Carla. *Unequal City: Race, Schools, and Perceptions of Injustice*. New York: Russell Sage Foundation, 2015.

Showalter, Elaine, and English Showalter. "Victorian Women and Menstruation." *Victorian Studies* 14, no. 1 (1970): 83–89.

Sizer, Theodore R. *Horace's Compromise: The Dilemma of the American High School*. Boston: Mariner Books, 2004.

———. *The New American High School*. San Francisco: Jossey-Bass, 2013.

Skocpol, Theda. *Protecting Soldiers and Mothers: The Political Origins of Social Policy in the United States*. Cambridge, MA: Harvard University Press, 1995.

Smith, A. Lapthorn. "Higher Education of Women and Race Suicide." *Popular Science* 66 (March 1905): 466–73.

Snellman, Kaisa, Jennifer M. Silva, Carl B. Frederick, and Robert D. Putnam. "The Engagement Gap: Social Mobility and Extracurricular Participation Among American Youth." *Annals of the American Academy of Political and Social Science* 657 (January 2015): 194–207.

Snyder, T. D., C. de Brey, and S. A. Dillow. *Digest of Education Statistics 2015*. Washington, DC: National Center for Education Statistics, 2016. https://nces.ed.gov/pubs2016/2016014.pdf.

Sobek, Matthew. "New Statistics on the U.S. Labor Force, 1850–1990." *Historical Methods: A Journal of Quantitative and Interdisciplinary History* 34, no. 2 (2010): 71–87.

Solomon, Barbara Miller. *In the Company of Educated Women: A History of Women and Higher Education in America*. New Haven: Yale University Press, 1985.

Spencer, John P. *In the Crossfire: Marcus Foster and the Troubled History of American School Reform*. Philadelphia: University of Pennsylvania Press, 2012.

Stansell, Christine. *City of Women: Sex and Class in New York, 1789–1860.* Urbana: University of Illinois Press, 1987.

Steele, Kyle P. *Making a Mass Institution: Indianapolis and the American High School.* New Brunswick: Rutgers University Press, 2020.

Steffens, Lincoln. *Philadelphia: Corrupt and Contented.* New York: S. S. McClure, 1903.

Steffes, Tracy L. *School, Society, and State: A New Education to Govern Modern America, 1890–1940.* Chicago: University of Chicago Press, 2012.

Sugrue, Thomas J. *The Origins of the Urban Crisis: Race and Inequality in Postwar Detroit.* Princeton: Princeton University Press, 2005.

———. *Sweet Land of Liberty: The Forgotten Struggle for Civil Rights in the North.* New York: Random House, 2008.

Thompson, Heather Ann. "Criminalizing Kids: The Overlooked Reason for Failing Schools." In *Public Education Under Siege,* edited by Mike Rose and Michael B. Katz, 131–140. Philadelphia: University of Pennsylvania Press, 2013.

Travers, Eva. "Philadelphia School Reform: Historical Roots and Reflections on the 2002–2003 School Year Under State Takeover." *PennGSE Perspectives on Urban Education* 2, no. 2 (Fall 2003). https://urbanedjournal.gse.upenn.edu/archive/volume-2-issue-2-fall-2003/philadelphia-school-reform-historical-roots-and-reflections-2002-.

Tyack, David B. *The One Best System: A History of American Urban Education.* Cambridge: Harvard University Press, 1974.

Tyack, David B., and Larry Cuban. *Tinkering Toward Utopia: A Century of Public School Reform.* Cambridge, MA: Harvard University Press, 1995.

Tyack, David B., and Elizabeth Hansot. *Learning Together: A History of Coeducation in American Public Schools.* New York: Russell Sage Foundation, 1992.

Tyack, David B., Robert Lowe, and Elisabeth Hansot. *Public Schools in Hard Times: The Great Depression and Recent Years.* Cambridge, MA: Harvard University Press, 1984.

Todd-Breland, Elizabeth. *A Political Education: Black Politics and Education Reform in Chicago Since the 1960s.* Chapel Hill: University of North Carolina Press, 2018.

Tompkins-Stange, Megan E. *Policy Patrons: Philanthropy, Education Reform, and the Politics of Influence.* Cambridge: Harvard Education Press, 2016.

Ugland, Richard M. "Education for Victory: The High School Victory Corps and Curricular Adaptation during World War II." *History of Education Quarterly* 19, no. 4 (Winter 1979): 435–51.

Useem, Elizabeth. "Big City Superintendent as Powerful CEO: Paul Vallas in Philadelphia." *Peabody Journal of Education* 84, no. 3 (2009): 300–17.

———. "The Impact of NCLB and Related State Legislation." In *No Child Left Behind and the Reduction of the Achievement Gap: Sociological Perspectives on Federal Educational Policy,* edited by Alan R. Sadovnik, Jennifer A. O'Day, George W. Bohrnstedt, and Kathryn M. Borman. New York: Routledge, 2013.

Warner, Sam Bass. *The Private City: Philadelphia in Three Periods of Its Growth.* Philadelphia: University of Pennsylvania Press, 1987.

Watson, Dyan. "What Do You Mean When You Say Urban." *Rethinking Schools* 26, no. 1 (Fall 2011).

Weir, Margaret. "Urban Poverty and Defensive Localism." *Dissent,* Summer 1994, 337–42.

Welch, Emmett H. "Duration of Unemployment in Philadelphia." Philadelphia, PA: Industrial Research Department, Wharton School of Finance and Commerce, March 1, 1932.

Welsh, Richard, Jerome Graham, and Sheneka Williams. "Acing the Test: An Examination of Teachers' Perceptions of and Responses to the Threat of State Takeover." *Educational Assessment, Evaluation and Accountability* 31, no. 3 (August 2019): 315–47.

Welsh, Richard O., and Sheneka M. Williams. "Incentivizing Improvement or Imposition? An Examination of the Response to Gubernatorial School Takeover and Statewide Turnaround Districts." *Education Policy Analysis Archives* 26, no. 124 (October 2018): 1–36.

Willits, Joseph H. "Some Impacts of the Depression upon the Negro in Philadelphia." *Opportunity*, July 1933, 200–219.

———. *Steadying Employment, with a Section Devoted to Some Facts on Unemployment in Philadelphia*. Philadelphia: American Academy of Political and Social Science, 1916.

Wolfinger, James. *Philadelphia Divided: Race and Politics in the City of Brotherly Love*. Chapel Hill: University of North Carolina Press, 2007.

Wood, Sharon E. *The Freedom of the Streets: Work, Citizenship, and Sexuality in a Gilded Age City*. Chapel Hill: University of North Carolina Press, 2005.

Woodruff, Clinton. "A Corrupt School System." *Education Researcher* 26 (December 1903): 433–39.

Works, George A. *Philadelphia Public School Survey*. 4 vols. Philadelphia: Philadelphia Board of Public Education, 1937.

Zeran, Franklin R. *Life Adjustment Education in Action*. New York: Chartwell House, 1953.

Zimmer, Ron, Suzanne Blanc, Brian Gill, and Jolley Christman. *Evaluating the Performance of Philadelphia's Charter Schools*. Washington, DC: Rand Education, March 2008.

Zschoche, Sue. "Dr. Clarke Revisited: Science, True Womanhood, and Female Collegiate Education." *History of Education Quarterly* 29, no. 4 (1989): 545–69.

Unpublished Works

Bornstein, Deborah. "The Search for Sanity: The Start of the School Year in One Classroom in One Philadelphia High School." 1998.

Clapper, Michael. "The Constructed World of Postwar Philadelphia Area Schools: Site Selection, Architecture, and the Landscape of Inequality." PhD diss., University of Pennsylvania, 2008.

Kean, Michael Henry. "Student Unrest and Crisis: The Response of an Urban Educational System." PhD diss., Ohio State University, 1972.

Martin, John. "The Role of the School-Community Organization in Maintaining Integration in Neighborhood Schools in Racially Mixed Areas of Philadelphia." PhD diss., University of Pennsylvania, 1967.

Phillips, Anne E. "The Struggle for School Desegregation in Philadelphia, 1945–1967." PhD diss., University of Pennsylvania, 2000.

INDEX

Figures and tables are indicated by page numbers followed by *fig.* and *tab.* respectively.

ACKNOWLEDGMENTS

First and foremost, I want to thank Philadelphia educators, families, and youth, particularly those at Germantown High School, who have been cheerleaders, listeners, and, most important teachers as I wrote this book. I could fill another book with my deep gratitude for their generosity and relentless fight to provide equity and justice in a city that I love. I'd especially like to thank Ted Domers, Deborah Grill, Lisa Haver, Jeanette Jimenez, Dan Lazar, Rosie Martin, Janel Moore-Almond, Lauren Overton, Dina Portnoy, Linda Singleton, Geoffrey Winikur, Bonnie Uditsky, and many others who have asked to remain anonymous. I would also like to thank the Germantown High School alumni/ae and youth who pushed me to listen more carefully and do more with this work. Through your stories, I was able to tell my own.

This book would not have been possible without the mentorship and support of two individuals named Michael. I met Michael Katz as a first-year graduate student at Penn. Michael used history to temper my idealism and naïveté while simultaneously letting me imagine how schools remained central to democracy and opportunity. And when I discussed my experiences at Germantown High School, he listened to my ideas and helped me refine my questions. Michael honored and cultivated my desires to integrate school practice, educational activism, and archival research. I only wish he could have seen this work in print.

Michael Silverman allowed me to be his shadow in three different institutions that he led. I often say that I learned more from Mike's mentorship than all of my graduate courses combined. Michael represents a model in school leadership—a compassionate listener, a focused practitioner, and a champion for the educators, families, and youth under his care. He gave me the confidence and knowledge to write about the things that matter the most to me: public schools.

I want to thank the members of my dissertation committee: Kathleen Brown, who asked big questions and reminded me to stay true to myself;

Mark Stern, who taught me to communicate numbers to a broad audience; Thomas Sugrue, who through his own scholarship and mentorship reminded me about the importance of grassroots, case-study history; and Stanton E. F. Wortham, who taught me how to listen carefully to people's words.

I have benefited immensely from the financial support that quite literally made it possible for me to write this book. I have never taken for granted the extraordinary support that I received as a graduate student at the University of Pennsylvania. For eight years, I had full funding from the Graduate School of Education and Graduate School of Arts and Sciences. In addition to this support, I have received funding for this project from Drexel University's School of Education and Barnard College, Columbia University.

Two fellowships came at pivotal times and sustained me. First, I received the Caperton Fellowship at Harvard University's Du Bois Institute (now the Hutchins Center). This fellowship gave me a full year of time and unparalleled resources to think critically about revisions to the book. I would like to especially thank Henry Louis Gates Jr. for his ongoing support and mentorship. I would also like to thank Krishna Lewis and Abby Wolf, two remarkable women and true friends. Krishna and Abby made it possible for me to move to Cambridge with a one-month-old newborn and ensured that I had all the support a mother-scholar deserves. They normalized the idea that it is possible to prioritize your family while doing your scholarship. I have never taken for granted what they did for me and will always be grateful to them and the entire Hutchins Center staff, especially Kevin Burke. My fellow fellows represented the model of collegiality and made my fellowship pure joy, especially Abongwe Bangeni, John Drabinski, Shose Kessi, Brian Sinche, and Diane McWhorter.

Ben Lewis and Giovanni Zambotti at Harvard's Center for Geographical Analysis and the staff at Harvard University's Institute for Quantitative Social Science were always available to support this work. I could not have done this without them and my incredible research assistant, Jack McGrath. Jack is the brains behind every map in this book. Anna Callahan provided critical advice on the map design.

I remained at the Hutchins Center for two more years as a National Academy of Education/Spencer Fellow where I continued to develop this work. I could not have finished the book without this support.

Thank you to my extraordinary team at the University of Pennsylvania Press. Bob Lockhart, my editor, stuck with this project through its many iterations and offered support in many key moments. Tamara Gaskell, who copyedited the manuscript, and Kimberly Giambattisto, who oversaw the production. Kathleen Kearns, my book developer, gave me the confidence and support to finish this work.

I also want to thank the anonymous reviewer who reviewed the first draft and to Harvey Kantor, whose own scholarship has had a profound influence on my work. Harvey reviewed multiple drafts for Penn Press and offered pages of critical feedback to push the manuscript forward. His insights are on every page.

I want to thank my teachers and advisors. From high school, I would like to thank Nancy Baun, my cello teacher, Charles Lucas, my history teacher, and Kenneth Shaw, my school counselor, who set me on this path. Attending Wellesley College was one of the best decisions I have ever made. My Wellesley professors modeled the combination of exemplary teaching and scholarship—something I try to emulate every day. In particular, I'd like to thank David Haines, Ken Hawes, Martina Königer, Sergio Parussa, Susan Reverby, Sally Sanford, Nathaniel Shiedley, Anita Tien, and Elizabeth Varon. At Penn, I'd like to thank faculty and staff including Earl Ball, Leslie Boyd, Sigal Ben-Porath, Lee Cassanelli, Amit Das, LaToya Floyd, Steven Hahn, Kathy Hall, Mike Johanek, Peter Kuriloff, Walter Licht, Doug Lynch, Torch Lytle, and Kathy Peiss. Jerry Murphy pushed me to dream bigger, Joan Goodman reminded me to stay true to myself, and Harris Sokoloff gave me time and space to think. No one did more for me at Penn than Rona Rosenberg, who I affectionately call my Penn mom. Rona always listened carefully, offered sound advice, and acted as my resident cheerleader in all ways. I'm so lucky to have her in my life.

As I worked on this book, I have called many institutions home. At Drexel, I'd like to thank Tina Richardson, Kristy Kelly, Val Klein, and Bruce Levine. At Teachers College, I'd like to thank Nafiza Akter, Courtney Brown, Steve Goss, Jeffrey Henig, Veronica Thomas, and Brian Veprek. Adele Bruni-Ashely is a wonderful colleague and friend, William Gaudelli represents the model of what academic leadership should be, and Yolanda Sealey-Ruiz is a fierce mentor and friend.

At Barnard College, I'd like to thank the wonderful people in the education program, Thea Abu El-Haj, Patricia Argueta-Medina, Lisa Edstrom, Maria Rivera Maulucci, Chandler Miranda, Jennifer Rosales, and Rachel Throop. I'd also like to thank Jennie Correia, Miriam Neptune, Alicia Peaker, and Mary Rocco. Provost Linda Bell provided critical support and advice. Corinne Kentor is an amazing teaching assistant, scholar, and colleague.

Finally, I would also like to thank Alondra Nelson for always making time to offer support along the way.

I have had the great fortune of teaching hundreds of students in the past two decades. My students and colleagues at the Steppingstone Foundation, especially Will Austin and Danielle Heard, taught me to take risks in the classrooms and to listen to my students' fears and dreams. The Calhoun School taught me what it is like to teach in a school without walls and the possibilities of progressive teaching and learning. Wayland Middle School let me stretch my wings and to understand why private funding matters. My students at Barnard, Columbia, Drexel, Penn, and Teachers College pushed me to think more deeply about the ways that injustice and inequity operate and to remember that solutions are possible. The world is a better place because you all are in it.

This scholarship rests on the work of archivists and journalists who have preserved and documented this history. I'd like to thank the individuals who have done so at Barnard College-Columbia University, Germantown Historical Society, Harvard University Libraries, the Historical Society of Pennsylvania, Temple University Urban Archives, and the University of Pennsylvania Van-Pelt Library. I'd like to offer a special thanks to the staff at the Free Library of Philadelphia who worked tirelessly to help me track down critical sources, even during years of dwindling public funds. I could not have written this work without the support and care of the staff and volunteers at the Germantown Historical Society, especially Alex Bartlett, Sandra Chaff, and Sam Whyte, or the words of Philadelphia journalists who have written about the city's public school system for decades, especially Mensah Dean, Dan Denvir, Orrin Evans, Kristen Graham, Dale Mezzacappa, and Paul Socolar, who made us realize years ago the importance of locally funded, independent, educational journalism. I am indebted to you.

I have benefited from the generosity of scholars who have commented on my work, including James Anderson, Lawrence Bobo, William Cutler, Mindy Fullilove, Karen Graves, Michael Hines, Brian Jones, Nick Juravich, David Labaree, Lisa Levenstein, Gary Orfield, Charles Payne, Jack Schneider, Carla Shedd, Christopher Span, Kyle Steele, and William Julius Wilson.

The members of my book workshop at Penn offered critical advice over many years. Thanks to Daniel Amsterdam, Ansley Erickson, Rand Quinn, Elaine Simon, Jon Zimmerman, and a huge shout out to Amy Hillier, who has been a constant source of inspiration and love. She showed me the magic of maps and remains someone I continue to lean on. Jon Hale and Jack Dougherty offered critical advice over many years.

I am fortunate to have many friends and colleagues who have showered me with their care, love, and time, especially T. Nana Mokoah Ackatia-Armah, Chris Agresta, Rumana Ahmed, Rasha Albani, Ari Betof, Blerta Braka, Meghan Burkins, Betty Chandy, Haig Chahinian, Tina Collins, Mary Conger, Helen Coster, Jennifer DiBara Crandell, Ricky Debnath, Eva-Dina Delgado, Christine Dobridge, Katrina Dornig, Rachel Fester, Wendy Green, Adam Goodman, Hilary Jansen, Abigail Jones, Gabe Kuriloff, Dorothea Lasky, Jessica Lautin, Stephanie Levin, Kimberly Leopold, Sam Leopold, Manja Lyssy, Sally Maxwell, Christina McBride, Julia McWilliams, Jay Mehta, Lisa Merrill, Julia Murray, Billy Oleson, Peter Pihos, Mary Kaye Rhude-Faust, Sarah Rodriguez, Robert Sember, Paul Serritella, Betty Tung, Adrienne Walker, Christoph Weidemann, and Lisa Ziemer. I'd also like to thank the incredible people in my New York City building: Alyssa, Celeste, David, Diana, Evan, Marcus, Najam, Nazia, Nick, and, of course, your incredible kids. You make New York City my favorite place to be.

Two friends, Ethan Hutt and Akira Drake Rodriguez, read countless drafts and supported me throughout the process. Anne Fleming represented a friend in the truest sense of the word—Anne believed in this project as if it was her own, reading drafts, sharpening arguments, and cheering me on. Her wisdom is all over this book. I miss her dearly.

Three women, Alfie Daniels, Marteena Jones, and Yinnie Tse, have been by my side for more than two decades. They answer the phone at any time of the day and remain constant sources of love and support.

I'd like to thank my family, who have supported me at every turn. I'd like to thank my in-laws, Michael and Susan Jacobs, for their support. My brother-in-law, Brian, has looked at every map, graph, and chart in this book at least a dozen times.

I'm part of a large Italian immigrant family, which has showered me with love my entire life. I'd like to thank my cousins, aunts, and uncles, especially my late aunt, Rosanna, who showed me the power of urban communities, pushed me to fight for justice, and supported me at every turn. I'd like to thank my sister, Christine, and her husband, Ed, who have listened to far too many conversations about this book and who I love beyond words.

I have dedicated this book to my parents, Lisa and Richard. I consider myself the luckiest kid in the world to have them as my parents. They have loved me unconditionally, and while they did not always have the advantages and privileges that I do, they always believed that I could do anything I set my mind to. They sacrificed a great deal to provide me with the experiences that I have had, laying bricks for me to walk on, reminding me to seize opportunities when I had them, and supporting me anytime life seemed tough. My parents, through their example, taught my sister and me to recognize and act on injustice when we saw it and to listen to people's stories and perspectives. They were and remain my first and very best teachers. My father passed away one week before I received my final book contract. I am sure he would have been beaming with pride if he could have held this book in his hands.

Finally, I'd like to thank my husband, Joshua, who has been my guiding light for more than half of my life. I am lucky to have a partner who allows me to be completely who I am and who is always in my corner. Our children, Luke and Sylvia, came into this world as this project moved from a dissertation to a book. Their presence, joy, and love have happily pulled me away from this work many times, but they have also motivated me to finish it. No one exemplifies the hope that I have for a more just and equitable future than they do. Being their mom is the most important work I do.